North Korea

the Bradt Travel Guide

Henry Marr
with Neil Taylor

edition
4

www.bradtguides.com

Bradt Travel Guides Ltd, UK
The Globe Pequot Press Inc, USA

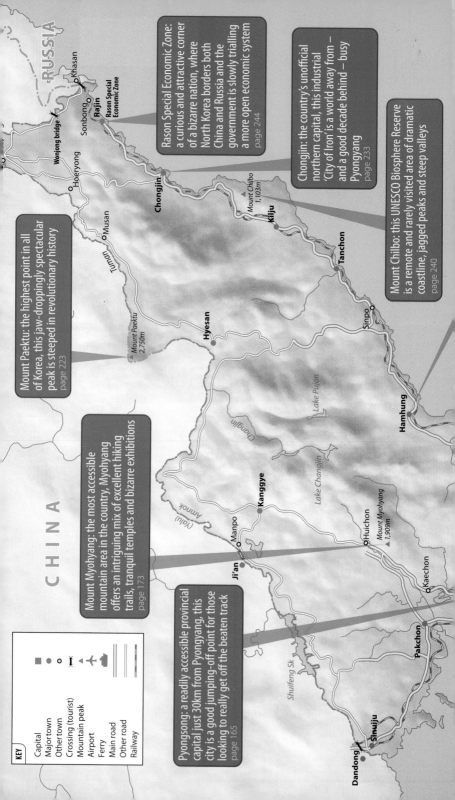

RUSSIA

CHINA

KEY
- ■ Capital
- ● Major town
- ○ Other town
- ✗ Crossing (tourist)
- ▲ Mountain peak
- ✈ Airport
- ⛴ Ferry
- ━━ Main road
- ━━ Other road
- ━━ Railway

Khasan

Wonjong bridge

Sonbong
Rajin
Rason Special Economic Zone

Hoeryong

Musan

Chongjin

Tuman

Mount Chilbo
1,103m
Kilju

Tanchon

Mount Paektu
2,750m

Hyesan

Sinpo

Lake Pujon

Changjin

Hamhung

Lake Changjin

Kangye

Amnok (Yalu)

Huichon

Mount Myohyang
1,909m

Manpo

Ji'an

Kaechon

Shuifeng Sk

Pakchon

Sinuiju

Dandong

Rason Special Economic Zone: a curious and attractive corner of a bizarre nation, where North Korea borders both China and Russia and the government is slowly trialling a more open economic system
page 244

Chongjin: the country's unofficial northern capital, this industrial 'City of Iron' is a world away from — and a good decade behind — busy Pyongyang
page 233

Mount Chilbo: this UNESCO Biosphere Reserve is a remote and rarely visited area of dramatic coastline, jagged peaks and steep valleys
page 240

Mount Paektu: the highest point in all of Korea, this jaw-droppingly spectacular peak is steeped in revolutionary history
page 223

Mount Myohyang: the most accessible mountain area in the country, Myohyang offers an intriguing mix of excellent hiking trails, tranquil temples and bizarre exhibitions
page 173

Pyongsong: a readily accessible provincial capital just 30km from Pyongyang, this city is a good jumping-off point for those looking to really get off the beaten track
page 165

Hamhung: a city where heavy industry meets pristine beaches, Hamhung makes a good base for those venturing to rarely visited Pujon and Mount Okryon
page 213

Mount Kumgang: a site of near-mythical status since the 7th century and famed across Korea, this beautiful corner of Asia has craggy peaks, a pristine coastline and, for now, almost no visitors at all
page 201

Pyongyang: the socialist Shangri-La, this misunderstood and secretive city has to be seen to be believed – and even then you may not believe your eyes
page 87

Panmunjom: the single-most poignant reminder of a divided nation, where troops from North and South stare at each other over the DMZ
page 144

East Sea of Korea

West Sea of Korea (Yellow Sea)

Yellow Sea

SOUTH KOREA

SEOUL

Japan (suspended)

Hyundai Asan (suspended)

Rail crossing (for tourists); land crossing suspended

Kosong

Mount Kumgang 1,638m

Demilitarised Zone (DMZ)

Wonsan

Imjin

Nam

Pyongsan

Cross-DMZ crossing point in joint security area (not for tourists)

Road and rail connection to Kaesong Industrial Zone

Kaesong

Panmunjom

Pyongsong

PYONGYANG

Sariwon

Haeju

Nampo

Mount Kuwol 954m

N

Bradt

0 50km

0 30 miles

North Korea
Don't miss...

Mount Kumgang
Revered by all Koreans, this near mythical mountain is simply breathtaking, particularly in autumn (KG/AWL) page 201

Monuments and palaces
Mix with the masses and bow before the 20m-tall twin statues of Kim Il Sung and Kim Jong Il at the Mansudae Grand Monument in Pyongyang (CM) page 107

Panmunjom and the DMZ
Visit the heavily militarised DMZ, marking the border between North and South Korea, and learn about the armistice in Panmunjom (CL/S) page 144

North Hamgyong
For those with the time to get to North Hamgyong, this lesser-visited corner of the country is a world away from the relative glitz of Pyongyang; pictured here, the provincial capital of Chongjin (CM) page 231

Pyongyang
A city like no other, the North Korean capital will enthral and confound in equal measure (T/S) page 87

North Korea in colour

above	A young pioneer places flowers outside the Mansudae Art Studio in Pyongyang — the capital is filled with monuments and statues depicting the Kims (EL) page 113
above left	Although the exterior has now been glazed, the Ryugyong Hotel in Pyongyang may end up taking as long as the pyramids to complete (NL/AWL) page 98
left	Students engage in a mass dance in front of the Monument to Party Foundation (CM) page 120
below	Pyongyang's ornate metro stations are considered to be palaces of socialism (EL) page 94

AUTHOR

Henry Marr's love affair with travel to the more unusual parts of Asia began at the age of 18, when he spent a month mountaineering in Kazakhstan. After a summer living in Tbilisi, his next adventure culminated with him spending two years in Ulaanbaatar, where his next-door neighbour was Mongolia's first (and only) cosmonaut. Seeking employment Henry returned to the UK and now lives outside London, where he satisfies his wanderlust by planning, promoting and escorting tours to niche destinations such as Abkhazia, Nagorno Karabagh and, of course, his true forte, North Korea.

CONTRIBUTING AUTHOR

Neil Taylor has worked closely with Bradt for 20 years. A former director of tour operator Regent Holidays, he was responsible for starting their tours to North Korea following an invite to Pyongyang in 1985. After retiring from Regent, he turned to travel writing, largely on the Baltics and on East Asia, and to guest lecturing on land tours and cruises to both these areas, which enables him both to keep up to date and to share his knowledge of these regions with other travellers.

AUTHOR'S STORY

Tired and jetlagged, it's 04.00 and I am writing the last little piece of the jigsaw that is this book from a Beijing hotel room. Soon, I will begin the all-too-familiar traipse to Beijing's glitzy yet often shambolic airport. These now familiar stopovers in the Chinese capital are always a sleepless blur – jetlag mixed with excitement – as I think of the imminent adventure: North Korea.

All these years on, I am no less excited now than I was on the morning of my first visit in 2005 – I still feel like a child on Christmas Eve in the days and weeks leading up to my next trip to the DPRK, and my time in the country is always a whirlwind of equally bizarre and fascinating experiences that I struggle to explain to people back home. It isn't easy to accurately describe North Korea to people who have not experienced it, but for over a decade I have managed to scrape together a living from arranging tours to the country; an unusual career choice, but one that at least allows me to regularly visit a country that could almost be described as my second home.

When my name came to the attention of Bradt, whose books I have used for many years, and they mooted the possibility of my writing this guide, I felt humbled and slightly bewildered – but, of course, said yes immediately. Over the subsequent weeks and months I have strived to pour my obsession with North Korea into these pages in the hope that you too may consider visiting the country while it still exists as I know it.

It will be breakfast soon, and I can already hear the murmur of traffic from the street some dozen storeys below me. So, I will sit here in this somewhat dated hotel room, deleting files from my laptop, removing the more questionable books from my Kindle and finishing off these last few emails before I, in essence, go dark for the next three weeks, leaving the real world behind as I catch a flight to North Korea. I can't wait.

PUBLISHER'S FOREWORD
Hilary Bradt

North Korea is not what you expect. When I visited in 2016 with Regent Holidays, I was surprised at the smiling people and what I believe is a genuine love for their past leaders and a desire for peace. Our guide throughout the visit was Carl Meadows, whose 15-year acquaintance with the DPRK and deep knowledge of the country made him the ideal tour leader. He has passed that knowledge on to Henry Marr to create the only comprehensive and accurate guide to North Korea in existence, helped by my old friend Neil Taylor whose enthusiasm for the DPRK sparked my interest in the first place. Not only is it accurate, it reflects the authors' fascination and appreciation of 'the world's most secretive nation'.

Fourth edition published January 2019
First published 2003
Bradt Travel Guides Ltd
IDC House, The Vale, Chalfont St Peter, Bucks SL9 9RZ, England
www.bradtguides.com
Print edition published in the USA by The Globe Pequot Press Inc,
PO Box 480, Guilford, Connecticut 06437-0480

Text copyright © 2019 Henry Marr
Maps copyright © 2019 Bradt Travel Guides Ltd; includes data © OpenStreet Map contributors
Photographs copyright © 2019 Individual photographers (see below)
Cover research: Pepi Bluck, Perfect Picture

ISBN: 978 1 78477 094 5

British Library Cataloguing in Publication Data
A catalogue record for this book is available from the British Library

Photographs AWL Images: Katie Garrod (KG/AWL), Nick Ledger (NL/AWL); Hilary Bradt (HB); Eric Lafforgue (EL); Carl Meadows (CM); Shutterstock: Anton_Ivanov (AI/S), Attila JANDI (AJ/S), junrong (j/S), Kanokratnok (K/S), Chintung Lee (CL/S), lebedev (L/S), nndrin (n/S), Truba7113 (T/S), mbrand85 (mb/S), Maxim Tupikov (MT/S); SuperStock (SS)

Front cover Arirang Mass Games (EL)
Back cover Pyongyang (CL/S); Mount Kumgang (HB)
Title page Juche Tower, Pyongyang (AI/S); Mural in Pohyon Temple (EL); Kuryong Falls (SS)

Maps David McCutcheon FBCart.S

Typeset by D & N Publishing, Baydon, Wiltshire and Ian Spick, Bradt Travel Guides
Production managed by Jellyfish Print Solutions; printed in the UK
Digital conversion by www.dataworks.co.in

Acknowledgements

Looking upon others for their help leads to nowhere

Kim Jong Un

Contrary to the brilliant wisdom of the Supreme Commander, I must admit that I have had to ask for a great deal of help from others in order to compile this book. Many of those who have assisted I cannot name in print for reasons that, if not yet obvious, should become so as you read this guide. They mostly know who they are and I am extremely grateful to them. Over the years, the cumulative days, weeks and months spent exploring my unofficial second home has afforded me the chance to see my beloved North Korea develop, ever so slowly, into a country that is becoming a better place to live in for all. All of my happy memories of travel and adventures are tinged with one sadness; being away from home for so long, away from those who I would have loved to have shared the experiences with the most. My utmost thanks accordingly go out to my wife, family and long-suffering friends who, when I am home, I equally bore and beguile with endless talk and tales of life north of the DMZ.

Despite all the assistance in amassing the information that can be found over the following pages any errors are my own; sporadically I have had to give (as a friend of mine was once overheard to say) 'a rough approximation of a guestimate' when I have provided certain details, as at times numerous 'official' sources have bombarded me with contradictory information. If you find any glaring errors I will of course be mortified, but do let the good people at Bradt know so that, should I have the honour of writing a fifth edition of this guide, they can be rectified. Particular mention must go to Neil Taylor for his passion to get this project off the ground, together with Hilary Bradt, Rachel Fielding and Laura Pidgley of Bradt Travel Guides for their patience and support from day one. Within the industry, Carl Meadows, Andrea Godfrey, Michael Voss and all at Regent Holidays in Bristol have provided unrivalled support and assistance, as well as Simon Cockerell of Koryo Tours, Geoffrey See and Ian Bennett of Choson Exchange, and Benjamin Griffin of Juche Travel Services. Invaluable information and a number of quotes in this book are taken from the countless pamphlets and books churned out by the uncredited and anonymous writers from organisations such as the Foreign Language Publishing House and Kumsong Youth Publishing House – they certainly have a way with their words and I would thank them if I knew who they were. Finally, I have been fortunate to have had some wonderful travelling companions to North Korea over the years but am particularly grateful to 'Comrade P', who has proven to be not just an excellent partner in crime but also a comically pedantic factchecker, always reminding me of little titbits of trivia to pepper this final text with.

Thank you all.

Contents

NOTE ABOUT MAPS

Several maps use grid lines to allow easy location of sites. Map grid references are listed in square brackets after the name of the place or sight of interest in the text, with page number followed by grid number, eg: [104 C3].

LIST OF MAPS

KEY TO SYMBOLS

—·—·—·	International boundary	Border crossing	
=:=:=	De-militarised Zone (DMZ)	Hospital/clinic, etc	
-------	Province boundary	Buddhist temple/monastery	
═══════	Main road (regional maps)	Pagoda	
▬▬▬▬	Railway line	Pavilion	
···········	Featured hike/footpath (regional maps)	Major zoo	
✈ ✈	Airport (international/domestic)	Garden	
--⛴--	Ferry route (passenger)	Department store	
▭	Railway station	Beach	
🚌	Bus station	Skiing	
M	Metro station	Funfair/theme park	
P	Car park	Waterfall	
🛈	Tourist information office	Lighthouse	
E	Embassy	Viewpoint	
🏛	Museum/art gallery	Archaeological/historic site	
🎭	Theatre/cinema	City wall	
🏢	Important/historic building	Stadium	
🏰	Historic castle/gate/fortification/bastion	Old town	
👤	Statue/monument	Urban park	
🏠	Hotel/inn, etc	Market/urban square	
✕	Restaurant		

Introduction

When I first visited North Korea there was far less information out there than we have today, and much of this so-called 'information' was vague, inaccurate or just plain false – an issue that still prevails. I do hope that this guidebook will help in some small way to dispel some of the misinformation and to portray the country more positively than it is largely presented on the global platform. The country isn't perfect, it has major problems, but I maintain resolutely that North Korea, or the Democratic People's Republic of Korea as it prefers to be called, is a far, far better place than the world is led to believe. Life in North Korea is very different from life anywhere else, but we are all human; believe it or not, its citizens have pretty much the same aspirations that I imagine most people the world over strive for. We have far more in common with North Korea than differences, and part of the xenophobia, which goes both ways, is rooted in the nation being so cut off from the international community that few really understand it, or the mindset of its people. Tourism, however restricted it remains, is one of the only means of cultural interaction between North Korea and the outside world; a few hours in the country will tell you far more than another hackneyed documentary or trite news exposé ever could.

It could well be George W Bush who inspired me to visit North Korea, his infamous 'Axis of Evil' speech spurring me on to visit what looked to be the ideal destination for an alternative holiday. Within a few minutes of touching down in Pyongyang on that first trip I fell head over heels in love with North Korea – a fascinating, bizarre, confusing country that I could take a thousand adjectives to only start describing, but should I have just two words to choose, would proffer 'parallel universe' as being the most apt. When I first started visiting North Korea, ten days was enough to visit almost all that was permitted. The guides would compile reports on the ideology of the group, try to engage in complex political discussion on Marxist-Leninism, and strictly monitor photography and movements. Nearly all North Koreans would be wearing a uniform of some kind, and besides propaganda books there was almost nothing available in the few shops we were allowed to visit. Although at first the guides – much like the Democratic People's Republic of Korea (DPRK) in general – seemed to have a cold exterior, it became quite apparent after just a few hours in the country that they, and almost everybody we met, were friendly, interesting and just plain *nice*. Putting politics to one side, the Koreans I met were all good-humoured folk with a somewhat veiled *joie de vivre*, quickly opening my eyes to their rich history, fascinating culture and beautiful land. I have never looked back.

The itineraries on offer then were more restricted than today but, quite often, the highlight – then and now – was not so much the 'sights' as the unscheduled encounters, adventures and experiences along the way. Like most travellers, on that first visit it was the monuments and grandiosity of Pyongyang, together with the famous DMZ that I was desperate to see. I had no real idea, for example, of Korean culture and cuisine, of their millennia of history or of the pristine national parks

Freedom of travel does not exist within North Korea. All citizens, save for the very elite, need reasons and permits to move around their own country, and in such a draconian system it is quite understandable that foreigners also have restrictions placed upon them. As a result, tourists are not permitted to move freely within the country and can only travel to and around North Korea as part of a prepaid, preapproved and fully escorted tour. Breaking the rules will, at best, ruin your day and your guides' week; at worst it will lead to your deportation or arrest.

A tourist group, be it a party of one or 20, will typically be allocated two local tour guides and a driver. Guides are normally with you from the moment you arrive in the country until the moment you depart, and will stay in the same hotels as you. They are generally passionate, good humoured and nearly always available to assist in any way, and will be your best window to understanding how all facets of the country work. Do bear in mind, though, that certain things in North Korea cannot be openly discussed and should be avoided (sex, history, politics and religion), and please do not push the conversation if you disagree with the guide, or do not get the response you are looking for. In addition, leaving your hotel without the guide's express permission is not possible and should not be attempted.

Although becoming slightly more relaxed in recent years, the myriad diktats relating to rules and requirements for incoming visitors are not always clear or expressed in writing – on arrival in the country, your local guides will clarify the current interpretation of what is and isn't acceptable conduct and you must adhere to their guidelines. If you violate regulations it can have serious and permanent consequences for the local guides, their families and future. It should go without saying, but foreigners, too, have been known to seriously implicate themselves with conduct that would be branded as a simple tomfoolery in the West – the sad fate of US student Otto Warmbier (page 35) should stand as a reminder to all that North Korea is not a conventional travel destination. Journalists posing as normal tourists have quite literally ruined people's lives just to deliver a mundane story on their experiences of sneaking out of their hotel at night, or similarly vapid 'exclusives'. For genuine tourists who break the more trivial rules, major implications are unlikely, but it will probably cause a heated argument and doubtless spoil the overall enjoyment of the rest of the tour, for both the offender in question and those travelling with

that blanket the country – all things, among others, that have persuaded me to return again and again to delve further into the hinterlands of this hermit kingdom. While the authorities used to focus tourism efforts on Pyongyang, trying to attract visitors with large-scale events such as the Arirang Mass Games, they have now realised that they have an awful lot more to offer; travellers interested in truly seeing the country can go further now than ever before, with all manner of new possibilities and special interest tours helping to slowly pull back the curtain inch by inch, year by year.

North Korea has come an awful long way from the dark days of the 1990s and the last few years have, somehow and despite sanctions, seen something of a construction boom in the capital. This started at the tail end of the last decade with the government striving to beautify the city for April 2012 – the 100th anniversary of the birth of President Kim Il Sung. Under Kim Jong Un the pace seems to be speeding up, with developments appearing across the capital, from water parks and funfairs to high-rise apartment blocks. Now even taxis can be seen across the city them. People have been known to be sent on the first flight back to Beijing, at their own expense. To put it bluntly, this is not a country where it is worth even remotely pushing the envelope. If you are happy to partake in the 'system', you will have an amazing experience. Tourists are 'invited' to North Korea and as such should act akin to a guest – respecting the values and traditions of the people. This warning is not meant to scare, and incidents are incredibly rare, but they do happen.

This book summarises almost everything a tourist could conceivably do in the country, and can be used as an armchair guide, to plan your own private tour of North Korea or to provide some inspiration on what you could see and do before you look for a tour operator and itinerary that best fits your requirements. Unless specified, all areas mentioned within the guide *should* be possible to visit, but things can change quickly in North Korea, with little or no explanation as to why. Telephone numbers, opening hours and other such vital details one would expect of any normal guidebook are not found within these pages as North Korea is not a normal country; all will run to schedule as prescribed by your local guide and the state-approved itinerary they have for you. The permits, papers and documents required for you to travel will all be handled for you, as everything is 100% prearranged. Essentially, this all means that travel to this staggeringly complicated country is, from the traveller's point of view, remarkably straightforward.

Once in the country, minor changes to your itinerary are possible, but certain logistical arrangements can take days, if not weeks to put in place – so please don't expect to be able to arrange a charter flight or visit to a remote county on the spot. Those on private and small-group tours will naturally be able to have a greater degree of local flexibility than larger groups, which tend to be more pressed for time and thus controlled somewhat more rigidly. Some groups may include a spot of spare time in their itineraries, but you will still have to stay together as one ('in single-hearted unity', as the guides often express it), and will be limited as to what you can do – an unscheduled walk in central Pyongyang or a trip to a bar isn't going to be a problem, but an impromptu factory visit or tour of the Supreme Court just won't be an option. Should you want to do something that is not in your itinerary, you should raise it as early as possible. Your guides will always strive to accommodate you, but ultimately the needs of the group come first.

and all manner of what is essentially private enterprise is creeping in across the country – as Bob Dylan sang, *the times they are a-changin'*.

This nation has the habit of getting under one's skin – it certainly has mine. People have been forecasting the fall of the country as we know it for the past 30 years, and could well be doing so for the next 30 as well. But with the momentous events of 2018, which nobody could have predicted just six months prior, quite what the next few years will bring is anybody's guess. For the first time in many years there is the prospect of real and irreversible change creeping in, ending decades of self-imposed isolation as Pyongyang, ever so slowly and somewhat reluctantly, is being dragged into the international fold. These are exciting times indeed. The country cannot be truly explained, accurately described, or even truly understood. Visiting is the best way to try and get your head around the place – but it could well leave you, like me, more confused than ever before.

Henry Marr

Part One

GENERAL INFORMATION

Location Northeast Asia, bordering China and Russia to the north, and South Korea (Republic of Korea) to the south.

Area 122,762km^2

Status Democratic People's Republic

Population 23,349,859 (2008 census)/25,370,000 (2016 estimate)

Life expectancy 75.5 (Women)/68.2 (Men)

Climate Combination of continental and oceanic, with short, hot and humid summers, and long, cold winters.

Capital Pyongyang

Other major cities Chongjin, Hamhung, Kaechon, Kaesong, Nampo, Sariwon, Sinuiju, Tanchon and Wonsan

Exports Mineral products (primarily coal briquettes) (44%), textiles (29%), machines (6%), metals (4.9%) animal products (4.1%) and other (12%)

Official language Korean

Religion In essence – Atheist

Currency Won (North Korean Won), although for tourists US dollars, euros and Chinese yuan are readily acceptable.

Exchange rate Confusing! See box, page 65.

National airline Air Koryo

International telephone code +850

Time GMT+9

Electrical voltage 220v, 60Hz

Weights and measures Metric

Flag Central red panel with a five-pointed star within a white circle, bordered on either side by a narrow white stripe and broad blue stripe.

National anthem Aegukka (애국가), translating as 'The Patriotic Song'

Most significant public holidays 1 January (New Year's Day), 8 February (Army Day), 16 February (Day of the Shining Star, Kim Jong Il's birthday), 15 April (Day of the Sun, Kim Il Sung's birthday), 1 May (May Day), 27 July (Victory Day), 15 August (Liberation Day), 25 August (Day of Songun), 9 September (Republic Foundation Day), 10 October (Party Foundation Day), 31 December (New Year's Eve)

1

Background Information

GEOGRAPHY

Located on the Korean Peninsula in northeast Asia, North Korea is encircled by a gang of four: China, Russia, Japan and, of course, South Korea. While North Korea is an island in the political sense, it isn't one in the literal; to the north the Amnok (or Yalu in Chinese) and Tuman rivers mark the 1,416km-long border with China and the tiny 17.5km-long connection with Russia. The southern border is a far less natural one – a 4km-wide and 238km-long demilitarised zone (which is in fact anything but 'demilitarised') that cuts the peninsula roughly in two: the Democratic People's Republic of Korea (also known as North Korea, or the DPRK) in the north, and the Republic of Korea (also known as South Korea, or the ROK) in the south. When the nation was divided between American and Soviet spheres of interest in 1945 no experts were consulted; it was through a cursory examination of a National Geographic map that the 38th parallel was chosen as the dividing line, although the present-day demarcation was fixed along the final battle lines of 1953 (page 17) – a little south of the parallel in the west, a little north in the east.

With Korea Bay and the West Sea of Korea (Yellow Sea) on one flank and the East Sea of Korea (Sea of Japan) on the other, the long coastline is a mix of tidal plains and sandy bays. Heading inland reveals a country that is 80% mountainous, with many deep narrow valleys and steep, heavily forested ranges crisscrossing the country. The highest point in the Korean Peninsula is the 2,750m Mount Paektu, an active volcano straddling the Chinese border. With so much hilly terrain, only 19.5% of the nation is used for arable purposes and the majority of farming takes place in the western half of the country, where the fertile coastal plains are far wider than those in the east. North Korea is just over 20% larger than its southern neighbour and has, at its last official count, an area of 122,762km², but land reclamation projects slowly push this figure up, one labour-intensive kilometre at a time. In the last census of 2008 the population was recorded at 23.35 million, a figure that is thought to have crept up by another couple of million in the last decade.

GEOGRAPHICAL DIVISIONS AND TERMS Although reclassifications occur from time to time to add to the confusion, the country is best divided into nine provinces, with Pyongyang and the Rason Special Economic Zone having extra-provincial status, making a total of 11 areas. The status of Sinuiju, Nampo, Kaesong and Mount Kumgang is confusing to say the least, but for the purpose of this book are described as being part of the main provinces in which they are located. Each region is afforded its own chapter within this book and they appear in the following order: Pyongyang, North Hwanghae, South Hwanghae, South Pyongan, North Pyongan, Chagang, Kangwon, South Hamgyong, Ryanggang, North Hamgyong and Rason Special Economic Zone.

자강도	Chagang
강원도	Kangwon
함경북도	North Hamgyong
함경남도	South Hamgyong
황해북도	North Hwanghae
황해남도	South Hwanghae
평안북도	North Pyongan
평안남도	South Pyongan
평양	Pyongyang
라진선봉경제특구	Rason Special Economic Zone
량강도	Ryanggang

PROVINCES

At a city (*si*) level, urban areas are divided into wards (*guyŏk*), which are then broken down again into neighbourhoods (*dong*). In rural areas, provinces are broken down into counties (*kun*), which are then further split into villages (*ri*). More populous parts of a county are referred to as *ŭp*, while some counties have a workers' district, known as a *rodongjagu*.

Places and features are generally given a geographical suffix, and it pays to know a few of these suffixes, as they occasionally slip into usage or translations. *San*, for example, means mountain, and a Korean speaking English is just as likely to call their highest peak Paektusan as they are to call it Mount Paektu. Other words that regularly drop into English explanations include *bong,* meaning hill, and *nam*, meaning south. Finally, *gang* means river, so should somebody ask you about the *gangs* in London they are more likely to be interested in the drainage basin of the River Thames or the locks on Regent's Canal than they are in the city's latest knife crime statistics.

CLIMATE

North Korea has a combination of a continental and oceanic climates, with the extreme northeast having something of a Siberian look and feel – forests of fir, spruce and larch can be found at higher altitudes. As a rule, winters are marked as being long, cold and dry, while summers are short, hot and humid – over 50% of annual precipitation falls during the East Asian monsoon rains of July and August, a time when flooding is common across the country. In a nation that has self-reliance or 'Juche' as one of its core philosophies, the lack of suitable farmland mixed with the propensity for droughts and floods ensures that putting enough food on the table is a never-ending battle – a battle that was lost in successive years during the 1990s and contributed to the famine of 1994–98. Energy shortages during bleaker years led to notable deforestation in the lowlands, further exacerbating flooding and reducing agricultural output, but current reforestation projects are trying to redress the damage done.

While it's apparent that toiling the land is a struggle, living off what lies beneath has the potential to be far easier. The ground is rich with metals such as gold, tungsten, zinc and molybdenum and, before economic sanctions hit, an estimated 40% of North Korea's GDP came from the sale of coal briquettes alone. With the country sitting on an estimated US$6–10 trillion dollars of mineral wealth, venture capitalists the world over have been keenly watching recent events unfold, in the hope that North Korea will open for foreign investment, dragging the dilapidated mining infrastructure into the 21st century.

NATURAL HISTORY AND CONSERVATION

A long coastline and significant range in altitude, from balmy beaches to chilly mountains, help North Korea sustain a rich and diverse ecosystem. A number of strictly protected national parks and wildlife sanctuaries dot the country, though being over 80% mountainous means that much of the DPRK's environment is safeguarded by its own topography, rather than the conservational status a national park may afford. The land that can be intensively toiled almost always is, and habitats, particularly in the lowlands, have transformed due to urbanisation and the collectivisation of agriculture. Recent years have seen some conversion of forest into agricultural plots, together with further degradation due to the growth in the demand for firewood, while successive droughts have caused forest fires and noxious insect damage. Forest is recorded at covering 73% of the DPRK's territory but some estimates put the actual coverage as low as 50%; thankfully, there are now structured systems in place that are striving to undo the damage done a generation ago. All things considered, however, the country presents itself well – most visitors are surprised at the often pristine landscapes found here, with a thick carpet of shrubs and dense forest often stretching far into the distance, the view only occasionally interrupted by a belching industrial plant of some form.

The ecosystem offers a surprisingly wide range of biodiversity for a country of its size, with just shy of 9,000 plant species, including a significant number of medicinal plants that are important in Eastern medicine. Within the animal kingdom, a total of 865 fish, 17 amphibians (including the Siberian salamander), 26 reptiles (including loggerhead and leatherback sea turtles, David's ratsnake and the Mongolia racerunner) and 105 mammal species are recorded. The long list of the latter includes such wondrous beasts as the Amur leopard, Siberian tiger, long-tailed goral, Sika deer, Mongolian wolf and Asian black bear. Not to be outshone, marine mammals include three varieties of seal and all manner of dolphins, porpoises and whales.

Within the ornithological sphere, BirdLife International note 33 Important Bird and Biodiversity Areas within the country, spread over 2,530km[2]. Of the 326 recorded bird species in the DPRK, 278 are migratory. The East Asian–Australasian Flyway, which passes through the Korean Peninsula, is one of the world's most important migratory routes, so the protection of the birds that use this (which include the critically endangered Baer's pochard, spoon-billed sandpiper and yellow-breasted bunting) is important work. While the coastal mudflats in neighbouring China and South Korea have dwindled, the slow pace of change, coupled with fewer polluting factories and the lower levels of fertiliser and pesticides used in the North, is making the DPRK an increasingly important habitat for these birds.

Many examples of the flora and fauna in the DPRK likely still only exist to the extent they do due to the country's slow economic development. Yes, the country does use pesticides and chemical fertilisers and yes, it has tolerated deforestation and the degradation of habitats and ecosystems, but the economy has been so hampered for so long that the rate of this environmental damage has been far slower than in many other parts of the world. Now that humankind is becoming increasingly aware of the environmental damage it is doing, it is hoped that, as and when North Korea finally does start to live up to its true economic potential, it can do so in a way that is more thoughtful, thus preserving the exemplary natural history of the country for many generations to come.

HISTORY AND ECONOMY

ANCIENT HISTORY Accounts in both North and South Korea claim 5,000 years of native history; excavations of pottery shards and stone tools provide evidence of human settlements from Neolithic times. Many excavations have taken place in the Pyongyang area – sadly, this became easier following the 1950–53 war as so much of the modern city was destroyed, allowing access to its foundations. Though there have been claims made in North Korea that humans in the peninsula originated there, there is in fact no reason to believe that societies in the North were any more or less sophisticated than their neighbours in the South.

The mythical emperor Tangun is given credit for founding Korea in 2333BC. In the North, he is regarded as a real person and tourists can visit his 'tomb' in the eastern outskirts of Pyongyang (see box, page 130).

THE RIVAL THREE KINGDOMS The period described as the Three Kingdoms, from 57BC to AD668, is accepted both by Koreans and by scholars abroad. The three kingdoms were the **Baekje**, the **Koguryo** and the **Silla**, stretching at that time into what are now the three Chinese provinces of Heilongjiang, Jilin and Liaoning. The period could probably also be referred to as the 'Four Kingdoms' as the Gaya region, based around what is now Busan on the southeast coast, was independent for most of this time, before being absorbed into the Silla Kingdom in AD562. Silla, based in the southeastern part of the country, eventually became the strongest of the three; by 668 it had conquered the other two, uniting the whole Korean peninsula, which it did with strong support from the Tang Dynasty in China (which came to power in 618). The Tang had concluded that an alliance with a largely unified Korea under its suzerainty was a satisfactory solution to the geopolitical issues of the peninsula. This alliance was useful in preventing incursions from what is now Mongolia; culturally, it left a widespread legacy that continued well after the end of the Silla Dynasty in the 10th century, which fell into decline in tandem with the Tang, on which it was so dependent.

THE KORYO DYNASTY Reigning between 918 and 1392, the Koryo Dynasty is held in high regard in the North, as it was both the first truly unified kingdom on the peninsula and also had Kaesong as its capital. However, the Koryo never achieved the strength of their Silla predecessors due to frequent attacks from non-Chinese

With centuries of foreign invasion, influence and meddling from the Chinese, Japanese, Russians and Americans, the Korean peninsula has understandably suffered under a dearth of accurate depictions of its past. This has, of course, been further impacted by the peninsula's division and regimes, making conventional scholarship impossible for many years.

The end of the military regime in the South in 1987 has changed this somewhat for both nations. For North Korea, this has been due to those who have fled over the border since then, many of whom have provided rather lurid accounts of the suffering they have faced throughout their lives. Of course, what is lacking still are accurate accounts from those who have stayed – not to mention those who have benefitted from the increasingly affluent lifestyle now possible in Pyongyang. Regular defections from the North Korean diplomatic corps unfortunately tend to have little impact on our knowledge of the country, largely on account of the authorities in South Korea ensuring that very little of what they reveal on high-level politics reaches the public domain; much of this is done to protect families left behind who might suffer further due to any publicity garnered by their 'black sheep'. One exception was in the publication in 2018 of *Password to the Third Floor* by Thae Yong Ho (currently only available in Korean), the Deputy North Korean Ambassador to London who defected with his family in 2016. However, Thae was, as a result, referred to as 'human scum' by the North Koreans and a regular meeting between Pyongyang and the South was cancelled in protest.

The North is becoming more willing to present history prior to the Kim family, but as it has to be accommodated within a Marxist framework and only covers events from within the current territory of the DPRK, it is impossible to take any publication from the country at face value.

tribes based across the Amnok River and then, from the 13th century, there were frequent successful raids by the Mongols. Japanese pirates became an increasing problem, too, and one of the Mongol pretexts for invading Korea was the need to deal with them. Never again would Koreans rule across the Amnok or the Tumen rivers, although Korean ethnic communities remain on the Chinese side to this day. They have always accepted Chinese rule and never attempted to join whatever Korean regime was in power on the other side of the rivers. Equally, no Korean regime has suggested expansion to incorporate them.

Despite Mongol raids, Chinese inventions continued to reach Korea. Block printing arrived early in the 11th century, and movable type in the mid 13th century, 200 years before Gutenberg introduced the latter to Europe. Koreans were therefore among the first non-Chinese to enjoy the regular production of books on a large scale, even if, to begin with, they were only written in Chinese characters. Of more long-term significance from that period was the gradual introduction from China of Buddhism, a spiritual force that would remain active until the mid 20th century and which also started to influence Korean art and pottery.

THE 500-YEAR DYNASTY In the late 14th century, General Yi Seonggye became increasingly powerful as he succeeded in defeating both the Mongols on land and Japanese pirates at sea at a time when the Koryo Dynasty was weakened by poor leadership. In 1392 he seized the opportunity of murdering the Koryo king and established a new dynasty: the **Choson** or **Yi** Dynasty as it is sometimes known. It ruled from 1392 until 1897, which inaccurately suggests 500 years of stability; in reality, from the end of the 16th century the opposite was the case. In 1396 the capital was moved from Kaesong to Hanyang, now part of Seoul, and would remain there.

The dynasty's most effective ruler, usually known as King Sejong The Great, was on the throne from 1418 until 1450. Because of his diverse talents, he was probably the best king Korea ever had: his administration was efficient and he took his Confucianist ethics seriously, his officials planned for the droughts and floods that have been a regular part of Korean history and his military campaigns were always successful, particularly against Japanese pirates. He also introduced the Hangul phonetic alphabet, still in use today (page 41), to replace Chinese characters, which was invaluable for increasing literacy, and supported scientists – considerable progress was made with clocks, rain gauges and sundials, among many other inventions. In the North, his name is barely mentioned, but of course neither are any other names between King Tangun and the rise of the Kim family in the 19th century. It has to be admitted, however, that prestige remained among officials who were able to write in Chinese characters.

The year 1592 was one of the most important in Korean history. On 24 May, the Japanese invaded Busan and fighting against Korean and Chinese troops ensued until the following February, when, for the first and only time in Sino-Japanese

KOREA'S ADMIRAL NELSON?

The most famous Korean of the 16th century was undoubtedly Admiral Yi Sun Sin (1545–98), who defeated the Japanese against extraordinary odds in repeated battles between 1592 and 1598. Not only was he a brilliant strategist, being able to deceive and then trap the Japanese ships time and time again, but he won great respect from all those he commanded. The Japanese were not interested in Korea as such, but needed a route through which they could protect themselves from the Mongols, Manchus and Chinese. With this aim in mind, they were happy to burn down both Pyongyang and Seoul between 1592 and 1597, before they were driven out by the Koreans with the crucial support of the Ming Dynasty rulers in China, who provided troops and supplies.

In 1596, the Japanese managed to infiltrate a supposed double agent into the Korean military, giving information as to where the next invasion would be. Not trusting this information, Yi refused to go to an area that he knew was rock infested and where his ships would come only to grief. This resulted in his arrest and torture, and near death. He was, however, spared from a formal death sentence and was instead demoted to the rank of an enlisted soldier. Not for the first time, he soon had to be brought back to a senior command, after the navy suffered a humiliating defeat, having failed to correctly assess likely Japanese movements. His crowning success was at the Battle of Myeongnyang in October 1597 where, with judicious knowledge of tides, currents, likely weather and sandbanks, Yi was able, with just 13 ships, to defeat an enemy that had around 330.

Yi was killed by a stray bullet in battle a year later, although news of his death was kept from his sailors for several crucial hours, and so – of course – from the enemy as well. He has often been compared to Admiral Lord Nelson for being able to, as it were, lead his sailors to victory from his death bed. It was another 300 years before the Japanese attempted to invade Korea again.

HENDRICK HAMEL

In 1653, a Dutch ship under the command of Hendrik Hamel was shipwrecked near Jeju Island, off the south coast. The crew had originally consisted of 64 men, but 28 drowned before they could reach the shore. The remaining 36 were captured and imprisoned by the Koreans, firstly being transferred to Seoul, and after a few months to Pyongyang, where they were kept for seven years – a further 11 of them died during this time. House arrest is perhaps the best description of their fate as they had jobs as bodyguards and were allowed freedom of movement within the town. Pleas by the sailors for their release, made both directly and via the Chinese, were rebuffed as the royal family did not want knowledge of their country to spread abroad. The ship owners had assumed the ship was lost, together with the entire crew, which was understandable given that the Koreans refused to allow messages to be sent to Japan. Hamel himself finally managed to escape with seven colleagues in 1667, reaching the Dutch community in Nagasaki (Japan), which was where he had hoped to arrive 12 years earlier. His journal, which remained largely unknown for 200 years, was translated into English in the 1990s and offers vignettes on several aspects of Korean life at the time, including gruesome and very detailed descriptions of executions, torture and floggings, which were conducted in public.

history, Chinese forces were victorious. The Japanese had initially been successful, with Seoul falling on 12 June, and Pyongyang a month later. However, Chinese forces crossed the Yalu River and over the next four months were able to take advantage of Japan's inability to keep its forces regularly supplied. As would happen so often in subsequent military history around the world, a successful initial Blitzkrieg was not followed by a clear occupation policy that could define and hold crucial lines of supply.

Following the defeat of the Japanese in 1597 (see box, opposite), subsequent dangers came from overland and from the Manchus who, by 1644, drove the Ming Dynasty out of Beijing and by 1683 ruled the whole of China. Realising that stability in Korea would help them in this aim, they attacked the peninsula in 1627 and again in 1636, briefly driving the royal family and the government to the island of Ganghwa. As a consequence, Korea then became a nominal tributary of China and showed no interest in contact with the outside world, a policy that China was largely adopting as well at that time, in contrast to its eagerness for trade along the Silk Road under earlier dynasties. Korea then had a period of peace for about 200 years. The Japanese retreated into their self-imposed isolation and the Manchu Dynasty in China, which formally came to power in 1644, remained strong through the 18th century, so the Chinese were not threatened from abroad. Korea has no choice but to follow this policy of isolation as adopted by its two great neighbouring powers.

Korea Opens Up Foreign vessels from several Western countries approached the Korean coast in the early 19th century, and their numbers increased after the opening of China during the first of the Opium Wars around 1840. Although negotiations for landing and trading started during this time, they were all peacefully repulsed by the Koreans who, like China and Japan at this time, saw no need for links further afield.

In 1853, the US gunboat *South America* visited Busan, though it arrived more as a wreck than as a pioneer in trade. The sailors were returned overland to China and were largely not allowed to return to their ship (only sailors needed to take away the ship were allowed back on board). In 1866, the USS *General Sherman* came up the Taedong River to Pyongyang to try to impose trade, firing towards the shore as the ship approached – before getting stuck on a sandbank. The exact sequence of events after that are uncertain, but all of the crew were killed – either burnt to death onboard, drowned as they attempted to swim ashore, or beaten to death after reaching land. It is now claimed in North Korea that the person leading the assault on the *General Sherman* was Kim Ung U, the great-grandfather of Kim Il Sung, though there is no evidence for this. A monument celebrating the sinking of this 'pirate ship' can be found in Pyongyang, near where another American ship, the USS *Pueblo*, was moored for many years (page 23).

During the 1850s and '60s, Ganghwa Island, in the mouth of the Han River, was the scene of a number of confrontations between Korea and various foreign ships – all of which were successfully driven away. However, in September 1875, the Japanese, alert to the increasing number of Western incursions in the region and open to foreign trade as a result of the 1854 Treaty of Kanagawa, approached the island with their ship *Unyo*. The subsequent battle was won easily by the Japanese, which consequently led to the signing of the Treaty of Ganghwa in February 1876. Japan victored with its gunboat diplomacy – despite Tokyo formally recognising Korea as an independent country the treaty was, in essence, designed along the same lines as the various 'unequal treaties' that were being imposed by Western powers in Asia at the time. The Japanese now had full trading rights with Korea. The crucial element of the agreement was extraterritoriality, which meant that Japanese nationals were not subject to Korean law in the ports of Busan, Inchon and Wonsan. Full diplomatic relations were established, with the Koreans told to correspond in Chinese or Japanese, not Korean.

The description of Korea as the 'Hermit Kingdom' first appeared in *Corea, the Hermit Nation* by William Elliot Griffis (1882), an American missionary and teacher who spent many years in both Japan and Korea. He noted the lack of cohesion at court and the risk that Korea would be swallowed up by 'jealous and greedy rivals'. He saw timber rights and mining concessions being sold to foreigners far too cheaply and noted the lack of a samurai class that was preventing Korea developing in the same way as Japan. He wrote: 'There is a total absence of an intelligent middle class which in the west is the characteristic of progressive actions.' The travel he arranged for several Korean officials to see the educational system in Japan was not a success; they were worried by the potential risks (namely a threat to their positions) posed by the introduction of widespread education. Griffis could, despite his frustrations, understand their view that the kingdom had enjoyed its own civilisation for 5,000 years and so they saw no need to replace it. The view of such Koreans was often 'we trouble no other nation, so why do they trouble us?', but Griffis also well understood the Japanese role in Korea as they pursued their policy of modernisation 'with the hot-headed zeal of the newly converted'.

The Korean royal family remained unconvinced of the need for reform, perhaps because the Chinese royal family thought likewise and both hoped that Western incursions were a tiresome temporary phenomenon that could in due course be dealt with. The only concession, if it could be called as such as it was granted by Korea under the imposed 'unequal treaties', concerned diplomatic links – during the 1880s a number of embassies were opened both in Korea and abroad. In 1882 a Treaty of Amity and Commerce was signed with the US, and formal diplomatic relations followed in 1883. The following year, Sir Harry Parkes, who had been British Ambassador to Japan for 18 years, but was by this time Ambassador in

Christianity had previously been banned in Korea since 1758, a year in which many Catholics were executed. However, the 1882 treaty with the US (see opposite) lead to an immediate influx of Presbyterian missionaries, whose activity was centred on Pyongyang. The first Presbyterian to arrive was Horace Allen (and his wife) in 1884, who came to serve as a doctor to the new foreign community. He was fortunately in Seoul when an assassination attempt was made on the Queen's nephew, Prince Min Yong Ik; Allen's modern treatment undoubtedly saved the prince's life and ensured a safe future for Presbyterian activity throughout the country. By 1910 there were 60,000 registered converts; Americans quickly delegated to Koreans who extended the work of the church well beyond proselytising, and also established its presence in the countryside. In many places, they brought the first school, the first medicine and the first introduction to science and engineering. The role of Presbyterians in Korean society continued to be felt until the early 1930s when ever-increasing Japanese control of the country inevitably led to their decline.

China, came to Seoul to sign a friendship treaty – conveniently at a time when the Korean court had just started to allow foreigners to reside within Seoul city walls. The necessary land for an embassy was bought for 1,200 Mexican dollars (at the time the main trading unit in East Asia), equivalent then to £225; the British Embassy in Seoul remains on that site today.

THE INCREASE IN JAPANESE INFLUENCE The Tonghak Uprising in 1894 was the culmination of attempts by this rural-based group to seize power in the face of increasing tax demands, but it was ruthlessly suppressed by Chinese and Japanese forces. Perhaps inspired by the Taipings in China, who ruled large parts of China during the 1850s, the Tonghaks combined religious fervour with a radical political streak, and, like the Taipings, had leaders who regarded themselves as divinely inspired. Neither the Tonghaks nor the Taipings could, however, organise a military or political programme that enabled them to overthrow the imperial regime, so both inevitably provided pretexts for foreign intervention. In the case of Korea, this led to clashes between the Chinese and the Japanese around Inchon, which eventually lead to the First Sino-Japanese War, in which the Japanese found Korea a very useful transit area as it intensified. The Treaty of Shimonoseki in 1895 brought this war to an end, and with it the end of Chinese suzerainty over Korea. In 1897 the Choson Kingdom formally became the Great Korean Empire, but this meant little as by 1910 Japan would have total control of Korea.

As they increased their influence in Korea, the Japanese were eager to sign treaties with other imperial powers, particularly with those who might be hostile to Russia, who had an interest in Korea and fought Japan in the 1904–05 Russo–Japanese War. Therefore, in 1902 they signed one with Britain that accepted Korea as being subject to Japan and the Japanese accepted a similar role for Britain in India. This Treaty of Alliance, as it came to be called, brought Japan into World War I on the Allies' side and signified their acceptance of continuing British rule in India, at a time when this was being increasingly questioned in India itself. In return, the Japanese absorption of Korea did not give rise to any outside objections. This process was carried out in two stages. From 1905, Japan presented Korea as a protectorate, and in 1910 the country was annexed, with the already minimal role of the royal family coming to an end. Japanese long-term strategy was clear from the start: Korea was to become a transit post to facilitate war with China. This was shown most dramatically in the building of the railway from Busan on the south coast to Seoul, which was then extended to join it up with the Chinese railway system. Like the other imperial powers at that time, the Japanese saw themselves as bringing the modern world to communities that had not yet been industrialised or, as they would have put it, 'civilised'.

KOREA UNDER JAPANESE OCCUPATION The Japanese takeover of Korea was formalised in a treaty signed in August 1910 by the Korean Prime Minister and the future Japanese Governor. However, as no member of the Korean royal family signed it, it was technically invalid (a fact noted by the South Korean and Japanese governments in 1965 when they formally declared it void). The Japanese quickly realised the potential Korea offered as an integrated part of their country. The northern area was rich, having mineral resources and mountain rivers to provide electric power, while the south was more agriculturally based (but subsequently poorer). Inhabitants of the Japanese island of Kyushu, closer to Korea by boat than Tokyo was by land, soon saw the potential as settlers.

Major independence demonstrations took place across Korea in March 1919, with around two million participants. The public stance of the Japanese at this time was that they were generating Korean prosperity and guaranteeing the safety of foreigners. Admiral Saito Makoto, Governor of Korea from 1919 to 1927 and again from 1929 to 1931, talked extensively about 'cultural cooperation', but what he was really working towards was cultural assimilation. Name changes were introduced such as Keijo for Seoul and Heijo for Pyongyang, and public speeches had to be spoken in Japanese. Cultural control increased during the 1930s, with the discouragement of Korean studies in schools and in universities. There was extensive migration (both voluntary and forced) from Korea to Japan during the occupation; it is estimated that by 1939 nearly a million Koreans lived there, a figure that would increase to two million by the end of the World War II.

The ruthless suppression of the March 1919 demonstrations by the Japanese – it is estimated that 47,000 people were either killed or seriously injured – indicated that other means of protest would have to be followed as military and/or open political activity in Korea itself was no longer possible. Most political activists

COMFORT WOMEN

The most controversial legacy of the Japanese occupation was the issue of 'comfort women', which was largely ignored for 50 years by Japan after the war, and even then was evaded and marginalised. An uncertain number of Korean women – estimates vary from 50,000 to 200,000 – were forced into prostitution by the Japanese army and kept at 'comfort stations' linked to barracks all over the Empire of Japan. To maintain morale and to prevent escapes, the women, as with the troops, were told that the Western forces were cannibals who would eat them alive were they to fall into captivity. The women who survived and were able to return to Korea usually felt too ashamed and distraught to discuss their experiences until they were very elderly. It is thought that most of the women involved were kidnapped in the southern part of the country; as a result, this remains an issue between South Korea and Japan today and not something that has often been raised by North Korea.

chose exile – indeed, Kim Il Sung himself spent 20 years in rural China and a further five in the Soviet Union (see box, page 20). The man who would become his first southern opposite number, Syngman Rhee, began to work with a Korean 'government in exile' based in Shanghai in the 1920s before moving to the United States. This exile group was largely made up of Christian northerners who had been centred around religious communities based in Pyongyang. Rhee himself led a very public life and was able to present the Korean case personally to both president Roosevelts (Theodore and Franklin), which in due course assured his role as the first leader in South Korea. There are, in contrast, minimal firm records of Kim's activities during this time, which enabled him, and even more his successors, to paint an unblemished record of constant revolutionary activity within Korea, leading, naturally, to the leadership.

The Japanese advanced further and further into China during the 1930s, having begun with an occupation of Manchuria in 1931. Having Korea as an integral part of Japan of course facilitated this advance, and some Koreans joined the Japanese military during this period and had successful careers in Manchuria. During World War II, although conscription started in 1939 for Koreans to work in Japanese factories, enlistment in the Japanese Army remained voluntary until 1944 and Koreans became notorious as prison guards for the Japanese. Nevertheless, as manpower shortages increased with the worsening military situation in the battles with the Allies, conscription became compulsory in 1944. There was, however, no fighting in Korea itself during World War II.

THE END OF JAPANESE OCCUPATION The Cairo Declaration of 1 December 1943, which concluded a conference in the city that was attended by President Roosevelt, Prime Minster Churchill and Marshall Chiang Kai-shek, pledged independence for Korea 'in due course' – inevitably angering Korean groups in exile who wanted independence immediately. Then, and at future conferences during World War II, Korea was very much treated as a tiresome sideshow to what were understandably seen as more important issues. As discussed with the Western powers at the 1943 Tehran Conference, Stalin agreed that the Soviet Union would enter the war against Japan once Germany was defeated. This was further confirmed at the Yalta Conference of February 1945, where he agreed that the Soviets would turn their attention to the Pacific War within three months of the war ending in Europe. Roosevelt had suggested at Yalta that a trusteeship between the US, UK, Soviet Union and China should rule Korea for the next 20–30 years. Stalin thought that five years could be sufficient, but the matter was not thought to be urgent as the leaders expected the war against Japan to continue for two to three further years. The power of nuclear weapons was yet to be realised.

With the commencement of the Soviet–Japanese War on 9 August 1945 the US became anxious that the USSR would strive to occupy the entire peninsula and hurriedly proposed the division of Korea along the 38th parallel – with the North occupied by the USSR and the South by the US. This line was arbitrarily chosen by the US as it roughly divided Korea in two, while keeping Seoul in the South. Prior to this division there had been no pre-existing geographical, historical or cultural boundaries between the two. The Soviets accepted the proposal, which was incorporated into General Order No. 1 for the surrender of Japan, and was issued on 17 August. As was the case with Germany, it was assumed that reunification would take place soon after, and both sides anticipated that it would be under their auspices; at this point neither considered a long-term division, although this was, of course, the outcome. Unsurprisingly, no Korean views were sought on the matter.

THE DIVISION OF KOREA The Soviets were initially uncertain whether to make Hamhung or Pyongyang the capital of the north, but the fact they considered this topic at all suggests that they immediately realised that Seoul would not be entering the equation. There was little knowledge of Korea among the Soviet authorities, partly because several Korean exiles were killed in the 1937 to 1939 purges. A communist party had to be established from scratch, as what little clandestine activity took place under the Japanese had centred on Seoul. Pyongyang was hardly a likely base for left-wing movements, with many religions active there, but very little industry. The party also had to contend with rival factions; although small, they were all still determined to have a role in the new country. One, formed by nationalist activist Cho Man Sik, was the Democratic Party of Korea; although it had no communist sympathies, because of its likely appeal to the population, it was forcibly merged by the Soviets into their communist party. Cho is sometimes referred to as the 'Ghandi of Korea' due to his determination not to use violence. He was arrested in 1946 by the Soviets when they realised he could not be used as part of their strategy for imposing communism on the North, and was probably among the 500 prisoners executed in a Pyongyang jail in October 1950, just before the communist retreat. Today, Cho is commemorated in the South, but, of course, not mentioned at all in the North.

Kim Il Sung arrived in the North a month after the Soviet forces, at the age of 33 (see box, page 20). He gave his first speech in October 1945 at a meeting clearly choreographed by the senior Soviet military figure in Korea, General Nicholai Lebedev; as a result, it was full of symbolic praise for Stalin. Kim was formally proclaimed leader in December 1945 – the month when the UN had proposed elections for the entire country. However, the Soviet authorities prevented the UN representatives from crossing the border, and no further attempt was made.

The Soviets were the only relevant outside power in the North's immediate post-war history as the Chinese were still fighting their civil war. The Korean local 'elections' held in November 1946 had a clear Soviet stamp on them, with just one candidate from the Worker's Party of North Korea in each constituency and a turnout of 99.6%. Meanwhile, the South banned the Communist Party and made it clear that any sympathisers should move to the north.

Much power in the North between 1945 and 1950, both on stage and behind the scenes, lay with the Soviet Governor and then Ambassador Terentii Shtykov. He implemented land reform in 1946, probably the most popular measure ever introduced in the country. He also had a close relationship with Stalin and the two of them were largely responsible for the 1948 Korean Constitution. It is also likely that he would have determined that Kim Il Sung would be formally nominated as Korean leader once power was handed over. Shtykov realised that Kim needed a high public profile to satisfy the nationalistic aspirations of the population and to give the impression that a Japanese occupation was not simply being followed by a Soviet one. By August 1946, the membership of the Worker's Party of North Korea reached 170,000, largely thanks to Kim. The party had been officially founded on 10 October 1945 by Kim and the Soviet administration, a day still commemorated every year in the North.

The Democratic People's Republic of Korea (DPRK) was formally inaugurated on 9 September 1948, now celebrated as Republic Foundation Day. The South Koreans had done the same on 15 August and were henceforth referred to as 'separatists' in North Korean propaganda. Both sides began to realise that war would be the only way to achieve unification, and frequent raids across the border were a clear indication of this. Nevertheless, both thought they could win this struggle on their own without the help of their previous occupiers.

KIM GU

One potential rival to Kim Il Sung was Kim Gu, who headed the Korean government in exile in Shanghai during the Japanese occupation and whose political activities, and hence his imprisonments, stretched back to imperial days. He committed his first assassination in 1896, when he was 20, of a Japanese businessman and would in due course be responsible for many more. He was lucky to escape execution for his crimes during the late imperial era. In Shanghai in the early 1920s, he was able to persuade the new Soviet government to provide 700 pounds of gold to finance his activities. When Shanghai fell to the Japanese in 1941, he fled to Chongqing, the temporary capital of the Chinese nationalist government. He wanted immediate independence and was opposed to the trusteeship agreed by the Allies at Yalta in 1945. He returned to the South immediately after the Japanese surrender, with a team of bodyguards and, some say, with a team of concubines as well. He had by then well-deserved his nickname of 'the assassin'.

Gu was no communist, but realised that talking to Kim Il Sung was essential if any form of reunification was to take place. The two met in April 1948 in Pyongyang, but it was clear that no common ground could be found. Kim Il Sung saw no need to compromise on the policies he had worked out with Shtykov and doubtless was already foreseeing a time when he would impose these on the whole Korean peninsula. Gu was nominated, against his wishes, as a presidential candidate in the South, but lost heavily to his life-long enemy, Syngman Rhee, who then arranged his assassination in June 1949, still seeing him as a potential threat. In 1998, Gu was posthumously awarded the DPRK's National Reunification Prize, and in the South the Order of Merit – an irony he would have appreciated, being so keen on reunification.

Soviet forces left North Korea in December 1948 and US forces followed suit in June 1949 (although 500 American military trainers remained) – somewhat ironic timing in light of what happened in June 1950. The Soviets left behind much of their equipment in the North and the US started giving significant military aid to the South.

THE KOREAN WAR BREAKS OUT It is unclear when Kim Il Sung first planned an invasion of the South, but he was clearly encouraged by the apparent ease with which the Chinese communists had taken control of their country in 1949. Given that the border along the 38th parallel was still relatively open, it would not have been difficult for Kim to receive regular reports on the weak state of the military in the South. Kim certainly discussed his plans often with Ambassador Shtykov, who supported the idea and reported positively to Stalin. The Soviet leader was sceptical to begin with, fearing a clash with the US that could lead to nuclear warfare, but in the end was won over by Kim, who came to Moscow in April 1950 for discussions. Kim continued to China where he garnered support from a confident Mao Zedong; fresh from defeating nationalist forces and having set up the People's Republic of China, Mao was sure that as the Americans had been forced to accept communism in China, they would do so in Korea too. By then, the Soviet Union had nuclear weapons and Mao did not think the Americans would risk a nuclear war over Korea.

The North attacked on 25 June 1950. The military in the South were largely off-duty and totally unprepared, partly because it was a Sunday. Although the invasion came from the North, it can be seen as a reply to repeated provocations from the South that had taken place along the border since it was established in 1945, rather than as a totally unjustified attack out of the blue. Kim was clearly the driving force behind the decision but final approval was sought and given by Ambassador Shtykov, following instructions from Stalin. The first few days were immensely successful for the North Koreans, with Seoul falling on 28 June. The UN ordered the immediate withdrawal of the North's army, citing that the Soviet representative on the Security Council, Jakob Malik, was not in attendance. Had he been, he would have undoubtedly vetoed the motion and the subsequent deployment of UN forces in the South to resist the invasion.

Kim assumed the South would surrender after the fall of Seoul and, as a result, he failed to make long-term plans or prepare for a response. However, on 30 June, US President Truman ordered ground forces from Japan to be sent to South Korea, who arrived on 4 July. Nearly 100,000 British troops joined the South Koreans and the US forces under UN control, which also included Australia, Canada, Belgium, France, Turkey and nine other countries. Overall command was under US General Douglas MacArthur, who had been Supreme Commander for the Allied Powers in Japan. Many of the deployed troops were as naive as the forces in the North had been, reckoning that it would only take a week to settle before they would return to Japan.

General MacArthur's master stroke was the attack on Inchon, which took place in mid September 1950 and led to Seoul being recaptured by UN forces towards the end of that month. It was planned impeccably, with earlier diversionary raids elsewhere to fool the North Koreans and with spies able transmit details of the local forces in Inchon. UN forces occupied the whole of the South by the end of October.

Had UN forces stopped at the 38th parallel (a policy recommended by the British), it is quite likely that the war would have ended after just five months. Sadly, however, this was not the case, and by November 1950 UN forces occupied most of the North, with Kim Il Sung having to flee to the mountains in the northeast. Concerned that UN forces might extend the war into China, the Chinese invaded the Korean border with 200,000 troops on 25 October, all well-trained by Peng Dehuai and most with fighting experience gained in the Chinese civil war that had finished a year earlier. Fortunately, the Chinese forces were also well-armed, as by now the Soviet supply of arms and food, which had been provided since the outbreak of war, were seriously dwindling. The Chinese were concerned that UN forces might cross the Amnok River and indeed many in the US military were keen to do so. However, President Truman would not allow this and US bombing stopped literally at the border in the middle of the river; a bridge was bombed to destruction on the North Korean side, but untouched on the Chinese side.

A bombing raid on the border town of Sinuiju on 8 November set the pattern for further raids over the next 2½ years; 300 US planes dropped 630 tonnes of bombs, reflecting an intensity that no British or German town faced during World War II. Indeed, the savagery of the war equalled that on the Eastern Front during World War II when there was not the slightest concern for human life. The only town to be spared from this onslaught was Kaesong (page 138).

General Douglas MacArthur had seemed the obvious choice as Commander of the UN forces given his experience in the Pacific during World War II, and his recent governmental experience in ruling Japan further increased his popularity. However, he failed in the guerrilla warfare that was needed to defeat the Chinese, who moved in small units at night and hid in the forests by day. (The US would have similar problems with the Vietcong 20 years later.) He also failed to appreciate the significance of the Chinese invasion until much too late, promising all who would listen that the war would end by Thanksgiving and the troops would be home by Christmas. His public advocacy of the nuclear option against China, which would never be US government policy, inevitably led to his dismissal in April 1951, along with his failure to visit Korea from his base in Japan or, perhaps more surprisingly, the US.

MOVES TOWARDS PEACE The Chinese counteroffensive in April 1951 failed as it was unable to dislodge UN forces from what became the ceasefire line, which ran north of the 38th parallel in the east, and to the south of it in the west. Fighting continued for a further two years, but not with the same intensity as during 1950–51.

The Chinese were put under great strain supplying their troops, given that roads and railways were constantly bombed by the Americans. Carrying backpacks through the night was the only supply route that was relatively dependable, but the loss of manpower inevitably led to a weakened morale among both the Chinese and the North Koreans. The Chinese commander Peng Dehuai went frequently to Beijing to warn Mao Zedong of the deteriorating situation. Equally the UN forces could not show any progress to satisfy electorates in Britain and the US, or to the other UN members who contributed troops and weapons.

Negotiations towards peace started in the summer of 1951 and took place in Kaesong and in Panmunjom. Once talks began, neither side wanted to disrupt them, meaning that Kaesong was spared the destruction the rest of the country had suffered. Fighting would continue elsewhere in the North to test the resolve of each side, but despite this there were no major victories; in due course, the cease-fire line became the armistice line. The ceasefire was further accelerated by the change in leadership among the Allies. In November 1952, after his election but before he was formally inaugurated as president, Dwight Eisenhower visited Korea and privately threatened the Chinese with nuclear weapons. In the Soviet Union, Stalin died in March 1953 and his successors had no wish to see Korea continuing as unfinished business. Similarly in Britain, the Conservatives won the October 1951 election and saw the war as unfinished Labour Party business that they wanted to bring an end.

A major stumbling block in peace negotiations was the exchange of Korean and Chinese prisoners of war, some of whom did not want to return. Exactly what their real feelings were was in many cases hard to ascertain, given that their future would be so unpredictable whatever choice they made. The Indian government did most of the work to bring both sides together and then to keep them talking but they did not take part in the negotiations themselves.

The Korean Armistice Agreement was signed on 27 July 1953 by the UN (not the US), China and the DPRK. South Korean president Syngman Rhee refused to sign it on behalf of the South, feeling that such a gesture would suggest acceptance of the division of the country, and therefore would represent a betrayal on his part. With this in mind, it is accurate to say that the Korean War was, in fact, a war that both sides won and both sides lost. Probably a million people were killed to restore the status quo of a country divided into two irreconcilable elements.

The border between the North and South, now known as the DMZ (Demilitarised Zone), became one of the most heavily guarded in the world. Not only has crossing it been impossible for all except a few UN officials, but there has also been no post or telephone contact between the two countries since it was drawn up, so family members who found themselves divided across the border, as many did, would never know the fate of their relatives. With the increase in bilateral negotiations between North and South during 2018, there could be considerably more border crossings here in the near future.

Although the land border was easy to delineate, the border at sea caused friction on several subsequent occasions. A Northern Limit Line nominally divides the North Korean mainland from Yeonpyeong and four smaller islands that belong to the South, even though they are well to the North of the cease-fire line. This tricky border still exists today – see box, page 153.

AN UNEASY PEACE? The decade or so after the 1953 armistice is the period in North Korean history about which the least is known. Very few Westerners visited, there were no diplomatic relations and, being understandably concerned with rebuilding their country, the North could not put great effort into presenting a case abroad.

Kim Il Sung spent much of 1953 consolidating his power at the expense of so-called 'enemies' – mainly communists from the South who came north when it was clear that the country was going to stay divided. A show trial with 12 defendants took place in August 1953, with extensive national publicity. The four charges were: plotting a coup, destroying the Communist Party in the South, working with the Japanese authorities during the occupation, and spying for the US. A detailed plan for the coup, and the composition of the government that would replace Kim, was presented. After a few weeks in prison, the defendants of course admitted guilt to all of these 'crimes', even though the accusations were totally false. In its form, the trial seemed to adhere to all legal niceties, being held in public, with journalists present and with defence lawyers as active as the prosecution. However, the trials were scheduled only when it was certain that

THE CHOLLIMA MOVEMENT

The Chollima is a mythical flying horse, akin to Pegasus from Greek mythology, that has its origins in Chinese classical texts from the 3rd century BC. Chollima literally translates as a 'thousand li horse', with a 'li' being a traditional unit of east Asian measurement (and two points in Scrabble), which equates, in modern Korean usage, to 393m. Accordingly, Chollima could gallop, or fly, almost 400km in a single day.

In the immediate post-war years, to say that North Korea was in dire straits would be an understatement. Cities were levelled, industry destroyed and the collective psyche of the nation, despite the best efforts of the propagandists, was near its nadir. As Kim Il Sung set out at this time to cement his power, the importance of rebuilding the decimated economy was paramount to national (and his political) survival. In late 1956, in preparation for the nation's First Five-Year Plan, a grand economic strategy designed to drastically improve the economy, Kim Il Sung launched the Chollima Movement, the most famous mass mobilisation campaign in the country's history. Inspired by similar movements inaugurated in the USSR by Stalin in the 1930s, and far more successful than China's Great Leap Forward (to which it is occasionally compared), the Chollima Movement urged the entire nation to work harder and better in order to smash production targets, increase output and generally achieve the unachievable, just like the mythical Chollima horse. This Stakhanovite movement, motivating workers through ideology (as they, of course, would not be rewarded financially) spurred on socialist emulation, as people gave their very all to exceed output, outdo their peers and smash targets by hundreds of percent to try and become 'Chollima riders', hero labourers that were glorified across the nation – a rare example in the nation's history where the people, not their leaders, were celebrated for their tireless efforts.

the defendants had been broken and would keep to the script. It is impossible to guess what was going through the defendants' minds as this charade was being performed; perhaps they hoped for reduced sentences, but this was in vain: ten were executed and two given long prison terms.

In the summer of 1955, the trial of Pak Hon Yong took place. Pak was DPRK Foreign Minister from the founding of the country in 1948 until his arrest in 1953. He had been an active resistance fighter under the Japanese and then worked to establish communist activity more openly in the South after the 1945 division of the country, before coming north in 1948. Unlike the show trial, no journalists attended and the official press gave it minimal coverage – perhaps there was uncertainty over whether Pak would keep to the script. It is likely Pak was executed in December 1955, although some scholars think he was kept alive a little longer to provide information on other 'traitors'. Either way, it is clear that Kim was acting very much as Stalin had done with his purges in the late 1930s, and no further public trials would take place until that of Jang Song Thaek in December 2013 (page 33).

August 1956 saw the first and last clear attempt to oust Kim Il Sung. Kim had been summoned to Moscow in July by Khrushchev for a supposed 'dressing down' as, having denounced Stalin in his 'Secret Speech' in February that year, the Soviet leader wanted to address Kim's dictatorial nature. Plotters in Pyongyang took advantage of Kim's absence to start their planning; however, the plot failed as they did not gain sufficient support from the Central Committee. Some of the plotters

1

With the movement being adopted with zeal across the nation, the First Five-Year Plan was deemed a success, and estimates state the North Korean GNP nearly doubled between 1956 and 1960, completing the already ambitions Five-Year Plan two years early. Of course, while deemed a success, endless overtime in arduous conditions is not sustainable in any environment. While the Koreans hail the Chollima Movement (and all their similar and subsequent mass mobilisation campaigns) as nothing but an absolute success, foreign economists state that these gains were little more than short term, as they exhausted workers, lead to a dip in the quality of manufacturing and distorted both resources and the economy. When the First Five-Year Plan came to an end, there was no chance for the nation's workers to take it easy for a while – it was immediately proceeded by the Seven-Year Plan which, due to its disappointing results, lasted a decade. Although the plans and schemes for upping production continued unabated, the workers themselves could not.

Decades on from the original Chollima Movement, 2012 saw the first mention of the Mallima Movement, a new campaign that evolved into 'Mallima Speed'; Mallima meaning 'ten thousand li horse' – ten times faster than its predecessor from the 1950s. Designed, like the Chollima Movement, to spur on the ideological enthusiasm and output of the nation and its workers, Mallima wasn't that much different from Chollima in reality – while almost any North Korean would publicly state that he or she would do anything for their leader, increasing one's already overstretched output ten, nay one hundred fold, is impossible, even for the most sedulous of citizens – still, it's a good soundbite and slogan with which to try and rouse the masses. Presumably a supersonic 'Sibmanlima' (one hundred thousand li horse) will be the next banner, helping to stir the proletariat into sending their economy, and Korean socialism, on an unstoppable and stratospheric path towards utopia.

KIM IL SUNG: FROM OBSCURITY TO DEITY

Considering that Kim Il Sung ruled North Korea for almost 50 years, very little is truly known about the second-longest serving non-royal head of state in the 20th century – pipped to the post by none other than Fidel Castro. The following sweeping summary is *believed* to be accurate, but until the various vaults in Moscow, Pyongyang, Beijing and elsewhere are opened, a little unintentional fiction may cloud the facts.

Kim Il Sung was born on the 15 April 1912, the very day that the *Titanic* plunged into the icy depths of the North Atlantic. Over 11,000km away from those cold waters, Kim was born in Mangyongdae, in those days a sleepy village near Pyongyang. Born Kim Song Ju (only adopting the *nom de guerre* Kim Il Sung, meaning 'becomes the sun', around 1935), his family were Christians and neither destitute nor wealthy – similar to many rural intellectuals they eked out a living and did better than most in Japanese-occupied Korea. Despite this, like so many others the Kim family left to try their luck in Manchuria, around 1920. It was here that Kim Il Sung attended a Chinese school and became fluent in the language, a talent that would see him in good stead with China in the decades to come.

At some point in the early 1920s Kim briefly returned home, but it is generally accepted that from 1925 through to 1945 he was, save for a few guerrilla forays into the northern borderlands of Korea, living in exile. It is known that Kim joined an underground Marxist group while living in China and, at the age of just 17, spent several months in prison for his political convictions. Shortly after his release Kim joined an anti-Japanese Communist guerrilla unit – clearly prison hadn't redeemed him. At this time many such forces were springing up across Manchuria and while they mostly had the same prime aim – routing the Japanese from the Asian mainland – their political affiliations covered the entire spectrum.

Although a united Korean People's Revolutionary Army probably never existed (contrary to the official line in North Korea), the 1930s did see various disorganised guerrilla units slowly unify while Kim Il Sung steadily rose through the ranks, highlighting both his credible leadership skills and military capabilities. His name was cemented as a notable military leader in 1937 when men under his command attacked a Japanese garrison on Korean soil (see box, page 230), an event that escalated both Kim's status among Koreans and his notoriety with the Japanese, just as the latter were strengthening their position in Manchuria. By late 1940 many senior guerrilla leaders had been killed by the Japanese, and Kim, a wanted and hunted man, fled into the comparative sanctuary of the Soviet Union.

Living in relative exile, Kim Il Sung enjoyed a period of stability for the first time in over a decade, the bulk of his time believed to have been spent in or near Khabarovsk, where it is believed his first son, Yuri (better known as Kim Jong Il), was born. The fact that Yuri's (as well as Kim's) subsequent children born at that time were given Russian names possibly reveals that he saw little prospect in an imminent return to Korea. In the summer of 1942 the Soviets created a military unit comprising former Manchurian guerrillas, the 88th Independent Brigade, and appointed Kim Il Sung as captain – clearly he had left a good impression on his hosts. Despite the countless Pyongyang-published hagiographies, Kim did not fight the Japanese in 1945 and only returned to Korea after its liberation to, it is believed, function as the deputy *kommendant* of Pyongyang, a position picked for him by the Soviets presumably as he was the highest ranking Pyongyangite that they knew and trusted.

Kim arrived in Pyongyang at a serendipitous time. With no strong domestic communist organisations or leaders, Kim Il Sung was a logical candidate for the Soviets to select as temporary ruler – somebody they knew, could trust and, they thought, mould. Almost by accident, Kim, seemingly through chance and circumstance and almost certainly not through any ambition for a political career, became the de facto leader of North Korea. He seemed to accept this role with reluctance at first, but it did not take long for his humility to transform into hubris. Still a military man at heart, Kim had been hardened by a decade of guerrilla activities in Manchuria and further inured to hardships in the late 1940s, with his second son, Kim Man Il, drowning in 1947 and wife, Kim Jong Suk, dying through childbirth complications just two years later. A widower at 37, Kim Il Sung consequently became more affirmative and, it seems, started to see himself as a real leader of a true independent nation, which the North became in September 1948 when the Democratic People's Republic of Korea was founded. Whether the traumatic experiences of losing his wife and son embittered Kim Il Sung and helped push him to war as a diversion from his personal troubles is an interesting theory, but one on which we can only speculate.

By the end of the Korean War in 1953, Stalin was dead, the Soviet Union was changing, and it was highlighted that China was a reliable ally that, at the time, didn't interfere too much in internal North Korean politics. Kim had finally established himself as a true leader and master tactician, playing the USSR and China off against each other for the mutual benefit of North Korea – a skill he used throughout his life to help keep the DPRK's economy afloat long after it should have sunk.

Although a personality cult around Kim Il Sung had been developing for years, it was in 1972, for his 60th birthday, that it began to truly escalate to the proportions we recognise today. After nearly two decades with no challenge to his leadership, and years of surrounding himself with only self-preserving sycophants from within his own Guerrilla Faction, perhaps Kim Il Sung began to believe the hype – it seems he relished the growth of his personality cult. In the bubble of North Korea, where by this time foreign influence had no real bearing on the politics of the country, the cult grew unchecked and unhampered into mindboggling proportions. This allowed for the installation of what is often referred to as the 'Kim Dynasty,' as Kim Jong Il's position as successor was affirmed in 1980, allowing for Kim Il Sung to spend his final years transferring absolute power down to his son. By the time of his death in 1994, Kim Il Sung was a god in the eyes of almost any North Korean, allowing him to be awarded, after his death, the title of 'Eternal President'.

Such a cult continues today with the adoration of his son – almost every room in the DPRK has a joint portrait of Kim Il Sung and Kim Jong Il, and all flats are obliged to have these doubles centre-stage on the living-room wall, checked by the police check to ensure that they are well maintained and regularly cleaned. This adoration (admittedly to a lesser extent) has also continued with Kim Jong Un, although given his different approach to his predecessors and the changing nature of the DPRK today, how such a cult will be maintained in the wake of a more open North Korea remains to be seen.

escaped to China, while others were demoted – a far more congenial fate than would have happened the previous year. It is likely that this opposition move failed because of the lack of a clear alternative leader, but also because of the genuine progress being made since the armistice to rebuild the country.

Following this, real dissent seems only to have taken place on an individual basis, with defections happening while abroad – something that became an increasing problem for the regime, and one which it never found a solution for. Yi Sang Jo, the Ambassador to Moscow, asked for political asylum there in September 1956, a year after he had arrived. It was a sign of the distance building up between the two countries that this was granted – and indeed that he requested it. The Korean press could not mention this event, but increasingly fewer references to the Soviet Union suggested this detachment to regular readers. The Chinese would, through the years, take an ambiguous stance on escapes and defections. They did not want to encourage them but equally, because of the large Korean community in the northeast of China, could not return all of those who were caught. The result has been that some refugees have been returned and others have made their way to third countries, from where the South Koreans can look after them. The Chinese guard the South Korean Embassy in Beijing to prevent refugees seeking access there, as they do not want to be seen publicly supporting the South in this way.

KIM INCREASES HIS POWER Although by now considered as the undisputed leader of the country, Kim Il Sung couldn't be guaranteed absolute power while rival political factions still existed in the the DPRK. Therefore, he began eliminating his political rivals at this time, picking off the three remaining factions that remained in the North one by one. In 1956, a milestone year in the communist world, a joint Soviet-Chinese delegation came to Pyongyang and threatened to depose Kim should he not supress his hostilities towards their political influencers in the country, namely the Soviet and Yanan factions. The threat of being toppled, together with Khrushchev's famous 'Secret Speech' that same year, did nothing to rein in Kim – in fact, it seemingly had the opposite effect. Short-term concessions were made, but this attempt to control Kim seemed to only reassure that in order to have absolute control, he had to distance himself from his prime patrons, who thought they could still treat him like their puppet. But this was not the same man of a decade earlier – the marionette of the late 1940s had cut all his strings and was now firmly in control. The attempts of the USSR and China to 'de-Stalinise' North Korea came to nothing. If anything, this failed attempt further tempered Kim's mettle and he continued in removing all potential rivalry. By 1962, Kim had absolute power.

Throughout the late 1950s and into the '60s, references in the North Korean press to the Soviet Union or to China were reduced, as they felt uncomfortable with both positions. The DPRK could not possibly support peaceful coexistence with the US, something which started under Khrushchev and continued under Brezhnev. A further sign of wariness towards the Soviet Union came through the DPRK accepting only observer status within COMECON (the Soviet-led economic organisation comprised of their member states and other communist countries) in 1957, but never increasing this to full membership. The DPRK was nervous that it would be plundered for its mineral resources, which would be exchanged for finished products on unfavourable terms. Equally, from 1966 they became frightened by the implications of the Chinese Cultural Revolution, which suggested what could occur when rigid central control is relaxed. If forced to choose, they would have to lean towards China given the long common border, the extensive trade and the outlet it provided to other countries. With perhaps a hint of arrogance, combined with a

A TALE OF TWO HIJACKINGS

The hijacking by the North of a South Korean aircraft on 16 February 1958 forced the South into direct talks with the North for the first time. The crew and all but six passengers were released in early March, and it is possible that all six were hijackers as no appeals for their release were ever made. However, the situation with the second hijack of a domestic flight from Gangneung en route to Seoul on 11 December 1969, was very different – it was forced to fly to the North Korean city of Wonsan. The crew of four and seven out of the 46 passengers were never returned; it seems they were given different jobs as occasional sightings of them were reported. The North claimed (implausibly) that they had all sought asylum, but contact with their families in the South was, of course, impossible. Hwang Yong Chol was two years old when his father Hwang Won was detained, and for years has been campaigning for his release. It has been galling for him that many other releases have been granted, but not that of his father. His younger sister, aged three months at the time, now lives in Britain from where she has continued to run a similar campaign.

sense for the absurd, election turnouts and support for the government were always alleged to be 100%, never a mere 99.9%.

A significant sign of Kim's confidence was the promotion of his son, Kim Jong Il (see box, page 30). First mentioned as a politburo member in 1974, he was publicly nominated as his father's successor in 1980. Kim senior would have seen the leadership paralysis in Moscow in 1953 after Stalin's death and the ousting of the Gang of Four in the wake of Mao's death in 1976. He wanted to plan a very different scenario, which he was now able to do.

At the start of the 1960s, the standard of living was higher in the North than in the South and in China, because of the effective and speedy rebuilding of the country after the War; as a result, a few ethnic Koreans started to move back from China and Japan to the DPRK. Perhaps because of this confidence, no moves towards making contact with the South were made during this decade. In fact, there is much evidence to suggest that the North still hoped to overthrow the government there. In 1965, there were 42 military incidents at the border generated by the North, and by the first six months of 1967 this figure had increased to 286.

As with the South, there was no contact with the US throughout the 1960s. However, an event on 23 January 1968 forced a very sudden change in this, with the capture of the USS *Pueblo* and its crew of 82. It was spying close to North Korean waters, but whether it actually entered Korean territory remains a matter of dispute. The Soviet Union was keen for the crew to be released quickly as they did not want the issue to interfere with the ongoing US–Soviet détente, which the war raging in Vietnam at the time was certainly doing. Nevertheless, the North Korean stand on the issue was clear: a '3A' policy of 'Admit, Apologise and Assure' (ie: admit the ship had illegally entered into DPRK territorial waters, apologise for this, and assure that no such intrusions would happen again). Such wording was not initially acceptable to the US government, however, and some congressmen even suggested the use of nuclear weapons against the DPRK. The North, in public at least, initially planned for US military retaliation, telling non-essential diplomats to leave Pyongyang and building bunkers across the country. In the end, though, such an admission was signed by members of the crew at Panmunjom, just before they crossed the border – something that assured their release but which they denounced immediately after they had left DPRK territory. The ship was not returned and is now a tourist attraction in Pyongyang (page 115).

It is possible that the *Pueblo* was seized as a distraction from a failed attack on the Blue House in Seoul, the residence of the South Korean president, which had taken place two days earlier on 21 January. A unit of 31 commandos had crossed the border into the South unchallenged, hidden in the mountains and then regrouped in Seoul, disguised in southern military uniforms. They were challenged about 100yds from the Blue House and a shoot-out ensued, killing many of the commandos and the president's bodyguards. In 1972, during the visit of the first delegation from the South to the North, Kim Il Sung claimed that the raid had been plotted by extreme leftists and that it did not reflect 'my intent, or that of the party'. This seems far-fetched, however, and he was not able to claim that the perpetrators had been caught and executed. The North Koreans were clearly hoping to take advantage of the intense fighting in early 1968 in Vietnam, in which South Korean forces were taking part. They gambled correctly that the US could not contemplate a second war in Asia at that particular juncture.

In 1969 South Korea accepted 'dual recognition', under which it was happy to establish diplomatic relations with any country that already recognised the North. However, it took a long time for other countries to take advantage of this, with the Soviet Union only doing so in 1990 and the Chinese in 1992. Nevertheless, travel between these two countries and the South started much earlier, as did trade and academic exchanges – factors that led to further isolation of the DPRK. Consequently, the North actually became more dependent on these two former benefactors, as other socialist countries started to take a greater interest in South Korea, unaware of the poorer living conditions that reflected the worsening food supplies in the North. Rationing increased, with food distribution replacing shops. In the South, however, there was consistent economic growth from 1960 to 1988.

The first agreement between the governments of North and South Korea was a joint declaration signed on 4 July 1972, which looked forward to peaceful reunification and demilitarisation and created a hotline between the two governments designed to prevent any further military clashes. That such a stage was reached after 20 years of non-communication can be seen as progress, particularly as it brought about the Three Principles of National Reunification (see box, page 129), which are still of import today.

The 1970s saw a further intensity in the personality cult around Kim, ironically as the economy went into decline. More statues appeared, as did badges on every lapel. Kim started to travel by private train, new palaces were built around the country, and his entourage grew larger and larger. Anti-Japanese propaganda practically stopped, probably in an attempt to generate trade and encourage more Japanese-Koreans to return 'home', although this was contradicted by the kidnaps described below. This decade also saw the North join the Non-Aligned Movement as the DPRK sought new allies and trading partners across the globe in a number of countries that were not formally aligned with the major power blocs of the day. This was, however, a time when excessive international borrowing led to defaults, which had never before happened in the communist world. Whatever other criticisms that were made in the West about the communist countries, it was taken for granted that loans were repaid on the nail. The country was exposed to international ridicule when it tried to tackle this problem by getting its diplomats in Scandinavia to sell duty-free alcohol and tobacco from their car boots on the street.

Another exploit during the 1970s, which brought not only ridicule but also condemnation, was the kidnap of Japanese citizens and their subsequent abduction to North Korea to teach Japanese and, to even occasionally take part in films. Speed-boats would scour isolated areas of the western coast of Japan, where individuals or couples would be seized and taken to Korea, whereupon they were considered 'missing persons' back home, as contact with their families in Japan wouldn't be remotely possible. This procedure was, of course, denied by the DPRK, although it was claimed that both Japanese and Koreans had escaped from Japan and were now living happily in the DPRK. It was only in 2002, when Japanese Prime Minister Junichiro Koizumi visited the DPRK on the first official visit since the end of World War II, that the Koreans admitted to 13 such abductions; Kim Jong Il gave a verbal apology, but not a written one. Eight people, it was claimed, had died and five were allowed to return to Japan, but this has remained a contentious issue between the two governments and there are still no diplomatic relations between the two countries.

THE BEGINNINGS OF A MARKET ECONOMY? Mao's death and the end of the Cultural Revolution in China in 1976 eventually led to the country rapidly becoming a market economy, happy to trade on a worldwide basis. Consequently, North Korean officials began to visit trade fairs in Beijing to test the water and see what might be relevant to them. There were hints that the North might open Special Economic Zones following the Chinese model, but in the end only one was created in earnest, in Rajin (page 244). It was at this point that Western tourism in DPRK also made its modest beginning, when Regent Holidays in the UK (page 50) and other similar specialist companies across Europe began to send tour groups.

Unfortunately, a terrorist attack in 1983 set back any hope of the DPRK becoming internationally respected. On 9 October, the South Korean President Chun Doo-hwan was on an official visit to Burma (now Myanmar) and was due to lay a wreath at the Martyrs' Mausoleum in Rangoon (now Yangon) when a bomb exploded and killed 21 people, including four members of his cabinet. The DPRK always denied any involvement in the attack, but one of the surviving gunmen confessed to being from the DPRK and to having been trained there. Such training clearly continued, as in November 1987 a South Korean passenger jet exploded mid-air after a bomb was planted by two North Koreans in the hope of sabotaging the forthcoming Olympic Games in Seoul. Coming five years after the previous terrorist outrage, this second attack assured that the DPRK's pariah status continued.

Despite the attack, the Seoul Olympic Games went off in 1988 without any further issues, and became an excellent medium for South Korea to advertise itself to the outside world. By then, 142 governments had established diplomatic relations with Seoul. Pyongyang had hoped to co-host the games, but expressed no interest in various compromises suggested by Seoul. If the DPRK wanted a better international profile, the Olympic Games would have been an ideal time to accept a modest form of participation, but in the end, Seoul stole the show, just at a time when it was also displaying democratic credentials.

However, in July 1989 the 13th World Festival of Youth and Students took place in Pyongyang, an event that took place every few years in the capital of a socialist country. It was a great success from a North Korean point of view, attracting over 20,000 foreign participants – a number that Pyongyang had never seen before and would not see again. The May Day Stadium (page 110) was built for the festival; it is estimated that US$4 billion was found (or borrowed) for this and many other prestige building projects, which began the detachment of Pyongyang from the rest of the country. The majority of the participants were delegates from the socialist countries that still existed as such in the summer of 1989. Many were able to have open discussions with Koreans, something that had never happened before – conversations could not be controlled, given the number of people involved. Some 100 participants came from the US, as did a smaller number – illegally – from South Korea. The festival was a high point for the North, giving it the international recognition and prestige that it had previously not experienced – something that was not repeated during the difficult 1990s.

THE TOUGH 1990s The beginning of the decade saw the almost outright collapse of global communism. All of the eastern European regimes toppled in the autumn of 1989, and a year later East Germany ceased to exist; the Soviet Union carried on until December 1991 when it broke up into 12 new countries, the three Baltic states having already declared re-independence that summer. As so many communist nations across the globe overthrew their regimes at this time, many assumed that North Korea would follow suit; however, given the block in the DPRK on news from abroad, it is perhaps not surprising that the regime did not feel too threatened by these events. That said, North Korea certainly suffered from the loss of the Soviet Union, although not to the same extent as Cuba, as trade with China continued more or less as normal. More and more, the North Koreans had to pay a world market price in hard currency for any imports, meaning that these had to be drastically reduced. Nothing was said publicly about belt-tightening, although it was impossible to maintain the standard of living to which the North Korean population had become accustomed.

The control on day-to-day activities, a characteristic of life in North Korea since its beginning, in no way lessened in the early 1990s. Radio receivers continued to be checked, with the aim of preventing listeners tuning into channels from abroad, self-criticism sessions akin to those of the Cultural Revolution in China continued on a weekly basis, as did constant classes in political history. Foreign students and the few foreign workers in North Korea were not allowed to visit local people at home. The concept of Songbun, a sort of caste system whereby family members were responsible for each other, became more intense (see box, page 38). Accounts by refugees often mention that a major deterrent to planning an escape was the knowledge that their direct family was bound to suffer, which at its worst could mean being sent to a labour camp. Estimates of the North Korean prison population peak around 1990, with a figure of 200,000 often being quoted. This compares with one of 150,000 in the early 1980s and a drop to 100,000 by 2010.

A lot of specific meetings and events took place during the 1990s, which will be noted below, but the famine that devastated the country from 1994 until 1997, with many longer-term effects on health, must be covered first. After the collapse of the USSR, gone was the ample supply of fuel that kept the power stations running and agricultural machinery fully functional. Gone, too, was a similarly plentiful supply of fertiliser that had been crucial in establishing and running the collective farms. In Imperial and Japanese times, it had been the South that provided the country's food and the North that delivered the industrial growth. Industrial output halved between 1990 and 2000, figures that are likely to have been much worse in agriculture.

During the 1990s, the Chinese were in an ambivalent position towards North Korea. By cutting off aid and seriously blocking refugees, they had the power to destroy the country. Their links with South Korea, particularly after the establishment of diplomatic relations in 1992, became ever closer. The personality cult around Kim Il Sung, and then from 1994 around Kim Jong Il, was a sore reminder of the cult around Mao in the late 1960s, an era the Chinese wanted to forget. Yet they could not countenance the idea of US troops on the other side of

JUCHE

To understand North Korean culture, you first need to understand the philosophy by which it is underpinned: Juche. Bringing together threads of thought from both Marxism–Leninism and nationalism, it is presented as a political theory 'beyond Marxism', in which man controls his destiny with no role for any religion. Although there is little detailed history about this philosophy, it is widely accepted that Kim Il Sung was the founding father, developing the ideals as he came to power. The first known reference to Juche came in a speech in 1955, but it wasn't until a speech in 1965 that the three fundamental principles of the ideology were set out: political independence (*jaju*); economic self-sufficiency (*jarip*); and self-reliance in defence (*jawi*).

Such ideals are clearly reminiscent of Marxism–Leninism, but a crucial element of Juche that sets it apart from similar schools of thought is the concept of a Great Leader, the role taken on by Kim Il Sung. In *On the Juche Idea*, published by Kim Jong Il around the time of his father's 70th birthday and considered the most authoritative work on the subject, it states that Kim Il Sung was critical of communism's elitist notions, and thought that the likes of Marx and Lenin were 'divorced from the masses'. According to Juche, in order for the masses to be successful, they need a strong leader to guide and encourage their progress – an ideal that was core in developing the cult of the Kims and the lasting strength of the one-man rule in North Korea. This focus on the supreme leader explains the lack of reference in the DPRK to earlier thinkers and leaders such as Stalin, Marx, Engels and Lenin, the likes of whom were always mentioned in China and in the Soviet Union. Indeed, the Great Leader is given almost deity-like status – flaws and imperfections are not mentioned or accepted, and no mistakes are ever admitted. The words of the Great Leader are always thought to be benevolent and true, while his actions are understood to be in the best interests of the masses.

Juche provided the DPRK with a cloak that combined socialism with nationalism and self-reliance, consequently allowing the country to stand in proud isolation from the rest of the world. In 1997, a Juche calendar was introduced by Kim Jong Il, with 1912 (the year of Kim Il Sung's birth) being Year 1 and 2018 being Year 107 (although the Gregorian calendar is still used in all communications abroad and in all references to dates prior to 1912). Despite its importance in Korea, the ideal result of the principle – self-sufficiency for the DPRK, in which they can stand alone with no help or assistance for the outside world – has, of course, not occurred. Indeed, Kim Jong Un refers to the idea much less than his father and grandfather, presumably an admission that economic progress can only be made by increasing, rather than reducing, links with the outside world. How such economic change will impact on the notion of a Great Leader remains to be seen.

the Amnok River, were the North to collapse, nor the surge in refugees that would result from any breakdown in authority in the North. Had the US ever suggested troop withdrawal from the South, the Chinese might have been less concerned with the continuation of the regime in the North, but it remained a useful buffer while they continued to see the US as a threat. In the early days of the DPRK, shortly after the armistice when the Chinese supplied 75% of the fuel and 66% of the food to the country, Mao Zedong described the relationship between the two nations as being as close as 'lips and teeth'. By the 1990s, however, they and the Russians were demanding prompt payment and no longer gave 'friendship' prices, which had a devastating impact on supplies.

The famine is one of the few events in North Korean history in which any hint of a problem has been officially revealed. The regime outwardly stated that 250,000 died as a result of the famine, something that required considerable courage for a nation otherwise unwilling to accept imperfection. (Of course much higher figures are suggested abroad, reaching up to three million deaths). The *Panorama of Korea* describes the famine as follows:

'In the 1990s, the country had a hard time called The Arduous March owing to the dissolution of the socialist market, the imperialist allied forces' moves to stifle the nation and successive natural disasters. But The Arduous March was concluded with the successful administration of Juche politics.'

This suggests that it was Juche (see box, page 27) that brought the famine to an end, but in reality the exact opposite was the case – it was foreign aid that saved them. For the first time since the armistice in 1953, considerable stocks of food were provided by UN agencies and about 300 street markets arose around the country, a totally informal means of trading, but one totally alien to the traditional socialist system that should have been able to distribute food fairly across the country. It is true that floods hit the country badly in 1994, but had international aid been sought earlier, and had the political environment been one in which officials could talk frankly to each other, the consequences would have been far less acute. A major problem for aid donors was the lack of information the government was willing to reveal and their unwillingness to allow relatively free travel to foreign aid workers around the country. Agencies could, without too much difficulty, supply basics such as flour and dried milk, but they needed to be sure that these goods went directly to parts of the country where they were needed most and were not stolen for private sale en route, or diverted to others, such as the military.

Housewives also played a pivotal role in alleviating the famine as they were able to devote their time to starting private businesses that could, in turn, generate income to buy food for their families. Some started cultivation in mountain areas that would be seen as unproductive under normal conditions. Others crossed the border into China to exchange North Korean goods for Chinese ones, most often food, which was in ample supply in China. At other times, the North Korean authorities would have put a stop to such activity, but they vaguely tolerated this during the famine. Later, because markets had become such a regular part of life for most people in the countryside, they were allowed to continue and still operate on an unofficial basis. Guides are nervous when tourists ask about them and discourage photography. Contact with relatives abroad was also allowed at this time, as they could supply crucial foreign currency, and thus access to special shops.

It is unclear how concerned Kim Il Sung was with this crisis, but he remained alert until the end of his life on 8 July 1994, when he died of a heart attack. There was an official mourning period of three years after his death, but in practice all that occurred for a more intense period of 13 days before the funeral was that all public entertainment and sport was cancelled. As was the case when Kim Jong Il died in 2011, it was two days after the death before his passing was officially announced.

Despite the struggles at home, the 1990s saw a slight thaw in relations with the US. DPRK research in the nuclear field had started in the 1960s after both the Chinese and the Soviets refused to help them in this field. On 21 October 1994 an

THE CURIOUS VISIT OF BILLY GRAHAM

The American evangelist Billy Graham visited the DPRK with his wife Ruth in 1992, who had grown up in Pyongyang as her parents had been missionaries in Korea. In 1972 he had preached to a million-strong audience in Seoul, leading the North to accuse him of being a witch-doctor. By 1992, however, the DPRK needed any friends they could get and therefore accepted his request to travel to Pyongyang. He presented Kim with a bible in public, but was not allowed to preach out-of-doors. He returned again in 1994, when Kim was still alive, and became the first foreigner to be allowed to preach in a church in the North. Kim told Graham on his second visit that like the climate outside, winter should also turn to spring in the context of US–Korean relations. The Grahams' son Franklin, who ran a charity called Samaritan's Purse, returned with Ruth in 1997 when the famine was at its worst, bringing agricultural supplies and dental clinics.

'agreed framework' was worked out between the two countries, with the Koreans agreeing to freeze work on and eventually dismantle their existing plutonium-based reactor at Yongbyon in exchange for a number of provisions from the US, the most important of which being the construction of two light water reactors for the production of energy and the supply of 500,000 tons of heavy fuel annually until the first reactor came online. The framework also called for a move towards the full normalisation of economic and political relations between the two. There would be many more such agreements, given the frequency with which they broke down, but these talks did, at least, ensure that some famine aid reached the North Koreans and reduced the prospect of war breaking out again on the peninsula. Discussions at meetings, and many fax and phone exchanges, were ongoing about the setting up of liaison offices in each capital, prior to full diplomatic relations.. However, in the summer of 1995, the North Koreans suddenly said that plans for these offices would have to be delayed indefinitely and nothing concrete has happened since; no reason was given for the change in policy, but the shift to a Republican majority in the US Congress (who were opposed to the agreement) in November 1994 had put a strain on relations in the months leading up to Pyongyang's decision to walk away from the table. The Kim–Trump summit in June 2018 may lead, in due course, to diplomatic relations.

In 1996, the US was granted limited access to the DPRK to search for troops missing in action from the Korean War. It is thought that about 5,000 unaccounted (MIA) troops died in what is now DPRK territory; 33 expeditions in all took place until 2005, with only 229 bodies being recovered. The regular operation stopped in 2006, probably because of US objections to a North Korean nuclear test, although the official reason given was a concern for the team's safety. At the time of writing in 2018, with a good political climate between the two countries, negotiations have started again on this issue.

KIM JONG IL IN POWER As per Kim Il Sung's wishes, Kim Jong Il came to power immediately on the death of his father, although he didn't officially become leader until 1997 after the supposed three years of mourning.

The election of Kim Dae Jung as President of South Korea in December 1997 had an immediate effect on inter-Korean relations. His background could not have been more different from that of Kim Jong Il; Kim Dae Jung had first stood for

THE LESSER KIM?

Officially it is said Kim Jong Il was born on Mount Paektu on 16 February 1942 (which is now a national holiday); however, it is more likely that he was actually born near Khabarovsk in Russia, exactly one year earlier. It is thought that he left school at the age of 16 and then studied to be an air-force trainee in East Germany. One of many rumours about his childhood is that he had a flying accident in Germany and therefore refused to travel by aeroplane again, although there is nothing in East German diplomatic correspondence referring to him being there at that time.

The circumstances under which Kim Jong Il came to power could not have been more different than his father's. Aside from his very early childhood, his upbringing and surroundings were those of a pampered royal, totally cut off from day to day life in his country. He 'ascended to the throne' at the age of 52, so at a time in life when he could assume that the system would outlive him, as he had known nothing else. His 17 years in power were never threatened, despite the fact that he ruled during the famine and he was the least imaginative of the three Kims to have been in power. Only one public remark has been recorded, a chant 'Glory to the Heroic Soldiers', and this was in 1992, before he became leader. He appeared in public fairly often, waving to the crowds at major state events, and 'giving guidance' all around the country, but never once did he give a speech. No other national leader, however they may have come to power, has been so isolated. The few Westerners who met him do give a more positive picture, namely that he was on top of his brief and could talk sensibly. His body language in public does, however, suggest an unease that was not characteristic either of his father or of his son. Plenty of lurid stories are told of his private life, some of which seem plausible, but we have little indication of whether he took much interest in the famine and what links, if any, he foresaw with the South and with the US.

the presidency in 1971, but election-rigging ensured that he lost. The Korean CIA, KCIA, arrested him in Japan in 1973 and hoped to kill him, something they would have achieved had the US not intervened. He was imprisoned in South Korea, and on one occasion in 1980 was sentenced to death, but, following the intervention of Pope John-Paul II, he was reprieved. His life alternated between being under house-arrest, in prison or in exile, usually in the US; his 'crimes' were simply the organisation of an opposition to presidents Park Chung-hee and Chun Doo Hwan. US Secretary of State Madeleine Albright met him in 1986 when he was under house arrest and drew a parallel with Vaclav Havel and Nelson Mandela, who at the same time were in prison, but who would both shortly become presidents of their own countries. The South Korean presidential elections of 1987 and 1992 were peaceful and Kim did creditably in both, but it was not until 1997, 26 years after his first attempt, that he finally won and made an immediate impact on all aspects of policy.

Kim Dae Jung will be long remembered for what became known as the Sunshine Policy, introduced in 1998, which attempted reconciliation with the North and for which he received the Nobel Peace Prize in 2000. He did not push for reunification, clearly a pipe dream 50 years after the war, given the stability of the North even with the effects of the famine. In the end, the South gave much more than it took, but a summit with Kim Jong Il was achieved, a rail line was rebuilt across the border, and tourist groups from the South were able to visit the Kumgang Mountains, a scenic area with no parallel in the South. About 250,000 people a year crossed the border, although the North had hoped for closer to one million. Such tours came to a sudden end in 2008, however, after a South Korean tourist was shot in circumstances which, a decade on, are still unclear (see box, page 206).

Separate North and South Korean teams were organised for the Olympic Games in Sydney in August 2000, but at the inaugural ceremony they marched together, perhaps a tangible result of the two leaders having met two months earlier. It is rumoured that the summit in June 2000 was only confirmed after the South paid US$500 million for the meeting to take place, and that it would only happen if Kim Dae Jung travelled to Pyongyang to meet with Kim Jong Il, which he duly did. The talks went well and as a result frequent contact at a lower level would continue on a regular basis.

Relations with the US also improved somewhat towards the end of the decade. William Perry, a former US Defence Secretary, visited North Korea in 2000 to prepare for a Clinton visit that, in the end, did not take place. As with most of such meetings, the aim from the US side was to ensure a renunciation of nuclear weapons in return for diplomatic recognition. On one visit, Perry agreed to the delivery of 100 tonnes of potatoes to the country; on another, he delivered antibiotics to a hospital. He commented on the new buildings, which made his hosts point out that they were necessary following the US bombing campaigns that hit every town in the North.

The number three in the DPRK hierarchy, Marshall Jo Myong Rok, visited Washington in October 2000, where he received a warm reception from Madeleine Albright and President Clinton. Jo was keen to push Clinton into committing himself to a visit to Pyongyang and suggested that a nuclear deal would be possible if he did. In the end it was agreed that Madeleine Albright would visit Pyongyang two weeks later. She spent 12 hours in all with Kim Jong Il and their talks varied widely. Albright describes these meetings in her book, *Fascism: A Warning*, in which she states that she found him 'pretty normal for someone whose father's birthday each year is celebrated as the Day of the Sun'. Kim expressed hopes for renewed diplomatic recognition and showed understanding of many world issues; he admitted that relations with China were poor and complained about the Russians too, as they had persuaded the North Koreans to grow corn that turned out to be suitable only for livestock.

Links with other countries also started to improve in 2000, when Australia, the UK and Italy all established diplomatic relations. The British Council started an English-language programme, with two teachers being sent from the UK to the North, and scholarships becoming available for North Korean students to study in Britain.

Despite the positive inroads made by Clinton, the election of George W Bush in 2001 led to a totally different US approach to the DPRK. Bush talked in his 2002 State of the Union address of North Korea as being part of the 'axis of evil', together with Iran and Iraq – a mantra that would be frequently repeated over the following years. There was little momentum in the new US administration to continue dialogue with North Korea; although occasional meetings between the two as part of the 'six-party talks', aimed at finding a peaceful resolution to international concern over North Korea's nuclear weapons program, did bring them to the table in Beijing a number of times from 2003 to 2007. Hostile commentators referred to Bush's ABC policy meaning 'Anything But Clinton' – Bush hoped to force regime change in North Korea, as he did in Iran and Iraq, and was not interested in coexistence.

Annual military exercises between the US and the South Korean forces, run jointly and very publicly in the South ever since the end of the war in 1953, always worsened the atmosphere whenever they took place, and understandably gave the North justifiable cause for alarm. A rare cessation of US war gaming exercises occurred in 1992 and 1994–96 when the 'agreed framework' still had momentum, but every other year in which these operations took place gave incentive for the North to develop its nuclear programme, with the first test taking place underground in October 2006. This programme should be seen as part of the DPRK's determination to become totally independent and therefore not beholden to any outside authority, which had so often been the fate of previous Korean dynasties. The DPRK nuclear programme has continued ever since, despite many talks on possible offers to the North that could persuade the country to give up its nuclear weapons. In his talks with Kim Jong Un in June 2018, President Trump offered to stop the annual military exercises but as these take place in March, it remains to be seen at the time of writing whether this will occur.

In 2003 construction of the Kaesong Industrial Zone (see box, page 143) began in the North, signifying a major breakthrough in inter-Korean relations. Situated 5km from the border, it became an important assembly and manufacturing centre for the South.

October 2007 saw a second inter-Korean summit, this time between Kim Jong Il and President Roh Moo Hyun, who had largely followed the policies of his predecessor Kim Dae Jung, but with much less determination. The final communiqué of this summit was full of aspiration, speaking of building 'a permanent peace regime', reducing 'military tension' and transcending 'differences in ideology and institutions' and listing practical measures that could help implement these, such as flights from Seoul to both Mount Paektu and Mount Kumgang, scientific exchanges, and a joint Olympics team taking the train from Seoul to Beijing via Sinuiju. In the end, though, none of these ideas materialised.

Perhaps the only event that can be partially credited to the summit took place in February 2008 – a visit to Pyongyang by the New York Philharmonic Orchestra. The programme started with both national anthems, and both national flags were displayed – a remarkable first. Journalists were granted internet access and ample international phone lines, and the concert was broadcast in full on television in both countries, so in that sense there was national exposure for it. At the same time, however, US Secretary of State Condoleezza Rice travelled to Seoul to attend President Lee's inauguration and commented: 'I don't think we should get carried away with what listening to the concert might do in North Korea'. The actions of the government that she served ensured that there were no cultural follow-ups to the event.

It was strongly rumoured that Kim Jong Il had a stroke in August 2008, and this was confirmed in early December by a French doctor, Francois-Xavier Roux, who had treated him at that time. He added that he felt Kim was still very much in charge. The doctor spoke more openly after Kim died, admitting he had been in a life-threatening coma and that his son was often at his bedside. The rumours were strengthened by Kim's failure to attend the 9 September celebrations of the 60th anniversary of the founding of the DPRK. This absence was not, of course, explained by the DPRK media, but they did mention the rumours as 'a Western conspiracy to sabotage the government' and many pictures were published of him, of course not dated, at public events. It would have been simplest to tell the truth, which was that he had had a stroke but that he had recovered from it. Unfortunately, in a country that hates to admit the slightest imperfection, this was not possible.

May 2009 saw a nuclear test by the North Koreans; as with US-Korean joint military exercises in the South, this gave rise to protests abroad but neither then, nor at any later stage, has a verifiable agreement seemed possible. The North wants a withdrawal from the South by US forces and the US wants complete freedom in the North to confirm that any work being undertaken there is not related to nuclear military activity. Good faith has never lasted long enough for either side to trust the other.

Serious military action was fortunately avoided in March 2010 when an incident at sea nearly led to military action: the sinking of the South Korean vessel *Cheonan* off the country's west coast, which resulted in the deaths of 46 members of the 104-person crew. At the time, it was alleged that the North Koreans had torpedoed the boat, but many other theories have subsequently arisen, including the explosion of a mine dating back to the Korean War. It is now unlikely that a definitive conclusion will ever be drawn. In November of the same year, the South Korean island of Yeonpyeong was shelled from the mainland after warnings had been ignored concerning South Korean exercises at sea that were allegedly trespassing across the Northern Limit Line (see box, page 153) into North Korean waters.

KIM JONG UN COMES TO POWER On 19 December 2011, the North Korean authorities announced that Kim Jong Il had died two days earlier from a heart attack, whilst travelling outside Pyongyang. Ten days of mourning was announced, and, as when his father died, no public entertainment was allowed during that period.

As little is known about Kim Jong Un's youth as is about that of his father and grandfather. He was most likely born on 8 January 1983, but this has never been confirmed in Pyongyang and it is not yet a holiday, unlike the birthdays of his predecessors. The only source of information for his childhood is a memoir by a Japanese chef, Kenji Fujimoto, who worked for Kim Jong Il as a sushi chef from 1988 to 2001, and describes the elaborate dishes he was requested to cook. We know that Kim was brought up separately from his elder brother Kim Jong Nam and that he was sent to a boarding school in Switzerland as a teenager, posing as the son of the ambassador to disguise his true identity.

Those hoping for more political and economic liberalism under Kim Jong Un were quickly disillusioned. Given the age at which he came to power, probably 28, and the fact that he had seen a Western country first hand, it is perhaps surprising that he has remained so inactive in the economic field. The concentration of wealth in Pyongyang and the increasing tolerance of private markets were both policies of his father, although neither was ever codified. Kim's first formal decision was The Leap Day agreement of 29 February 2012, which saw the US provide 240 tonnes of food to the North in return for the nominal stopping of nuclear and missile tests and uranium enrichment. However, as with many of these such agreements over the years, it was broken on 13 April with a failed satellite launch. Many tourists were in Pyongyang at that time to see celebrations for the 100th anniversary of the birth of Kim Il Sung, and were told that the launch 'had not been a complete success'.

North Korea conducted its third nuclear test in February 2013, an act that escalated tensions between the DPRK and, seemingly, the entire world. As hostilities ratcheted up an outburst of strong rhetoric came from the North, in which Pyongyang-based embassy staff were advised to leave, given the alleged threat of warfare breaking out from the South. However, this was contradicted by the fact that tourists were still welcome; no embassy withdrew any staff, nor did any foreign office advice suggest that there was any danger in travel to the DPRK. The hotline at Panmunjom was cut (page 24) and the 1953 armistice was declared invalid. Yet, as quickly as these steps were taken, they were withdrawn on 15 April. Later in 2013, the dismissal and execution of Kim Jong Il's brother-in-law Jang Song Thaek was extraordinary due to the publicity given to it. Jang was married to Kim's

1

sister, Kim Kyong Hui, and had a range of senior posts; during Kim Jong Il's final years, when he was suffering from the stroke he had in 2008, it was thought that Jang may, to some extent, have taken his place. However, he was accused in the North Korean media of a vivid array of crimes, including 'plotting to overthrow the state, womanising, gambling and selling the country's resources at cheap prices', and he was called a 'despicable human scum worse than a dog'. His real 'crime' is unknown – was it his alleged support for liberal economic reforms, or did it have more to do with Kim Jong Un consolidating his power? Jang's arrest at a Workers' Party meeting on 8 December, attended by several hundred members, was shown on television, as was his trial. His execution was announced shortly afterwards. Because of a story circulated in the Chinese press claiming that Jang and five accomplices had been stripped naked and thrown to 120 ravenous dogs, the DPRK Ambassador to Britain took the unusual step of denying this and confirming to Sky News that Jang had been shot. Despite the media claims, it is safe to presume that in actuality family issues were involved as well; Kim Kyong Hui was certainly not executed in 2013 and was pictured at events over the following year or two.

THE INTRODUCTION OF UN SANCTIONS The date of the seventh Party Congress – a meeting of the WKP to review their work since the last congress, instil loyalty to the leadership and elect members to certain organs of leadership – was announced on 30 October 2015 for May 2016. By giving the date so far in advance, and even by holding a congress at all – the previous one had taken place in 1980 – showed how confident Kim Jong Un now was of his authority and how determined he had become not to take the Chinese road of attempting to allow economic reforms while keeping firm political control. In his speech at the Congress, he referenced 'the filthy wind of bourgeois liberty, reform and openness blowing in our neighbour'; although he did not name China specifically, his target was perfectly clear and reinforced his determination to distance himself from the more liberal policies of Jang Song Thaek and continue in the way of his father. Had Kim had any reservations about this policy, he would not have used such a public forum to declare it. He was following the Soviet and Chinese models for these Congresses, in that they signalled the end of any internal debate. Indirectly, he admitted food shortages were still a problem in his passionate references to the needs for self-sufficiency in food and for local sources for fuel to be found. Although North Korea has ample coal, something that has always been a staple export, it does not have oil; to this day, Kim is reluctant to be too dependent on China for it, given his ideological differences with the regime, but importing from Russia adds several thousand miles of transport costs.

An 'export' from the North that seemed to be increasing in 2016–17 was that of labourers, largely to the Middle East, China and Russia. Due to the UN sanctions policy, increasingly tightened since their introduction in 2006 as a result of the DPRK's first nuclear test, this should stop by the end of 2019, though in reality that seems unlikely to happen, as the labourers will start their journeys through Russia or China. Given that nobody involved wants publicity for this kind of 'business', accurate figures are hard to obtain. Some estimates suggest that about 65,000 such workers were abroad in 2000, and that it had risen to 150,000 in 2017. Most labourers are married and take the work to give their families a better standard of living than would be possible if they stayed at home. It seems that no coercion is involved in choosing this work, but recruitment procedures have not been clarified in any media. It is not known for definite how much of the wages workers keep and how much goes back to North Korea to support their families and to provide desperately needed foreign currency for the regime, but it has been suggested that as much as 80% of the money earned goes back to Korea. In the Middle East and Russia, it is thought that the labourers are largely involved in construction – most recently for the 2018 World Cup in Russia and for the 2022 tournament in Qatar – while in China many are employed in small businesses in the north-east of the country.

The UN first imposed sanctions on North Korea in 2006 when their first nuclear test took place, and they have been nominally tightened on several occasions since then. Concerning imports, the aim is to prevent anything of military significance reaching North Korea, while with exports the aim is to cause economic harm. Therefore, the country is fortunate that neither China nor Russia has taken the UN sanctions policy too seriously. Inevitably, given the lack of sensible statistics from any of these three countries, the exact impact of the sanctions is hard to judge. There is no doubt that exports in coal, iron and seafood have suffered, as neither country can afford to be seen to be blatantly ignoring sanctions. Kim visited China in 2018, for the first time since coming to power, not just once but three times in as many months, before and after the Trump summit, but at the time of writing no public changes in policy had emerged. However, China has expressed in public the view that UN sanctions should be reviewed and, whatever distaste the governments may have for each other, they realise that they should work together on dealing with the US.

North Korea flung itself into the international headlines again in 2016 with the arrest of US student Otto Warmbier, who had travelled to Pyongyang on a short tour of the country, en route to a study abroad programme in Hong Kong. After celebrating on New Year's Eve, Warmbier allegedly managed to get into a staff area of the hotel and steal a propaganda poster, and was consequently arrested on 2 January as the group was checking in for their departure flight. Almost two months later, Warmbier was forced to give a press conference, in which he admitted to his crime, before being tried a few days later. The trial itself lasted just an hour, at the end of which he was given a sentence of 15 years hard labour. While he was in prison, his health dramatically deteriorated and he entered a vegetative state; although the North Koreans claimed that he was contracted botulism, this was never substantiated. In June 2017, he was medically evacuated to the US in a coma and died two days later. An inquest confirmed that he had not been physically mal-treated in Korea, but his parents blocked a full autopsy that might have clarified what caused his death. Following Warmbier's death, US citizens were strongly advised not to travel to North Korea, and a few months later the State Department issued a blanket travel ban, which is still in place today.

2017 AND 2018: TWO VERY DIFFERENT YEARS

On 13 February 2017, Kim Jong Nam, the half-brother of Kim Jong Un, was murdered at Kuala Lumpur International Airport by two women who smothered his face with a nerve agent. The two suspects were quickly arrested, but four North Koreans, older men who were allegedly the brains behind the attack, left Malaysia for Pyongyang the same day. Kim Jong Nam had been living in Macau since 2003, largely as a playboy (it is reported that he had two wives and a mistress). In 2001, he was caught on arrival at Tokyo Airport with a forged Dominican Republic passport and subsequently arrested. Further scandal came in 2012, when a book of interviews was published in which he made it clear that he thought his youngest brother was incapable of leading the country and that without major reforms the North Korean regime would collapse. Both of these factors doomed his chances of succeeding his father, even though he was the eldest child, and there were several rumoured attempts at killing him once Kim Jong Un was in power.

In September 2017, shortly after the North provocatively tested a hydrogen bomb, President Trump proclaimed at the UN that the 'Rocket Man is on a suicide mission for himself and for his nation. He is obviously a madman who does not mind starving or killing his people. He will be tested like never before.' Kim Jong Un's collected response a few days later upped the ante: 'I will surely and definitely tame the mentally deranged US dotard with fire.'

In contrast to 2017, Kim Jong Un started 2018 in a very different mood (despite the fact that he declared the nuclear button was on his desk at all times and that the US mainland was now within reach of his nuclear warheads). On New Year's Day he suggested talks with the South about joining teams for the Winter Olympics that would be held in Pyeongchang in February 2018. Several countries, including the US, had expressed concern about potential security issues at the games so participation from the North could help put such concerns to rest. Initially there had been considerable opposition to this policy in the South, on the basis that the North was not offering any tangible benefits in return, so their charm offensive should be rejected. However, by mid-January it had been agreed that athletes from the two regimes would march together at the opening ceremony, as they had done in 2000, 2004 and 2006 and that there would be a joint women's hockey team. Ten athletes from the North competed in other sports. The Seoul government firmly supported this initiative, and felt that an immediate and positive reaction to Kim's speech was called for, although amongst the general public in the South, opinions were much more mixed.

Kim Yo Jong, the sister of Kim Jong Un, led the delegation (the first member of the Kim family to travel south since the 1953 armistice) and made it clear that she was happy to meet South Koreans and Americans, both formally and informally. However, the US Vice-President, Mike Pence, showed that he wanted to avoid all contact with her delegation, emphasising this by bringing Fred Warmbier, father of Otto (page 35), and by very publicly meeting defectors from the North now living in the South.

Despite this, US policy towards North Korea changed soon after the games, probably because of South Korean pressure. Over Easter 2018, Mike Pompeo, at the time Head of the CIA but shortly to become Secretary of State, visited Pyongyang, although details of his visit were only revealed by President Trump two weeks later when he said 'good things are happening'. This was proved on 27 April when Kim Jong Un and President Moon Jae-in met at Panmunjom on the southern side, and Moon remarked that Panmunjom was now a centre of peace, not of division. An unprecedented rapport was clearly established between the two leaders, and both were able to talk impromptu to the press afterwards, even though no details of their discussions were revealed. On 11 May, after talks in Washington with the South Korean Foreign Minister, Mike Pompeo expressed the changed mood in the US administration by saying 'If Chairman Kim chooses the right path, there is a future brimming with peace and prosperity'. A day later, a similar view came from David Beasley, the head of the UN World Food Programme, who had just returned to the UK having spent four days in the DPRK. Interviewed on BBC Radio 4's *Today* programme, he said that 'North Korea's leaders are open to change. They are turning a new page in history. There is a genuine desire to move forwards.'

On 12 June, Kim Jong Un and President Trump met in a landmark summit in Singapore, despite threats from Trump to cancel it a few days earlier in reaction to heightened North Korean criticism of US military action in the South. However, both sides realised that more was to be gained than lost by proceeding. Although no detailed negotiations took take place, this allowed for a general communiqué that did not involve any serious or immediate commitments. That the meeting took place at all was what mattered. To the North, it gave the prestige of their leader being seen on the world stage, and to the US, the chance to start solving a problem on which little progress had been made since 1953.

A BRIGHTER FUTURE? While Kim Il Sung could limit his circle of leaders abroad to those who operated in a similar manner, able to embark on projects in a totally whimsical manner and to dispose of opponents likewise, Kim Jong Un is having to face up to the outside world far more regularly and to countries, apart from China and Russia, where he is unlikely to see the same face in four years' time. At the time of the 12 June 2018 summit, many comments were made as to how differently Kim Jong Un had projected himself in comparison with his father and his grandfather. It was noted that he enjoyed a sightseeing tour of Singapore and allowed this to be shown on North Korean television. At the April summit with President Moon Jae-in, he talked and joked openly with him; in fact, laughing and joking seems to be the image he wants to project, just as much as that of the serious statesman. A cursory look at film of his father on public occasions, so frequently sulking and looking bored, makes this contrast instantly obvious.

Whatever the long-term results of the summit are, together with other moves being made separately by South Korea, it is probably safe to predict that the isolation of North Korea is finally coming to an end. Though still relatively small in numbers, more of the population is now travelling abroad – or at least have access to the world outside North Korea through electronic media smuggled in from China and South Korea. As is the case in China, North Korea will likely struggle to continue to block all access to foreign media and Western views. And although North Korean refugees, whether in the South or in communities such as New Malden to the south of London, may find life disconcerting and far tougher than they expected, returning home is almost entirely out of the question.

With the Kims, comparisons are still obviously made with intense religions that take over every aspect of private and public lives. Tourists are told on arrival that Koreans respect their leaders and that foreigners must do likewise, even if their behaviour at home is totally different. Those who fall out of line are quickly sent back to China. If plans materialise for a massive tourism resort at Wonsan (see box, page 194), how will the hosts cope with the drunken escapades, criticism of the regime, and the fraternisation between staff and guests that is bound to take place? Will tourists come in the first place, if they cannot use their mobile phones and require round-the-clock Wi-Fi? Specialist tour operators around the world have taken tours to North Korea for 30 years or so, and their clients have valued the experience, precisely because it is so different from tourism elsewhere. The mass market will not make such concessions.

In China, following Deng Xiaoping's ascent to power in 1977, many 'non-persons' who had fallen out with Mao Zedong were rehabilitated, but there is no sign of such movement in North Korea, nor of admitting that some people outside the Kim family had a crucial role to play in the establishment of the regime. That Kim would want to make personnel changes in his regime after his father's death is perfectly understandable; what is not is the need he felt to execute his uncle for the crime of wanting closer relations with China, which will probably happen anyway as 'sanctions' are seen to be ever more meaningless. Secrecy is another issue that needs to be tackled. The Singaporean photographer Aram Pan, who travels frequently to North Korea, perhaps summarised this best when he wrote: 'We still know more about the ocean and outer space than we do about North Korea.' Only when he is proved wrong will we know that the DPRK has finally changed.

North Korea is a hard-line nation that, while often classified in the West as a totalitarian dictatorship, outwardly promotes itself as a democratic multi-party state, with the three main parties being the Workers' Party of Korea (WPK), Korean Social Democrat Party (KSDP) and the Chondoist Chongu Party (CCP). The WPK have been in power since North Korea came into existence in 1948 and currently hold 607 of the 687 seats within the Supreme People's Assembly, the highest organ of power in the land.

All parties work within the framework of Juche (see box, page 27), North Korea's official state ideology, claimed to have been penned by Kim Il Sung, and all parties are closely allied with each other. There is no soapbox banter between the opposing groups here – there is one leader, and nobody dares question him. The various organisations and groups, such as the State Affairs Commission, WPK Central Committee and Cabinet, exist as bureaucratic, paper-shuffling and rubber-stamping organisations, and a good deal of Kremlinology needs to be administered to work out who really holds the power and makes the decisions.

When it comes to elections, all candidates are put forward by the Democratic Front for the Reunification of the Fatherland, an organisation allied with all parties and often claimed to be completely controlled by the WPK. Voting is compulsory and the electorate are often presented with just one choice – indeed, voter turnout at the last election in 2014 was reported at a staggering 99.97%, as abstaining or spoiling your ballot is not a sensible option. For all the pomp of the assemblies, cabinets and congresses that North Koreans often wax lyrical about in an attempt to validate their 'democratic' system, the real decisions in the murky world of Korean

SONGBUN

In the late 1950s, Kim Il Sung created a murky system of ascribed status known as Songbun, a caste or class system ascribed to every citizen aged 17 or over. Although everybody is aware of this chilling system, they are not informed of their own status within it – examining one's footing in life is as good an indication as any as to where one is positioned.

The government has a file on everybody and citizens are designated as either a member of the core, wavering or hostile class. Within these three classifications, 51 sub-classifications exist – allowing any official running a check (on a now digitised system believed to be called 'Faithful Servant 2.0') to really get down to the bare bones of your heritage and status. Files are routinely checked, monitored and updated, and individuals are not just judged on their own merits, but also the lives of the previous three to six generations of their family.

The core class is said to comprise approximately 30% of the population, and is largely made up of descendants from revolutionaries, war heroes and those who died fighting for their country, as well as those who were peasants, labourers or factory workers around the time of the DPRK's founding. The wavering class accounts for around 45%, and comprises families with people who may have lived in (or moved to) the South or China, or families that may have had merchants, intellectuals and such within them. Finally, the hostile class, accounting for the bottom 25% or so, are descendants of landlords, capitalists, political prisoners, those with a religious background, those who fought for the South in the Korean War and those who are considered to be 'against' the party.

politics appear to be made elsewhere and behind closed doors, by the select well-connected few. Questioning those who hold the power and make the real decisions in these corridors of power is not an option – subordinates shouldn't question their superiors, and the risks of doing so are often far too high. And so continues the system, in perpetuity.

PEOPLE

Every country has the government it deserves

Joseph de Maistre

The Korean psyche, both North and South, is built on a varying degree of mistrust of the outside world. While international trade and relations undoubtedly shaped Korean culture into what it is today, importing religious and political ideals along with a great deal else, it has also led to attacks, occupation and war, be it from the Mongols and the Manchus in feudal times to the Japanese and Americans in the modern age. The 20th-century history of Korea was defined by foreign meddling, division and mass upheaval, with Japan, the USA, China and the Soviet Union/Russia (among others), all getting involved in affairs that many Koreans feel they could have settled themselves, should they have been allowed to do so. The status quo continues to this day. All the interference within Korea has understandably led many to take a dim view of outsiders, particularly when the external nations with said interest in Korea seem to approach the Koreans with an air of superiority. Under such a climate, Joseph de Maistre's famous words, as occasionally quoted when North Korea is discussed, are a little unfair – both

How one is received, where one is schooled and what job one may ultimately be given all comes down to Songbun. A talented pupil from the hostile classes will almost never be as successful as a core class dullard – some citizens just have to come to terms with the fact that they should know their place and, save for a miracle, nothing will change that. Songbun dictates how people must conduct themselves, as one's actions will not only have an effect on their own Songbun, but that of their family also. This is true of marriage, too – few would marry somebody of a lower Songbun, as this would drag down their status. In Pyongyang, a city reserved for the crème de la crème, people have an increasingly poor understanding of life outside of the capital, as Pyongyangites almost always marry from within, preserving their status and reinforcing the bubble. When the entire bubble that is the DPRK came close to bursting during the famine (page 26), it was those of the lower caste that were the least likely to have access to food and medical care, and as a result these were the people that starved.

It is not easy to elevate one's status, but it is very easy to be downgraded. In modern North Korea, one's Songbun is still important, but wealth now holds significant sway. Experimenting in a little capitalism, which in the past affected one's Songbun, is now quietly acceptable. As a market economy slowly opens, those with capital are afforded a little social mobility, as palms can be greased to try and help one climb up the slippery pole. But of course, the people with the bulk of the money to start with are the core class.

Koreas had their governments forced upon them by external forces, events that they had no control over.

Divided into spheres of Soviet and US interest, those living in the Soviet North, like it or not, had a Stalinist system forced upon them. Although the Soviet Union departed Korea, moved on and slowly liberalised, North Korea became increasingly hard-line, surviving a brutal three-year war with the US-/UN-allied South and slowly transforming into an isolationist state living under a personality cult. The experiences in Korea from 1945–60 alone saw the departure of the Japanese, the division of Korea, the Korean War and the rise of the cult of Kim Il Sung, while a second defining period from 1991–2011 saw the collapse of the USSR, the death of Kim Il Sung, the Arduous March and famine, the rule and death of Kim Jong Il and the arrival of Kim Jong Un – all momentous events that will have had a profound effect on the psychology of the nation, both collectively and individually.

North Koreans work hard and keep their head down. Days are long, and of what little 'leisure' time there is, much is spent bettering oneself through political studies, self-criticism classes or 'voluntary' work. But the oft-portrayed stereotype of a mindless drone is a cheap shot and wholly inaccurate – North Koreans are a surprisingly well educated and cultured people who have a genuine lust for life, with hobbies and interests not a world away from our own. On a personal level, I find it far easier to relate with North Koreans that I do with people from many other nations I have visited and, bizarrely, there are some interesting cultural comparisons between Britain and Korea; nations on the fringe of their respective continents, enduring a complicated relationship with their neighbours, who they share similarities with but are also wholly different from.

While the Western world celebrates individualism, independent thinking in North Korea can be dangerous, creativity is stifled and few dare to put their head above the parapet. Though nobody speaks of such things, everybody knows that it is very easy to fall foul of the system, and the scars of others have taught them caution; certain things are simply never discussed and one's guard is almost never lowered, even to close friends and family. Accordingly, many citizens walk a tightrope almost every day, being careful not to trip up, for the slightest mistake can lead to a sudden and hard fall from grace. Such a life which, while perceived as normal (as nobody has ever known any different), must put intense psychological pressure and anguish on the entire nation.

Foreigners visiting North Korea will not be kowtowed to – Koreans expect and deserve to be treated on an equal footing, with respect for their culture and customs. Friendships are slow to develop, but even one-time visitors who make the effort will see bonds start to form, while regular travellers to the country can cement genuine lifelong friendships. Sadly, many of the problems in North Korea's international relations are down to the lack of regard shown to this proud homogenous nation, with a good deal of media coverage on the DPRK being offensive and intolerant at best, and veiled racism at worst.

LANGUAGE

The Korean language is estimated to be spoken by approximately 77 million people worldwide and, while various dialects exist, it should be highlighted that the North and South still share their mother tongue. A member of the Koreanic language family, Korean is, according to modern linguists, the most widely spoken example of a language isolate – ie: a language with no demonstrable genealogical relationship with any other. Much like with English, somebody's accent and speech can reveal where they are from; at least nine core dialects can be found across the peninsula.

Despite being a language isolate, a significant proportion of the vocabulary is Sino-Korean, either directly borrowed from written Chinese or coined in Korea or Japan using Chinese characters. To a lesser extent, some words have been borrowed from Mongolian and other languages. Since the division of Korea in 1945, the language spoken in the North and South has slowly diverged; while the South now has a great deal of English lexical borrowing, the North has not only tried to curtail the import and usage of foreign words, but has tried to eliminate some Sino-Korean words altogether in favour of native Korean words. Accordingly, it could be argued that the language used in North Korea is more traditional and authentic than the one spoken in the South. But in the propaganda war of dialects the North is losing; South Korea and its vibrant contemporary culture has been riding a wave of global popularity in recent years and learning Korean (or rather, the Southern dialect), has become incredibly fashionable. Cottoning on rather late in the day, the North Korean authorities are now apathetically promoting language courses for foreigners looking to learn the real thing in Pyongyang – after all, no textbooks in the South are likely to include such phrases as 'loyalty to the leader is the highest expression of patriotism' or 'let's go to see a mass gymnastic display!'

The language is agglutinative and has 24 letters in all – ten vowels and 14 consonants, using both single vowels and diphthongs. The alphabet was traditionally written vertically from top to bottom, but horizontal writing from left to right is now the norm. Korean language generally lacks grammatical gender but does have an extensive system of honorifics to reflect the speaker's relationship to the subject of the sentence, and speech levels to reflect the speaker's relationship to the audience. Before the 1443 creation of Hangul, the Korean alphabet, by Sejong The Great, Koreans used classical Chinese alongside native phonetic writing systems. Far simpler than Chinese script, Hangul was developed to promote literacy and to establish a cultural identity for Korea through a unique script. Each letter is based on a simplified diagram of the patters made by the mouth, tongue and teeth when producing the sound related to the character, a writing system many linguists consider to be the world's most logical. This simplified script was a major step in educating the masses but met with much resistance from the elite in its early days. Despite the first Hangul manuscript being published in 1446 (a handy document explaining this new script), it was not until 1894 that Hangul was finally adopted for official use, with the first Hangul newspaper arriving two years later.

RELIGION AND BELIEFS

Outwardly, North Korea presents itself as an irreligious nation, one that has transcended to a higher plain: communism. Religion is largely frowned upon and thought of as backwards – something that was promulgated in the feudal days to oppress the masses. Save for a few pseudo-monks at the occasional monastery, your chance of meeting anybody that openly appears to be religious is almost nil. However, much like the rest of the world, centuries of religious beliefs have naturally permeated into the country's culture, with many contemporary customs and beliefs still rooted in the five core faiths that held sway across the centuries.

Korean shamanism is ancient and predates Buddhism, which came to the peninsula in the 4th century AD. Upon arrival, Korean **Buddhism** developed a few distinct forms of its own and quickly grew in popularity in the south, becoming the state religion for the Silla Kingdom in 552. Despite its rapid adoption in the south, Buddhism was slow at making inroads in the north and it was not until the unified Koryo Dynasty of 918–1392 that it became prevalent across the entire peninsula. Despite Buddhism being widely accepted during the Koryo era, it was at this time that another belief arrived: **Confucianism**. Much like with Buddhism, Confucianism was adapted somewhat to make it more palatable for Koreans, and neo-Confucianism took hold. It was in the early years of the Choson Dynasty, which lasted from 1392–1897, that neo-Confucianism ousted Buddhism to become the main belief system, a time that marked the beginning of centuries of Buddhist repression.

In the late 18th century a third religion arrived from beyond Korean shores – **Christianity**. Intense missionary activity across Korea, accelerated by increased contact with the West, led to a rapid growth in the number of Christians, with Pyongyang becoming such a hotbed of Christian activity in the late 19th and early 20th centuries that it has been referred to as the 'Jerusalem of the East'. The Christian fervour was to be short-lived, however, as when the Japanese arrived in 1910 they took a hostile view of Christians, allowing the fifth main pre-Kim belief to flourish – **Chondoism**. This Chondoism has its roots in Confucianised indigenous shamanism and was a religious reaction to the Western encroachment of Korea, and was more acceptable to the Japanese who tolerated this 'Eastern learning'. With the collapse of the Japanese Empire and the division of Korea, the North quickly became a hard-line communist state, with little time for religion. Many Christians fled to the US-allied South, banking (and rightly so) that their beliefs would be tolerated there. Chondoism, a more home-grown system of beliefs, was just about accepted and continued to be tolerated in the DPRK, as it is viewed more as a utopian peasant movement than a religion. The Chondoists even have their own political party, the Chondoist Chongu Party, who, as of the last elections in 2014, hold 22 of the 687 seats in the Supreme People's Assembly.

Despite the faiths that have arrived on Korea's shores over the centuries, religion in contemporary North Korea does not exist in any real sense. There is no freedom of religion and the few temples, churches and such found in the country are either preserved as cultural relics or constructed and maintained for primarily political purposes. Official figures of the number of Shamans, Buddhists, Christians and Chondoists are quoted – but these are unverifiable and seem only to be presented to try and appease the many vocal naysayers outside the country who lambast the DPRK for its lack of religious freedom. Religion is occasionally used as a political tool, to impress big nations and big businesses when North Korea is striving to improve relations or cut a business deal. Occasionally a foreign delegation comes into town and what appears to be a rent-a-mob congregation is rustled up, to warm the pews and act like it's all business as usual – a charade that Pyongyang is happy to keep up in order to appease governments and win contracts.

With a knack of adopting and amending religions and beliefs from elsewhere, the DPRK has adapted Marxism-Leninism into their new prevalent belief system – the state ideology, known as **Juche** (see box, page 27). With Kim Il Sung as the creator and figurehead, he is almost considered as a Confucius mark II; not a god, but the Great Ultimate, the Eternal President. Accordingly, while religion does not truly exist in the DPRK, the personality cult that has been going strong for over 50 years has arguably created an entirely new religion, and a fundamentalist one at that, with the Juche Philosophy as its scripture. Kim Il Sung, who removed all religion from the country, has made himself into a deity, with all North Koreans wearing a badge depicting either him or his son, Kim Jong Il, on their chest.

EDUCATION

Education is universal and state-funded, with literacy, much like voter turnout at elections, reported at 100%. Compulsory schooling lasts for 12 years, with five years of elementary school (ages 7–11), three years of middle school (ages 11–13), three years of high school (ages 14–16) and at least one year of college or further education beyond that. Thereon, a high proportion of students will go on to university or higher learning, with men's studies almost certainly being interrupted by national service. Thanks to this, many men are nudging 30 by the time they start their non-military careers.

North Korea's educational system has a narrow view and follows the party line – from their first steps, the next generation are being indoctrinated and completely immersed into the system, taught to idolise the Kims while being presented with a version of history very different from our own. Discipline and technical ability is high, with science, technology, languages and maths being of great importance. However, it is the hours of classes in subjects such as 'Socialist Morality and Law', 'Revolutionary History of Our Great Leader Kim Jong Il' and 'The Childhood of our Supreme Leader Kim Il Sung' that help programme the students into good loyal citizens with a collective mindset. Outward forms of self-expression and a questioning intellect are not encouraged.

Upon stepping out in their not-so-wide world, graduates, by and large, have an education which, while it may stand them in good stead in North Korea, would place them on the backfoot in the outside world; an awful lot needs to be unlearnt for those few who do leave the country. With an educational style quite alien to the West, foreign visitors in the DPRK are often shocked and impressed upon meeting North Korean students, who are almost guaranteed to be impeccably behaved, extremely polite and, in certain fields, years ahead of their Western counterparts, but in others far behind.

Educational institutes, from kindergartens through to universities, often feature on conventional tours of the country, as the government is proud to highlight the Machiavellian system it has instilled in generations of North Koreans. Visiting these educational establishments will normally include a brief visit to the dedicated classrooms assigned for disseminating lessons on the great leaders where, in Kim Jong Il's words, the seeds of 'absolute loyalty to the party and leader' are sown.

CULTURE

ARCHITECTURE When it comes to architecture, North Korea has its own inimitable style, with heavy influences from the Stalinist and brutalist schools. Lashings of concrete fuse with occasional Eastern influences, pastel shades and curious lines – all coupled with such immense scale that the country has some truly spectacular examples of architecture, with countless startlingly unique structures jutting out from a sea of uniformity.

Despite the ravages of war, some pre-20th-century architecture exists, with preserved city gates, fortification walls, temples and traditional housing to be found across the country, particularly in Kaesong. Surprisingly, a few Japanese colonial buildings also stand, although they will rarely be pointed out as such. Regardless, what enthrals almost all visitors is the fascinating modern architecture of the country, much of which was created from a blank canvas after the massive destruction of the Korean War.

Before the end of the war, Kim Il Sung was already drawing up plans for building a socialist utopia: cities of wide streets and boulevards and high-rise residential blocks, with striking buildings and monuments sprinkled along axes and arteries. The focus, as always, would be on Pyongyang, but, once the armistice was signed, grandiose schemes were rolled out across the country. Redevelopment in the immediate post-war years was slow and initially more Soviet than it is now, but in the 1970s and 1980s, which could be called the golden years of North Korean architecture, cities transformed into the forms as they largely present themselves today, with the majority of the most impressive examples of architecture being constructed during this period.

Kim Jong Il's 17 years at the helm coincided with the Arduous March and extreme austerity measures, which meant construction either slowed down or completely ground to a halt. But in the final years of his rule, as the economy was spluttering back to life, so too did development. Under Kim Jong Un a construction boom has been taking place, with a great deal of what has been coined 'retro-futuristic' designs permeating many projects. Contemporary architects, a few generations on from those who rebuilt the country in the post-war years in predominantly Soviet and brutalist styles, are homegrown – they have only ever known the DPRK, have had little external influence on their education from international thinking and certainly do not subscribe to *The Architectural Review*. In such an isolated environment, design has evolved on a different tack, making North Korea one of the most visually fascinating countries on earth.

LITERATURE

The book is a silent teacher and a companion in life.

Kim Il Sung

Non-fiction in North Korea can be incredibly heavy, in both content and physical weight, with page after page, chapter after chapter, of word-for-word speeches made by the great leaders. Any aspiring member of the WPK would do well to voraciously devour these texts and, ideally, memorise them. Kim Il Sung's *Collected Works* run to 50 volumes, while the *Complete Works* currently tops out at 100 volumes. Besides the works of leaders past and present, there are also seemingly countless books on Juche, imperialism, socialism and the war. They are all fascinating to dip into, but largely unreadable given their density.

Fiction, bar a couple of stellar examples such as *The Sea of Blood*, isn't a great deal lighter, as there are essentially two types of novels from North Korea: those that deal with the revolutionary traditions, and those depicting the situation today. Even folk tales, comics and children's books portray a message, which likely goes over the head of the readers, but plants a seed of thought. Children are unlikely to join the dots and realise the symbolism behind the bullying red, white and blue cockerel, who goes out of his way to spoil everything in the land for all the other peace-loving animals. (Thankfully, the cockerel drowns in this famous tale, peace across the land is restored and, of course, the children are delighted.)

PAINTING

Art not related with the revolution, art for its own sake, is useless.

Kim Jong Un

Traditional art remains strong today in North Korea, with landscapes and scenes of ancient and feudal Korea a polar-opposite to the equally common socialist-realist works, for which the country is so famous. Artists, whatever the genre, are considered highly skilled and their works are occasionally exhibited internationally.

BUYING ART: DIFFERENT STROKES FOR DIFFERENT FOLKS

Hilary Bradt

I didn't expect to come home from North Korea with a picture. It was yet another surprise in a country full of surprises. During my 18-day visit it became obvious that in a country where everyone has a job, however mundane and unrewarding, artists do not do too badly. Provided, that is, that they have the skill to portray heroic postures and joyful faces in a wide variety of media. The smiling leaders, surrounded by happy peasants and profitable endeavour (steel works, agriculture and, of course, soldiers) pop up all over the place and in a huge scale.

In the vast Mansudae Art Studio in Pyongyang (page 113) over 1,000 artists beaver away producing public works and commissions, and around 4,000 staff are employed to keep the whole operation going. Artists here probably live a more secure life than in many countries as they don't have to worry about selling their work and they receive a regular salary and privileges – providing they follow the rules. Abstract or semi-abstract art does not exist; it is all representational. But once sculptors have honed their skills by assisting in the creation of Kim images they can take on commissions of giant portraits of foreign leaders. Two enormous statues of Robert Mugabe are still in the studios, prevented from reaching their destination in Zimbabwe by international sanctions. The low cost of the work, and the skill at producing it on such a huge scale, has made art one of North Korea's most high-profile and profitable exports – African dictators are particularly fond of it. Artists have travelled to Angola, Benin, Chad, Togo, the DRC and Ethiopia to complete their commissions and earn millions of dollars in valuable hard currency.

I love buying paintings, so was excited that our itinerary included visits to two art galleries. I had no idea what sort of art would be on offer. When we entered the first one, about midway through the tour, my heart sank. There, in the first two rooms, were paintings of the beaming leaders in a variety of scenic backgrounds. I should have guessed. The third room was more interesting, at least to one member of our group, in that in had patriotic oil paintings that didn't feature a leader. The person in question was making his eighth visit to North Korea and wanted to add to his collection of posters and paintings. He bought an oil painting of joyful peasants celebrating a good harvest.

It was at the second gallery, in Wonsan, that I hit the jackpot. The first couple of rooms were predictably uninspiring, but things became interesting when I spotted the oil paintings of scenery that wouldn't disgrace an upmarket British gallery. A piece depicting Kuryong Falls (page 205) particularly caught my eye; the style was almost Impressionist, with far freer brush strokes than the patriotic paintings. I loved it and bought it for a bargain 30 euros.

But that wasn't all. In another room was a painting that stopped me in my tracks. It glittered. It was of a pine and birch forest, the sort that we had driven through near Mount Paektu. The misty sun brightens the still water of a woodland lake and reflects the surrounding pine trees. Looking closely I could see it was created not from paint but from shavings of different coloured minerals. I'd never seen anything like it, and I bought it. It was only later that I learned that this was jewel painting, unique to North Korea, and created literally with jewels. Or semi-precious stones, at any rate. It now has a permanent place on my sitting room wall – a unique reminder of an extraordinary trip.

The Mansudae Art Studio in Pyongyang (page 113) is believed to be the largest centre of art production in the world, and it's possible to arrange a tour of the studio, as well as the Korean Art Gallery and many other small studios across the country. Small hand-painted posters and screen prints are available from €25 or so, with fine art creeping up into the multiple hundreds, or even thousands, of euros. If you are hoping to pick up a piece of art, it is advisable to bring a poster or drawing tube from home, as tracking down any packaging locally can be difficult.

POTTERY The oldest examples of earthenware on the peninsula date back to 8000BC. Though influenced by Chinese ceramics, Korean pottery developed its own, arguably superior, style over the subsequent millennia, and in turn influenced Japanese ceramics. The arrival of celadon in the latter years of the Silla Dynasty saw a conceptual shift in Korean ceramics, as these pale green-blue designs slowly incorporated native influences. The high-water mark in Korean pottery is largely considered to be the 12th century, the middle period of the Koryo Dynasty, thanks to the invention of the inlaid celadon or *sanggam* technique, with elegant pieces of the time incorporating designs such as stylised fish, insects and birds, and key-fret, foliate and geometric patterns. Koryo celadon started its decline with the Mongol invasions of Korea and by the time of the neo-Confucianist Choson Dynasty styles had started to change, partly due to the waning Buddhist influence within the culture. Choson pottery was typically white porcelain and simpler, with less decoration, although sanggam techniques remained present in *buncheong,* a form of dark stoneware which, together with Choson pottery, largely replaced the more eye-catching celadon pieces of the Koryo days.

Modern North Korea does, to an extent, celebrate its pottery – a few outlets make attractive reproductions of Koryo celadon vases and such, which means that while the art isn't exactly flourishing, the skills are at least kept alive.

MUSIC All music in North Korea will portray a message of some form, one that is very different from contemporary Western music. Song titles such as 'Let Us Defend Socialism', 'The General is the Great Champion' and 'Pride of the Girl Soldier' tell you all you need to know about the accepted subject matter.

Folk and classical music still cling on, and the National Symphony Orchestra perform a repertoire of both Korean and international pieces, often erring towards blasting out rousing bombastic numbers and martial pieces – just as one would expect. Modern music of all genres is designed to be accessible and catchy, with lyrics delivering a clear message, after all, in Kim Jong Un's own words, 'an excellent song is a weapon more powerful than a gun or aircraft'. Songs are occasionally of love (for the family, the party and *occasionally* the opposite sex), but the most common recurring themes are doused in propaganda – celebrating the party, its leaders and armed forces, or delivering vital messages, such as increasing potato production. Pop music is normally twee and has an air of familiarity, like something from a light entertainment show from the 1960s, and is often delivered by glamorous coiffured ladies or burly baritones. These polished family-friendly numbers often use electric guitars, synthesisers and saxophones, but the sound produced is more like 1970s Soviet pop music, refreshingly different from almost anything you will have heard in decades, or will likely ever hear again.

Those looking for rousing military music should track down a CD or two from The Korean People's Army Merited Chorus, while something more classical may crop up at the Moranbong Theatre, where the State Symphony Orchestra regularly perform. A couple of pop stalwarts, who have released multiple dozens of albums between them over the years, are the Pochonbo Electronic Ensemble and the Wangjaesan Light Music Band, some of whose album covers are so wonderfully kitsch they are worth purchasing for the novelty value alone. The Moranbong Band have been dubbed North Korea's answer to the Spice Girls, though this moniker is slightly unfair – the band are extremely talented. Founded in 2012 and said to be have been personally selected by Kim Jong Un, these dashing debutantes dragged North Korean music (almost) into the 21st century. At their inaugural televised performance just a few months into Kim Jong Un's leadership, Korea – and the global media – was shocked by the high heels, comparatively racy dress and their choice of songs, including such decadent imperialist numbers as 'My Way' and the theme from *Rocky*, as they shared the stage with dancing and waving Disney characters such as Winnie-the-Pooh, Snow White and the Western world's favourite verminous couple. 'Is this it?' the world asked. 'Is North Korea opening up?' asked the learned journalists, before predicting imminent glasnost. 'Is it *finally* happening?' The answer was no.

THEATRE AND OPERA   Modern theatre is predominantly modern North Korean, so will always carry an overt political and social message, following the party line to the bitter end. Accordingly, the highly polished production values are often more memorable than the content, which can be quite predictable.

Occasional foreign plays are performed also, but the exposure to and interest in Western classics is limited. Expect to see Koreans 'chalking up' to play Caucasian characters, often with added sideburns and prosthetic noses.

Korean Revolutionary Opera is an art form in itself and has to be seen to be believed – performances are infrequent, but truly awesome. See box, page 105 for more information.

CINEMA

The cinematic art has become a powerful ideological weapon which greatly inspires the working people to the revolutionary struggle and construction work.

Korean Film Art (1985), Korean Film Export & Import Corporation, Pyongyang.

The first North Korean film, *My Home Village,* was released in 1949 and follows the tale of a forlorn peasant farmer who discovers the revolution, joins the guerrillas and (thanks to Kim Il Sung) plays his part in routing the Japanese from his village and country, liberating Korea. Huzaah! All features henceforth have carried weighty and overt ideological messages, where the state, community and nation wins in the face of adversity. Plotlines can be simple – a plumber struggling to convince the carefree corner-cutting managers of a building project that the inferior pipework they propose to fit in a tower block will not meet the needs of the residents, or a little more complex, such as in *Pulgasari,* set in feudal times, where a Godzilla-like creature helps oppressed citizens overthrow a corrupt monarch. Films are typically set in either feudal times (highlighting the struggle of the masses), times of war (nearly always with Japan or the US), or the modern era (when the tales are largely of selflessness and steering those who have strayed back onto the true path of the revolution). Personal sacrifice is a common theme, with many giving their all, even their lives, for victory, whatever that may be.

Exposure to world cinema is severely restricted, so Korean cinema has a captive audience, and the state has produced hundreds of films over the years. Cinemas are found all over the country, ranging from small screens on co-operative farms to grandiose civic buildings in Pyongyang. Filmgoing is a popular form of escapism, just as in the West, with many actors and actresses being household names, even decades on from their defining role. Some real gems do exist, with *The Sea of Blood* (1968), *The Flower Girl* (1972) and *Salt* (1985), among others, all being considered classics. The peak of Korean cinema is generally thought of as the 1970s and 1980s, a time when Kim Jong Il, who was slowly assuming the role of prince regent, was heavily involved in the art. A cinephile rumoured to have had over 20,000 videos and DVDs in his collection, Kim Jong Il came to redefine North Korean cinema, with his 1973 treatise *On the Art of the Cinema* and 1987's *The Cinema and Directing* being his manifestos on how to steer domestic filmmaking in a new direction.

Kim Jong Il's obsession with cinema is highlighted in a story so unbelievable that it could have been the plot of a Hollywood blockbuster. In the late 1970s a famous South Korean power couple, Shin Sang-ok and Choi Eun-hee – he a prized director and she a coveted actress – were abducted from Hong Kong, allegedly at the orders of Kim Jong Il, in order for them to help him realise his vision for North Korean cinema. The couple seemed to accept their fate and settled in Pyongyang, making a number of blockbusters for Kim Jong Il in the 1980s, including *Runaway* (1984), where the budget was so large a real train was exploded for the finale. By 1986 the couple decided to run away themselves, defecting to the West while in Vienna. This intriguing tale is the subject of a 2016 British documentary, *The Lovers and the Despot*.

2

Practical Information

WHEN TO VISIT

Gone are the days when the country would close its doors to tourists during the depths of winter – travellers may now visit year-round. However, access to far-flung areas can be restricted during the icy depths of winter and during the sudden summer rains that can turn rural roads into a quagmire, so more comprehensive tours are best undertaken from early April to late June and late August to late October, when it is generally cool and dry. Weather aside, visiting in the low season can be very rewarding, as so few travel to the country it may feel like you have the entire place to yourself. Those looking for pomp and ceremony might consider timing their visit to coincide with a national holiday or special events, but do bear in mind that around major celebrations the country can seem deceptively bustling with many tour groups and foreign delegations in town, the crowds often overshadowing the overall spectacle of the anticipated celebrations.

HIGHLIGHTS

Pyongyang must be a contender as the most fantastical and bizarre capital city on earth and offers all manner of wonderment. With so much to see and do in this near-alien world, the city can leave even the most seasoned traveller utterly stupefied, with the fascination all further magnified due to the absolute bizarreness of it all. There is much more to see beyond Pyongyang, however. Mounts Myohyang and Kumgang are both accessible mountain areas that showcase the very best of the country's overlooked and beautiful natural beauty, while for many the holy grail of North Korean travel is Mount Paektu, known locally as the 'sacred mountain of the revolution', which can only be reached by chartering a vintage aircraft – an adventure in itself. The east coast has countless pristine bays and beaches, all slowly leading north to remote North Hamgyong Province, arguably the 'real' North Korea and a world away from the relative glamour of Pyongyang – a worthy inclusion for hardy travellers.

SUGGESTED ITINERARIES

The scope of tours grows with each passing year, but if you have fewer than six nights to spend in North Korea it would be best to focus on the southwest of the country, taking in Pyongyang, Kaesong, the DMZ and, time permitting, Mount Myohyang. Other attractions that could be incorporated into a brief tour include Nampo, Pyongsong and Sariwon. With a week or more to play, consider a foray into the southeast, with areas such as Hamhung, Wonsan, Mount Kumgang and Masikryong all accessible on both private and group tours.

More in-depth and complex tours, often for groups only or on select dates due to logistical necessities, can enable you to really get off the beaten track, making use of overnight train journeys or chartered aircraft to get up into the remote northeast. Such comprehensive tours can be two to three weeks in duration and cover almost everything it's possible to see or do – a wonderful prospect should you have the time, money and inclination.

TOUR OPERATORS

The number of operators offering tours to North Korea has mushroomed in recent years. The list we include below is by no means comprehensive; a cursory investigation on the internet will reveal more. As any tourist heading to North Korea is obliged to travel as part of a fully organised and escorted package, advertised prices are generally for a complete tour, including all accommodation, meals, transport and entrance fees. The prices and range of tours vary from one operator to another and it is well worth checking exactly what is and isn't included in the cost of any package, as many of those 'too good to be true' prices are likely to be just that. A few questions that you should ask of any operator include:

- Whether they work directly with North Korea, or through another tour operator
- The minimum and, more importantly, maximum size of their groups
- The nationality/language/demographics of their typical group
- How your visa will be arranged and obtained
- Exactly where the tour starts and ends
- What financial bonding and protection they hold
- Any exclusions in tour prices
- How the trip will be paid for

Conventional tours may last anything from two or three days to upwards of three weeks. As the possibilities within the DPRK expand so does the range of experiences on offer. While on investigation the country may sound expensive to visit, tour costs are, with all things considered, remarkably good value for money, as essentially everything that can be included will be. Of course, different tour operators pitch their services differently: some focus on price, piling high and selling cheap, others focus on service and some on the overall experience. All tours will ultimately be handled by the small number of organisations in North Korea licensed to arrange tours, such as KITC (Korea International Travel Company) and KIYTC (Korean International Youth Travel Company), but direct contact with these organisations is difficult. It is far easier and almost always cheaper to arrange your trip through one of the agencies listed below.

UK

Juche Travel Services 2A High St, Thames Ditton KT7 0RY; m 07754 670186; e info@juchetravelservices.com; w juchetravelservices.com; see ad, 1st colour section. Offers private, group & special-interest tours including aviation, education & sporting trips.
Lupine Travel 23 King St, Wigan, Lancashire WN1 1DY; 01942 497209; e info@lupinetravel.co.uk; w lupinetravel.co.uk; see ad, 1st colour

section. Operating budget tours to an eclectic mix of unusual destinations since 2008.
Regent Holidays 6th Flr, Colston Tower, Colston St, Bristol BS1 4XE; 020 3588 2971; e regent@regentholidays.co.uk; w regentholidays.co.uk; see ad, inside back cover. A pioneer of the unusual, Regent have been operating private trips & small & specialist group tours to the country since 1985, with excellent customer service and attention to detail. ABTA bonded & ATOL licensed.

USA

New Korea Tours 1748 Aspen Glen Dr, Hampden, CT 06518 \ +1 203 613 5283; e mark@ newkoreatours.com; w newkoreatours.com

AUSTRALIA

Uri Tours e info@uritours.com; w uritours.com

CHINA

Explore North Korea \ +86 159 4154 5676; e tours@explorenorthkorea.com; w explorenorthkorea.com; see ad, 2nd colour section

Koryo Tours \ + 86 10 6416 7544; e info@ koryotours.com; w koryotours.com; see ad, 2nd colour section. Often imitated but rarely bettered – few know the DPRK as well as this firm. Involved in a variety of North Korean projects in addition to tourism, such as documentaries & art exhibitions.

Krahun e info@krahun.com; w krahun.com. Specialising in tours to Rason & North Hamgyong.

KTG DPRK Tours \ +86 24 2284 3816; e info@ north-korea-travel.com; w north-korea-travel. com; see ad, inside front cover. Shenyang-based operator offering budget rates & small tour sizes.

Young Pioneer Tours \ +86 159 9965 3436; e tours@youngpioneertours.com; w youngpioneertours.com; see ad, 2nd colour section. Budget adventure travel firm operating tours to an increasing number of off-the-wall & off-the-beaten-track destinations.

GERMANY

Korea – Reisedienst Weidkampshaide 10, D-30659 Hannover; \ +49 (0)511 647 8616; e info@nordkoreareisen.de; w nordkoreareisen. de. Mainly catering to Germans, this company has been offering tours to North Korea since 1990.

Pyongyang Travel Krossener Straße 23, 10245 Berlin; \ +49 (0)308 562 5802; e info@pyongyang- travel.com; w pyongyang-travel.com. Founded in 2013, this company offers tours to an exciting mix of unusual destinations in addition to North Korea.

SINGAPORE

Choson Exchange e team@chosonexchange. org; w chosonexchange.org. A non-profit organisation pursuing deeper engagement with the country through various projects, including sending skilled volunteers to North Korea to provide training in business & entrepreneurship.

SPAIN

Viatges Pujol Córcega 214, 08036 Barcelona; \ +34 933 219 303; e viatgespujol@viatgespujol. com; w coreanorte.com. One of the few specialists offering tours conducted in Spanish.

SWEDEN

Korea Konsult \ +46 73 981 0372; e postmaster@koreakonsult.com; w koreakonsult. com. One of the biggest players in mainland Europe, offering pretty much the whole gamut of tours in the country.

RED TAPE

VISAS Save for the rarest of circumstances, all travellers to North Korea will be travelling via China or Russia, compounding the red tape required to visit. Those passing through China should ensure that their passport is valid for at least six months from the date of entry, while those passing through Russia will require a passport valid for six months beyond the expiration date of their Russian visa. Both Russian and Chinese visas will take up a full page of your passport and require additional space for entry and exit stamps. Almost all nationalities require a visa to China or Russia, and you will likely need double-entry visas, assuming you return from whence you came. However, citizens of 53 countries can currently spend up to 144 hours visa free in Beijing under the Transit Without Visa Scheme (TWOV). This scheme only applies if you arrive directly into Beijing by air from another country, and are travelling directly out of Beijing, by air, onto a third country (ie: North Korea). The rules are a little complex with a few clauses and exceptions, but most travellers happy to fly in and out of North Korea from China can now avoid the headache of applying for a costly Chinese visa and spend a few days exploring Beijing in the process. Shanghai and Shenyang, an occasional route of entry to

2

North Korea, also operate a TWOV scheme, for 144 and 72 hours respectively. Your tour operator will be able to clarify criteria for these visa exemptions, as they do change and are not well publicised.

The DPR Korean visa must be obtained in advance, and a tourist visa is always single entry/exit and valid for the precise duration of your trip. Before one can apply for a visa, your invitation/approval to visit the country must be obtained. This normally takes a couple of weeks, but has in extreme cases been arranged in just a few days. Regardless, many tour operators are reluctant to take bookings with less than four to six weeks' notice due to the complications in arranging tours to the country. The earlier you book the quicker you should get your visa and the more polished your tour will likely be. You will not see your approval document; it is essentially a message sent to your nominated DPR Korean Embassy, normally by fax, granting permission for your visa to be issued.

Your tour operator should handle all the documentation in order for your visa authorisation to be granted and as an absolute minimum will require a colour scan or photocopy of your passport together with your home address, contact details and full employment information. The Pyongyang authorities essentially want to know who you are and what you do, and to make sure you are not involved in journalism or similar fields. The details required of you will be clarified by your tour operator, most of whom are well versed in the protocol, processing these applications day in, day out. They will also be able to inform you of the precise requirements, as they vary somewhat depending on your nationality, residency and the nominated embassy issuing your visa.

Only once your visa authorisation has been issued can the visa be applied for. This is a straightforward exercise as the issuing embassy will now have full permission to issue your visa. They will require at least one completed visa application form and at least one passport photograph, but again, requirements differ. Some tour operators include the visa fee in their costs, while others charge. The visa cost is an arbitrary but reasonable figure that differs from one embassy to the next. Many tour operators issue the majority of their clients' visas through Beijing for ease. In this instance the visa is a document separate to your physical passport, so can be obtained on your behalf and handed to you locally, typically a day or two before your trip commences. Other DPRK embassies affix a full-page visa to your passport – a great souvenir, but this does often mean giving up your passport for a few days or having to go to an embassy in person.

Obtaining a visa is normally far easier than one would expect and as long as you have been accurate, honest and truthful in your application they are almost never refused. The only people who normally find it difficult to obtain visas to North Korea are journalists (who really must not try to sneak in posing as tourists), together with those travelling on South Korean or Japanese passports. Protocol changes with the diplomatic ebb and flow and though North Korea was accepting tourists from the US at the time of writing, the US Department of State will invalidate the passports of any traveller who does so, unless they have obtained a Special Validation Passport (which is extremely unlikely to be issued). In addition, US citizens may not enter or exit the country at the Sinuiju border and a small number of hotels do not accept US travellers, but rules change and should be checked in advance with your operator.

Visas have been known to be extended in-country for people wishing to prolong their trip. On obtaining your visa, particularly if you collect it yourself, it is recommended to double and triple check that all numbers, dates and details match your passport and plans, as certain embassies have a reputation for making mistakes. Once in North Korea all the permits, papers, documentation and registrations will all be handled for you by your guides. Accordingly, they generally like to keep hold of your passport for the duration of your trip, which will make touring the country easier for all parties concerned.

IMMIGRATION AND CUSTOMS On arriving in North Korea, you will normally be required to complete three forms: a health and quarantine declaration card, an entry/exit card and a customs declaration. The health and quarantine card is a rather simple document asking which countries you have visited in the last ten days, with a checklist of symptoms of illnesses and prohibited items that you will hopefully not have. Ticking any boxes on this form, indicating you are unwell, or bringing in any of the restricted items (such as eggs, meat and seed cultures) is not recommended. The entry/exit card is also a simple form, with no questions that should be difficult to answer. The customs declaration stumps the most people, as visitors should declare the amount of cash (and in which currencies) they are carrying – it's easier to note this in advance than count it all out in the queue. Regardless, how much cash you are bringing in is not really an issue. You must, understandably, declare items such as weapons, but also any GPS devices, mobile telephones, communications means and all books and publications. If your camera or telephone has a built-in GPS device this is vaguely acceptable, but a standalone GPS device, or standalone communications device such as a radio or walkie-talkie is not. Customs are essentially looking for the things that you clearly know you shouldn't be carrying (page 63). The contents of your laptop, mobile telephone and any other electronic media may be inspected as well, but checks are normally cursory – they will typically glance over your belongings and tinker with your telephone for 30 seconds or so before waving you on. It is all relatively easy and far less daunting than most expect it to be. Should you have any inoffensive but prohibited items there is normally recourse to leave these at the airport and collect on departure (or have officially sealed and kept on your person to present on exit, should you be arriving overland).

EMBASSIES AND CONSULATES The majority of the embassies in Pyongyang are located in Taedonggang District. Apart from the large Russian and Chinese embassies, these are small diplomatic outposts; any consular assistance that may be afforded to you will be limited, particularly when you are outside the capital, as even diplomats cannot freely explore the country. Many embassies encourage that you inform them of your travel plans in advance.

The Chinese Embassy has been known to quickly issue visas to stranded travellers in the past, but this is not recommended and should only be considered as a last resort. The Swedish Embassy is a protecting power for the United States and can provide limited assistance to unrepresented EU nationals, while the British Embassy can provide some assistance to most unrepresented Commonwealth citizens. All of this information is fluid and should be checked in advance of travel. The following list isn't exhaustive, but covers the main embassies in Pyongyang. Travellers in North Hamgyong and Rason should note the two consulates in Chongjin. It has been known for Chinese visas to be obtained in Chongjin, but really, do not come this way unless you have all in place in advance of travel!

Embassies in the DPRK

ⓔ Brazil 3 Munsudong, No 41 Ground Flr, Taedonggang District, Pyongyang; ☏ (2) 381 7955; e brasemb.pyongyang@itamaraty.gov.br

ⓔ Bulgaria Munsudong, Taedonggang District, Pyongyang; ☏ (2) 381 7343; e embassy. pyongyang@mfa.bg

China Kinmaul-dong, Moranbong District, Pyongyang; ☎ (2) 381 3116; e chinaemb_kp@mfa.gov.cn

Chinese Consulate Chonmasan Hotel, Chongjin City; ☎ (073) 230802; e consulate_chongjin@mfa.gov.cn

Czech Republic Taedonggang Kuyok 38, Taehakgori, Puksudong, Pyongyang; ☎ (2) 381 7021; e pyongyang@embassy.mzv.cz

Germany Munsudong, Taedonggang District, Pyongyang; ☎ (2) 381 7385. e info@pjeongjang.diplo.de

India 6 Munsudong, Taedonggang District, Pyongyang; ☎ (2) 381 7215; e amb.pyongyang@mea.gov.in

Indonesia Munsudong, Taedonggang District, Pyongyang; ☎ (2) 381 7425; e pyongyang.kbri@kemlu.go.id

Mongolia Munsudong, Taehakgori 19, Pyongyang; ☎ (2) 381 7323; e pyongyang@mfat.gov.mn

Pakistan Bldg No 23, Compound 53, Munsu St, Taedonggang District, Pyongyang; ☎ (2) 381 7479; e parep.pyongyang@gmail.com

Poland Munsudong, Taedonggang District, Pyongyang; ☎ (2) 381 7325; e pjongjang.amb.sekretariat@msz.gov.pl

Romania Munsudong, Taedonggang District, Pyongyang; ☎ (2) 382 7336; e romania.dprk@yahoo.com

Russia Somun-do, Central District, Pyongyang; ☎ (2) 381 2101; e embassy@rusembdprk.ru

Russian Consulate Chongjin City; ☎ (073) 230203; e chondjin@dks.ru

Sweden Somun-do, Central District, Pyongyang; ☎ (2) 381 7485; e ambassaden.pyongyang@gov.se

United Kingdom Munsudong, Taedonggang District, Pyongyang; ☎ (2) 381 7980; e pyongyangenquiries@fco.gov.uk

DPRK embassies and missions abroad

The North Korean government maintains around 50 embassies, consulates and missions across the globe; the number increases in one part of the world as new business ventures are explored, while it decreases elsewhere as diplomatic spats ensue. They are generally wary of strangers and are reluctant to assist people without an appointment with information on visas, tourism and such; some barely manage to answer the phone at all. A few seem unable or unwilling to issue visas, but your tour operator will clarify the best course of action, as where you can or should obtain your visa from will depend on a number of factors, including your nationality and place of residence. Once more, this list isn't exhaustive and it should be noted that it's best to let your tour operator do the introductions here, so that the relevant office (and person) is expecting to hear from you.

China 11 Ritan Bei Lu, Jianguomenwai, Beijing 10060; ☎ +86 10 6532 1186; Beiling Dajie, Huanggu, Shenyang 110034; ☎ +86 24 8685 2742

France 47 Rue Chauveau, Neilly-sur-Seine, Paris; ☎ +33 1 47 47 53 85

Germany Glinkastrasse 5–7, 10117 Berlin; ☎ +49 302 062 5990

Hong Kong Suite 1101, 11F Chinachem Century Tower, 178 Gloucester Rd, Wan Chai; ☎ +852 2803 4447

Italy Viale dell'Esperanto, 26, 00144 Rome; ☎ +39 6 5422 0749

Mongolia Huvisgalchdiin St Chingeltei, Ulaanbaatar 151560; ☎ +976 11 326153

Russia Mosfilmovskaya St, 72, Moscow 119590; ☎ +7 499 1436231; Ul Dikopoltsev, 28, 680000 Khabarovsk; ☎ +7 4212 336283

South Africa 958 Waterpoort St, Faerie Glen, Pretoria; ☎ +27 12 991 8661

United Kingdom 73 Gunnersbury Av, London, W5 4LP; ☎ 020 8992 4965

United States of America (Permanent Mission to the UN) 820 Second Av, 13th Flr, New York, NY10017; ☎ +1 212 972 3105

Vietnam 25 Cao Ba Qrt St, Hanoi; ☎ +84 24 3823 3008

BY AIR The sole passenger airline within the country is **Air Koryo** (w airkoryo. com.kp). The carrier is often mocked in the Western media as being the 'world's worst airline' or as a 'one-star airline'; titles that are unfair and wide of the mark, as Air Koryo is not only reliable but also proffers an enjoyable and authentic North Korean experience that harks back to the golden age of jet travel, with immaculate air stewardesses, a complimentary meal and service with a smile. International flights are all operated by Tupelov Tu-204 or Antonov AN-148 aircraft, the oldest of which was manufactured in 2007. Rumours of Air Koryo being 'blacklisted' by the European Union continue to circulate, but this ban only applies to the older aircraft in the fleet, which now only operate domestically – so do note that should you fly internally it will almost certainly be against the advice of the EU! Baggage allowance is 23kg in economy class and 30kg in business.

Internationally, Air Koryo operates reliable scheduled flights from Pyongyang to Beijing, Shenyang and Vladivostok. In addition, they occasionally serve Shanghai, but only as and when demand sees fit. Over the years they have tried and failed to launch services to destinations such as Dandong, Shenyang, Khabarovsk and Bangkok; but these are essentially chartered services prone to cancellation – the only reliable year-round connections are to Beijing, Shenyang and Vladivostok. While the airline has a website this struggles to function

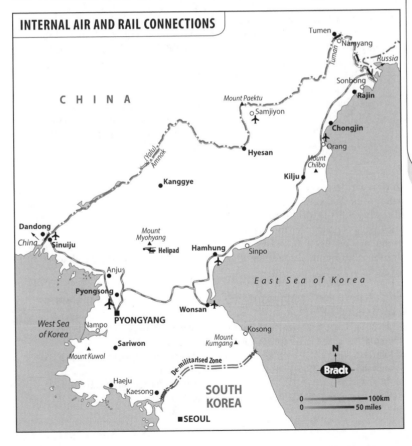

INTERNAL AIR AND RAIL CONNECTIONS

Those wanting a memorable experience can charter aircraft to get to some of the more far flung corners of the country, and this is still the only means for tourists to reach Mount Paektu. Many tour operators incorporate a charter flight into their more comprehensive itineraries and the cost for larger groups doesn't have to be prohibitively expensive. All available aircraft are based in Pyongyang and operators can essentially name the date and routes that they wish to fly, with the costs creeping up as more sectors and overnight stops are added. Charters can be anything from a leisure flight over Pyongyang or a one-day jaunt to Mount Paektu up to a one-week charter taking you all over the country, with the aircraft almost certainly waiting on the tarmac while you enjoy your travels. At the time of writing, flights could be chartered to and between the following airports:

- Uiju (UJU; for Sinuiju)
- Samjiyon (YJS; for Mount Paektu/Ryanggang Province)
- Orang (RGO; for North Hamgyong and Rason Special Economic Zone)
- Sondok (DSO; for Hamhung and South Hamgyong Province)
- Wonsan (WOS; for Wonsan and Kangwon/Mount Kumgang)

The model chartered will typically depend on economies of scale, but the most common aircraft used is an Anotonov An-24. Other aircraft available include the Ilyushin Il-18, Ilyushin Il-62, Tupelov Tu-134 and Tupelov Tu-154. For the deep-pocketed enthusiasts, it has been known for groups to charter flights in a cargo plane, the Ilyushin Il-76.

In addition to aeroplanes, Air Koryo offers a fantastic Mil Mi-17 helicopter for scenic leisure flights over Pyongyang and for day trips to Hyangsan (page 174). Theoretically, visitors may also charter helicopters to whizz them to the ski slopes of Masikryong or hiking trails of Mount Kumgang, but whether anyone has ever done this is another matter.

and, regardless, your tour operator will almost certainly have contracted rates and group discounts – it is best to leave it to the professionals as trying to liaise directly with the airline could well be a taxing and fruitless exercise. Demand for flights is greater during the high season (late March to late October), and the frequency of flights increases accordingly. All schedules listed below are from summer 2018 and all times are local. Historically, schedules have changed little over the years.

Flights between Pyongyang (FNJ) and Beijing (PEK)

Flights on Tue & Sat operate year-round. Flights on Thu run in the high season &, if demand requires it, Mon & Fri.

Pyongyang–Beijing (JS151) Dep 09.00, arr 10.00; Mon & Fri

Beijing–Pyongyang (JS152) Dep noon, arr 15.00; Mon & Fri

Pyongyang–Beijing (JS151) Dep 08.50, arr 09.50; Tue & Sat

Beijing–Pyongyang (JS152) Dep 13.05, arr 16.05; Tue & Sat

Pyongyang–Beijing (JS251) Dep 10.35, arr 11.35; Thu

Beijing–Pyongyang (JS252) Dep 14.00, arr 17.00; Thu

Flights between Pyongyang (FNJ) and Shenyang (SHE)

Operate on Wed & Sat year-round.

Pyongyang–Shenyang (JS155) Dep 11.50, arr noon

Shenyang–Pyongyang (JS156) Dep 13.55, arr 16.10

Flights between Pyongyang (FNJ) and Vladivostok (VVO)

Operate on Mon & Fri year-round.

Pyongyang–Vladivostok (JS271) Dep 08.30, arr 11.00

Vladivostok–Pyongyang (JS272) Dep 12.20, arr 13.00

Besides Air Koryo, just one other airline, **Air China**, serves the country. Sadly, though, they just cannot make up their mind about what they want to do with their undersubscribed Pyongyang service, which currently operates only in the high season, as they seem to cancel, postpone and alter schedules with such frequency that tour operators are reluctant to endorse this route with them. After pulling the service altogether in 2017, Air China relaunched the Beijing–Pyongyang route for summer 2018, promoting thrice-weekly flights on Mondays, Wednesdays and Fridays (in both directions).

BY RAIL

To/from China North Korea is well connected by train to China and many tour operators include arriving or departing by rail as a standard feature of their tours. Four trains a week operate between Beijing and Pyongyang (and vice versa), while a daily service now also operates between Dandong and Pyongyang (and vice versa). All times given are local.

The Beijing–Pyongyang service departs from Beijing Railway Station at 17.27 on Mondays, Wednesdays, Thursdays and Saturdays and arrives into Pyongyang the following day at 18.45. In the opposite direction, it departs Pyongyang on the same days at 10.25 and arrives into Beijing at 08.38 the following day. Tickets exclude meals but there is a restaurant car, though it gets very busy at dinner time, so you'll need to be quick in grabbing a seat if you want a meal. Note that the restaurant car in China only accepts Chinese currency, while the Korean restaurant car will normally also accept euros and US dollars. Regardless, stock up on snacks and drinks – it is customary to share and share alike with your travelling companions.

This route is essentially a domestic service with a few international carriages attached; departing Beijing most carriages are only going to Dandong, while departing Pyongyang most carriages are only going as far as Sinuiju – just a handful of carriages are shunted over the border. Accommodation within the carriages will be in relatively comfortable mixed-sex four-berth compartments, and a basic toilet and washbasin can be found at each end of the carriage, as can a samovar. The entire border experience can be lengthy, with the scheduled layover for formalities taking around 2 hours in each country (so expect 4 hours in total), but it is an experience to remember and the officials are all affable enough. The train does pass through a number of Chinese cities including Tianjin and Shenyang so you could, theoretically, arrange to board or disembark in one of these interim stops, incurring a small reduction in the ticket price as a result. Much like with air tickets, tour operators will generally have contracted rates for train tickets into and out of the country, so there is little to no benefit in your trying to arrange these independently. Procedure and protocols change, but in Dandong travellers normally disembark the train for passport and customs checks, while in Sinuiju formalities normally take place within the carriage.

The daily Dandong–Pyongyang service departs Dandong at 10.00 and arrives in Pyongyang at 18.45; in reverse, it leaves Pyongyang at 10.25 and arrives in Dandong at 16.23. This service is typically in a six-berth compartment (often referred to as third class), but is very comfortable for a day train. A restaurant car is normally, but not always, included on this service.

To/from Russia What was for years the forbidden rail line linking Pyongyang with Russia, this route is now permitted for foreigners to use; an epic journey through some wonderfully remote parts of both countries. The service is still hampered by delays, so a degree of flexibility and an open mind is essential. Seven times a month, train 007 is scheduled to depart Pyongyang at 07.50 for Rason. This train *may* depart one day earlier, and the precise date of operation is normally only confirmed 30 days in advance. The service is scheduled to take 29½ hours to reach the northeastern corner of North Korea (and passes through Hamhung and Chongjin en route), but can in fact take much longer. The goal is to ensure that the train arrives in Tumangang, on the border with Russia, in time to couple with the Moscow-bound train, which is fixed to depart Tumangang six times a month, on the 4th, 8th, 12th, 18th, 24th and 28th. The trains within Korea comprise ageing four-berth sleeping compartments with no restaurant car – bring plenty of supplies and wet wipes to wash with. A samovar in the carriage dispenses hot water.

While this route may be undertaken in reverse it remains even more complicated to do so, as the precise date of the train from Russia can jump around – it is best to check with tour operators as developments for this route are moving much faster than the trains themselves.

BY ROAD
To China The land borders between Dandong and Sinuiju (page 182), Tumen and Namyang (page 231) and Yanbian and Rason (page 249) are open to travellers with the relevant permits and arrangements in place.

To South Korea Crossings with the South are all severed, but by the time this book has gone to print connections could well have resumed to spots such as the Kaesong Industrial Zone (by road and rail) and Mount Kumgang, which at its peak was accessible by rail, road and sea.

BY SEA Connections with the outside world have all dried up – talks of resuming the service to Niigata in Japan (see box, page 196) remain just that, while the attempts to arrange cruises between Russia and North Korea have permanently run aground. Should the diplomacy of 2018 come to fruition, connections with Japan, South Korea and Russia may well resurface.

HEALTH *With Dr Felicity Nicholson*

Medical facilities in the country as a whole are basic, particularly in rural areas. Hospitals and clinics in the latter are usually able to offer only the very minimum medical care. Clinical hygiene is poor, anaesthetics are frequently unavailable, and electricity supply to the hospitals (even in the capital) can be intermittent; you should try to avoid serious surgery if you can. Take any medications you are likely to require with you as supplies are limited and can be very difficult to buy. There are no reciprocal health-care agreements with the UK, so ensure that you have comprehensive medical insurance and that you carry adequate supplies of any prescribed medication that you usually take.

TRAVEL CLINICS AND HEALTH INFORMATION A full list of current travel clinic websites worldwide is available on **w** istm.org. For other journey preparation information, consult **w** travelhealthpro.org.uk (UK) or **w** wwwnc.cdc.gov/travel (US). Information about various medications may be found on **w** netdoctor.co.uk/travel. All advice found online should be used in conjunction with expert advice received prior to or during travel.

VACCINATIONS The only requirement for vaccination is for a yellow fever vaccine for travellers over one year of age entering North Korea from a yellow fever endemic area. However, there is no actual risk of the disease in North Korea. With regard to other vaccinations, it is wise to be up to date with diphtheria, tetanus, polio, hepatitis A and typhoid. For longer trips or trips to more rural areas, especially in July and August when rainfall is heaviest, the **Japanese encephalitis** vaccine is recommended. Health-care workers, those working with young children and people on longer trips are advised to get the **hepatitis B** vaccine. A **rabies** vaccination is ideally advised for all travellers as it is unlikely that North Korea will have all the treatment needed to protect against developing rabies if you're bitten by an animal. This is even more important if you're heading to more remote areas as it will take even longer to reach help.

Tuberculosis (TB) is spread through close respiratory contact and occasionally through infected milk or milk products. It is very common in North Korea with an incidence of more than 409 cases per 100,000 population. With this in mind, it's worth considering the BCG if you have not had this vaccination before and are likely to be mixing with the local population for stays of three months or more. However, experts differ over whether a BCG vaccination against tuberculosis (TB) is useful in adults: discuss this with your travel clinic.

PERSONAL FIRST-AID KIT It's worth taking a first-aid kit with you to North Korea, containing at least the minimum of:

- A good drying antiseptic, eg: iodine or potassium permanganate (don't take antiseptic cream)
- A few small dressings (plasters/Band-Aids)
- Suncream
- Insect repellent; impregnated bed net or permethrin spray
- Aspirin or paracetamol
- Antifungal cream (eg: Canesten)
- Ciprofloxacin or norfloxacin, for severe diarrhoea
- Tinidazole for giardia or amoebic dysentery
- Antibiotic eye drops
- A pair of fine-pointed tweezers (to remove caterpillar hairs, thorns, splinters, coral, etc)
- Alcohol-based hand rub or a bar of soap in a plastic box
- Condoms or femidoms

FOOD SAFETY Use bottled water for drinking and brushing teeth. Avoid dairy products, which are likely to have been made with unpasteurised milk, and boil milk (or use powdered or tinned milk, using pure water in the reconstitution process). Ensure meat and fish are well cooked and served hot. Be wary of pork, salad and mayonnaise, and always cook vegetables and peel fruit. If in doubt: PEEL IT, BOIL IT, COOK IT OR FORGET IT.

LONG-HAUL FLIGHTS, CLOTS AND DVT

Any prolonged immobility, including travel by land or air, can result in deep-vein thrombosis (DVT) with the risk of embolus to the lungs. Certain factors can increase the risk and these include:

- History of DVT or pulmonary embolism
- Recent surgery to pelvic region or legs
- Cancer
- Stroke
- Heart disease
- Inherited tendency to clot (thrombophilia)
- Obesity
- Pregnancy
- Hormone therapy
- Older age
- Being over 6ft or under 5ft

Deep-vein thrombosis causes painful swelling and redness of the calf or sometimes the thigh. It is only dangerous if a clot travels to the lungs (pulmonary embolus). Symptoms of a pulmonary embolus (PE) – which commonly start three to ten days after a long flight – include chest pain, shortness of breath, and sometimes coughing up small amounts of blood. Anyone who thinks that they might have a DVT needs to see a doctor immediately.

PREVENTION OF DVT
- Wear loose, comfortable clothing
- Do anti-DVT exercises and move around when possible
- Drink plenty of fluids during the flight
- Avoid taking sleeping pills unless you are able to lie flat
- Avoid excessive tea, coffee and alcohol
- Consider wearing flight socks or support stockings, widely available from pharmacies

If you think you are at increased risk of a clot, ask your doctor if it is safe to travel.

COMMON MEDICAL PROBLEMS

Malaria There is a very low risk of malaria due to the benign *Plasmodium vivax* throughout the year. The limited risk is confined to some southern areas, but malaria tablets are not advised for anyone. Prevention against mosquito bites is paramount, however, so it is advised to use insect repellents containing 50–55% DEET from dusk until dawn (the mosquitoes that carry the disease emerge at this time). It is also wise to wear clothing to cover arms and legs, and to make your sleeping accommodation as mosquito-proof as possible.

Rabies Rabies is carried by all mammals but the most likely culprits are dogs and related species, and bats. It is passed on to humans through a bite, scratch or saliva on skin or on mucous membranes. You must always assume any animal is rabid as they can appear quite healthy, and seek medical help as soon as possible.

Meanwhile, scrub the wound with soap under a running tap or while pouring water from a jug. Find a reasonably clear-looking source of water (but at this stage the quality of the water is not important), then pour on a strong iodine or alcohol solution of gin, whisky or rum. This helps stop the rabies virus entering the body and will guard against wound infections, including tetanus.

Pre-exposure vaccination for rabies is ideally advised for everyone, but is particularly important if you intend to have contact with animals and/or are likely to be more than 24 hours away from medical help.

If you are bitten, scratched or licked by any mammal, then advice should be sought as soon as possible though it is never too late to seek help, as the incubation period for rabies can be very long. Those who have not been immunised will need a full course of injections and will also need a blood product called Rabies Immunoglobulin (RIG), injected around the wound. RIG is very hard to come by as there is a worldwide shortage, and it is extremely unlikely that it will be available in North Korea so a potential rabies bite could mean evacuating to a country that has supplies (eg: Hong Kong). If you have had all three doses of rabies vaccine before the exposure, you would only need to get two further doses of the rabies vaccine. Anyone who is immunocompromised must let the treating doctor know as more doses of post-exposure vaccine would be required. Although the vaccine is moderately expensive the course of rabies vaccine provides long-term cover (unless you are a vet working abroad when regular boosts or blood tests are recommended).

TREATING TRAVELLERS' DIARRHOEA

It is dehydration that makes you feel awful during a bout of diarrhoea and the most important part of treatment is drinking lots of clear fluids. Sachets of oral rehydration salts give the perfect biochemical mix to replace all that is coming out of you, but you'll find that other recipes taste nicer. Any dilute mixture of sugar and salt in water will do you good: try cola or orange squash with a three-finger pinch of salt added to each glass (if you are salt-depleted you won't taste the salt). Otherwise, make a solution of a four-finger scoop of sugar with a three-finger pinch of salt in a 500ml glass, or add eight level teaspoons of sugar (18g) and one level teaspoon of salt (3g) to one litre (five cups) of safe water. A squeeze of lemon or orange juice improves the taste and adds potassium, which is also lost in diarrhoea. Drink two large glasses after every bowel action, and more if you are thirsty. These solutions are still absorbed well if you are vomiting, but you will need to take small sips at a time.

If you are not eating you need to drink three litres a day plus the equivalent of whatever is going into the toilet. If you feel like eating, take a bland, high carbohydrate diet. Greasy, heavy foods will probably give you cramps. If the diarrhoea is bad, if you are passing blood or slime, or if you have a fever, you will probably need antibiotics in addition to fluid replacement. A dose of norfloxacin or ciprofloxacin repeated twice a day until better may be appropriate (if you are planning to take an antibiotic with you, note that both norfloxacin and ciprofloxacin are available only on prescription in the UK). If the diarrhoea is greasy and bulky and is accompanied by sulphurous (eggy) burps, one likely cause is giardia. This is best treated with tinidazole (four x 500mg in one dose, repeated seven days later if symptoms persist).

And remember that, if you do contract rabies, mortality is 100% and death from rabies is probably one of the worst ways to go.

Ticks and related diseases There is a possibility of tick-borne diseases in North Korea, including tick-borne encephalitis (Far East strain) and Lyme disease. Ticks are more prevalent during the summer months so travellers walking in forested areas should wear cover-up clothing including long trousers tucked into boots, socks, long-sleeved tops and a hat. Always check for ticks at the end of the day, paying particular attention to the hairline and behind the ears as ticks can easily be missed.

Ticks should ideally be removed as soon as possible as leaving them on the body increases the chance of infection. They should be removed with special tick tweezers that can be bought in good travel shops. Failing that, you can use your finger nails: grasp the tick as close to your body as possible and pull steadily and firmly away at right angles to your skin. The tick will then come away complete, as long as you do not jerk or twist. If possible, douse the wound with alcohol (any spirit will do) or iodine. Irritants (eg: Olbas oil) or lit cigarettes are to be discouraged since they can cause the ticks to regurgitate and therefore increase the risk of disease. It is best to get a travelling companion to check you for ticks. Spreading redness around the bite and/or fever and/or aching joints after a tick bite suggest that you could have an infection that may require antibiotic treatment, so seek advice.

HIV/AIDS While North Korea still publicly declares itself as HIV-free, there are still risks of this infection and other sexually transmitted diseases, whether you sleep with fellow travellers or locals. The majority of HIV infections in British heterosexuals are acquired abroad. If you must indulge, use condoms or femidoms, which help reduce the risk of transmission. If you notice any genital ulcers or discharge, get treatment promptly since other infections increase the risk of acquiring HIV. If you do have unprotected sex, visit a clinic as soon as possible; this should be within 24 hours, though may be considered up to two weeks, for post-exposure prophylaxis.

SAFETY

Crime against foreigners in North Korea is so low it is practically unheard of. Tourists are essentially respected guests and are treated accordingly. Despite having a poor name in the Western media and the occasional news story of tourists being arrested, one would have to be wilfully stupid to actually get arrested or into any bother while in the country; noting a few basic rules will ensure you have a safe trip:

- Tourists are not permitted to walk freely within the country, and must stay with their guide throughout. Do not attempt to detach yourself from your group or sneak out of your hotel at night.
- Tourists must not break photographic restrictions that are in place. In North Korea it is nearly always 100% obvious what should not be photographed – if in any doubt, always ask your guide.
- Tourists must not make any negative or derogatory comments regarding the North Korean government and its policies, philosophy or leaders, past or present. Particular importance is placed on the 'history' of the DPRK and the life and works of Kim Il Sung, Kim Jong Il and Kim Jong Un. Even behind closed doors, negative comments may cause offence and any overheard remarks

could have serious repercussions. Please keep any opinions you may have to yourself.

- Images of leaders should be treated with respect, and not folded, creased or marked.
- Tourists must not discuss religion with any Koreans unless prompted, and must not show, distribute or leave any religious texts/leaflets or the like in Korea. Many of the Westerners arrested in recent years were involved in proselytising Christianity. If you must take any religious texts with you to Korea this should be for personal use only, and read in the privacy of your hotel room.
- There are restrictions on what you may take into the country with you. Any publications that could be considered by the North Korean authorities to be offensive to the 'supreme dignity, ideology, system or culture of the DPR Korea', together with films (or such materials) of any nature made in South Korea are strictly forbidden. Furthermore, anything deemed as being pornographic is strictly forbidden.

Bar these unique conditions in North Korea, the typical safety concerns that apply across the globe should be noted: accidents are rare but road safety is poor, tap water should be avoided, and all medication that you may need should be brought with you. Health and safety standards across the country are a long way behind the West. Ensuring you have full travel insurance coverage is vital, and do remember that, especially with little chance of having access to the internet, a printed record of your insurance details should be kept on hand. It is recommended to bring enough cash with you to cover any emergency, as credit cards remain useless.

For the safety of your local guides and the Koreans you meet with on your travels, please ensure that any travel blogs, social media posts or publishing you may be involved in subsequent to your trip is cautious in content, as this will likely be seen by the DPRK government (who do scour the internet and wider media for coverage of their country). Undercover reporting and certain articles have resulted in serious implications for tour guides, creating serious and permanent implications for them and their families.

WOMEN TRAVELLERS There are no particular safety problems that women should be concerned about, but as North Koreans dress rather modestly, scantily clad women (and men for that matter), may be stared at; most in the country have never heard of, let alone seen, a miniskirt.

GAY AND LESBIAN TRAVELLERS Homosexuality isn't illegal in the country, but many in North Korea insist that this is because it doesn't need to be, as homosexuality is a Western 'disease' that doesn't 'afflict' Koreans – there is no need to ban something that doesn't exist. Such naivety highlights that sex and sex education is taboo – the country is, publicly at least, almost puritan. Same-sex couples travelling to North Korea will almost certainly be thought of as just heterosexual friends and it is best to gently maintain this allusion, as even public displays of affection between heterosexual couples can still cause a commotion.

TRAVELLING WITH KIDS North Korea isn't the most family-friendly destination, but children will likely be fawned over, particularly if they are blonde-haired and blue-eyed toddlers, as few people will have ever seen a 'foreign' baby. Family life is important in Korea so you will be fussed over, but don't expect to easily find baby food, nappies, car seats or any such items – bring everything you require. Conventional tour itineraries are not family friendly, but a private trip tailored for a family could be a most enjoyable – if bizarre – experience for children and parents alike.

WHAT TO TAKE

Despite an improving situation in North Korea, many goods that anywhere else in the world would be easy to obtain are difficult to locate here, particularly as almost all shops and markets are closed to foreigners. Thus, bring everything you need with you as otherwise you will likely go without or waste a good chunk of your time and tour trying to track down that elusive item. Electricity is 220v/60Hz, and electrical sockets do vary dependent on who the North Koreans were trading with when the hotel was constructed. Most rooms have a sizzling and sparky universal adaptor lead, but a universal adapter plug is recommended. A few other vital items include:

- Printed copies of all your travel documents (including your passport and visa)
- Batteries, chargers, memory sticks, adapter plug and other such electricals
- First-aid kit and all required medicines and personal hygiene supplies
- A towel (towels in many hotels can be very small and thin)
- Torch or headtorch (power cuts can be expected)
- Spare glasses and contact lenses (if required)
- Insect repellent, sunscreen and sunglasses
- Tea/coffee (for personal use, if required)
- Small day bag or overnight bag
- Sewing kit.

To try not to stick out even more than you inevitably will as a foreigner clothing should preferably be edging just slightly towards the more formal side of casual. While casual clothes are generally fine and it is unlikely that your guides will pass any comments, in Pyongyang it is better to dress 'smart-casual' so that you do not feel underdressed when compared with the locals. For certain sites, such as the Kumsusan Palace of the Sun (page 124), a dress code applies.

If you're planning on trekking in North Korea you should bring all equipment with you from home, including sturdy walking boots and appropriate clothing

TIPPING

Tips are not obligatory or expected, but the compulsory guides and drivers typically do a fantastic job and should be recompensed accordingly. Your tour operator will be able to give guidance as to a suitable amount depending on the size and nature of your tour. From time to time you may have additional local guides, most likely in the provinces, when hiking on Mount Myohyang or Mount Kumgang or touring remote museums, for example. Incomes outside of Pyongyang are lower than in the capital, so tips for these local guides, who may be with you for anything from an hour or two up to a few days, are always greatly appreciated. Tipping service staff is still not customary, but a small gesture will be gratefully received.

including waterproofs, hats and gloves. Campers will almost certainly need to bring tents, sleeping bags and all associated paraphernalia with them.

You may want to bring some postcards of home or family photographs to allow your guides and the people you encounter to see a little of how you live. Furthermore, bringing any snacks, fruits or chocolates for personal use (or to share with your new comrades) is recommended, as familiar snacks will be few and far between.

MONEY AND BUDGETING

While a few domestic card systems are slowly popping up in the country, for tourists the most important thing to remember is that credit cards, travellers' cheques and

IT TAKES WON TO KNOW WON

In North Korea the majority of visitors will not handle or use Korean won. Perhaps this is best, as a very confusing system of exchange rates exist, but just in case the opportunity does arise to pay in won, it may help to understand what it is worth.

You will likely be told by your North Korean guides that there are approximately 130 won to the euro, and you will indeed see in hotels and shops a printed exchange rate along these lines. A local beer in said shop would likely be advertised as being sold for 65 won – thus €0.50. If you tried to pay 65 won in this shop for your bottle of beer you would be politely informed that no, in this shop you can only pay in hard currency. Fair enough – pay €0.50 and your purchase is complete.

However, while the advertised exchange rate may be around 130 won to the euro, the actual exchange rate in Korea is something like 9,000 won to the euro. Should you visit a normal local shop and try to purchase a beer the asking price would not be 65 won (which in reality is less than one cent in euros) but more like 4,500 won, or half a euro. While this is all very confusing, should the price of something seem incredibly cheap, or incredibly expensive, it is best to clarify what the exchange rate being used is. Tourists can normally only pay in won in Rason (in the far northeast) and in one or two shops in Pyongyang – where you can thankfully exchange money at the actual exchange rate. Confused yet?

other forms of payment are almost completely useless in North Korea – you will require cash only, so you should bring all necessary money with you. If you run out of money you are essentially high and dry, so take more than you anticipate spending; on almost every trip I have been on I have known at least one person to run out of money due to overzealous spending, resorting to borrowing from other travellers – far from ideal.

Local currency is the won, a completely different won from the identically named money used south of the border. This is a closed currency that cannot be obtained outside of North Korea or taken out of the country when you leave. That said, it is unlikely that you will actually use any won while in North Korea as tourist transactions are normally always conducted in euros, US dollars or Chinese yuan. For now, the authorities prefer foreigners to use these aforementioned foreign currencies and are somewhat reluctant for foreigners to pay in won, although this is slowly changing. Accordingly, almost all establishments that you will frequent as a tourist will request payment in either euros, US dollars or yuan, and may well provide change in a different currency from the one you paid in. The currency of choice seems to vary from one shop to the next but whichever currency you take, ensure that all notes are clean and crisp – notes with small tears, markings or heavy folds will likely be refused. Also, do bear in mind that seemingly every cash till in the country is emptied out overnight – take as many small-denomination notes as you

KEEP YOUR EYES ON THE ROAD!

On almost any visit to the DPRK you will likely have at least a couple of long road journeys. While this may sound tedious, and the road quality may generally be quite poor, you must avoid the urge to drift off and instead keep your eyes open – a few hours looking out of the window as the countryside rolls by is truly fascinating.

First you may notice the military checkpoints, often on county lines or on entering certain cities. Passing through these is *normally* a straightforward affair, as you will hopefully have the required permit to pass, but at the more remote checkpoints telephone calls may have to be made as the guards can be a little unsure quite what to do when a foreigner arrives – it makes one feel full of relief, quickly turning into self-importance, when the all clear is given with a textbook salute, coupled with a genuine smile.

Perhaps you will notice the cosmos flowers, which often border the roadside for kilometre after kilometre, tendered by locals who tirelessly maintain the roads, often only with basic tools. Or the hitchhikers, sometimes young conscripts, who run out and wave when they see a vehicle approaching, only to back away looking sheepish when they realise they are trying to travel in a vehicle especially designated for transporting foreigners (page 68). In a country with so little traffic the roads are, worryingly, an ideal playground for children, who will often wave and laugh as they see a foreign face pass by. In very remote areas it has been known for children to run to the side of the road and bow at any passing vehicles – for anybody in a car *must* be important. And of course, in a country without much traffic what better place to dry corn than on the road itself?

Any traffic you encounter is often overloaded with passengers. Locals, who 15 years ago would have looked very bemused at the sight of a passing foreigner, will now normally wave and smile. Said locals could well be travelling in – believe it or not – a wood-burning truck. Spotted all over rural Korea just a few years ago, can possibly obtain as providing change is always a struggle, and is often proffered in the form of chewing gum, bottles of water or such. Some locations will accept euro coins as well; these are like gold dust in Pyongyang, as is a crisp one dollar bill. Chinese currency has become increasingly popular in North Korea of late, so at the time of writing I would recommend taking half of your cash in either euros or US dollars and the rest in yuan. In the northern border areas of Korea (such as Sinuiju and Rason), yuan is normally the only readily accepted currency, so do alter the mix accordingly if spending extended time in these regions. If departing Korea on the train to China, Chinese yuan are a necessity – once in China you will only be able to pay for services (such as meals in the restaurant car) in that currency.

Almost all organised tours will have all main costs included and paid for in advance, so by the time you arrive in Pyongyang all flights, train tickets, accommodation, meals, transport, guiding fees, etc, should be fully covered. Consequently, you will only need to pay for incidentals such as laundry, souvenirs, postcards, drinks and tickets to any special events. Some people can spend a week in North Korea and spend only €100, while others can spend much more. For a general tourist, allowing €40 per day (or equivalent) should suffice, but remember – if you run out of cash there is no means of obtaining more. Do take more if your tour coincides with national holidays (when celebrations are likely and tickets required for them), you are keen on purchasing any artworks or if you expect to

these trucks are slowly disappearing; a nod to the improving economic situation. Adapted to be powered by gasifying wood chips, these trucks bellow smoke at an alarming rate, and can often be smelt before they can be seen. While they will hardly be awarded any prizes for alternative fuel development, there is a real enterprising ingenuity here, highlighting the defiant 'make do' attitude that is so prevalent across the country.

The occasional good stretch of straight road could well be a highway strip, a section of road built to allow the landing of military aircraft. Highway strips, first constructed in Nazi Germany, are something of a Cold War legacy these days, but of course in North Korea the war never really ended and dozens of these strips can be found across the country. Many roads too are full of simple defences – large, presumably concrete, pillars can be spotted all over, typically when the road passes through a small cut in the rock or valley. These pillars, typically with a weak point at the base, are designed so that a small detonation could quickly block the road – a simple defence against any invading army. Tunnels and bridges in the country normally have a small sign marking their date of construction, and while the year of construction may vary, almost all tunnels and bridges were bizarrely completed, on perfect schedule, on 15 April, Kim Il Sung's birthday.

The above is just a drop in the ocean of some of the weird, wonderful and often unique things one may see on these certainly anything but boring road journeys. The authorities in North Korea are often accused of just showing visitors what they want to show them, but if you keep your mind and eyes open and on the road you will see and learn a great deal. Everything has its place and reason; should you see something unusual don't be afraid to ask, but any question may be met with embarrassment and suitable vagueness from your hosts – some things are best left unsaid.

make international phone calls or purchase an international SIM card. Indications of some typical costs (as of summer 2018) are as below:

- Local beer (bottled): €0.50–2
- Local beer (draught): €1–4
- Mineral water (250ml bottle): €0.25–0.50
- CDs or DVDs of local music/film: €5–12
- Small book: €1–5
- Book of postcards: €1–2
- Stamps: €1–2 each
- International phone calls: €2–6 per minute
- Artworks: from €30
- Tickets to events: €10–300

GETTING AROUND

As a tourist, all of your transport will be pre-arranged and serve you from start to finish. This will normally be a private vehicle, anything from a car to large bus depending on your party size. Most of the vehicles on offer are cheap Chinese brands that were not designed for the pot-holed rural roads of North Korea, but are comfortable enough when all is considered. Do not expect the likes of seatbelts, however.

MIND THAT CAR!

While it may sound like a dull thing to learn, the colours, numbers and text on any North Korean number plate will tell you a lot about a vehicle – allowing you to predict who will be saluted, who will be stopped and who will be searched.

COLOURS While there are minor variations in the colour of a number plate, the absolute majority of number plates will have a base colour that is either blue, black, yellow or green.

Blue (formerly white): This belongs to a state-owned company. In a country where almost everything is controlled by the state there are a lot of state-owned company vehicles. This is what you will almost certainly be travelling in while in the country.

Black: These are military vehicles, or vehicles owned by companies and organisations tied to the military. Like the blue number plates, the very large armed forces in the DPRK mean that these are very common.

Yellow: Something of a rarity and seldom seen outside of Pyongyang, this is a privately owned vehicle. The only people likely to own such a vehicle are likely to have received this as a gift from the state (by winning an Olympic gold medal or the like), or have relatives overseas that could gift it to them. There really are not many of these about and most are old vehicles, imported from Japan when ties were closer and relatives less distant. Should you spot one with a number higher than 2000, please do send in a photograph.

Green (formerly blue): This is an embassy/NGO vehicle. If an embassy vehicle, the first two digits will denote the country, and the following digits the

While a number of cities have bustling buses, trolleybuses and trams, these are generally 'not for tourists' and off-limits – if they can be accessed it is only by private charter. Accordingly, public transport within cities, bar the possibility of incorporating the 'standard' Pyongyang Metro tour into a city tour, is not yet viable.

Intercity travel is also normally by private vehicle, but long-distance travel by scheduled passenger train is now possible to the cities of Sinuiju, Hamhung, Chongjin and Rajin – a recent and exciting development. Meticulous planning is required, as other than the daily service to Sinuiju, these trains run just a few times a month. Air Koryo is slowly trying to launch domestic flights to destinations such as Wonsan and Orang, but to date these have been so unreliable and prone to eleventh-hour cancellation that they cannot be relied upon. However, private charters in the country are becoming increasingly common (see box, page 56).

ACCOMMODATION

There is no shortage of accommodation in the country; Pyongyang alone has a few thousand rooms allocated for accommodating foreign visitors. Until recently the chronic lack of visitors to North Korea had sent many hotels along a seemingly terminal path of decline as they struggled to keep their heads above water. Thankfully, most hotels are now slowly on the up, some are even refurbishing for the first time in decades, and it is optimism, not damp, that fills the air. All hotels

hierarchy of the vehicle attached to that embassy. As the USSR was the first country to open an embassy in the DPRK, they were designated the number 01. This number has since been inherited by the Russian Embassy, and as the Russian ambassador is the most important person at the Russian Embassy he or she is the *numero uno*, and thus drives a car with a green number plate, numbered 01 01.

NAME AND NUMBER The initial characters on the number plate will normally designate the province that said vehicle is registered in. While a Pyongyang-registered vehicle is arguably the most prestigious plate, a vehicle from Pyongyang driving in a remote province such as Ryanggang may be viewed with more suspicion than a locally registered vehicle.

Provinces aside, the first two digits on the number plate will normally designate what type of business the vehicle is involved in. While this information is not well publicised, you can be sure that every traffic lady or checkpoint guard will know every number and nuance – and will be well aware, for example, that '74' designates a vehicle appointed to handle tourists.

THE INEVITABLE EXCEPTIONS Of course, being North Korea there will always be exceptions. The date 27 July, written locally as 7.27, is 'Victory Day', an increasingly important date in the country. Of late, some vehicles have appeared that have no text at all and start with 727 followed by additional seemingly random digits – these are Pyongyang bigwigs but they are *still* a little less important than those who drive the expensive vehicles with plates that contain a bold red star by a one-, two-, or three-digit number. Should you spot one of these it's best to keep clear, as these chaps are not likely to stop for anyone!

have their quirks and even the very best, while comfortable, still have their nuances that will never quite elevate them to the five-star rating they claim. Rooms are almost always designated to be occupied by two people; some tour operators' policy is to strive to twin single travellers up with strangers, while others may insist that single travellers pay a supplement and have the room to themselves.

Despite the improvements, there are no international five-star options in the country just yet. Hotels are often categorised as deluxe, first, second and third class, but it has been so many years since many of them were classified as such that many are now far worse, or better, than their official ranking displays; it's best to ignore such rankings and decide for yourself. Even in deluxe hotels little foreign language is spoken, check-in can be slow and things such as Wi-Fi, room service, concierge and international menus essentially do not exist. 'Guaranteed' 24-hour hot water may not materialise and paying bills or making purchases from hotel shops and bars can be just as convoluted as they may be in a remote co-operative farm shop. Service is with a smile; it's just a little slow and confused.

Standard hotel rooms across the country typically have two single beds, and those wanting double-bedded rooms will likely need to upgrade to superior rooms – availability is rarely an issue. Rooms themselves are generally *comparatively* comfortable, but missing or broken lightbulbs, hard mattresses, slow lifts and dodgy plumbing can be expected in all but the very best options. Note that should you find a couple of bottles of water in your bathroom this *should be* boiled water, intended for brushing your teeth. Many hotels have a confounding range of facilities to keep guests entertained, from bars and restaurants to bookshops and bowling alleys; those with time and an inquisitive nature may find exploring the public areas of their hotel an interesting part of their time in the country. Most hotels do have a sauna or bathhouse of some sort, so those desperate for a scrub down will normally manage, somehow. You will be able to make international telephone calls from virtually all hotels, but check the prices (page 81).

Outside of Pyongyang the range of accommodation is more limited and, bizarrely, in some cities in which one would expect to find good hotels there are none, and in cities where one would expect to find only bad hotels there are some real diamonds in the rough. Unless stated otherwise, all hotels include breakfast as standard. Staff at every hotel will check your room once you have checked out and all items must be accounted for – towels, booklets and such should not be removed from your room.

Tour operators and their Korean partners naturally have their preferred hotels, so if joining a group you will likely have little say as to where you stay, but if you are arranging your own tailored trip to the country you can by all means decide where you would like to bunk down for the night. However, in a country where the state decides all, you may find yourself being moved from one hotel to another with little explanation. Given that some of the basic hotels are only ever-so marginally cheaper than the mid-range options, whoever is handling your trip may be reluctant to put you up in some of the more tired hotels – is it really worth discomfort to save just a few dollars a day?

EATING AND DRINKING

FOOD Acknowledging the famine of the 1990s, many Westerners employ a spot of gallows humour when it comes to wining and dining in North Korea, likely asking mocking questions in advance of travel along the lines of 'will I be fed?' or 'do I have to take all my own food with me?' Yes, acute malnutrition still exists in parts of the

Providing price codes for North Korea is somewhat irrelevant as tourists may not book a hotel directly and are unlikely to just pitch up at a restaurant unannounced – everything is perfectly stage managed and almost always prepaid. The prices of hotels and restaurants are agreed as part of long-standing agreements and not made public. Some hotel receptions advertise astronomical walk-in rates, but these have no bearing on reality and are presumably there because somebody somewhere read a book on hotel management and thought it a good idea. Hotels in North Korea are categorised into deluxe, first, second and third class but, as mentioned elsewhere, hotels haven't been reclassified insofar as these ratings should be disregarded.

Tour packages in North Korea are normally pitched at the mid range, so hotels and restaurants priced in the **$$$** bracket (as detailed below) are the norm and should incur no surcharges. Those looking to save money can look at the **$** or **$$** options, but the saving is negligible and the drop in quality noticeable. To splash out, **$$$$** or **$$$$$** options can incur steep supplements. For restaurants, budget places are normally off-limits, but if you want to splurge, superior restaurants can push up the prices.

HOTELS
$$$$$	A supplement of over €25 per night.
$$$$	A small surcharge of €10–25 per night.
$$$	Standard tour pricing. No surcharges/discounts.
$$	A small reduction of approximately €5 per night.
$	A reduction of up to €10 per night.

RESTAURANTS
$$$$$	A supplement of over €10 per meal.
$$$$	A small surcharge of up to €10 per meal.
$$$	Standard tour pricing. No surcharges/discounts.
$$	A small reduction of approximately €2–4 for a meal.
$	A very inexpensive and basic meal or snack, saving €5 or so.

country but remember, you will be a guest, a VIP of sorts; looking at Kim Jong Un's frame it is clear that the important are well fed in North Korea.

Breakfasts are normally a pretty basic affair and will typically always be taken at your hotel. Depending on the hotel and the number of guests the meal may be a take it or leave it selection served at your table, or a self-service buffet of Korean and vaguely European dishes such as bread and fried eggs. It's all perfectly edible but nothing to get particularly excited about. North Koreans are not big tea and coffee drinkers; if you desperately need a shot or two of caffeine in the morning you would do well to consider bringing your own supply, together with UHT milk or creamer. If you are served coffee it will likely be weak and depressing. Requests for more, or stronger, coffee will likely cause a kerfuffle and induce frowns from the waitresses, who will be shocked at your brazen temerity.

Lunches and **dinners** are normally far more impressive, and will typically be Korean through and through, although some restaurants try to make the occasional Western-leaning dish to appease visitors after eight days in a row of your side

KIMCHI

A staple food at any Korean table, *kimchi* is engrained in the culture of the peninsula and comes in hundreds of varieties. Made from salted and fermented vegetables with all manner of seasonings, this typically spicy and healthy dish dates back at least 2,000 years. Generally served as a side, it is also incorporated into some main meals such as stews and pancakes. Kimchi is so important to Koreans that the South's 'Korean Atomic Energy Research Institute' spent five years and millions of dollars in creating 'space kimchi', so that when their first astronaut, Yi-So-yeon, went up in 2008 she could enjoy the taste of home. At that price, it hopefully tasted out of this world.

dish being kimchi, so you may suddenly be presented with French fries. When in Pyongyang and larger cities you will likely mix your dining between restaurants in the city and in your hotel, but in more remote parts of the country many meals will feel like they're taken within the confines of barracks. Most hotels can arrange a packed lunch with little bother. For lunches and dinners, dishes are normally served up akin to many parts of Asia, with numerous communal selections materialising one after another. So much food is served that often one doesn't know when the gluttonous onslaught will end, but the last dish to be served is typically a watery soup together with boiled rice (*bap*), which will likely have some other grains, vegetables, seafood or meat mixed into it. The dishes served vary across the country; inland, meals will normally always include one or two meat dishes such as pork or chicken, while in coastal areas meals often include a fair few seafood dishes, including squid, crab and all manner of bivalves. In the poorer mountainous areas, potato is a major staple in the kitchen and on the table, as little else can be encouraged to grow in these harsher climes.

Regional specialities Many regional dishes and specialities exist in the country and there is plenty of opportunity to enjoy dishes such as cold noodles (*naengmyeon*), where noodles (typically buckwheat) are served up in a spicy broth with vinegar, radish and a varying range of other ingredients thrown in, all served up cold. Also popular is *bibimbap* (which literally means mixed rice but is a meal in itself), normally served piping hot in a stone pot with sautéed and seasoned vegetables together with chilli, soy sauce, egg and sliced meat – simply delicious. Other notable dishes include *pansangi* (page 139), Korean hotpot (*sinseollo*) and a variety of delicious barbecues, often with their own regional nuances. Korean cuisine, which just a few years ago was little known in the West, is becoming increasingly popular in the wider world and the food found in the North is arguably more authentic than in the South, where foreign influence has crept in. Numerous Korean cookbooks are in print these days and one can even pick up some Pyongyang publications, should you really want to know how to prepare the real thing. Koreans normally use metal chopsticks, but nearly all restaurants will be able to find a few knives and forks for those who struggle with their manual dexterity.

Dietary requirements In a country where people starved less than three decades ago, the notion of having a dietary requirement is an alien one that Koreans struggle to get their head around. Yes – vegetarians, vegans and coeliacs will be catered to (there is always rice after all), but they will have to be a little relaxed and open minded, accepting that they will have a more limited range of dishes than most. You will need to clarify to your guide as to exactly what you can and cannot eat, and keep good humoured when they inevitably say things along the lines of, 'I understand you are vegetarian, but will this beef be OK, as it is the best beef in all of Bukchang County?' Food intolerances should be clarified to your guides also, but those with serious allergies are advised to pack any emergency medicines and be extremely cautious with their food.

DRINK **Tap water** should be avoided. You may be told locally that it is safe to drink, but given the ready availability and low price of bottled water it really is not worth taking the risk. An increasing number of inexpensive domestically produced **soft drinks** and juices are available. Sadly, the ever popular 'Crabonated Cocoa' drink is now carbonated and crab free. Imported canned coffees and juices are widely available for when the bottled water gets a little mundane. Familiar Western brands, including that symbol of Americana, Coca-Cola, are rare but occasionally turn up, often in the unlikeliest of locations.

Alcohol has long been the opiate of the masses in North Korea, and while public drunkenness is not nearly as endemic as in parts of western Europe, an increasing disposable income and number of bars make a perfect cocktail for a night out, although the real spit and sawdust drinking dens (they do exist) are normally kept off the tourist trail. Koreans do enjoy a drink, and **beer** is typically served at lunch and dinner. Self-proclaimed experts agree that North Korean beer is rather good and far better than what is churned out in the South. The boom in the number of micro-breweries is an unforeseen result of the diminishing role of Pyongyang's centralised economy and supply chains, with many hotels and cities now making their own special brew. Major beers in the country include Taedonggang (see box, page 101), Ryongsong and Ponghak. Traditional and refreshing *makgeolli*, a lightly sparkling off-white rice **wine**, is a little weaker than beer and worth trying at some point if you can track it down, but it is considered a simple drink for country bumpkins – your Pyongyangite guides may consider it beneath them to

A NIGHT ON THE TILES

The authentic 'local' beer bars in North Korea, which foreigners can sometimes wrangle a visit to, do have familiarities of home about them, but also have a few curious features and customs rarely found elsewhere. The bars are normally brightly lit and have no seating – everyone stands around elevated tables, presumably so nobody can ever get too comfortable. The floors are generally paved with glossy white ceramic tiling – perfect for the barmaids who scurry around brushing away monkey-nut shells and mopping up spillages, but not suitable for the occasional person who has had one too many. To save repeated trips to the bar, drinkers often purchase all the planned drinks for their session in one go, so it isn't unusual to see a customer with five beers lined up in front of him, slowly drinking one increasingly warm beer after another. Bars are predominantly male, but female customers are often just as evident as they would be in many bars and pubs in the Western world. These somewhat clinical-looking drinking dens feel quite welcoming and innocent in their own special way; as divisive topics of conversation such as politics, sex and religion are almost certainly off the table, there is presumably only sport to argue about.

drink. The most common tipple for serious drinking is **soju**, a traditional and inexpensive colourless rice wine of around 20–25% alcohol. More a spirit than a wine, soju is to drink as kimchi is to food – transcending the table to become a touchstone of the culture. Other spirits are made in Korea and imported drinks such as Vietnamese vodka, Eastern Bloc wines and faux-Scotch whisky can be found gathering dust in hotel bars across the country, normally needing to be purchased by the bottle (with no refunds).

Coffee is not popular, and save for heading to some of the more upmarket hotels in Pyongyang, getting a coffee that aficionados would call 'decent' is not easy – it's often simpler to just do without. As mentioned prior, if you need a daily hit of real coffee you may want to consider bringing supplies with you, together with UHT milk if required, as otherwise you may be limited to the 'coffee' occasionally served at breakfast. **Tea** is popular and often served at meals, but is not remotely as important as it is in China, where it is of course something of a national obsession. It's typically green or herbal and won't be served with milk, so if you want a strong cup of builder's tea bring your own supplies, as restaurants are normally happy to accommodate Westerners and their whimsical ways.

SMOKING Despite nonchalant efforts from the government to stub out the practice, around half of North Korean men smoke. Kim Il Sung smoked, as did Kim Jong Il, as does Kim Jong Un. The habit is so acceptable that Kim Il Sung is depicted in occasional oil paintings with a cigarette in hand, smiling away, and Kim Jong Un always seems to be clutching a cigarette when he is filmed out and about – even when standing next to a primed intercontinental ballistic missile.

Cigarettes are cheap and a selection of brands of varying quality and harshness are manufactured across the country, while those tightening their belts smoke roll-ups, using strips torn from newspapers for rolling paper. It is almost expected that men will smoke, but for women to smoke is taboo and almost never seen in public. Smoking in restaurants, bars, on trains and in public areas is common, even when prohibited. It is only in recent years that some people are starting to realise that the non-smokers around them may not enjoy all the secondhand smoke, but huffing and puffing away while gesticulating that you are not enjoying the smoky atmosphere will likely have zero effect. As public areas in Korea tend to be large, places are rarely too smoky, so smokers and non-smokers can exist together in relative harmony – except for on trains, when the smell is hard to avoid as it wafts down the corridor. Hotels mostly allow smoking in the rooms and the concept on non-smoking floors doesn't exist yet, but with guests few and far between, rooms with the odour of stale cigarette smoke are rare.

PUBLIC HOLIDAYS, NOTABLE DATES AND FESTIVALS

1 January *New Year's Day*
8 February Army Day
16 February *Kim Jong Il's birthday*
5 March Farmer's Day
8 March International Women's Day
15 April *Kim Il Sung's birthday*
1 May *May Day*
1 June International Children's Day
6 June Chosun Children's Union Foundation Day
3 July Day of the Strategic Forces

8 July Memorial Day of the death of Kim Il Sung
27 July *Victory Day*
15 August *National Liberation Day* (Independence from Japan)
25 August Day of Songun
5 September Education Day
9 September *Republic Foundation Day*
10 October *Foundation of the Workers' Party of Korea*
16 November Mother's Day
24 December Kim Jong Suk's birthday
27 December Constitution Day
31 December *New Year's Eve*

Visiting the country during a public holiday or over a notable date/festival can show the country at its best. The dates marked above are just the more significant ones of note – there are more! Few of these days are actual days off, as in reality a 'public holiday' is a working day for almost all in this workers' paradise. Celebrations vary – on the minor dates such as Farmer's Day or Mother's Day, life will just be a little more jovial down on the farm or at home with the family, but for the more significant dates (as highlighted in italic), larger festivities are typical. Exactly what will take place is never normally known until the eleventh hour; the atmosphere may just be a little more relaxed with people picnicking in the parks and enjoying a spot of leisure, but it is also possible on major days that mass dancing in the city squares, dazzling firework displays or large parades may take place. It is also common on these special days for celebratory orchestra, opera, circus or sporting events to occur and it is possible to attend these events, with tickets purchased locally through your guides.

Military parades are far less frequent than media footage may lead you to believe and foreigners cannot normally get anywhere near Kim Il Sung Square when the bigwigs are in the podium, but it has been known for a few lucky groups to catch a glimpse of this spectacle from the edge of Pyongyang. Celebrations are normally always larger if the holiday in question is a quinquennial year or landmark anniversary.

In addition to the above dates, **Lunar New Year** is held in January or February and marked with a few special events, as is **Daeboreum**, the first full moon of the lunar calendar, which takes place a fortnight later. Held in late summer or early

CHUSEOK

Very different from the well-publicised events that take place on some of the more militaristic or nationalistic holidays, Chuseok, literally meaning 'autumn eve' is a harvest festival of old that has survived many dynasties and will likely also outlive the present epoch. Taking place from the 14th to the 16th day of the eighth lunar month (typically falling between mid-September and early October), this holiday honours traditions by visiting ancestral homes, visiting the graves or urns of the deceased and partaking in traditional sports, dances and games such as *ssireum* (Korean wrestling) for the men and *ganggangsullae*, a jovial dance performed exclusively by women that incorporates singing and gaming. As with many autumn festivals the world over, a great deal of folk games, feasting and drinking takes place, so it's not just the fallen wrestlers that come to with a sore head the following morning.

autumn, **Chuseok** is a harvest festival where ancestors and deceased relatives are also honoured (see box, page 75).

SHOPPING

Unsurprisingly, the socialist paradise isn't a shopper's paradise, and those looking for antiques or pre-Kim curios will come home empty handed. Although such items exist, they will likely not see the light of day under Kim Jong Un's watch, for, in his own words, 'selling the prestige of one's country and nation is a treachery'. The most interesting purchases for visitors are in the wonderful array of books published in the country, together with the stamps, badges, socialist-realist artworks and other more conventional souvenirs along the lines of the 'I love Pyongyang' T-shirts and novelty figurines of ladies in traditional dress. Most hotels will have a bookshop of some form and taking in a couple of souvenir and art shops will be a normal feature on typical itineraries. Some of the socialist trinkets on offer are so wonderfully unique or kitsch that they make the perfect souvenirs or gifts, and even the thriftiest travellers normally find they just cannot live without some of these items, such as CDs of the Pochonbo Electronic Ensemble or a tailored Kim Jong Il-style suit. Receipts or documentation for any purchases should be kept, especially for more expensive items, as on departing the country you may well be asked to provide such paperwork.

Besides mementos of your visit from the tourist-orientated outlets, you may well take in conventional shops such as the Kwangbok Area Shopping Centre or Rakwon Department Store in Pyongyang, chiefly worth visiting to highlight what is available to the more moneyed locals as the items on sale are of limited interest to most. They are, however, also worth visiting to stock up on drinks and snacks should you have any long journeys ahead of you. Except in Rajin (page 252), markets across the country are off-limits to tourists, as the government doesn't want to acknowledge that its hard-line, centrally planned economy needs a spot of help from market traders (and the flourishing capitalist revolution they have kickstarted) to help keep the system ticking over.

In the last few years it has become increasingly common for restaurants, museums and almost anywhere tourists may visit to have a gift shop to try and induce you to part with your hard currency, but without the pushy sales patter often found elsewhere. While a lot of the items on offer are similar from one venue to the next, the golden rule applies – if you want it, buy it, as, alas, you may never see that booklet about the Kumsong Tractor Plant again. As shopkeepers' grasp on the fluctuations and values of differing foreign currencies is limited, prices jump around a little from one shop to the next, but they are generally fairly consistent – shopping around for smaller items is not worth your time or money. Should you be buying more expensive artworks, such as paintings, a little haggling may be acceptable, but prices are normally pitched fairly.

The majority of shops are off-limits to foreigners, primarily as they are not geared up to accepting foreign currency or handling foreigners, and they don't quite know the protocol of how to sell an item that is normally dispensed only to locals under the provision of a ration coupon. Tourists and their cameras staring at and snapping pictures of locals going about their daily lives has also pushed some of the more well-known department stores in Pyongyang to close their doors to foreigners as they are, after all, shops, rather than attractions. Should you want to see a 'real' shop, the general stores at some of the co-operative farms are normally happy for you to have a quick nosey. Regardless of where you do shop, transactions can normally be a drawn-out and complicated affair, involving chits, receipts, rubber stamps and up to three or more assistants all with a distinctly different role. Patience is a virtue.

ARTS AND ENTERTAINMEMT

MUSEUMS Museums, regardless of their *raison d'être*, all have a heavy political angle and can be so sprawling that those with very limited time in the country or only a passing interest may want to consider omitting them completely. Generally open by appointment, your tour will normally be along a prescribed route, with little chance to pick and choose what you want to see. There is essentially nothing labelled in any language other than Korean, but your guides will, as ever, be on hand. Don't get me wrong, there are some wonderful museums to be found across the country, but the overall outcome of visiting many of them often teaches you more about the North Korean mindset than it does of its history. Pick and choose them wisely!

LIVE ENTERTAINMENT Theatre, circus and orchestra performances are held frequently across the country, and tourists can readily attend events in Pyongyang. As schedules are only announced at the last minute, those interested in attending these well-polished events should inform their tour operator in advance and remind their local guide on arrival in the country, who will try and work his or her magic to arrange tickets for you. Ticket prices are far more than locals would pay, but markedly less than prices back in the West, and will normally place you in one of the better seats. The circus and orchestra are largely non-political, but a few surprises such as flags, slogans and wobbly clowns pretending to be drunken GIs can pop up from time to time. Theatre performances may be anything from Shakespeare or Chekhov to modern revolutionary output and will almost certainly be in Korean only. The best thing one can catch on stage in Pyongyang is one of the less frequent Korean Revolutionary Opera performances (see box, page 105). If you have an opportunity to go, jump at it.

CINEMA While cinema is an important art form in the country (page 47), the chance to catch a film is few and far between. Occasionally, tour guides arrange private screenings of classics such as *The Flower Girl* or *A Broad Bellflower* in Pyongyang, but this is expensive and a little contrived. Korean feature films can be picked up on DVD in bookshops across the country for a fraction of the price that it costs to book out a cinema. A rare exception is the biennial (held in September on even years) Pyongyang International Film Festival, when the red carpet is rolled out and an array of films are shown across a number of cinemas to select locals and visiting foreigners.

SPORT Domestic and international sporting and cultural events can also be attended, with matches and competitions in fields such as wrestling, taekwondo, synchronised swimming and table tennis drawing in the crowds. Every February the Paektusan Prize International Figure Skating Festival is held in Pyongyang, while a number of events take place each spring for the April Spring Friendship Art Festival. The annual Pyongyang Marathon is also held in April and has become an increasingly significant fixture now that it is open to non-professionals, drawing in a few hundred visitors each year, but nothing drags in tourists like the Mass Games (see box, page 78).

MASS GAMES

Mass games, or mass gymnastics, is an artistic and gymnastic display where large numbers of performers conduct a highly choreographed and regimented performing arts spectacle, emphasising group dynamics over the individual.

The first mass gymnastics events in North Korea took place back in the early days of statehood, arguably deriving from similar spectacles that were taking place in Stalin's Russia and a handful of other nations. By the early 1970s, with their economies near level pegged, both North and South employed mass games as an art form, but when the South's economy really started to take off Seoul more or less abandoned these collective displays, rolling them out in 1988 for one last swansong, the Seoul Olympics. The North, however, spent decades elevating and improving mass gymnastics to unbridled levels, transforming them to a socialist-realist spectacular.

The most famous event of its kind in North Korea, and the world, is the Grand Mass Gymnastics and Artistic Performance Arirang, simply referred to as Arirang. This Guinness World Record-breaking event took place for just a few weeks each year from 2002–05 and 2007–13, its 100,000 performers delivering an indescribable 90-minute extravaganza from, where else – the only place that could host it – the world's largest stadium. Imagine the opening ceremony of the Beijing Olympics but bigger, better and more polished, or a Nuremberg Rally, albeit with acrobats, fireworks and children dressed as rabbits. The entire event is so mind boggling, so bizarre, and so packed full of iconography, nationalism and state worship that it could only be North Korea. The event has to be seen to be believed and, even then, you will not believe your eyes.

But are the Mass Games about to be consigned to the history books? The logistics and cost of organising such an event, even if impossible to measure in real terms, is astronomical. Nothing took place from 2014–17; it seemed that the event just couldn't be justified, even by the North Koreans. But in 2018 a new Mass Games resurfaced, to celebrate the 70th anniversary of the country's foundation, titled The Glorious Country. Was this just one last hurrah? Your guess is as good as mine.

PHOTOGRAPHY AND VIDEO

The rubrics relating to photography and video in North Korea are opaque, but generally less restrictive than most visitors imagine them to be. With no clear guidelines, the interpretation of 'rules' on what is and isn't permissible can vary from one guide to the next. From time to time a journalist posing as a tourist visits the country; when news of this discovery reaches Pyongyang it understandably causes panic among the local guides, who react by becoming a little harsher for some months in their interpretation of what is and isn't allowed. Regardless, don't begrudge your guides as they don't make the rules – it would be much easier for them to say you can photograph whatever you like; they are merely protecting themselves and you.

Except for the actively encouraged photographs with your military guides at the DMZ, anything of a military nature, such as checkpoints, fortifications and army vehicles is strictly prohibited. This can be frustrating, as there will almost always be one or two soldiers, conscripts or uniformed men and women among any crowd. In a rural environment, photographing people engaged in manual labour such as working in the fields, pulling an ox and cart or maintaining the roads will be actively discouraged. Poverty, construction sites and anything else that doesn't promote 'beauty' (in the eyes of your guide, not the beholder) shouldn't be photographed. When driving through the countryside or travelling by train you will likely be told to take no photographs whatsoever, as this keeps things simple for your guides. Restrictions are often most severe in the lesser-visited areas of the country such as in North Hamgyong Province, where breaches in protocol can result in all cameras and memory cards being inspected, to the embarrassment of the guides and frustration of the group. Upon arriving in the country, guides will almost always inform you of the current rules, and it really is not worth spoiling goodwill for a blurred shot of somebody's grandmother carrying a sack of potatoes. If there is ever any inkling of doubt as to whether something may be photographed, always ask first.

The majority of problems arise when locals are photographed without giving their permission. When tourists hit the streets of North Korea many suddenly act akin to the paparazzi; just as you, dear reader, wouldn't take kindly to being jumped upon and photographed when you are out shopping or enjoying a picnic with your family, neither do North Koreans. Most people are happy to be photographed, but you should politely ask first.

In sensitive areas (such as borders and airports) it is better to just put your camera away, as by having it around your neck you are tempting fate, inviting bored officials to 'ask' to inspect your camera. These chaps are pretty savvy with a camera and know how to look through your folders, find hidden files and delete anything not to their liking.

Technically, lenses of over 150mm are prohibited, as are powerful optical zooms and high-specification binoculars/telescopes, but these rules are largely ignored these days by customs officials as technology has advanced too quickly for them to keep up. The more professional-looking equipment you bring with you, the more likely you are to be quizzed at the border, but unless you are bringing in top-end kit together with all manner of tripods, lenses and paraphernalia, you are unlikely to have any issues.

MEDIA AND COMMUNICATIONS

The official line is delivered domestically through a variety of outlets including newspapers, radio, TV and the intranet.

WEBSITES, PUBLICATIONS AND PERIODICALS Internationally, the country disseminates the party line and some background information on the country through several news outlets such as the Korean Central News Agency (w kcna.kp), Naenara (w naenara.com.kp) and Rodong Sinmun (w rodong.rep.kp/en), the official voice of the Central Committee of the Workers' Party of Korea. A few English-language newspapers and periodicals, such as *Korean Today*, *Foreign Trade* and *The Pyongyang Times* (w pyongyangtimes.com.kp) are normally handed out on Air Koryo flights and are available to buy in bookshops across the country – all giving a feel of the current political climate and North Korean psyche; with many articles relating to the brilliant leadership of the Kims, the puppet clique running South Korea, those dastardly Yankees or the Japanese imperialists. Many titles can now be downloaded and perused at your leisure via the official Publications of the DPRK website (w korean-books.com.kp).

TELEVISION AND RADIO Radio and TV sets are pre-tuned to North Korean stations only and must be checked and registered with the police to stop persons from attempting to tune into foreign channels. There are just three major TV channels, with Korean Central Television being the only one providing guaranteed daily programming, normally broadcasting 8 hours a day during the week and a little longer on weekends. Broadcasting naturally starts with the national anthem and ends each evening with another anthem, *Our Shining Country*. A few dramas and feature films are broadcast each day, but the bulk of programming is monotonous, with such heavy doses of the military, politics and propaganda that most just turn off, as they can't tune out. Still, as a tourist it is worth watching from the comfort of your hotel room to try and get your head around the officially prescribed mentality and, if anything, to catch the weather forecast (normally at 19.25 and 22.25 each evening). In the better hotels in Pyongyang and some of the top-end hotels elsewhere, the television in your hotel may proffer a small and fuzzy selection of foreign channels, which chop and change from time to time, and are occasionally switched off altogether. If working, you should normally have one English-language news channel, be it the BBC, CNN or Al Jazeera, together with a few Chinese and Russian stations.

As you are not allowed to bring a radio with you (unless it is a built-in function of your telephone, tablet or such), you won't be likely to listen to any, but some older hotels do have a built-in radio set within the bedside table, which may or may not work. Other than rousing martial music to help you get out of bed there isn't much worth listening to, but you may be able to pick up the Voice of Korea (w vok.rep.kp), formerly Radio Pyongyang, which broadcasts in a few languages, including English.

TELEPHONES, POST AND INTERNET Despite what you might assume, it is possible to keep in contact with the outside world, although this is costly and can be time-consuming to arrange. Although mobile telephones are near-ubiquitous these days, yours will not work as a communications device unless you purchase a special and costly SIM card, which will only work for making/receiving international calls and texts, as it works on a different network from the one locals use. These SIM cards are expensive and *should* be available at the airport but can be quite elusive – often requiring driving to a few different offices or hotels to find a manned desk selling them. Unless you really must be in touch 24/7 with the outside world, there is little

PYONGYANG CALLING

North Korea's domestic telephone network, both mobile and landline, is a complicated one. The locals' landlines and most numbers only work domestically, so even if you obtained the telephone number of somebody in North Korea who you wished to call, it would be impossible for you to do so from your own country, and vice versa for them to call you. Yes, theoretically you could try and go through the switchboard (remember those?) on ☏ +850 2 18111, but you will realistically only manage to get connected to a number with a 381 or 382 prefix – numbers designated to organisations that have a reason to interact with the outside world, such as embassies and hotels. Should you purchase a local SIM card for your mobile telephone you will still not be able to make normal domestic calls, but can make a pseudo-international call to a number starting with 381 or 382. In such a scenario, should you be in Pyongyang and wish to inform the British Embassy that you require treatment at the Friendship Hospital, you would need to make what is akin to an international call to the Embassy to inform them of your predicament, while only a Korean would be able to call the hospital for you from his or her telephone (on ☏ 3827 688, if you must know).

benefit in spending what could be a few hours of your sightseeing programme to arrange this, particularly if you are on a short- to medium-length tour. Do bear in mind that these cards only appear to be available in Pyongyang and come with prepaid credit; should you run out of credit a repeat trip to find a counter selling the SIM cards will be required. For the conventional tourist it is far better to do without and, should you need to call home, do so from your hotel, as all but the most basic hotels have a communications centre of sorts, some of which are so wonderfully archaic that using them is quite the experience. Landline or mobile, it goes without saying that your calls will be listened to, so be nice. At a few spots in the far north and far south of the country your telephone may pick up a Chinese, Russian or South Korean network but be cautious here as technically this is prohibited; you don't want to be shopped to the authorities by the local jobsworth.

Note too that international phone calls can be expensive; calls placed from your hotel can cost anything from €1.50 to €10 (or more) per minute. Prices for calling from mobiles tend to be almost identical to calling from a landline.

The internet is, for all intents and purposes, unavailable. It is possible, with some time, form filling and at significant cost to obtain a SIM card with mobile data, but this is primarily aimed at foreign residents and regular visitors to the country, not tourists. Some hotels have a computer allowing you to send an email from their own account (for a high fee calculated by the kilobyte), but note these may well disappear in the recipient's junk box. Although it is often restricted completely, a couple of hotels such as the Potonggang and Hyangsan flirt with providing actual and full internet access from a communal computer, but prices are eye-wateringly expensive. Again, all use is strictly monitored and accessing anything you shouldn't, such as South Korean websites, pornography or anything which may be derogatory about North Korea (and its leaders), is not a good idea. It's best to put the internet to the back of your mind and enjoy being disconnected from the modern world for a few days – it's remarkably refreshing to have an actual dinner conversation in North Korea, without people looking down at their phones every 5 minutes.

Postcards and letters can be sent from most hotels in Pyongyang and the service is reliable, taking anything from five days to one month to arrive. The DHL office in Pyongyang seems desperate for business and will normally come to your hotel to pack and ship larger items. Expect all post to be thoroughly inspected.

CULTURAL ETIQUETTE

North Koreans are hospitable and generally forgiving of most social faux pas. Traditional values are rooted in Buddhism and Confucianism, so age and social standing are important factors in human interaction that visiting foreigners will largely be excused from understanding. Koreans are generally respectably dressed, and can look slightly aghast when they see scruffy foreigners or travellers with visible tattoos, body piercings, dreadlocks and other such alien modes of outward self-expression. Public displays of affection are rare and frowned upon; touching, patting or backslapping is something reserved more for friends than strangers. Kissing a woman (or man for that matter), on one or both cheeks can cause great embarrassment and blushing, but once you know somebody well enough the reverse can be a problem – handshakes can linger for, what is for Westerners, an uncomfortably long time.

It is considered uncouth to blow your nose at the table, and recommended to be discreet if you need to do so. It is custom that others, preferably the host, should refill your drink, so if your glass is constantly refilled just leave it full once you are suitably quenched (or sozzled). Similarly with food, it is not expected for you to clean your plate – should you do so more food may materialise. If you need to call somebody's attention you should wave them towards you with your palm facing down, not up (as if you are swimming with one hand). The western wave (with the palm facing up) is the Korean gesture for summoning a dog. Shoes should always be removed when going into homes and temples and you shouldn't point the soles of your shoes or feet at others.

While there is an awful lot more to the above, all will be forgiven as you stumble from one faux pas to the next, learning as you go along with a few smirks and laughs from your hosts. What is harder to forgive and what causes the majority of problems in the country is insulting any facet of the 'supreme dignity, ideology, system or culture of the DPR Korea'. Kim Il Sung, Kim Jong Il and Kim Jong Un are almost deities and, like it or not, the personality cult they have instilled should be viewed akin to a fundamentalist religion. Questioning, joking or mocking the system will be a sure-fire way to gravely insult your guides, likely ruining your trip

TIME FOR CHANGE

In the early 20th century, Korea adopted a standard time of GMT+8.5, a time zone that existed for just a few short years. In 1912, shortly after the Japanese annexation of Korea, the time was realigned to GMT+9, the same as their new Japanese masters. After liberation from Japan on 15 August 1945, reverting back to their pre-colonial time zone was hardly a priority, so both Koreas stuck with Japanese time until Pyongyang decided in 2015, with just ten days' notice, to implement the order that the North would revert back to their former time zone on the 70th anniversary of liberation. North and South now ran on two different time zones.

Fewer than three years later, on the occasion of Kim Jong Un's historic meeting with South Korean President Moon Jae-in on 27 April 2018, Kim Jong Un mooted the North could move back in line with the South, noting that (as quoted in the *Rodong Sinmun*) 'it was a painful wrench to see two clocks indicating Pyongyang and Seoul times hanging on a wall of the summit venue'. Just two days later Kim Jong Un announced that the country would indeed revert back. The very next day the Supreme People's Assembly jumped into action and issued a concise 79-word decree, essentially saying, 'get it done.' Four days later and only eight days after Kim Jong Un, seemingly off the cuff, had suggested it, the clocks of North and South were synchronised once more, now both running on what is essentially Japanese Standard Time.

Granting that the clocks in North and South Korea now run on the same time, one would assume that their calendars are also in sync, but thanks to the North's introduction in 1997 of the Juche calendar, they are not. Adopted on the third anniversary of Kim Il Sung's death, the Juche calendar replaced the Gregorian calendar, with 1912 (the year of Kim Il Sung's birth) becoming Juche 1. The few and minor events in history that may have happened before Kim Il Sung's birth are still referred to using the Gregorian calendar, but everything beyond it is referred to in Juche years. Accordingly, the country was founded in Juche 37, Kim Jong Il died in Juche 100 and the Gregorian year 2025 will be Juche 114. As this is all somewhat confusing, the Gregorian year is often slipped in, in parentheses, after the Juche year, highlighting that even the locals struggle with this concept from time to time.

in the process. Any conversations on such things, even among your group or in the privacy of your hotel room are best avoided, as walls have ears; allegedly, sometimes quite literally.

DOING BUSINESS IN NORTH KOREA

by Ian Bennett and Geoffrey See of Choson Exchange

If North Korea is an unlikely tourist destination, it is an even more improbable place for outsiders to do business. For decades it has been all but closed to foreign investors, both culturally from within and through sanctions from the international community. Coupled with a crumbling infrastructure and patchy track record of safeguarding foreign assets, few have opted to take the plunge and even fewer have come out of it successfully.

But things are changing. A network of SEZs (Special Economic Zones) across the country was started in the 1990s and expanded under Kim Jong Un. Many of these can still be filed in the 'yes, it's a muddy field, but think of the potential' category, but it is not hard to see how that potential could be tapped if relations with the international community improve and joint ventures start to spring up.

Like many other countries in the region, business deals in North Korea are founded on personal relationships. High-level contacts are useful but only get you so far; with North Korea's shifting internal politics, if an official falls out of favour then their influence vanishes. Underpinning this with nurturing relationships at ground level helps reduce this risk. It also requires patience and diligence in information-gathering. With a top-down approach to government and no regular access to the internet, information silos and rumours abound. Two different North Korean business partners may give contradictory responses to the same question; they are not necessarily acting in bad faith, they just have different information sources. We were once told by a trusted contact at the Investment Commission that a double taxation treaty with Singapore had been in place for the past two years, but then the Ministry of Finance told us that such a treaty had never been signed.

The opacity of North Korea's structure means potential investors have to spend time establishing who the real decision makers are. Authorisation for a business opportunity can usually be traced back to one of the arms of the state; establishing which ministry- and adjunct committee and subcommittee is essential, as well as identifying the relevant and empowered stakeholders within those organisations.

With the absence of a clear legal precedent in many areas, whether or not a deal succeeds will depend on these people – so think about what they need, how your interests are aligned, and how can you help them. Think from their point of view, bring a lot of patience, and if the domestic and international situations are also favourable you may be successful.

Choson Exchange is a non-profit organisation pursuing deeper economic engagement with the country through various projects, including sending skilled volunteers to North Korea to provide training in business and entrepreneurship. Since 2009, they have brought over 100 foreign volunteers to North Korea to mentor and network with over 2,000 Koreans in entrepreneurship, business and economic policy.

2

Essentially everything you are told about the leaders, the Korean War (and who started it) and the Workers' Party is gospel. Images of the leaders are considered sacred too, so books depicting any of the Kims should be well kept and newspapers should be carefully folded, so that the image of the leader isn't creased. If photographing statues of the leaders, it should be the entire statue, not just part of it. Furthermore, at certain times you will be expected to bow before statues or effigies of the leaders, and may even see the embalmed bodies of Kim Il Sung and Kim Jong Il lying in state at the mausoleum – if you know you cannot be respectful here you should rethink visiting North Korea altogether.

Criticisms of almost anything in ultra-nationalist North Korea, such as a poor road, should be guarded, as this can be construed as a criticism of the government as, after all, they are responsible for the road. It really is all terribly confusing and many travel to the country neurotic that they are going to spark a diplomatic incident – very, very few do. Travellers are far more likely to have a fall out with other members of their tour than one of their effervescent hosts – you really would have to be going out of your way to get into trouble in North Korea, but there are blurred lines that should never be crossed and certain things than can never be freely discussed. Your guides will often engage in discussions of politics, history and such, but should you disagree with their stance it is best to steer the conversation elsewhere; some things are best left unsaid. Finally, should you have gone too far and said or done something you know you shouldn't, an immediate and sincere apology, with a spot of self-criticism thrown in for good measure, is the best course of action. Digging your heels in will only ever exacerbate the situation.

TRAVELLING POSITIVELY

Tourism to the DPRK helps employ thousands of people, brings vital money into the economy and, perhaps more importantly, allows for some small cultural interactions with the outside world that would otherwise be near non-existent. With more foreign visitors heading to North Korea year on year, an increased reliance on tourism has had its part in helping to slowly bring the country into the international fold. Furthermore, realising the importance of tourism, it could be argued, has drawn some government spending away from more questionable projects into much-needed infrastructural development.

Owing to the very nature of North Korea, few charities are active within the country, but some of the tour operators working in the DPRK have their own grassroots projects, which they are able to monitor through regular visits. North Koreans are very proud people and are reluctant to receive handouts, although some established charities do exist, such as UK-based Love North Korea Children (w lovenkchildren.org), who feed impoverished children through a number of bakeries in the country.

Just by visiting North Korea you are channelling money to the government – due to the very nature of their economy there is no way of avoiding this. Regardless of this, tourists and the money they spend help in their own infinitesimal way to keep the country, and its people, afloat.

Part Two

THE GUIDE

3

Pyongyang (평양)

The very name 'Pyongyang' stirs up a range of evocative thoughts and images in the mind of almost anybody who hears it; while some may envisage it as a socialist Shangri-La, the majority sadly picture this misunderstood and secretive city, which is so rarely out of the news, as something diametrically opposite – as a city of 3.3 million deranged communist automatons. Vilified in the 21st century, the world's easternmost 'Axis of Evil' capital has struggled for years to accurately portray itself to the outside world, with the global media preferring to denigrate Pyongyang, as it does the entire country, rather than attempt to understand it, or approach it impartially.

This obsessively centrally planned city, where seemingly everything has its place and purpose, was designed as a workers' utopia and is the pride of North Korea, where Kim Il Sung was born, dreams are made and the former leaders are laid to rest. This is the epicentre, the beating heart, without which the nation could not survive. In 1953, following the destruction of the Korean War, Kim Il Sung strove to create what was – in his eyes – perfection from a near-blank canvas. The blueprint for this city was socialist-modernist, with wide streets, utilitarian high-rises, grandiose civic buildings and world-class public facilities, all complemented by parks and greenery. There is no denying that Pyongyang is impressive – there are few cities where the word 'unique' can so justifiably be used – but of course the original vision has not been completely realised, and if you look for faults you will find them in abundance. Still, there is a great deal to impress, charm and surprise in this mysterious capital, where the slight undercurrent of a Cold War atmosphere always prevails, injecting a permanent drip of adrenaline into every second spent in the city.

Under former dynasties and long before the devastation of the Korean War, Pyongyang was a walled city, and though today the walls that protect citizens from the outside are merely bureaucratic, they are just as insurmountable. Those that live in the capital are undoubtedly the chosen few – the lucky ones. Pyongyangites are largely blessed by their heritage; of the younger generations almost everybody was born in the city, incongruous to most Asian cities where rural–urban migration is a pressing issue. Owing to their Songbun (see box, page 38), Pyongyangites have poor knowledge of what lies beyond their sanctuary, just as those in the hinterlands have little knowledge of life in the ivory tower of the capital. Pyongyang is not North Korea – it is the emerald city that everybody else in the country strives to reach. To see only the capital, with its bombastic monuments and monumental edifices, will give an unbalanced view of the country as a whole – but to see it is truly something to behold.

Should you be mature in years and fortunate enough to have visited the USSR in the 1960s, China in the 1970s or Albania under Hoxha you may have an idea of what to expect; but for the rest of us Pyongyang is the last city standing, a relic of

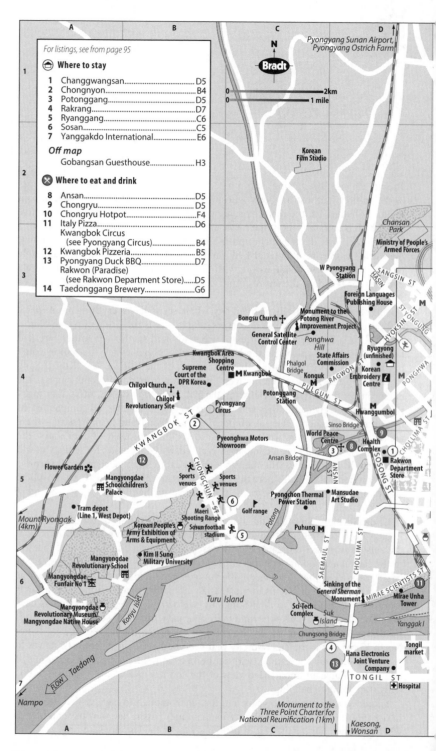

For listings, see from page 95

Where to stay

1 Changgwangsan................................D5
2 Chongnyon....................................B4
3 Potonggang....................................D5
4 Rakrang..D7
5 Ryanggang......................................C6
6 Sosan..C5
7 Yanggakdo International..................E6

Off map
   Gobangsan Guesthouse....................H3

Where to eat and drink

8 Ansan..D5
9 Chongryu..D5
10 Chongryu Hotpot............................F4
11 Italy Pizza......................................D6
   Kwangbok Circus
      (see Pyongyang Circus)...............B4
12 Kwangbok Pizzeria..........................B5
13 Pyongyang Duck BBQ......................D7
   Rakwon (Paradise)
      (see Rakwon Department Store)...D5
14 Taedonggang Brewery......................G6

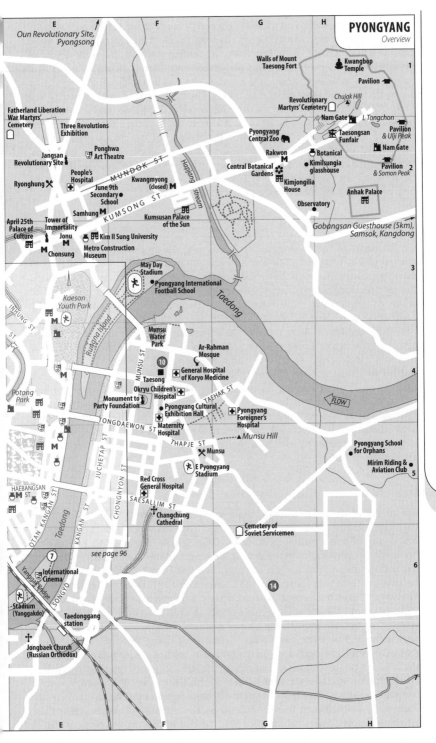

PYONGYANG
Overview

E | F | G | H

Oun Revolutionary Site, Pyongsong

Walls of Mount Taesong Fort

Kwangbop Temple

Pavilion

Revolutionary Martyrs' Cemetery
Chujak Hill

Nam Gate
L Tongchon

Pavilion & Ulji Peak

Nam Gate

Taesongsan Funfair

Pyongyang Central Zoo

Rakwon

Botanical

Central Botanical Gardens

Kimilsungia glasshouse

Kimjongilia House

Pavilion & Somon Peak

Observatory

Anhak Palace

Gobangsan Guesthouse (5km), Samsok, Kangdong

Fatherland Liberation War Martyrs' Cemetery

Three Revolutions Exhibition

Ponghwa Art Theatre

Jangsan Revolutionary Site

Ryonghung

People's Hospital

Kwangmyong (closed)

June 9th Secondary School

Samhung

Tower of Immortality

Jonu

Chonsung

Kim Il Sung University

Metro Construction Museum

April 25th Palace of Culture

Kumsusan Palace of the Sun

MUNDOK ST

KUMSONG ST

Hapjong stream

May Day Stadium

Pyongyang International Football School

Taedong

Kaeson Youth Park

Rukna island

Munsu Water Park

Ar-Rahman Mosque

Taesong

General Hospital of Koryo Medicine

Okryu Children's Hospital

Monument to Party Foundation

Pyongyang Cultural Exhibition Hall

Maternity Hospital

Pyongyang Foreigner's Hospital

Munsu Hill

FLOW

Pyongyang School for Orphans

Mirim Riding & Aviation Club

Potong Park

TONGDAEWON ST

THAPJE ST

Munsu

E Pyongyang Stadium

Red Cross General Hospital

SAESALLIM ST

Changchung Cathedral

Cemetery of Soviet Servicemen

HAEBANGSAN ST

Taedong

see page 96

International Cinema

Stadium (Yanggakdo)

Taedonggang station

Jongbaek Church (Russian Orthodox)

Yanggak Bridge

SONGYO

INHUNG ST

MUNSU ST

JUCHETAP ST

CHONGNYON ST

OTAN KANGAN ST

KANGAN ST

Pyongyang

1

2

3

4

5

6

7

89

communism that soldiers on while almost everywhere else has moved on – in many ways feeling more akin to a dystopian city from celluloid than an actual place you'd expect to find here on earth. But change is coming – streets that were devoid of traffic a few years ago now have cars, shops with once-barren shelves are now full of goods, and a small but growing middle class show us that while all Pyongyangites are equal, some are more equal than others. The Pyongyang of tomorrow may well be a better place than it is today for the millions who call it home, but the Pyongyang of today could not be more fascinating. An increasingly electric atmosphere fills the city, as if after decades in the wilderness the prospect of real change is just around the corner, one that will define the Pyongyang, and North Korea, of tomorrow. Whatever the country becomes in the years to come, it appears unlikely that it will be of the nature envisaged back in 1948, when the country was founded with the help of Georgia's infamous hot-headed son, Joseph Stalin.

GEOGRAPHY

On the banks of the Taedong River, Pyongyang sits on mineral-rich and fertile alluvial plains, with just a few low hills (chiefly in the northeast and northwest) causing inconveniences to the urban planners. With a humid continental climate, the city receives approximately 940mm of precipitation per year, over half of which comes down as rains in the hot monsoon months of July and August. By contrast, winters, from November to March, are cold and dry, with Siberian winds providing additional chill. The navigable Taedong leads to the port of Nampo and the West Sea of Korea (Yellow Sea), approximately 50km away as the crow flies, while lesser rivers such as the Sunhwa, Potong and Hapjang all flow through north Pyongyang into the Taedong, helping to keep the city cooler and greener than it would otherwise be. As the beating heart of the DPRK, the road and rail infrastructure here is the best in the country, with the Pyongyang–Sinuiju railway a vital and well-maintained lifeline with China. The worst-offending heavy industry is largely found elsewhere in the country and the air in Pyongyang is clean when compared with most Asian capitals – a pleasing contrast to those arriving from Beijing.

HISTORY

For much of its early history, Pyongyang was little more than a provincial backwater, standing by as Seoul and Busan developed as major trading centres. The first record of it as a trading post for the Chinese dates from 108BC, presumably because of its convenient location near the mouth of the Taedong River. The city has had its ups and downs over the centuries, and even ascended in its status to become capital of both the ancient old Choson Dynasty (of which relatively little is known) and later, the larger Koguryo Dynasty, a claim it held from 427AD for over 200 years, until the collapse of this dynasty in 668. Thereon Pyongyang, which was still of notable importance on the peninsula, was overshadowed by other settlements in Korea for many years. Centuries of changing borders, falling and rising dynasties, civil wars and foreign invasions, such as the Japanese invasions in the late 16th century, all left an imprint on the fabric of Pyongyang, but one that is often hard to spot these days. In modern North Korea, pre-20th-century history is somewhat elusive on the streets of the Pyongyang; save for the few forlorn city walls, gates and temples, there is little to overtly remind the casual visitor than anything happened here before April 1912, when Kim Il Sung was born, as that is how the history is written locally, and thus how it will continue to be portrayed under the current dynasty.

A large influx of Christian missionaries in the second half of the 19th century took Pyongyang as their base; most were from America, but there were also contingents from Australia, the UK and Canada. Some accounts of the city at this time refer to it as being the 'Jerusalem of the east', and the missionaries here were not solely concerned with religious enlightenment but also in spreading education and medicine around the country. By the beginning of the 20th century, there were around 100 churches serving Pyongyang's population of 40,000. The Japanese frowned on Christianity, however, and though it continued to be practiced, its promulgation dwindled from the start of their formal occupation in 1910.

Pyongyang was written into North Korean history on 25 August 1945, when the Soviets declared that it would become the northern capital of the new divided Korea. With its history of religious leanings and very small-scale industry, the city was an unlikely central base for the new communist party, but the Soviets had to make do. In 1947, two years after the Japanese retreat (but before the Korean War), Soviet journalist V Perlin described the city:

> The streets of Pyongyang abound in the most sudden and glaring contrasts. Within a few paces of the smooth central streets, we find labyrinths of narrow gloomy alleys. In the heart of the city, tiny Korean houses with close-barred doors and windows alternate with smart mansions and business buildings, only recently occupied by Japanese banks. A glittering motorcar may hoot frantically and in vain at a stubborn bullock, yoked to an ancient two-wheeled carriage, blocking traffic at the corner. A lady of fashion walks down the street, exactly one step behind her husband, a stout gentleman in European dress. Custom forbids her to walk at his side. A woman's place is in the rear. A year and a half ago, every 11th resident of this town was Japanese. Now there is not a single Japanese to be seen.

Such as description could, of course, have been given for many medium-size Asian cities, which expanded without planning constraints and where the poor and rich lived cheek by jowl. It is significant, though, that no political colour is included in this description, although it was written by a Soviet journalist at a time when communism was taking control of the DPRK. Clearly it had not yet put its stamp on the capital.

This was to change during the Korean War, when UN bombing physically destroyed most of the Christian buildings in the city, as they destroyed everything else – many of them were, ironically, situated on what was to become Kim Il Sung Square (page 102), nowadays the site of the military parades determined to show the power of totally non-Christian forces. At the end of the war in 1953, when conditions were at their very worst, Soviet writer Vasili Kornilov reported:

> The residents of Pyongyang had to begin life in the devastated city by ascertaining which streets could be used without danger of being blown to bits by delayed action bombs, how to reach the nearest bomb shelter and the times of day when the air raids usually occurred. To mark out the danger spots, sappers surround them with empty petrol drums. As often as not, these drums bear a crude chalk drawing of a bespectacled face and the legend in Korean 'President Truman'. When they want to warn their fellow-citizens of the presence of a delayed-action bomb, the townsfolk do not say 'Avoid that street. There is a time-bomb there'. They say 'Don't go that way. Truman's there'.

It is perhaps crude to say so, but the bombing undoubtedly helped the communist regime to assert its power. To residents in the North, the US, South Korea and capitalism were all represented by this one persistent, devastating and inexcusable activity. No government propaganda was needed to supplement the total destruction all around. The city was rebuilt by the Soviets in the aftermath of the war, but sadly North Korean secrecy has prevented us from establishing exactly what plans were made. Similarly we have no idea as to why particular buildings were erected. Clearly Kim Il Sung must have given constant 'guidance' and shown that the development of Pyongyang took precedence over most other activities except perhaps defence. This development admittedly abated somewhat during the famine in the mid 1990s (page 26), with the most visible intrusion of reality being the failure to complete the 105-storey Ryugyong Hotel (see box, page 98).

Madeleine Albright, Secretary of State under Bill Clinton, visited Pyongyang in October 2000. Her description of her arrival could have equally well have been written by anyone in President Nixon's entourage during his visit to Beijing in February 1972, when the Chinese capital had wide roads, prestigious buildings but a largely lethargic air about it. In her book, *Fascism: A Warning* she writes:

> Arriving in Pyongyang in October 2000, I found a capital city like no other. From airport to guesthouse, our motorcade encountered not a single car. The trees had colour, leaves turning with the season, but the brownish fields appeared thirsty for rain and the sagging barns looked desperate for paint. There were no streetlights, so driving downtown in the evening, we were directed to the right road by a pair of bone-like fluorescent sticks held by a policeman (or –woman) whose body was made invisible by the surrounding blackness.
>
> In daylight, the Pyongyang I saw was a metropolis of bustling sterility, with ant-like columns of workers and bureaucrats walking or pedalling away on battered bicycles occasionally making room for Cold War-era Russian Volgas, small jeep-like trucks and the government's multihued fleet of sedans.

It was only really in the last decade of Kim Jong Il and the early years of Kim Jong Un's leadership, when the country was finally recovering from the famine of the 1990s, that Pyongyang began to make the leap towards modernisation. This was, however, at the sacrifice of potential development elsewhere; while visitors will notice (and no doubt appreciate) the better roads between the main towns, the improved hotels and the willingness to now show almost all parts of the country, the difference with Pyongyang becomes more accentuated each year. Glimpses at passing villages and towns, where tourists do not stop, show a level of poverty that should by now, 70 years after the establishment of the regime, have been eliminated. Sadly, checkpoints are viewed as necessary on all the roads out of Pyongyang. In theory, these are for 'security', but in reality they are to ensure that access to the capital is only granted to those with permission to visit, or with proof of long-term residency.

Those able to live there are in an environment that soon should be able to call itself 'cosmopolitan'. Restaurants serving foreign food are opening, and more goods from China and the outside world are in the shops. This is clearly not the capital of a country suffering too badly from sanctions. It is difficult to predict whether this dichotomy will present political difficulties in due course for the regime. In many other dictatorships in Asia and Africa, the contrast is far greater and regimes that countenance this happily survive. A solution for the regime could be greater investment in the other major towns, which could then offer a goal to the population that at present only Pyongyang provides.

GETTING THERE AND AWAY

For now, almost all travellers will initially arrive in Pyongyang by air or rail (see page 55 for details). Pyongyang Sunan Airport [88 D1] is a 26km drive north from the city centre; a 20- to 50-minute drive from almost every address in the capital. Arriving by rail, Pyongyang Station is smack in the centre of town and within walking distance of a few hotels (should you be permitted to do so).

GETTING AROUND

Like all good socialist cities, Pyongyang prides itself on its cheap and affordable public transport, but as a 'normal' foreigner you will be obliged to travel the city by private transport, with your hosts providing a suitable vehicle that will be at your beck and call. Traffic in the city, while increasing, is very mild and private transport remains the quickest, if not necessarily the most enjoyable, way of getting from A to B at any time of day. Bear in mind that you will still have to pay for your assigned private vehicle even if you decide to explore a bit on foot or by bike (with your guide, of course).

ON FOOT AND BY BICYCLE Parts of the city can be explored (as always, with a guide) on foot, with an increasing number of prescribed routes allowing those with the time and inclination to see things at a slower pace. Bicycle tours can also now be arranged, but you are not able to freely cycle around the city.

BY TAXI An increasing number of taxis can be found in Pyongyang, from ageing models from the last century to modern cars, some hailing from the Pyeonghwa Motors Plant. Taxis are comparatively expensive for locals, but an explosion in their numbers highlights that many modern Pyongyangites have some level of disposable income. They are normally found parked up near hotels frequented by Koreans, and outside the railway station, larger department stores and restaurants. It is unlikely that you will need to use a taxi, but it would be possible to use one (with a guide) if necessary.

TRAMS, TROLLEYBUSES AND BUSES Trams, trolleybuses and buses cover a large network across the city and out into the suburbs, often at little more than a crawl. Judging by these often-jam-packed vehicles and long queues, services may not be as regular as your guides will lead you to believe. Tickets, like the metro, cost five won and are thus essentially free – which helps explain their popularity. Some of these charabancs are of a staggering vintage, having travelled millions of kilometres over the years – calculable as many vehicles have a red star painted on their side, each star denoting 50,000km of safe driving. Quite what 'safe driving' means isn't altogether clear. Sadly, public transport is generally off-limits unless you wish to charter an entire vehicle – a popular option for enthusiasts wanting to travel aboard these classic models of yesteryear that are increasingly hard to spot anywhere else on earth, save for in transport museums.

The **tram** network comprises three main lines and first opened in 1991, running Czechoslovakian-built tramcars along 53.5km of track. A short fourth line, the Kumsusan Line, transports pilgrims to the Kumsusan Palace of the Sun in immaculate Swiss cars, operating on a different gauge from the three main lines. It's now possible to charter a tram from the West Tram Depot (in Mangyongdae District) to Pyongyang Station (and occasionally beyond); an excursion that allows a couple of fleeting photography stops on the way, much to the bemusement of the bus conductor and those poor souls waiting at the stop – who will not be permitted to board.

The metro has been steeped in mystery and speculation since it opened in 1973, with rumours of secret lines leading to palaces, military installations and massive nuclear bunkers all helping provide additional excitement to a journey that costs, in Western terms, a fraction of a penny. These rumours circulate with another laughably contrary one: that just two stations exist (Puhung and Yonggwang, the ones most commonly used by tourists) and that all the busy commuters are actors.

Work started on the Pyongyang Metro in the 1960s and the first of the two lines, Chollima, opened in 1973 with the second line, Hyoksin (literally meaning 'renewal'), coming two years later. Envisaged as a larger network, long-proposed extensions ground to a halt when the economy derailed in the late 1980s, although rumours of the resumption of works re-emerged (not for the first time) in 2018. With just 17 stations (two of which are closed) the metro isn't extensive, but what it lacks in length it makes up for in its depth and architectural splendour – making it one of the world's most impressive systems and an absolute must for any visitor to Pyongyang.

Despite original plans, the entire network is firmly on the north bank of the Taedong. With a few exceptions, stations are not named after the area in which they are located, and instead have strong socialist names such as 'Triumph', 'Victory' and 'Red Star'. Because of this, a spot of local knowledge is required to navigate the system. Stations and tunnels are deep; while figures are not given, estimates put some of them at 110–120m or more underground – which would make them the deepest in the world. This depth, combined with multiple sets of heavy blast doors at the bottom of the escalators, allows the entire network to double up as an emergency citywide bomb shelter.

Architecturally akin to the best Soviet-era metro systems of the USSR, stations often start marbled and minimalist, with piped music echoing down the advertising-free escalator shafts. Escalators and foot tunnels lead through the blast doors to the often cavernous platforms, where the overwhelming and lavish socialist-realist designs unfold and come to the fore, with statues, mosaic murals, bronze reliefs and chandeliers.

The rolling stock was originally purchased new from China, but since the 1990s secondhand carriages from East and West Berlin have been incorporated into regular usage. In 2015, one new test train, purported to have been made in the DPRK, was unveiled – its bright modern features appearing out of place compared with all the vintage wagons that ride these rails. A possible sign of things to come,

Trolleybuses were introduced in 1962 and bump and grind along with quite a racket. Some of the vehicles in the fleet date back to the 1960s and the bulk of the cars were constructed in Korea, although a few Turkish and Czech trolleybuses have been imported in recent years. Much like with the trams, it's possible to charter a trolleybus, typically travelling from behind Department Store No 1 in the city centre, over the Okryu Bridge and finishing up near the Romanian Embassy in Taedonggang District.

Finally, public **buses** operate all over, and are largely a mishmash of ageing and secondhand vehicles from the world over. The oldest operational bus in the fleet, a 1950s Skoda, may be chartered for a novelty tour of central Pyongyang. A plaque adorns the dashboard to commemorate Kim Il Sung catching this very bus on 2 June 1954 – saving it from the scrapheap and keeping it on the road ever since.

these few new carriages are the only ones that do not have framed portraits of the leaders within them, atypical of all else here, as even deep underground one cannot normally escape politics.

Trains run every 2–7 minutes dependent on the time of day, and the system ostensibly runs from 06.00 to 21.30, with a single journey costing just five won. As part of a tour, tourists typically travel one stop from Puhung to Yonggwang, chiefly as these are considered the two most impressive stations. In response to the rumourmongers, tourists may now also travel on from Yonggwang to Kaeson, bypassing the three intermediary stations. It's also possible to arrange a comprehensive tour that takes in almost every station – a fascinating 3 or so hours.

RIDING THE RAILS When on the metro there is often no indication as to where you are in the city – locals just know. While visitors are unlikely to use the metro as a form of transport at present, a bit of context as to nearby sights may help.

CHOLLIMA LINE

Puhung (*Rehabilitation*): Mansudae Art Studio/Potonggang Hotel (1.1km)

Yonggwang (*Glory*): Pyongyang Station/Koryo Hotel

Ponghwa (*Signal Fire*): Party Founding Museum/Haebangsan Hotel (550m)

Sungni (*Victory*): Mansudae Fountain Park/Kim Il Sung Square/Grand People's Study House

Tongil (*Reunification*): Mansudae Grand Monument/Chollima Statue/Moranbong Park

Kaeson (*Triumphant Return*): Arch of Triumph/Kim Il Sung Stadium/Kaeson Youth Park/Moranbong Park

Jonu (*Comrade*) (Interchange): April 25 House of Culture/Metro Museum/Chinese Embassy

Pulgunbyol (*Red Star*): Three Revolution Exhibition (1.2km)

HYOKSIN LINE

Kwangbok (*Restoration*): Kwangbok Area Shopping Centre/Pyongyang Circus (800m)

Konguk (*National Foundation*): Potonggang Station

Hwanggumbol (*Golden Fields*): Gyonghung Beer Bar

Konsol (*Construction*) (closed): Ryugyong Hotel

Hyoksin (*Renovation*): Fatherland Liberation War Museum (900m)

Jonsung (*Triumph*) (Interchange): April 25 House of Culture/Metro Museum/Chinese Embassy

Samhung (*Three Origins*): Kim Il Sung University/June 9th Secondary School

Kwangmyong (*Brightness*) (closed): Kumsusan Palace of the Sun

Rakwon (*Paradise*): Pyongyang Central Zoo/Central Botanical Gardens/Taesongsan Funfair (700m)/Revolutionary Martyrs' Cemetery (1.2km)

⌂ WHERE TO STAY

For some reason a myth has developed that anybody staying in Pyongyang has no choice of accommodation. Tales permeate that all and sundry are put up on a mysterious island in central Pyongyang – in the heart of the city, but detached from it and all it offers by the Taedong River, which provides a natural barrier to stop anyone who dares escape. Allegations of bugged rooms, secret floors and mysterious guests all make Yanggak Island sound more like Tracy Island, but the reality is, sadly, a little less exciting. The Yanggakdo International Hotel on Yanggak Island is indeed where a good deal of visitors stay, but chiefly due to the fact that it is the largest hotel and one of the better options in Pyongyang.

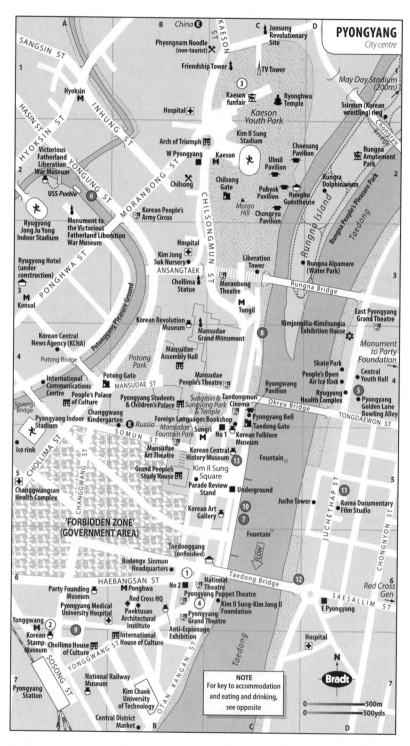

PYONGYANG
City centre

- China **E**
- SANGSIN ST
- KAESON ST
- Phyongnam Noodle (non-tourist) ✕
- Friendship Tower
- Jonsung Revolutionary Site
- May Day Stadium (200m)
- HASIN ST
- HYOKSIN ST
- INHUNG ST
- YONGUNG ST
- Hyoksin M
- Hospital ✚
- Arch of Triumph
- Kaeson funfair ③
- TV Tower
- Kaeson Youth Park
- Ronghwa Temple
- Ssireum (Korean wrestling) ring
- Chongryu Bridge
- Victorious Fatherland Liberation War Museum
- USS Pueblo ⑥
- Kim Il Sung Stadium
- Ulmil Pavilion
- Choesung Pavilion
- Rungna Amusement Park
- MORANBONG ST
- W Pyongyang
- Kaeson M
- Chilsong
- Chilsong Gate
- Chilsong
- Moran Hill
- Pubyok Pavilion
- Hungbu Guesthouse
- Chongryu Pavilion
- Rungra Dolphinarium
- Taedong
- Ryugyong Jong Ju Yong Indoor Stadium
- Monument to the Victorious Fatherland Liberation War Museum
- Korean People's Army Circus
- CHILSONGMUN ST
- Rungna Island
- Rungna People's Pleasure Park
- Ryugyong Hotel (under construction)
- PONGHWA ST
- Hospital ✚
- Kim Jong Suk Nursery
- ANSANGTAEK
- Chollima Statue
- Liberation Tower
- Rungna Alpamare (Water Park)
- Konsol M
- Moranbong Theatre
- Rungna Bridge
- Tongil M
- Korean Revolution Museum
- Mansudae Grand Monument
- Kimjongilia-Kimilsungia Exhibition House
- East Pyongyang Grand Theatre
- Korean Central News Agency (KCNA)
- Potong Bridge
- Potong Park
- Potonggang Pleasure Ground
- Mansudae Assembly Hall
- ⑧
- Monument to Party Foundation
- International Communications Centre
- Potong Gate
- MANSUDAE ST
- People's Palace of Culture
- Mansudae People's Theatre
- Skate Park
- People's Open Air Ice Rink
- Central Youth Hall
- Sosong Bridge
- Pyongyang Indoor Stadium
- Changgwang Kindergarten
- Pyongyang Students & Children's Palace
- Sungmin & Sungyong Park & Temple
- Taedongmun Cinema
- Ryongwang Pavilion
- Ryugyong Health Complex
- ⑤
- Pyongyang Golden Lane Bowling Alley
- Ice rink
- CHOLLIMA ST
- CHANGGWANG ST
- SOMUN ST
- Russia **E**
- Mansudae Fountain Park
- Foreign Languages Bookshop
- Sungri M
- No 1
- Pyongyang Bell
- Taedong Gate
- Korean Folklore Museum
- Okryu Bridge
- TONGDAEWON ST
- Changgwangsan Health Complex
- Mansudae Art Theatre
- Korean Central History Museum ⑬
- Fountain
- Grand People's Study House
- Kim Il Sung Square
- JUCHETHAP ST
- ⑪
- Korea Documentary Film Studio
- Parade Review Stand
- Underground
- ⑩
- Juche Tower
- CHONGNYON ST
- 'FORBIDDEN ZONE' (GOVERNMENT AREA)
- Korean Art Gallery ⑦
- Fountain
- FLOW
- Taedonggang (unfinished)
- Rodongv Sinmun Headquarters ①
- No 2
- National Theatre
- Taedong Bridge ⑫
- Red Cross Gen
- SAESALLIM ST
- HAEBANGSAN ST
- Party Founding Museum
- Ponghwa M
- Red Cross HQ
- Pyongyang Puppet Theatre ④
- Kim Il Sung-Kim Jong Il Foundation
- E Pyongyang
- Yonggwang M ②
- Pyongyang Medical University Hospital
- Paektusan Architectural Institute
- Pyongyang Grand Theatre
- ⑨
- Korean Stamp Museum
- Chollima House of Culture
- International House of Culture
- Anti-Espionage Exhibition
- Hospital ✚
- YONGGWANG ST
- SOSONG ST
- National Railway Museum
- Kim Chaek University of Technology
- OTAN KANGAN ST
- Taedong
- Pyongyang Station
- Central District Market
- N
- Bradt

> **NOTE**
> For key to accommodation and eating and drinking, see opposite

0 ———— 500m
0 ———— 500yds

Some of the more tired hotels in Pyongyang often quietly quote two figures when it comes to how many rooms they have, one being the total number of rooms, and the other being the number of rooms which that are *actually* functioning as such. Yes, by local standards the hotels are very good, but by Western standards they generally are not. What they are is fun, quirky and unmistakably North Korean. Should you delve down to the more basic hotels in Pyongyang, you may well have no hot water at all – some cannot even offer 24-hour running water. A bathtub full of cold water in your room is a sign that water only runs at select times – this water is intended for manual flushing and cold washing.

At the time of writing, the Taedonggang Hotel is closed for complete renovation while the Sojaegol Guesthouse does not accept 'normal' visitors. Despite works starting back in 1987, the world-famous Ryugyong Hotel remains unfinished (see box, page 98). Note that although we have given the number of rooms for each hotel listed, not all of them will be functioning when you visit.

⌂ **Changgwangsan Hotel** [88 D5] (420 rooms) Just off Chollima St, near the Rakwon Department Store, Air Koryo offices & the ice rink, the Changgwangsan is just about serviceable, with a small range of facilities. It has recently undergone a rather tasteless facelift with a garish glass frontage hiding its delightfully retro 1970s architecture. **$$**

⌂ **Chongnyon Hotel** [88 B4] (520 rooms) The only hotel to boast an outdoor pool (albeit usually without any water), the Chongnyon ('Youth') sadly lost its youth many moons ago. Located on the corner of Kwangbok & Chongchun streets, the hotel is so damp, dire & dilapidated that most of the rooms were mothballed years back. Until a major refurb takes places it should only be considered by those with a twisted sense of humour. **$$**

⌂ **Gobangsan Guesthouse** [89 H3] (24 rooms) Air Koryo has recently branched from being solely an airline to a company that provides a variety of services, offering everything from taxis & petrol stations to soft drinks – & now guesthouses. The Gobangsan is all shiny tiles & comfortable rooms, but not quite the '5-star luxury' they claim. The management feel that it is a true honour to stay here, & are therefore often reluctant to accept bookings from foreign visitors. **$$$$**

⌂ **Haebangsan Hotel** [96 B6] (83 rooms) Located next to the secretive headquarters of *Rodong Sinmun*, the North Korean equivalent of the Russian newspaper *Pravda*, the Haebangsan is a basic but appealing option in the heart of the city. Most guests are North Korean or Chinese, so those interested in sacrificing comfort for the chance of rubbing shoulders with a few 'characters' may want to consider this option, which has a smattering of facilities including a bookshop, restaurant & bar. Proximity to the Taedong River proffers the chance of evening strolls (with a guide, of course). **$$–$$$**

⌂ **Koryo Hotel** [96 A6] (495 rooms) Occupying 2 45-storey towers in the city centre, this hotel has a staggering array of facilities & is arguably the best option for tourists with limited time in Pyongyang, as so much is right on the hotel's doorstep. It also has a marginally greater air of exclusivity about it than the other go-to tourist stalwart, the Yanggakdo. Rooms have a lovely retro 1980s feel, with the plastic bathrooms looking like something from the crew cabin of a cruise ship. The small on-site supermarket is a good spot to stock

THE RYUGYONG HOTEL

Back in the 1980s, the North Korean leadership thought big when it came to prestige projects, with epic feats of civil engineering such as the West Sea Barrage (page 164), together with countless grandiose monuments and buildings still being churned out at an admirable rate, despite gradual economic decline. So, in 1987, when construction started on what would be the world's tallest hotel, a London Shard-esque 105-storey building, the Ryugyong, nobody really batted an eyelid. The plan was that it would be ready within two years, in time for for the 13th World Festival of Youth and Students in June 1989. However, dogged from day one by complications, many of which were down to overly complex design features such as diagonal lifts and not one but five revolving restaurants, the project slowly ground to a halt, much like the Korean economy, in 1992.

Work on the Ryugyong stopped for 16 years, leaving the hotel as a concrete shell as the country soldiered through the Arduous March; even the myrmidons of Kim couldn't justify working on such a vanity project when people were starving. As the economy slowly spluttered back to life, so too did work on the Ryugyong in 2008, with the Egyptian company Orascom kickstarting things, allegedly as a precondition of their being granted a monopoly to run a 3G mobile network in the country (which they also had to install and pay for). The plan was that it would be ready for 2012, the 100th anniversary of Kim Il Sung's birth. However, the grand-opening date came and went, along with a good chunk of Orascom's investment, as they soon came to realise that doing business with North Korea was very rarely a profitable venture. In 2012, Kempinski toyed with running the hotel before running a mile and then, once more, all slowly started to grind to a halt. Clad in glass but, as far as we know, essentially a hollow shell on the inside, little appeared to take place on the construction site for a few more years until 2017, 30 years after works started, when once more construction appeared to resume. It remains to be seen, however, whether the Ryugyong could finally be set to open its doors in the near future.

up on supplies before heading upcountry. **$$$–$$$$**

🏠 **Moranbong Guesthouse** [96 C1] (9 rooms) The closest thing to a boutique hotel in Pyongyang, this is a friendly little mid-range place tucked away in a secluded spot on Moran Hill. Given its long running, size & service it is favoured by locals & longer-term visitors, & is thus almost always fully booked. Even if you are not staying, the good-quality bar & spa facilities are open to non-guests. **$$$$**

🏠 **Potonggang Hotel** [88 D5] (113 rooms) The Potonggang has always typically catered more towards officials, dignitaries & business visitors than tourists, & this is reflected in its service & prices. Given its size, the hotel does not have such a dizzying array of facilities as the

other top-end options. This formerly attractive building has undergone a pretty tasteless change to its façade of late, but it's what's on the inside that counts – comfortable, well-maintained rooms, piping hot water & a decent b/fast. **$$$–$$$$**

🏠 **Pyongyang Hotel** [96 B6] (198 rooms) This 5-storey hotel near the Pyongyang Grand Theatre is rarely used by tourists but is comfortable enough if you're looking for something a bit different, & is home to the city's highly regarded Arirang Restaurant (page 100). Undergoing gradual refurbishment, its prime location near the Taedong River & Kim Il Sung Sq makes it a good option for those who have the time to enjoy escorted city walks, although rooms are best described as 'functional'. **$$–$$$**

🏠 **Rakrang Hotel** [88 D7] (29 rooms)
Although it opened back in 2010, the Rakrang, located on the south bank of the Taedong, has only recently started to accept foreign guests. Despite its small size, there's a surprising range of facilities on offer, including bars, billiards & a barbers. **$$$–$$$$**

🏠 **Ryanggang Hotel** [88 C6] (330 rooms)
Beauty is only skin deep; while looking good from the outside, once inside all manner of horrors will unfold. This hotel in west Pyongyang could be a good option, though it will almost certainly close soon to undergo much-needed refurbishment. For now, expect door handles to come away in your hand, unlit corridors & flashbacks from *The Shining*. **$$–$$$**

🏠 **Sosan Hotel** [88 C5] (530 rooms) Located in sleepy west Pyongyang, the Sosan was a mothballed dive that barely functioned before a massive refurbishment in 2015 turned it into a contender as one of Pyongyang's best hotels. There's a range of facilities including a swimming pool, a bookshop, bars & restaurants. In the summer months a range of pop-up food stalls often materialise in the grounds of the hotel, from where you may be able to walk to the Ryanggang over the road (& breathe a sigh of relief when you see where you could have stayed!). **$$–$$$**

🏠 **Yanggakdo International Hotel** [89 E6] (1,001 rooms) The largest hotel in the country with 47 storeys, the Yanggakdo offers all manner of facilities to potentially keep one busy for days on end, with a great bookshop, many bars & restaurants, a swimming pool, sauna, karaoke, tailor, casino, micro-brewery & much, much more. Once you do get up to your room there is far less excitement – rooms are perfectly functional, clean & comfortable, albeit a little frayed around the edges. **$$$**

✖ WHERE TO EAT AND DRINK

The country has seen a transformation since the not so distant days of the Arduous March. While locals starved, the tiny numbers of foreign travellers coming this way were thankful just to be fed. Food was bland and, at times, bordering on inedible. Restaurants were empty and dimly lit, crumbling linoleum flooring was *de rigueur* and diners had two options: take it, or leave it. In the past decade Pyongyang has enjoyed a culinary revolution, one which is slowly trickling down to the provinces. The number of restaurants and bars in the city is growing at an incredible rate, service has improved and the quality of all on offer is a polar opposite to what was served a generation ago. Food is generally Korean, or occasionally vaguely pan-Oriental as, of course, Pyongyangites have never really known anything else. All hotels have at least one restaurant, sometimes many more, and dining in the revolving restaurants of the Yanggakdo or Koryo is recommended for the views alone. Hotels frequented by foreigners are more likely to have a stab at offering Western dishes, but even then you'll find that it's more likely to be the chefs' interpretation of what foreigners like to eat – you may be better sticking to the foods they know best.

Locals love to barbecue and picnic when the weather is warmer, and on weekends and holidays between May and September the city parks and hills are often busy with groups of friends and families tucking into all-afternoon parties, which can become rather raucous in their own, innocent way.

RESTAURANTS While there are hundreds of restaurants that would happily serve you, a paying customer, the number of dining options available is generally limited to those restaurants that have an agreement in place with the tour operator arranging your package. That said, restrictions are slowly easing, and it isn't inconceivable that tourists may soon be able to eat and drink almost anywhere they wish in the city – of course this will likely mean paying for your guides and driver also, so it could be a costly night out! For now, however, we have listed some of the options that you are more likely to visit as part of your tour.

Other restaurants on the radar that you may consider visiting include the Ryonmot Restaurant in the north of the city, the Hyangmanru and Chongchun restaurants (both on Kwangbok Street), the Songsan in Mangyongdae and the Tongchonho in Taesong which, 'unlike the restaurants in the hurly-burly metropolis, this restaurant is nestled in the gorgeous mountain'.

In addition to the places listed below, a few of the state-run tour operators own their own restaurants, with imaginative names such as the KITC Restaurant and Golden Cup Restaurant as a clue as to who operates them. These restaurants only really cater to tourists and are often pushed by the tour operators – service is usually better than in other restaurants, but the atmosphere can be somewhat lacking.

Central Pyongyang: the north bank

✗ Ansan Restaurant [88 D5] Part of an international complex near the Potonggang Hotel & allegedly under the direction of the Central Committee & Ministry of Foreign Affairs, this quiet spot, which specialises in both Korean & Japanese cuisine, has a touch of class. The small hotel here may in the future accommodate normal tourists – with a bit of work this could be a lovely boutique hotel. $$$$

✗ Arirang Restaurant [96 B6] In the Pyongyang Hotel, this classic restaurant has been churning out fine food for decades. Highly regarded by locals & the few foreigners who dine here. $$$$

✗ Chongryu Restaurant [88 D5] On the Potong River, behind the ice rink, this restaurant can accommodate 1,600 people & offers over 120 Korean dishes. Along with the Okryu Restaurant, the food here is about as traditional as it can get – a Pyongyang institution about to enter its 7th decade. $$$$

✗ Italy Pizza [88 D6] A new pizzeria on Mirae Scientists St. Thanks to its location, tourists looking for a taste of home often come here – locals are still a bit wary of touching dairy so may well opt for the ever-popular raw liver dish instead (which is thankfully not one of the pizza toppings). $$$$

✗ Mujigae (Rainbow) Restaurant [96 C5] A flashy 120m ship moored on the Taedong near Kim Il Sung Sq, this 4-deck complex can cater to 1,230 guests at a time, but the high prices make it feel more like the *Mary Celeste*. $$$$$

✗ National Restaurant [96 B7] In the basement of the International House of Culture & close to the Koryo Hotel, this is a fun option with quirky decorations & occasional music shows. The local speciality is grilled meat & seafood – cooked right at the table. $$$$

✗ Okryu Restaurant [96 C4] Possibly the most famous restaurant in the city, the Okryu is located on the north bank of the Taedong & serves a range of traditional Korean dishes – their Pyongyang cold noodles are regarded as the very best in the country. $$$$

✗ Pyolmuri Restaurant [96 A6] Better for snacks & drinks than for a main meal, the Pyolmuri (near the Koryo Hotel) is more of a café than a restaurant & strives to offer a few dishes with a Western slant – the first of its kind in the city. $$$$

✗ Pyongyang No 1 Boat Restaurant [96 C5] Though now dwarfed by neighbouring Mujigae (see left), this humbler restaurant offers up a more relaxed & fun experience. It's all pretty staple Korean fare, but the staff are jolly &, should they have enough custom, will likely take the boat out for a brief jaunt along the river. $$$

✗ Rakwon (Paradise) Restaurant [88 D5] This bright & modern restaurant has its own micro-brewery & offers up classic Korean fare in a friendly setting near the Changgwangsan Hotel. $$$$

✗ Vienna Café [96 C5] Attached to the Central History Museum, this small café serves up some of the best coffee in town at near-European prices; a good refreshment stop during the winter months. $$$$

Central Pyongyang: the south bank

✗ Chongryu Hotpot [89 F4] A favourite of tour groups, this restaurant near the Romanian Embassy gives diners all the raw ingredients to prepare their own hotpot at the table, making it an ideal option for anybody with dietary requirements, as they have complete control over what goes into their food. Waiting staff are, thankfully, on hand to assist those whose skills do not lie in the kitchen. $$$

✕ Golden Lane Bowling Alley
[96 D4] With a downstairs bar & a couple of basic upstairs restaurants, this venue is often packed full of locals thanks to its central location & reasonable prices. A great spot for people-watching & attempting to mingle with the regulars. $$$

✕ Taedonggang Diplomatic Club [96 C6]
In Tongdaewon District, the Diplomatic Club offers delicious Korean food & a limited range of Western dishes in this restaurant/leisure centre/entertainment complex. It's a popular haunt for local diplomats, so you may well be rubbing shoulders with officials from the nearby Syrian & Mongolian embassies. $$$$

Mangyongdae, Taesong and Pyongyang environs

✕ Kwangbok Circus Restaurant [88 B4]
This is a great & often overlooked option in west Pyongyang attached to the circus, where the speciality is do-it yourself BBQ meats. $$$$

✕ Kwangbok Pizzeria [88 B5] The original Italian in town – a taste of Italy for a respite from Korean cuisine. $$$$

✕ Pyongyang Duck BBQ [88 C7] Diners cook their food at the table at this delicious & ever-popular option on Tongil St. Thankfully, the fantastic 1980s décor has not yet been replaced in the name of 'progress'. $$$

✕ Taedonggang Brewery Restaurant [89 G6]
A fair way out of town, this restaurant is normally the closest you can get to the Taedonggang Brewery. It serves up a number of beers & good food. Often only open by appointment. $$$

BARS Knowing full well that they have a captive market, hotel bars in Pyongyang stay open late, often until the last drinkers decide enough is enough and stumble to their rooms. For those looking for something just a little less sedentary, many hotels also offer karaoke, billiards, table tennis and other innocuous pursuits to keep guests busy. Should you head out with your chaperones, public bars and restaurants normally close earlier than those in the hotels.

♀ Mansugyo Bar [96 A2] One of the few regular bars that tourists may visit (sadly the excellent Gyonghung Bar is not accepting tourists at present as they 'bothered' the regulars). Sinking a couple of beers here while rubbing shoulders with the local lads is a merry way to spend an hour (or 2)! $$

♀ Taedonggang Bar No 3 [96 D5] Near the Juche Tower, this bar is all rather bling, but a good spot for mid-afternoon refreshment before continuing your urban exploration. $$$

TAEDONGGANG BEER

Considered the DPRK's premium lager, Taedonggang (literally, Taedong River) comes in a few varieties and seems to go from strength to strength as it increasingly dominates the domestic market, but its past is arguably more interesting that its present and future. This brewery in Pyongyang's Sadong District originally hails from Wiltshire, specifically the Ushers of Trowbridge brewery, which closed in 2000. Dismantled, sold and shipped from England to North Korea and rebuilt brick by brick, Taedonggang started brewing in 2002 and hasn't looked back. In 2016, the brewery hosted the first **Taedonggang Beer Festival**, held – where else – on the banks of its namesake river. The outside world seemed shocked at the prospect of a beer festival taking place in Pyongyang – presumably people never thought that North Koreans enjoy tucking into a few beers just like billions of others do the world over. Judging by the looks of a few people the morning after, it appears that some may have enjoyed themselves a little too much.

ENTERTAINMENT AND NIGHTLIFE

The preferred evening entertainment in Pyongyang is normally sitting around the restaurant table picking at leftovers, chatting, drinking and toasting to friendship, peace, loved ones and the like; the men often smoke and slowly get sozzled while the ladies retain their decorum to the last. Drunken debauchery, genuine nightclubs in the Western sense and venues trading in the sins of the flesh are either non-existent or the closest guarded secret in the country, although all sorts of saucy shenanigans are alleged to take place in the palaces. While your guides may roll their eyes at the suggestion, for many the most excitement of an evening could well be an accompanied city walk, allowing you to marvel at how dark, safe and sleepy Pyongyang is as the witching hour approaches, in what must be one of the quietest capital cities on earth.

SHOPPING

Public markets are off-limits and the closest you will likely get to an authentic department store or supermarket is the Kwangbok Area Shopping Centre (page 121). Though no shopper's paradise, the dazzling array of bizarre souvenirs available in Pyongyang induces most visitors to go home with a fair few quirky trinkets such as CDs, badges, models of major monuments and socialist-realist artworks.

The Foreign Languages Publishing House is the main printer in town and they churn out everything from tiny pamphlets to excess-baggage-inducing coffee-table books about the exploits of the greats and such like. Most hotels will have a bookshop of sorts and their main outlet is in the city centre, near Kim Il Sung Square [96 C4]. This bookshop occasionally sells artworks and propaganda posters, but fine art is best sourced at outlets such as the Mansudae Art Studio (page 113), where works by merited artists can cost in the thousands of dollars. Philatelists should head to the Korean Stamp Museum [96 A7] near the Koryo Hotel, and most of the larger hotels have a tailor that you can use to have a suit or dress knocked up in the local style. Owing to their guiding philosophy of Juche, an awful lot of goods are manufactured in Pyongyang, and they are ostensibly available to you, too. So, while the tourist shops don't sell locally made accordions or megaphones, for example, it doesn't mean that they aren't available. If you are desperate for a particular item, mention it to your guide – you may be surprised with the result. The friendly DHL office in the same block as the Ministry of Foreign Affairs will, for a pretty penny, ship worldwide. They are normally happy to come to your hotel in Pyongyang to pack and process your shipment.

WHAT TO SEE AND DO

CENTRAL DISTRICT (CHUNG) (중구역) With a wealth of interest in a relatively compact area, Pyongyang's Central (Chung) District is the crème de la crème of this showcase city, home to mind-boggling buildings, secret government quarters, monuments, museums, mystery and more. There is something here for everyone, and enough to keep you entertained and baffled in equal dose as you stagger and stumble from one surprise to the next.

Kim Il Sung Square [96 C5] The heart of the nation, Kim Il Sung Square will be instantly recognisable to anyone who has ever seen North Korea on the evening news – being home to the key military parades, mass dances, torchlight processions and other such spectacles that have become such a distinctive image of the country. Standing at the back of the 75,000m² square with the Taedong River behind you, the

Korean Art Gallery is to your left and Korean Central History Museum to your right. Immediately in front of you, the smiling images of the leaders will beam back at you, the small stone in front of them being Point Zero, from where all road distances in the country are measured. These portraits adorn the **Parade Review Stand**, from where the generals and majors lord and laud over the masses during parades and such. The parades, celebrations and events are held with far less frequency than one may expect and, unless you have friends in very high places, you won't get within a mile of the square when the really big guns do roll in, though you may manage to rub shoulders with the locals from a suitable spot at the side of the road a little way out, to try and catch a glimpse of a tank or two (hundred). Behind the parade stand, the large traditional building providing the backdrop to the Square is the ten-storey **Grand People's Study House** (see below). Heading to the west of the square, the building to your left is the **Ministry Of Foreign Trade**, while to your right is the **Headquarters of the Workers' Party of Korea**. The parade ground itself is flanked by the **Cabinet Secretariat** and the **Ministry of Foreign Affairs**; all highlighting just how important this area is.

Like the square itself, the **Korean Art Gallery** [96 C5] was built in 1954. It contains 22 display rooms, exhibiting everything from 4th-century tomb murals to 21st-century oil paintings depicting the construction of the latest hydro-electric dam. There are some stunning pieces on show here and lovers of socialist-realist art will be in their element. Across the square, the **Korean Central History Museum** [96 C5] claims to squeeze over 110,000 objects into its collection. The museum is a little dank and dusty and explanations are all a little over-simplified and politicised at times, but if you have any interest in the country before Kim Il Sung was born – and a couple of spare hours – then it's worth the visit. However, most tourists these days come just for the Vienna Café (page 100), which has its own entrance on the southeast corner of the building.

The Grand People's Study House

The museums on the square are overshadowed in more ways than one by the big draw on the square: the Grand People's Study House [96 B5]. With some 30 million books and over 600 rooms able to accommodate 12,000 visitors each day, the study house is hailed by the local guides as 'an important centre for intellectualisation for the whole of society'. Language courses, specialist lectures, computer classes and a wide range of ostensibly free programmes take place here that all and sundry may attend, as long as you have your Pyongyang-issued library card to hand. The cavernous building opened in 1982 and is a sight to behold – draped and caked in so much marble, granite and grandiosity that this could *only* be North Korea, but in case you need reminding of where you are, the two clocks adorning the front of the building play the 'Song of General Kim Il Sung'. Tourists typically enter through the VIP east entrance, where one of the most impressive light fittings in the country illuminates a stone statue of a seated Kim Il Sung reading a newspaper, a faint smile on his lips. Behind him, a moody mosaic of Mount Paektu provides a suitably revolutionary backdrop to this wonderfully over-the-top room. From here, your tour will take in a plethora of rooms such as a study and reading room or two, together with a language class, 'book-lending stand', lecture hall and an audio/video room. Year in, year out, visitors in the oft-empty audio/video room will likely be availed the opportunity of listening to a bootlegged CD by The Beatles or Simply Red – given the lack of people in the room Mick Hucknall's dulcet tones are clearly enough to scare most away from further forays into the world of Western pop. The tour will likely culminate in squeezing into a lift to take you up to the grand viewing balcony, which affords unparalleled views down to Kim Il Sung Square, across central Pyongyang and over to another of Kim Il Sung's birthday presents, the perfectly aligned Juche Tower.

The 'Forbidden Zone' and Haebangsan

Behind the Grand People's Study House, the Haebangsan-dong, Changgwang-dong No 2 and Sochang-dong areas are very much off-limits to foreigners and locals alike, although your driver will cleverly skirt around town in such a way that you may not even realise you are making detours to avoid entering these parts, which house many offices, residences and facilities for the very top echelons of the government and military. Along the southern boundary of this hidden forbidden zone, Haebangsan Street is home to the Haebangsan Hotel (page 97) and the office of the *Rodong Sinmun* newspaper [96 B6], controlled by the Workers' Party of Korea. Heading west, buildings such as the **National Theatre**, **Anti-Espionage Exhibition** and **Pyongyang Puppet Theatre** [96 B6], the last a rare example of Japanese colonial-era architecture, will also be bypassed, as even your guides cannot pull the necessary strings to get you inside. The **Party Founding Museum** [96 A6], just beyond Ponghwa Metro Station, is another Japanese colonial building that takes visitors back to how the DPRK all started; it is this very building that functioned as party headquarters in those early days. Inside the grounds lie the house where Kim Il Sung lived in 1945–49, while the garden pond is possibly the spot where Kim Jong Il's baby brother, Man Il, drowned while they played together, something Kim Jong Il seemingly never truly recovered from.

Changgwang, Yokjon and Yonggwang streets

To the southwest of the museum lies Changgwang Street [96 A6], which runs south for 800m to Pyongyang Station (page 113). This well-manicured avenue (locals have been spotted maintaining the grass verges with scissors, dustpans and brushes) has a good number of restaurants, but the first major building of note is the **Koryo Hotel** (page 97), one of the biggest and best places to stay in the city. The **Korean Stamp Museum** [96 A7] is just a couple of doors down from the hotel and is more shop than museum – it's well worth popping in for a quick look, though, as besides stamps it offers prints and souvenirs that you may not see elsewhere.

Around the corner and near the river, transport buffs may want to take in the **National Railway Museum** [96 A7]. Despite its name, this museum is more about politics than the railways, with oversized oil paintings brushing over history and lashings of marble flooring leading you from one echoey hall to the next as you learn where the leaders travelled by train and of the exploits of the merited engineers who built it all. Your tour will finish with a splendid diorama depicting father and son on site in a dramatic railway construction scene, followed by visiting a handful of historical locomotives and wagons. The blocks behind the museum are home to the blue-roofed **Central District Market** and **Kim Chaek University of Technology** [96 B7], but these areas are out of bounds.

The major road leading northeast from the station is **Yonggwang Street** [96 A7], an approved walking route for tourists. From west to east you will pass a cluster of shops and restaurants before you come to the **Chollima House of Culture** [96 B6] and the **International House of Culture** [96 B7], a largely ignored complex built in 1988 to promote cultural exchanges with the outside world. The building is also home to an exhibition hall of folk musical instruments from a number of non-aligned and developing countries, exhibits that excite few locals and even fewer tourists. Not many people come here, but the **National Restaurant** in the basement (page 100) is as fine a spot as any for dinner.

A detour to the road behind Yonggwang, near the Pyongyang Medical University Hospital, will take you to the **Paektusan Architectural Institute** [96 B6], where interested parties can, by appointment, get a brief insight into the grand urban plans of tomorrow, possibly meeting with an architect or two in the process. The ostentatious painting in the reception of the institute, a stylised montage of almost every notable Pyongyang building and landmark, is something to behold and it's almost worth coming to the institute for this alone. Back on Yonggwang, on passing the Otan Children's Park the road ends with the **Pyongyang Grand Theatre** [96 B6], a monumental building at the southern end of Sungri Street. The theatre, which has over 2,200 seats, is home to the Phibida Opera Troupe, famed for their Revolutionary Opera (see box, below). Performances are rare, but if you are fortunate to be in town while something is on you should jump at the chance – the scale of these shows is epic.

The route from here to Kim Il Sung Square (1km away) is often covered as a walking tour of the city, passing the **Pyongyang Hotel** (page 98) and the **National Theatre** [96 B6], as well as the **Taedonggang Hotel** [96 B6], which has been undergoing refurbishment for some years. For a change of scenery, you could also walk along the pedestrianised riverbank towards the square, which will lead past floating restaurants such as the Mujigae Restaurant (page 100) and the back of the headquarters of the Kim Il Sung-Kim Jong Il Foundation (see box, page 106).

Taedong Gate and Ryongwang Pavilion   Heading northeast from the square, the **Taedong Gate** [96 C4] or Taedongmun is a photogenic slice of the days of old, a juxtaposition to the high-rise buildings of nearby Changjon Street. This was the eastern gate of the inner castle of Pyongyang Castle and dates back to the 6th century, although the current structure is from 1635. It is claimed that the iron chain hanging from the upper storey of the gate was taken from from the *General Sherman*, the American ship that sunk on the river in 1866. The next little building

---

KOREAN REVOLUTIONARY OPERA

North Korea's socialist-realist themes wonderfully tread the boards at the Revolutionary Opera, where the stage productions are so fantastically flamboyant and production values so high that a performance cannot fail to impress even the most seasoned theatregoer. These melodramatic routines, influenced by the style of opera that developed during the Chinese Cultural Revolution, glorify all that is great in the world of North Korea, with socialism and the indomitable Korean spirit winning out in the end in a battle of good against evil.

The five Revolutionary Operas are largely credited as being either written or produced by either Kim Il Sung or Kim Jong Il, and Kim Jong Il's book, *On the Art of Opera,* is the go-to tome on the subject. The first, and arguably most famous, opera, *The Sea of Blood* is reputed to be a father/son effort and premiered in 1971, with the plot reflecting the 'burning hatred' of the Korean people against Japanese imperialists that 'turned the country into the sea of blood'. *The Flower Girl* followed in 1972, and teaches 'that the people of a stateless nation who have been deprived of their own sovereignty are more dead than alive'. *Tell O' the Forest* and *The Song of Mount Kumgang* also push the overt anti-Japanese theme, while the fifth and final opera, *A True Daughter of the Party,* is the only one set in the Korean War.

in this strip of land houses the **Pyongyang Bell** [96 C4], which weighs 13,000kg and dates to 1726; although it once tolled at dawn and nightfall to inform the locals of the curfew, this came to a halt in 1894. The last historical building of note before coming into Okryu Street is the **Ryongwang Pavilion** [96 C4]. Constructed in 1111 but rebuilt in 1670, the pavilion is as good a place as any in this pocket of Pyongyang to rest up and enjoy a spot of people-watching, this being a popular location for student artists to work on their city- and riverscapes. Beside the pavilion, a small stone, the **Monument To Kye Wol Hyang**, commemorates this *kisaeng* (akin to a geisha) who assisted in the assassination of a Japanese commander in the Imjin Wars, losing her life in the process. She is now considered a heroine for her sacrifice, with books and a popular TV drama serialising her life.

North of Kim Il Sung Square

Immediately to the north of Kim Il Sung Square, the **Korean Folklore Museum** [96 C5] covers everything from the primitive age to the 19th century across seven halls, but is rather forlorn and in need of significant renovation. Around the corner from the museum, the **Foreign Language Bookshop** is a must-see shopping stop and a great spot to witness one of Pyongyang's many glamorous traffic women doing their thing at this important junction. Opposite the bookshop, going into the large **No 1 Department Store** [96 C5] is *verboten*, but if you have arranged a private trolleybus tour of Pyongyang (page 94) you may enjoy a spot of window shopping while the logistics for the charter, which starts from here, are finalised. Some of the streets beyond here were redeveloped in 2012, the centenary of Kim Il Sung's birth, with new apartment blocks, restaurants and facilities being constructed in a development known as **Changjon Street**. This was one of the first significant developments unveiled in Kim Jong Un's era and is home to the **Mansudae People's Theatre** [96 C4], where the sexy sirens that are the Moranbong Band have been known to perform, their routines getting an awful lot of the Alpha Double-Plus men who manage to obtain tickets very hot under the collar. The striking theatre, which seldom opens its doors to foreign visitors, is a little garish in its design and would sit better in Beijing than Pyongyang, but is seen as another symbol of modernity in a city where the classic architecture of yesteryear is under increasing threat, all in the name of 'progress'.

Just to the south of the Changjon Street development, on Sungri Street, the two-screen **Taedongmun Cinema** [96 C4] was built in 1955 but underwent significant renovations in 2008. This attractive building with faux Greek columns is the flagship building for screening domestic premieres to a select VIP audience. Facing the cinema, the **Pyongyang Students and Children's Palace** [96 B4] was established in 1963 and is very similar in content and function to the Mangyongdae Schoolchildren's Palace (page 122), although this is the original and best (according to those who studied here). Gifted students come here after school to hone their skills in a number of specific fields. Over 500 rooms give extra-curricular classes in all manner of subjects, from embroidery or boxing to meteorology – seemingly everything is covered, including the performing arts, with a tour typically culminating in a top-notch performance that highlights the sheer talent of these children. The palace is typically open for tours and performances on Tuesdays only.

Behind the Children's Palace, the **Sungnyong Temple** and **Sungin Temple** [96 C4] are so long forgotten that they will almost certainly not be pointed out to you – should you wish to have a nosey round a fair few telephone calls may need to be made to find somebody to unlock the doors of these small buildings, which date to 1429 and 1325 respectively. Of more interest will be the **Mansudae Fountain Park** [96 B5] at the southern foot of Mansu Hill, with its fountains and paved grounds providing a cool respite on those hot summer days. The 'Snow Falls' sculpture of 28 dancing ladies gives a nod to the impressive performances that must take place in the building immediately behind it, the famous **Mansudae Art Theatre** [96 B5], which is only accessible, it seems, to the elite. Those with the time, willing legs and a willing guide may walk from here to the Mansudae Grand Monument (see below), passing the Hakdanggol Fountain Park as you go. To the west of the theatre, the **Russian Embassy** [96 B4] dominates a large site, its prime location telling of former times, with the USSR having such an integral role in the foundation, development and survival of the DPRK. This area is on the northern edge of the aforementioned 'Forbidden Zone'; many of the local kiddies attend the **Changgwang Kindergarten** [96 B5], where visitors will likely enjoy a spot of play time, take in a polished song and dance routine or two and likely come away feeling that the East Asian teaching methods could well shake up a few classrooms back home.

The **Mansudae Assembly Hall** [96 B4] on Mansu Hill is the seat of the Supreme People's Assembly. In the past, this 1980s building with its main 2,000-seat plenary hall featured on more select tours of Pyongyang, but these days visits are incredibly rare, though well worth requesting. The hall lies approximately 400m to the south of the **Korean Revolution Museum** [96 B3], which has over 90 rooms all covering various facets of the revolution in minutiae. Apparently it takes a week to properly look around the museum, so should you visit, do request a concise tour of just the highlights, which may include a short and distressing video showcasing the news of the death and subsequent period of national mourning for Kim Il Sung, complete with screaming children and grief-stricken citizens collapsing in shock as the world as they knew it fell in on itself.

Mansudae Grand Monument [96 B3] The big draw on Mansu Hill is the unmissable landmark that is the Mansudae Grand Monument, the 20m-tall twin statues of Kim Il Sung and Kim Jong Il. Originally built in 1972 for Kim Il Sung's 60th birthday, the statue of Kim Jong Il was added hastily in 2012, after his passing. Kim Il Sung's statue was tweaked when his progeny was placed beside him – the father's formerly stern face has aged and mellowed, now wearing a smile, his outstretched right arm and body language appearing to say to his son, 'just look at what we have achieved', as they look out proudly across the skyline of their city. When Kim Jong Il's statue was initially unveiled he wore a jacket, akin to his father's, but within a few months this was changed and he now appears in a more casual parka, as he so often wore in his later years. Behind the statues a 70m-long, 12.85m-high mural of Mount Paektu forms a strong revolutionary backdrop, while they are flanked by two bellicose group sculptures, depicting 229 figures in total (120 on the right and 109 on the left, if you must know).

A visit to this grand monument is serious; all visitors are 'expected' (read: obliged) to present flowers and bow, and generally to be polite, deferential and to carry themselves with a sense of decorum at all times. Hats and sunglasses should be removed and you will be expected to all line up in a row (if in doubt, just mimic what all the locals are doing), while your host says a few words. Photography is permitted, but you well be 'asked' (read: ordered) to do this after respects have been paid, and to ensure that any photographs of the leaders are of their full bodies, not cropped in any way. Locals may well ascend to the monument by the steps from Sungri Street below, but weak-willed Westerners are expected to be too lazy to manage this and will normally take a shortcut, approaching via the small car park to the south of the monument. The importance of this spot, which has a constant stream of visitors, cannot be stressed enough, this is hallowed land for these semi-divine men and is, along with the Kumsusan Palace of The Sun (page 124), the most sacred spot in the country – if you are not prepared to bow or be respectful it is best not to go at all as you will only cause problems and offence.

To the northern corner of the monument and overlooking Chilsongmun Street below, the **Chollima Statue** [96 B3] symbolises the Chollima Movement (see box, page 18). The photogenic monument comprises a 32m pedestal with a 14m bronze statue atop it, depicting a worker and peasant riding Chollima – the legendary winged horse, akin to Pegasus, that can travel approximately 400km a day. The worker is holding a document from the Central Committee of the Workers' Party of Korea while the peasant holds a sheaf of rice, as they valiantly surge forward. Next to the base of the statue and visible from Chilsongmun, three large propaganda billboards used to show some striking anti-US artworks, but the vitriol has been toned down of late, to the annoyance of most tourists.

Moran Hill and around

From Okryu Street it's a short walk to the southern fringes of **Moran Hill** [96 C2] or Moranbong. This sprawling parkland, the so-called 'garden of the capital', boasts forested hilly grounds and a network of paths rising to 95m above sea level. A leisurely couple of hours can easily be spent in this park, which is an extremely popular spot for Pyongyangites to wind down as they take in the views, enjoy a picnic or pressgang passing tourists into joining them for a spot of singing and dancing. Finding a suitable spot to sit and watch the world go by is most enjoyable, so if your time and guides permit this is exactly what you should do, ideally on a Sunday when the grounds are busiest. The hill is home to over 180 varieties of tree and 120 species of flower, but it's the overall atmosphere and scenery that makes Moran Hill stand out. Peppered with historical relics such as remnants of the walls of the inner fort of Pyongyang Castle and the Ulmil Pavilion, the grounds are home to over 1,500 years of history, from the Koguryo-era through to the Kim Dynasty.

In the southern fringes of the park, the Youth Open-Air Theatre will be bypassed, with most visitors making an initial beeline for the **Liberation Tower** [96 C3], a 30m-tall monument built to commemorate the Soviet Union's 'involvement' in the liberation of Korea. Constructed in 1946 but rebuilt in 1985 this monument is, like the Friendship Tower (page 112), one of the few overt references to assistance from foreign powers in those early days. The Kumnung Tunnel runs under the ground here and from this hillock a good vista of Rungna Islet and the opposite bank of the river is an indicator of the views to come as you press on.

An alternative path on the southern slopes of Moran Hill leads to the **Moranbong Theatre** [96 C3], home of the National Symphony Orchestra of the DPRK. The theatre opened in 1946 and last underwent refurbishment in 2006. The attractive building (which in 1948 held the first session of the Supreme People's Assembly where the foundation of the DPRK was declared) has a seating capacity of 800 and performances, which you can attend with prior arrangement, take place a few times each week.

A little to the west of the theatre, **Chilsong Gate** [96 C2] (the 'gate of love') was originally a 6th-century northern gate of the inner fort, but what stands today is a reconstruction dating to 1712. Slowly ascending, the various paths will take you by other relics of days gone by, such as the Tongam Gate and Chongryu Pavilion, but the most impressive vista is arguably from **Ulmil Pavilion** [96 C2]. Built in the 6th century as the northern command post for the inner fort of the walled city, the pavilion was rebuilt in 1714 and proffers a good panorama, particularly to the north and east. Your guides will plead ignorance, but the traditional green-tiled roofed buildings below you, between Ulmil and the river, comprise the **Hungbu Guesthouse**, where heavyweight heads of state such as Castro, Tito, Gaddafi and Ceauşescu all stayed back in the good old days. On the eastern flanks of the hill, the Chongnyu Cliffs drop steeply down to the river, so it is an ideal location to secrete a VIP compound; should you want to try and get a closer look at the guesthouse you could always ask to visit the **Pubyok Pavilion** [96 C2] or to head up to Choesung Pavilion, the highest point in the park – but the answer will likely be no.

Tongsong-dong and Potongmun-dong
From the heights of Mansu Hill down to the Potong River, a fair few places of interest can be found in the neighbourhoods of Tongsong-dong and Potongmun-dong. The **Rakwon Department Store** [88 D5] is a hard currency shop selling imported foodstuffs and goods to the same type of people who can afford to eat in the Rakwon (Paradise) Restaurant next door (page 100). You may want to come here to stock up on supplies, but the most interesting thing for most is to see the curious selection of goods on sale and to ponder how and why they ended up here – such as Argentinian beer.

Occupying an entire city block to the north is the **Changgwangsan Health Complex** [96 A5]. Opened in April 1980, this sprawling four-storeyed building can accommodate up to 16,000 visitors a day and has a bathhouse, indoor swimming pool, wading pool, barbers, massage, beauticians and more. The swimming pool includes diving boards and a 2,028-seat auditorium, and is used for competitions and occasional synchronised swimming performances (which the North Koreans can do *very* well). The health complex accepts foreigners, but to a confusing timetable – if you fancy a spot of pampering or paddling in a wonderfully retro North Korean setting then this is the place. From the Chongryu Restaurant, just around the corner, a leisurely walk of 1.4km will take you past the ice rink, Pyongyang Indoor Stadium and People's Palace of Culture, finishing up beside the Potong Gate. The **ice rink** [96 A5], like so many buildings in Pyongyang, opened in April 1982 and is a striking piece of architecture, with its conical shape and 24 supporting pillars appearing like the blades of an ice skate. If you want to pop in for a quick look inside the 6,000-seat rink it shouldn't be a problem, but the venue is best seen in February when it hosts the Paektusan Prize International Figure Skating Festival.

Next door, the 20,000-seat **Pyongyang Indoor Stadium** [96 A5] hosts occasional events, but most visitors come this way on national holidays, as the grounds in front of the stadium often host mass dances. The final grandiose building on the block is the **People's Palace of Culture** [96 A4], which hosts a number of domestic and international cultural events and is often the allocated venue for the few foreign acts and artists who venture to Pyongyang. Performances open to tourists here have been known to happen, but are extremely rare. The last stop on this stretch will be the **Potong Gate** [96 A4] or Potongmun. With a granite base topped with a two-storey pavilion, this was the western gate to the central fort of Pyongyang. Originally built in the 6th century, the gate was rebuilt in 1473 and again in 1955 after the devastation of the Korean War. Despite being listed as National Treasure No 3, you will not stop here unless you ask, and it may not even be pointed out, such is the general disinterest in such things among the proletariat of Pyongyang.

Rungna Island

Accessible via either Rungna Bridge or Chongryu Bridge, Rungna Island [96 D2] sits on the Taedong to the northeast of Kim Il Sung Square. The island is all about sports and entertainment, with its southern portion dominated by the **Rungna People's Pleasure Park** [96 D2], home to a small outdoor waterpark (Rungna Alpamare), the Rungna Dolphinarium, which has recently become even more popular now that seals have been added to the repertoire, a mini-golf course and the Rungna Amusement Park. Opened in 2012, this offers rides such as 'Octopus' and 'Sky Drop', while those wanting to try and shake off their tour guides would be recommended to explore the 990m^2 maze which, it is claimed, was designed with the help of Kim Jong Un. Do bear in mind, though, that the amusement park operates in a similar fashion to the Kaeson Youth Park, with vague opening hours that appear to be something of a national secret (page 112). The working schedules of all the spots in the park are confusing, erratic and limited – if you fancy a few hours of fun and frolics you will need to get your guides to check in advance.

To the north of the Chongryu Bridge, the Rungrado 1st of May Stadium, normally just referred to as the **May Day Stadium** [89 F3], has either 150,000 or 114,000 seats, depending on who's counting, but even the conservative count makes it the world's largest stadium. Completed in 1989, the stadium hosted the opening and closing ceremonies of the 13th World Festival of Youth and Students as well as, more famously, Arirang – better known as the Mass Games (see box, page 78). Local men, who have nearly all done some form of national service, will tell you that the stadium resembles a parachute, while women (these same men will tell you), think it looks like a magnolia flower. Interested visitors can, by special arrangement, arrange a tour of the stadium, which in 2015 was renovated into a bright, modern facility. Tours typically take in the pitch and many of the interior facilities, such as training and meeting rooms.

If you haven't had enough sport already, the northern tip of the island is home to the **Pyongyang International Football School**, a boarding school training up the football stars of tomorrow. This modern complex opened in 2013 and homes hundreds of children from across the country. Finally, a **ssireum (Korean wrestling) ring** is tucked away on the island. This open-air ring is sporadically used for traditional events such as the Grand Ox and Gold Bell prize National Wrestling Championship, which is held for a few days during Chuseok, a harvest festival that takes place each year from the 14th to the 16th day of the eighth lunar month (typically being September or early October).

Yanggak Island

Cut off from all the fun of Pyongyang by the Taedong River and only accessible by the Yanggak Bridge, Yanggak Island [89 E6] (its name meaning 'sheep's horn' – reflecting how it looks on a map if you *really* use your imagination) is home to the infamous **Yanggakdo International Hotel** (page 99), where a good portion of all foreign visitors to the country stay. Heading from the hotel on the north tip of the island towards the south, you will first come to the **Pyongyang International Cinema House** [89 E6], a six-screen cineplex perplexingly used for the biennial Pyongyang International Film Festival and practically nothing else. The southern portion of the island is home to the 30,000-seat **Yanggakdo Football Stadium** [89 E6], which regularly holds domestic matches and occasional international games. Behind the stadium, **Yanggakdo Sports Village** opened in 2012 and and boasts of its modern training facilities and sporting alumni. The village is also home to the Kigwancha (Locomotive) Sports Club, a club belonging to the Korean State Railways that is famed for its men's and women's football teams. While not a normal spot on tours of Pyongyang, special-interest sports groups occasionally come this way.

MORANBONG (모란봉구역) Immediately to the northeast of the Central District, Moranbong literally translates as 'Peony Hill', the name of the sprawling and densely forested hill and parkland that takes up a significant portion of this district.

In the south of the district, to the northwest of Mansu Hill, the **Kim Jong Suk Nursery** [96 B3] is named after Kim Il Sung's wife and a visit here will allow you to see these little nippers take their very first tentative steps on the road of the revolution. Of course, this is one of the best nurseries in the country; its location alone is enough to prove that these children, from 2½ to four years of age, were born with a silver spoon – or chopsticks – in their mouths. Regardless, it is a pleasure to see these happy healthy children, many of whom are boarders, as they are taught to 'love labour, treasure national and public wealth and treat their friends so fondly'. Heading west from the nursery the road comes to the Potong River and Yongung Street, where the first building of note is the **Korean People's Army Circus** [96 B3], open with far less frequency than the larger Pyongyang Circus (page 121). The soldiers put on an impressive act, with some of the trapeze and high-wire spectacles being so nervewracking they can be hard to watch. Built in 1964 but refurbished at least twice since, the circus accommodates up to 1,600 people and the occasional bear. If the circus isn't open you can always opt to drown your sorrows a few hundred metres further up the road at the **Mansugyo Bar** (page 101).

The **Arch of Triumph** [96 B2] in central Moranbong is a major city landmark that all visitors should take in, even if just for a brief photography stop. Unveiled on Kim Il Sung's 70th birthday (he was a very lucky boy – he was also given the Juche Tower and a few other gifts on this day), this 60m-tall arch is not only 10m taller than the paltry Arc de Triomphe but also 7.5m wider. Comprising 10,500 granite blocks, the arch has a small number of rooms, lifts and an observation platform, which is often closed, so if you are keen to ascend it may be worth asking your guide to telephone ahead. The face of the arch is inscribed with the lyrics to the 'Song of General Kim Il Sung', while the years 1925 and 1945 denote the 20 years Kim spent on the road of national liberation. The four columns of the arch bear intricate reliefs, but the most impressive aspect of the arch (as with many monuments in the country) is its ostentatious scale.

East of the Arch, the **Kim Il Sung Stadium** [96 C3] is at the foot of Moran Hill, and those looking for a longer foray on foot into the park would be recommended to enter from here (or the Kaeson Youth Park) with a guide and slowly meander south along the network of footpaths towards the Liberation Tower or Moranbong Theatre. The stadium lies on a patch of land where Kim Il Sung delivered his first public speech after liberation on 14 October 1945. At the time, Kim was essentially an unknown, but the event is painted in the country as a watershed moment, of the triumphant return of a hero. The stadium itself was originally built by the Japanese in 1926 but Girimri Stadium (as it was then known) didn't survive the Korean War. Moranbong Stadium replaced it in 1969 but it was rebuilt and renamed the Kim Il Sung Stadium in April 1982 – another 70th birthday gift for Mr Kim. The stadium was last refurbished in 2016 and boasts 40,000 seats, hosting domestic and occasional international football matches, all of which may be attended.

At the northwest end of the stadium, the **Autographic Monument of Triumphal Speech** is a large mosaic mural depicting Kim's aforementioned speech. The square in front of the mosaic doubles up as a car park for the Kaeson Youth Park, but is best seen on national holidays, when it's often a popular spot for mass dancing. To the northeast of the square, the **Kaeson Youth Park** [96 C1] opened in 1984 but was massively overhauled in 2010 with new, imported rides. The park is normally open in the early evenings during the warmer months, most commonly on Fridays, Saturdays and public holidays. In addition to the rides, the park has a number of food outlets and the forlorn **Ryonghwa Temple** [96 C1] within its grounds. Foreigners pay elevated prices to enjoy the rides (much like at all funfairs in Pyongyang), the only upside of which is that one does not have to join the queues, which can be *very* long.

Conspicuous from anywhere in this part of town, the 150m-tall **Pyongyang TV Tower** [96 C1] is another landmark building in the capital. The restaurant about three-quarters of the way up the tower (thankfully accessed via a lift with a backup generator) was one of the best in Pyongyang and proffered wonderful panoramic views of the city, but sadly tourists have not been able to visit for some years. Do ask if it is possible, however, as it will surely reopen at some point.

The **Friendship Tower** [96 C1] sits on a small hillock to the west of the TV Tower. Constructed in 1959 in memory of 'the Chinese People's Volunteers who helped the Korean people with blood in the Korean war', this 30m-tall tower is far less impressive that the Liberation Tower; nevertheless, a quick photographic stop cannot hurt, as it is also a good spot for views of the TV Tower. You can impress your guides by informing them that the tower comprises 1,025 blocks, symbolising 25 October, the date China joined the war. Just 500m from the Friendship Tower, the **Jonsung Revolutionary Site** [96 C1] was a command centre during the Korean War and contains a small network of underground tunnels and meeting rooms used by Kim Il Sung from 1951–53. The museum adds a little clarity in this lesser-visited site, which those with more than a passing interest in the Korean War would do well to consider visiting.

In a wedge of land between Pipa Street and the Ryonghung River, the monolithic **April 25th House of Culture** [89 E3] is not open to tourists, as the two theatres, with 6,000 and 1,100 seats respectively, typically hold major military events and official state ceremonies, such as the 7th Congress of the Workers' Party of Korea, held in 2016. At the end of the line in Moranbong, near Jonu Metro Station and at the west end of the avenue that leads to the mausoleum, the **Metro Construction Museum** [89 E3] houses an extremely impressive diorama of Kim Il Sung giving on-the-spot guidance down at the coalface, but only railway enthusiasts will gauge much interest in the other exhibits, which are more concerned with the depths of a personality cult than they are the impressive metro system.

PYONGCHON (평천구역)
Hemmed in by water on three sides and with the railway and Sosong Street marking its eastern boundary, Pyongchon District is something of an industrial zone for Pyongyang, with numerous factories keeping

Pyongyang running and most tourists away. Still, there are a few places of interest here, starting with one of the capital's landmark buildings, **Pyongyang Station** [96 A7]. While a station has been here since 1906, the current building dates to 1958 and its impressive façade is archetypical 1950s socialist architecture, capped with a clock tower, two bronze statues of workers and the omnipresent portraits of Kim Il Sung and Kim Jong Il. A small food court can be found outside the station catering to domestic travellers and Pyongyangites, while the nearby trolleybus, tram and metro stations add to the general hubbub, making this one of the most animated spots in the entire city. Even if you are not travelling by train, a quick visit to see the exterior of the station is recommended. Unfortunately, the interior is normally only possible to visit should you be arriving or departing by train, but it can't hurt to try your luck and ask.

Pressing on, in the north of Pyongchon a green strip of land of approximately 900m by 200m is home to a vaguely delineated area assigned and designed with foreigners in mind with, from east to west, the **Ansan Complex** [88 D5], **World Peace Centre** [88 D5] and the **Potonggang Hotel** (page 98) all located here. The latter two sights are associated with the Unification Church, better known as the 'Moonies', who have done a lot of work behind the scenes in the country over the years (see box, page 114).

Heading further south, the **Mansudae Art Studio** [88 D5] is a massive state-run complex that produces everything from tourist trinkets to the giant bronze statues of the great leaders scattered all over the country. With around 4,000 employees it is believed to be the largest centre of art production in the world. While the majority of the works are for domestic consumption, the artists here are considered true specialists in their field; their creations can be found from Angola to Zimbabwe and include the Angkor Panorama Museum in Cambodia and the African Renaissance Monument in Senegal.

The studio opened in 1959 and a tour of the 120,000m^2 grounds will be rather brief, taking in the large studio shop and a number of artists' studios where you will be able to see some of these masters at work. It is alleged that the various badges of Kim Il Sung and Kim Jong Il worn by all citizens are manufactured here under armed guard but, alas, you will not be able to independently verify this, nor will you be able to see anything depicting the leaders being worked on – this would be tantamount to sacrilege. The shop has some truly wonderful items for sale, but as most visitors are unlikely to be carrying thousands of dollars on their person many of the grander items take years to find a home.

A little south of the art studio lies **Puhung Station** [88 C5], almost certain to be the starting point of any tour of the Pyongyang Metro (see box, page 94). Pushing further south along Saemaul Street, look west and **Pyongchon Thermal Power Station** [88 C5] will come into view; this is an off-limits station generating power for central Pyongyang. The sprawling complex looks like something from a dystopian nightmare; its external appearance, often masked in a cloud of thick deep grey smog, may help explain the chronic power shortages in the country.

Further south still, on the Taedong River and just to the east of Chungsong Bridge, is the **Monument to the Sinking of the USS** *General Sherman* [88 D6], but these days the **Mirae Scientists Street**, which starts 500m east from the monument, is the big draw in this neck of the woods. Formally opened in 2015, this strip of approximately 1km by 200m is another of Kim Jong Un's grand construction projects, developed to house some of the institutes and employees of the nearby Kim Chaek University of Technology. A 53-storey residential building, **Mirae Unha Tower** [88 D6] is the tallest structure on this street, which is also home to

Sun Myung Moon, or Rev Moon as he is largely referred to in the West, was born in North Pyongan in 1920. Founder of the Unification Church or 'the Moonies' as they are colloquially referred to, Rev Moon converted to Christianity at a young age and led a highly controversial life, coupling his beliefs as a messiah claimant with decades of involvement in fields such as politics, business and race relations.

Rev Moon opposed communism and was even imprisoned in the North for his views. An enemy of the state, he fled to the South in 1950, where he founded the Unification Church four years later, with his self-penned *The Divine Principle* their guiding scripture. As the Unification Church grew so did Rev Moon's status, wealth and power – he transcended religion to become something of an international statesman, using his wealth and message of peace to try and influence political and religious leaders across the world. He lived for many years in the USA and became something of a household name – the 'mass weddings' and allegations of the brainwashing of followers made for great headlines. In 1991 Rev Moon visited North Korea, returning for the first time since he had fled more than four decades prior. The red carpet was rolled out as he met with Kim Il Sung in a high-profile effort to bridge the gap between the two Koreas. The two septuagenarians, one claiming to be the second coming and the other promoted domestically as a near deity, put old political and religious differences aside – kickstarting an amicable relationship between the DPRK and the Moonies that still exists. Until his passing in 2012, Rev Moon worked with the highest echelons of the North Korean government to strive to reconcile North and South, chiefly through economic co-operation, with Pyeonghwa Motors being just one example of a joint venture he set up with seemingly altruistic intent and moderate success.

shops, restaurants and all manner of local facilities. In the right light, and possibly through rose-tinted glasses, this bright modern development is a picture postcard of a worker's paradise.

POTONGGANG (보통강구역) Encircled by the Potong River and its canals, Potonggang District is bisected almost perfectly by the Pyongui Line, the main north–south railway and lifeline with China. The bulk of interest lies to the east of the tracks, with the **Ryugyong Hotel** [88 D4] being the landmark embarrassment in this part of town (see box, page 98). In the shadow of the Ryugyong, the **Korean Embroidery Centre** [88 D4] (also going by the name Pyongyang Embroidery Research Institute and similar variants) is one of those sites most likely visited as an emergency filler when plans go awry, but many find a stop surprisingly enjoyable. Inaugurated in 1947, the centre is in a two-storeyed Korean-style building that has developed over the years into a national centre for the teaching and preservation of traditional embroidery techniques. Although the tour starts rather dryly, with a little too much background history on mechanised techniques and the like, it becomes more interesting as you take in a number of rooms where the friendly and seemingly all-female staff produce some exquisite pieces, all leading seamlessly to the on-site shop, where a small selection of 'here's one I made earlier' embroideries are available.

To the northeast of the Ryugyong Hotel, the **Ryugyong Jong Ju Yong Indoor Stadium** [96 A2] opened in 2003 and is another of Pyongyang's impressive and underused public venues. The stadium hosts concerts and sporting events, most of which are open to foreign visitors, should something be on while you are in town. It was here that Kim Jong Un sat with Dennis Rodman as they watched the Harlem Globetrotters in 2013, to the bemusement of the outside world and North Koreans alike. The eponymous Jong Ju Yong was the founder of South Korea's Hyundai group and one of the world's richest men, spending considerable time (and even more money) in an effort to normalise relations between North and South.

Victorious Fatherland Liberation War Museum [96 A2] The big draw in Potonggang is this mammoth museum built in 1953, relocated in 1974 and massively overhauled and extended into its current guise in 2013. As the truism goes, 'history is written by the victors'; as the North *of course* won the war, the interpretation of history in this museum is very different from our own, but it is best not to question the guides and lecturers, all of whom are ostensibly in the military. The museum is normally entered via the Monument to the Victorious Fatherland Liberation War Museum, a 360m-long approach to the main museum that was originally constructed to mark the 40th anniversary of the signing of the armistice. This area, a mix of garden, war memorial and captured hardware is lined with ten groups of rhapsodic militaristic sculptures all leading to the main *Victory* monument. Amendments in 2013 moved a mass of captured and destroyed US/UN equipment to the flanks of the grounds, with two 180m-long open sheds containing tanks, artillery, helicopters and such, but the *pièce de résistance* sits on the Potong Canal: the **USS *Pueblo*** [96 A2], a highlight of the museum tour. Aboard the *Pueblo* you will likely watch a wonderful 14-minute documentary, directed, of course, by the victors, before being shown briefly around the ship. Your circumscribed tour will take in a decadent ice-cream dispenser, the in-port cabin, bridge and, most importantly, the 'Crypto Room', which leaves no doubt as to what the Americans were really up to on this 'environmental research ship'.

Once inside the museum itself, you will take in just a few of the many rooms, too much for some, too little for others. It is all extremely one-sided, a heavy dose of propaganda that can be hard to wash down as it is delivered with little fact or impartiality – just as one would expect. Military buffs looking for answers about the movements of specific regiments or intricacies of a specific battle will come away with nothing, as seemingly everything was perpetrated by the 'Yankee bastards'. Facts backed by proof are a bit thin on the ground here, so the visit is just as much a journey into the mindset of the North Koreans as it is a 'museum'. China barely gets a mention and the focus is primarily on the lead up to, and early days of, the war, when things were on the up. Losses, failures and mistakes are not discussed – after all, the war was a Victory with a capital V, and everything is black and white. While the focus of the museum is on the Korean War, a few exhibits relate to post-1953 events, with the capture of the USS *Pueblo,* the shooting down of the EC-121 surveillance aircraft in 1969, and the downing of a OH-58C helicopter in 1994, for example, all being covered in morbid detail. While much of the content can (but shouldn't be) questioned, the craftsmanship of the exhibits cannot – this is world-class through and through, with the waxworks in particular being so eerily realistic that you dare not stare them too long in the eye, just in case. The tour culminates in a seeing-is-believing, jaw-droppingly impressive 360-degree diorama of the Battle of Taejon, one of the North's early tactical victories against US forces. Trying to digest everything you have taken in while striving to filter some fact from the fiction, you will be outside once more, politely agreeing with the museum guide seeing you off as to who started the Korean War, while possibly promising to yourself that you really must read up a little more on the war when you get home.

From the Potong River to Ponghwa Hill
Heading south as you follow the Potong Canal back towards the river, the **Potonggang Pleasure Ground** [96 B3] is a sliver of park along the canal's north bank that is rarely visited, but should you fancy playing (and likely losing) a game of tennis or basketball this place is the best bet for a few minutes of humiliation. Heading west from here, on the far side of Sinwon Street, the **Korean Central News Agency** [96 A4], will not be pointed out to you. The nearby 14-storey **International Communications Centre** [96 A4] somehow soldiers on and may be visited should you need to visit this building which boasts to be fully equipped with 'international telephones, fax and voicecast facilities', but in this day and age it is somewhat obsolete, even in Pyongyang. Finally, a few good restaurants and bars can be found near the Hwangumbol Metro Station, a number all stretched out in a row along the west side of Gyonghung Street and a couple to the south, in the Ryugyong-dong No 1 area. The majority of these establishments cannot decide if they want to welcome tourists or not, as they permit then bar foreigners with such frequency that your Korean guides have largely given up trying to ascertain the current sentiment, but it's worth investigating further.

There is little to see to the west of the Pyongui Rail Line; almost all to the south of Pulgun Street, including Potonggang Station, is essentially industrial of some kind, while the bulk of land to the north of Pulgun and Ragwon streets on **Ponghwa Hill** [88 C4] is inaccessible. Ponghwa is home to executive housing (which is occasionally used by the more senior visiting journalists and politicians) and the headquarters of the **State Affairs Commission** [88 D4], both hidden from view. One of the few things you may visit on this stretch of the river is the 1971-constructed **Monument to the Potong River Improvement Project** [88 C3], but almost nobody ever does and your guides may not even know how to find it. Arguably the most exciting thing about this over-the-top stone monument is its proximity to the **General Satellite Control Center** [88 C4]; mission control for North Korea's space programme, which is just 120m away, but may as well be on the moon as you will not be allowed any closer.

SOSONG (서성역)
Sosong District stretches around the north of Potonggang and Moranbong districts and although it covers a relatively large area there is little to see in this part of town; a good chunk of land is industrial and governmental, and therefore inaccessible. Entering from Sochon Street in the southwest of Sosong, the **Foreign Languages Publishing House** [88 D3] could be a fascinating visit for bibliophiles looking for some seriously unusual titles, but for now the only foreigners passing through these doors are the few lonely translators revising and proofing some very weighty texts. **West Pyongyang Railway Station** [88 D3] won't get a look in, so will be bypassed at relative speed as you are taken northeast along Mudok Street. At some point you will likely detour away from Mudok Street, as the road bisects the massive grounds of the **Ministry of People's Armed Forces** [88 D3], complete with reservoir, underground facilities, hospital, stadium and much, much more.

Detour around the ministry complete, the last vestiges of the city proper in this part of town can be found along Podunamu Street, with the road leading towards a trio of nearby sites, starting with the **Jangsan Revolutionary Site** [89 E2], which is one of the most accessible places in Pyongyang for those that want to see just how far a personality cult can stretch. It seems that as a teenager Kim Jong Il planted a tree or two here, which somehow makes him the integral player in the construction of the Wasandong–Ryongsong motorway. As of 2017, it is alleged that 7.1 million people have visited this spot, which comprises a few preserved single-storey buildings and, of course, some impeccably planted trees. Unless you have the time for a very dry excursion while silently chuckling to yourself at the futility of it all then there really is no need to help get the total visitor tally up to eight million.

In the north of Sosong, beyond end-of-the-line Pulgunbyol Metro Station, lies the **Three Revolutions Exhibition** [89 E2], a sprawling slab of concrete and cavernous exhibition halls, which primarily display the manufacturing achievements of the country. The grounds comprise six main halls and are akin to a deserted North Korean version of Disney's Epcot Centre. Halls are dedicated to fields such as heavy industry, technical innovations and agriculture. Most find the Electronics Industry Hall, essentially a Saturn-shaped planetarium replete with scale-models of various Korean rockets and satellites, together with the Light Industry Hall and all its wonderful array of domestic products (bizarrely, much of which is impossible to find in the shops), of the greatest interest. The open-air exhibition of locomotives and tractors can get a certain type of traveller very excited, while the large monument at the head of the grounds is worth a photo stop if you have the time (it's a round-trip walk of 1.5km from the entrance).

To the west of the Three Revolutions Exhibition, where the urban sprawl ends and the airport roads starts, lies the **Fatherland Liberation War Martyrs' Cemetery** [89 E2], which was consecrated in 2013 to mark the 60th anniversary of the Korean War. The cemetery, which is logically taken in when heading to/from the airport or beyond, has an edifying stone memorial tower as its centrepiece, composed of a rifle, bayonet, flag and a Republic Hero medal. The tower is flanked by two smaller but no less impressive stone monuments, and behind these over 500 fallen fighters are at rest, their graves set out over nine tiers on a gentle slope of Tolbak Hill. Atop Tolbak, just 350m away, an anti-aircraft artillery battery is tucked away, highlighting that although these poor souls passed decades ago, the war footing continues regardless.

Finally, in the northeast of Sosong is the **Ponghwa Art Theatre** [89 E2], which contains a 2,000-seat and an 800-seat theatre. Attending a performance at this theatre, which comes under the remit of the foreboding-sounding Ministry of People's Security, is rarely possible, but the doors occasionally open during the Pyongyang International Film Festival and also opened in 2015, when the Slovenian group Laibach performed here.

SONGYO (선교구역), TONGDAEWON (동대원구역) AND TAEDONGGANG (대동강구역)
Pyongyang's central south bank, comprising the three districts of Sonyo, Tongdaewon and Taedonggang, have a lot less to offer than the north bank of the Taedong River, but a handful of sights, including a couple of major monuments, will certainly bring you this way.

Arriving on the south bank by way of the Yanggak Bridge, **Songyo District**, has very little of interest, being home to a few light industrial plants and an awful lot of concealed-from-view old-fashioned housing – a world away from the socialist utopia found along the many high-rise boulevards elsewhere in the city. Such housing, considered an embarrassment in Pyongyang, is hidden away from prying eyes, so your chances of a stroll through the backstreets of Songyo in districts such as chiefly single-storey Jangcung-dong No 2, are slim.

Passing the **Taedonggang Railway Station** [89 E6] and heading north along Chongnyon Street, the shops and restaurants here are essentially all *verboten*. It's somewhat ironic that one of the only doors in this part of town that you may be able to pass through are the ones that almost nobody living here would want to: those of the **Changchung Cathedral** [89 F5]. This Catholic cathedral opened in 1988 – a time when the allusion of religious freedom was promulgated by the government in an attempt to woo foreign friends. With no resident bishop or priest, masses are conducted just a handful of times each year by visiting foreign clergy, so catching a service here may require a little divine intervention.

Tongdaewon District, bookended by the Taedong Bridge at its southern end and the Okryu Bridge to its north, is of more interest than Songyo. The **Taedong Bridge** [96 C6] was originally constructed in 1922 and at one time went by the moniker of 'Japanese Bridge', a nod to those who ordered its construction. Destroyed twice in 1950, first by the retreating communists and secondly by the retreating US forces who had just finished rebuilding it, the current incarnation was erected once hostilities had ended. The **Okryu Bridge** [96 C4] is far less exciting, a girder bridge dating to 1960.

The east of Tongdaewon is home to the **East Pyongyang Stadium** [89 F5] and ostensibly accessible **Munsu Hill** [89 G5], a forested park rising to 82m above sea level, but nearly all the sights of interest are located within a few hundred metres of the riverbank. Heading north along Juchethap Street, the **Taedonggang Diplomatic Club** (page 101) is open to both diplomats and those who never quite made the grade; these days anybody with hard currency is welcome. Often frequented by embassy staff and NGOs, facilities include a restaurant, banquet hall, dance hall, swimming pool and more, and is thus as good a place as any in the city to enjoy a relaxing evening.

Beyond the club, a 1km-long and approximately 200m-wide embankment stretches all the way to the Okryu Bridge, with the Juche Tower as its focal point. This pedestrianised embankment is lined with grand granite sculptures, depicting such scenes as 'Juche-oriented industry' and 'Impregnable Fortress', together with manicured gardens and water features. The 170m-tall **Juche Tower** [96 D5] is the highest stone tower in the world and dominates the skyline of central Pyongyang. Often referred to as 'The Tower of the Juche Idea', the 150m column is topped with a 45-tonne, 20m-tall metallic torch, its perpetually flickering red glow symbolising the 'immortality of the Juche idea'. Unveiled on 15 April 1982, Kim Il Sung's 70th birthday, the exterior of the tower is made from 25,550 white granite blocks, one for each day of his life (the 17 leap days he had lived up until that point were seemingly overlooked by the designer, purported to be Kim Jong Il). In front of the tower stands a striking 30m-tall bronze statue, a sculpture of a worker, farmer and intellectual who is said to symbolise the indomitable Korean spririt, each holding aloft an implement, being a hammer, sickle and writing brush respectively, the three tools converging to form the symbol of the Workers' Party of Korea, and is reminiscent of Moscow's famous *Worker and Kolkhoz Woman*. In the middle of the Taedong River are two large fountains that shoot water as high as 150m into the air during holidays and celebrations.

The Juche Tower is aligned with Kim Il Sung Square and the Grand People's Study House on the opposite bank of the Taedong, while the **Korea Documentary Film Studio** [96 D5] and apartments to the east of the tower provide additional alignment – the urban planning perfectionists really must have had a field day with this project. The base pedestal of the tower has, on its eastern wall, a niche adorned with hundreds of marble and jade plaques presented from a plethora of friendship parties, political groups and such associations – a veritable who's who of weird and wonderful organisations the world over.

You will normally enter via this alcove, though there is another entrance to the tower. Inside, additional plaques overspill into the entrance hall and the souvenir shop charges elevated prices to the captive visitors awaiting the lift. Beneath you, a subterranean floor is normally bypassed; a basic café, toilets and other facilities are located here, but typically closed.

Unless you suffer vertigo, a trip up (and back down) in the lift to the viewing balcony at the base of the torch costs €5 and is a must. The charge has not changed since euro banknotes were first introduced, so don't be surprised if the price has doubled by the time you visit. From the top, a commanding view of central Pyongyang will help you pinpoint where you have been and where you are headed next, and affords unrivalled views of Kim Il Sung Square and the Grand People's Study House.

As you are driven further along Juchethap Street you will enter **Taedonggang District**, with the road parallel to the river becoming Munsu Kagan Street and home to the **Ryugyong Health Complex** [96 D4], **People's Open Air Ice Rink** [96 D4] and the **Skate Park** [96 D4]. These three venues all opened in 2012 and tourists may visit, but rarely do. Opposite this trio, the **Pyongyang Golden Lane Bowling Alley** [96 D4] offers 40 lanes of fun, together with billiards, arcade games and a couple of restaurants. The lanes opened in 1994 and remains as popular as ever; a great spot to wind down among all the local families and friends that often pack this place out on evenings and weekends.

To the north, the **Central Youth Hall** [96 D4] and **East Pyongyang Grand Theatre** [96 D3] both hold concerts and performances, with the latter hosting the New York Philharmonic when they came to town in 2008, the first major cultural exchange between North Korea and the USA. The Mansudae Art Troupe often perform in this 3,500-seat theatre and catching a concert here, or indeed at any theatre in Pyongyang, is highly recommended. Opposite the theatre, the **Kimjongilia-Kimilsungia Exhibition House** [96 D4] is open year-round, with the antechamber having a permanent display of the two eponymous flowers (see box, below). The entire building is only fully open a handful of times each year (and typically always for the birthdays of the former Mr Kims), for the Kimjongilia-Kimilsungia Flower Exhibition, when elaborate floral displays take over the entire building, often incorporating all manner of socialist iconography into the designs:

Pyongyang   WHAT TO SEE AND DO

FLOWER POWER

While the national flower of the country is the magnolia, it is far less important than the Kimilsungia and Kimjongilia, which are celebrated far and wide and dominate (other flora barely gets a look in) the Kimjongilia-Kimilsungia Flower Exhibition. The Kimilsungia is a violet hybrid orchid created by an Indonesian botanist in 1964. Should you attend the flower exhibition you will be told that Kim Il Sung's 'peerless character is fully reflected in the immortal flower' – it's best to nod and agree. Kim Jong Il's namesake flower is a bright red perennial begonia, cultivated by a Japanese botanist and presented to Kim Jong Il in 1988 as a token of friendship between Korea and Japan. The importance of these flowers to the nation is confounding, with songs, symposiums and hothouses across the country working round the clock to study, nurture and propagate them. When Kim Jong Il passed in 2011, his body was surrounded by Kimjongilia flowers, thus elevating the flower's status to even giddier heights.

water features, model rockets and polystyrene dioramas of Mount Paektu are all common themes.

The big draw inland from the riverbank is the **Monument to Party Foundation** [89 F4], which also goes by a handful of similar names. Best approached by the grass avenue that leads towards it for full dramatic effect, this monument was built to commemorate the 'brilliant history' of the Workers' Party of Korea. Erected in 1995 for the 50th anniversary of the party's foundation, the 50m-high monument (one metre for each year), is made of granite and depicts three clenched fists, one holding a hammer, one a sickle and one a writing brush – the party symbol. A 50m belt surrounds the three fists, symbolising 'the single hearted-unity of the leader, party and people', while the 70m pedestal beneath it symbolises that the party's history stretches back a further 20 years to 1925, when the anti-Japanese 'Down with Imperialism Union' was born. Sitting in 25,000m² of grounds, two red tower blocks, staggered in their height and painted red, provide a fitting backdrop to the monument, representing the flying red flag of communism. The monuments and grounds are all neatly aligned with the Mansudae Grand Monument – a fine example of socialist urban planning. The fact that Kim Jong Il was born on 16 February, or 2.16 as written in Korea, and that these two monuments are 2.16km apart is no coincidence. The interior of the belt has bronze reliefs of predictable content, and bears the slogan: 'Long life the Workers' Party of Korea, the organiser and guide to the victory of the Korean people!' Additional symbols, numerology and numbers can be found all over the site (and in buildings across the country), such things often being the yardstick of North Korean architecture. Beyond the grounds, behind the monument, the **Pyongyang Cultural Exhibition Hall** [89 F4] is more of a shop than an exhibition, but has some interesting photographs and a decent range of souvenirs.

Located on a bend in the Taedong River, the northern tip of the district starts near **Chongryu Bridge** [96 D1], a 1990s construction linking the area with Rungna Island and the north bank. Here lies the **Munsu Water Park** [89 F4], which opened in 2013 and covers 15ha of indoor and outdoor facilities, including all manner of pools and slides (together with restaurants, bars and a barber), all offering hours of fun for a modest fee.

Heading inland from the river a large number of educational establishments and nearly all of Pyongyang's embassies can be found compacted into a rather small area of Taedonggang District, together with the offices of various NGOs and housing for 'long-term residents'. Understandably, a fair few restaurants and shops, such as the **Taesong Department Store** [89 F4], are peppered around the area to accommodate these comparatively wealthy local residents. The only mosque in Korea, the **Ar-Rahman Mosque** [89 F4] is technically on Iranian soil as it is within the grounds of their embassy, but foreigners may, for now, attend Friday prayers by pre-arranging it direct with the embassy.

Although you can normally only visit the Friendship Hospital if you have a legitimate reason, a trio of nearby clinics provide triage and more to Pyongyangites, with the Okryu Children's Hospital, Pyongyang Maternity Hospital and the General Hospital of Koryo Medicine all on the same street and all being showcase facilities that regularly feature on city tours. The **Pyongyang Maternity Hospital** [89 F4] is arguably the most interesting of the three. Completed in 1980, the building's shape is designed to suggest the outstretched arms of a mother reaching for her baby – but you would likely need to be have had an epidural mixed with serious painkillers to even come close to spotting this. With 1,500 beds, almost anybody born in Pyongyang since 1980 was born here, and a tour of the facilities will normally include meeting a mother (who may well tell you that universal free medical care came into 'force' on 1 January 1953) and her little bundle of joy. The **Okryu Children's Hospital** [89 F4] opened in 2013 and is another grandiose new building for the Kim Jong Un era. With over ten wards and dozens of departments it is a rather odd excursion, but one that those with a passing interest in health care may want to consider. Finally, should Western medicine not be your thing, a trip to the **General Hospital of Koryo Medicine** [89 F4] may open your eyes to some of the popular Eastern treatments that are still strongly advocated in the country.

MANGYONGDAE DISTRICT (만경대구역) This suburb in west Pyongyang is a place of nobility, as it is where Kim Il Sung was born on 15 April 1912 (the day the *Titanic* sank). Of course, as the president was born here, his old stomping grounds *have to* look smart; Mangyongdae is one of Pyongyang's most impressive districts, and you could easily spend a full day taking in the grandiose architecture, visiting a number of the imposing civic buildings and enjoying some leisure time in the parks and hills around the Mangyongdae Native House and Mount Ryongak.

On crossing the Potong River and entering Mangyongdae via the Phalgol Bridge, you will be escorted along Kwangbok Street, a 4.5km-long avenue that is home to over 25,000 families and is arguably, along with Tongil Street (page 128), the finest example of socialist-brutalist residential architecture in the city. The first major stop is the **Kwangbok Area Shopping Centre** [88 C4], the only 'normal' supermarket tourists are permitted to visit in the country. Kwangbok is also the only spot outside of Rason (page 252) where you can exchange your hard currency for Korean won, as only local currency is accepted here. While visiting a supermarket may not be on the top of most people's 'must see' list of things to do in Pyongyang, it makes for an interesting excursion, allowing you to see and purchase a wide range of local products that you will not encounter anywhere else – and it's the ideal place to stock up on last-minute supplies before heading upcountry. While the ground floor is dominated by a supermarket, the first and second floors include clothing and a food court – prices, by Western standards, are very reasonable. The range of goods available to Pyongyang's burgeoning middle class seems to grow at an alarming rate, in stark contrast to the barren shelves of yesteryear, and nowhere in the country better highlights that North Korea is in the early stages of a massive consumerist and social transformation. Besides the food court, there is a handful of good restaurants near (and one under) the shopping centre, all of which are rather generic in content and cuisine, and may well feature on your tour.

Just a short way west along Kwangbok Street, the **Supreme Court of the DPR Korea** [88 B4] is rarely visited by people freely electing to do so, but it's possible to arrange a fascinating tour that takes in the three chambers and provides the lowdown on the laws of the land. The court is the highest organ in the country's judiciary, and trials of foreigners are always held here, so avid followers of North Korean news may well recognise the interiors. The lawyers that escort guests here are surprisingly honest and happy to discuss their laws, trials, constitution and cases, but this really is not a suitable spot to be too antagonistic.

Outside and free once more, a far more light-hearted stop is the **Pyongyang Circus** [88 C4]. Holding numerous performances each week, typically mid afternoon, this 3,500-seat venue is normally packed full of children and conscripts in equal measure. Circus is an art form in North Korea, and the acrobats and trapeze artists are up there with the very best, having won prizes the world over for their polished routines. A visit is highly recommended, but be warned, occasional animal routines still feature. A short walk further along Kwangbok Street leads to the **Pyeonghwa Motors Showroom** [88 B4], next door to the Chongnyon Hotel (page 97). Those interested in checking out the latest models assembled by Pyeonghwa can have a quick (escorted) nosey around the showroom, and even pick up the printed specifications for a selection of models, which is as close as you will get to a test drive.

At the Chilgol Overpass, a short detour to the northwest would take you to the **Chilgol Revolutionary Site** [88 B4] (where Kim Il Sung's mother was born) and on to the small **Chilgol Church** [88 B4]. Pilgrimages to both sites are possible for devout followers, but they really are best avoided by the casual traveller. The church is normally only open on Sunday mornings and only then by prearrangement (allegedly so that a congregation can be rustled up in time). It is Chilgol Church that, it is claimed, Kim Il Sung was dragged along to as a child, for his mother was in regular attendance. Another Protestant church – **Bongsu Church** [88 C3] – can be found in Mangyongdae, near the west bank of the Potong River. The current church, which seats 1,200, was built in 2008 and paid for by Presbyterians from the South. Like any church in North Korea, nobody seems to know what is and isn't real; are the congregation devout, or is it all smoke and mirrors?

The **Mangyongdae Schoolchildren's Palace** [88 A5], similar to the Pyongyang Students and Children's Palace (page 107), is an extra-curricular activity centre extraordinaire, catering daily to over 5,000 of the most gifted pioneers. Constructed in 1989 but massively refurbished in 2015, the complex includes a gymnasium, swimming pool and literally hundreds of rooms where the gifted youngsters typically focus on just one discipline for hours each day – day in, day out. A plethora of classes are taught, from accordion to xylophone, table tennis to taekwondo. A tour, which is normally only possible on Thursdays during term time, is highly recommended; the education style in the DPRK is clearly very different from in the West and the results are startling. A visit, which will include a selection of classrooms, will normally culminate with an immaculately polished 90-minute performance in the palace's theatre, showcasing the staggering talents of these children, who would largely wipe the floor with their counterparts the world over.

To the northwest of the western end of Kwangbok lies Mount Ryongak (see opposite), while to your south is **Mangyongdae-dong** [88 A6], where Kim Il Sung was born. This green heavily wooded area is home to a number of places to eat and some exclusive seats of education, with the Mangyongdae Revolutionary School and Kim Il Sung Military University, among others, training up the next generation. Approaching from the north, the western terminus **tram depot** [88 A5] is normally the starting point for public transport enthusiasts to enjoy a ride along the rails to the city centre, while the **Mangyongdae Funfair** [88 A6] can entertain up to 100,000 people a day, but is normally overlooked these days. The funfair is generally open on warmer weekends and certain national holidays (akin to the Taesongsan Funfair; page 125); when open most of the fun to be had is in people-watching. The park has the feel of an out-of-season seaside town, sleepy and dilapidated, and at any given time many of the rides are under repair, but thrill seekers can release their inner-child by riding the rollercoaster or hitting the arcades.

Pushing on, the **Mangyongdae Native House** [88 A6] is a common stop on all tours of the capital. Many moons ago a small village stood here, but the area has been cleared of all homes except for one; the birthplace of President Kim Il Sung. In pristine grounds, the ancestral family graves and Mangyongdae Revolutionary Museum are normally bypassed as you head directly to the family home that is so clean, fresh and new that cynics may question its authenticity. A visit to the humble thatched huts where Kim Il Sung grew up is something of a pilgrimage, and will be followed by a trip to the local well (that you may drink from) and a walk up Mangyong Hill. Mangyong Hill (its name translates as '10,000 views', a clue as to the panorama from the top) is home to a handful of spots that those who have totally succumbed to the Kim personality cult may consider unmissable, such as 'Rainbow-Catching Pine Tree' and 'the Wrestling Site where the President trained his body and mind', but only the view from the top of the hill is truly a must.

Travelling east from Mangyongdae along the north bank of the Taedong River, the road passes Konyu Islet and speeds towards central Pyongyang, but a turnoff at the Sonnae Bridge leads to Chongchun Street, which leads back to the Chongnyon Hotel and the Chilgol Overpass on Kwangbok Street. This area, often referred to as 'the Sports Village' or 'Chongchun Sports Street', is home to an array of impressive sporting facilities and stadia, all built to host the 13th World Festival of Youth and Students, held in 1989. The buildings are typically closed unless you are attending an event, but just to walk along Chongchun to take in the scale of the buildings, and their architecture, is a pleasant diversion. At the southern end of Chongchun, the **Ryanggang Hotel** and the **Sosan Hotel** (page 99) are getting a little more custom these days, as is the nearby **Maeri Shooting Range** [88 B5] where you can let off steam (and see that your guides' stint in the armed forces was not a total waste) as you try your hand at target practice. Both sports pistols and rifles can be fired for a nominal fee, but animal lovers may want to steer clear of the outdoor rifle range, where you can shoot pheasants and win dinner in the process. Behind the shooting range, the **Korean People's Army Exhibition of Arms and Equipment** [88 B5] opened in 2012 and is generally off-limits to 'normal foreigners', but those interested in checking out some of the finest military hardware in the country may want to see if access has eased.

A final stop in the district is usually the 292m-tall **Mount Ryongak**, the highest point in the city. A narrow road winds most of the way up the hill, and a few trekking paths also wind around and up to the top, Tae Peak. A scattering of cloisters and pavilions can be found on the upper reaches of the hill, with the views of Pyongyang becoming more impressive as you ascend. Local restaurants compete in arranging barbecues at one of the picnic grounds near the foot of the hill, which is also home to the Mangyongdae Children's Camp and the **National Gifts Exhibition House**. A far more compact and accessible (but less impressive) version of the International Friendship Exhibition (page 175), the National Gift Exhibition House displays gifts presented by ethnic Koreans (ie: those from North, South and anywhere else) to the leaders. Security and setup is similar to what you can expect at the International Friendship Exhibition in Mount Myohyang, so anticpate having to leave belongings in the cloakroom and to go through airport-style security checks, albeit without the long queues. As it plays second fiddle to the Friendship Exhibition this site is largely ignored by people as they instead head north for the real deal. However, if you cannot get to the International Friendship Exhibition in Mount Myohyang, or have been and just have to see more, there is some fabulous stuff to be found here, from a chair made of deer antlers to a painting of Kim Jong Il riding a tiger, prints of which are sadly not available in the gift shop.

TAESONG DISTRICT (대성구역) Northeast of central Pyongyang, Taesong is home to some major and truly fascinating must-see sites. The big draws in this part of town are the Kumsusan Palace of the Sun and the various points of interest on and around Mount Taesong, which on weekends is often packed full of locals enjoying an escape from the daily grind. Many of the leisure spots in Taesong are only really

in full swing on certain days and times of year; while the Taesongsan Funfair is a lovely experience on May Day and hot summer weekends, don't expect the same experience on a wet Tuesday in November.

Entering Taesong from the west as you travel along Kumsong Street you will likely pass under one of the dual arches that form the trident **Tower of Immortality** [89 E3], constructed in 1997 to commemorate the 'Immortal President', whose embalmed body lies just 3km away. This tower is the blueprint for many smaller towers that have sprouted across the country, all showing reverence to Kim Il Sung and, subsequently, Kim Jong Il. A hefty chunk of the hallowed land that leads towards the mausoleum was developed recently in what must be one of Kim Jong Un's greatest architectural achievements so far, with the **Ryomyong New Town** officially opening in 2017. Visitors may enjoy a walk in this prestigious and aesthetic residential area, where the tallest building tops out at a staggering 82 floors, making it the tallest completed building in the country.

The sprawling **Kim Il Sung University** [89 E3], further along Kumsong Street, is the highest seat of learning in the land. Founded in 1946, the university has impressive facilities and an alumni that includes Kim Jong Il and Kim Jong Un; clearly the elite who graduate from here have a bright future ahead of them. By appointment, visitors may tour the university for a somewhat contrived excursion that often takes in the Revolutionary Museum, e-library and indoor swimming pool. Sadly, visits seem to be timed so that you will see almost no students whatsoever – perhaps they are all hiding in the giant on-site bunker (you can't check – it's not included on the tour). A more relaxed setting is the nearby **June 9th Secondary School** [89 F2], just a few hundred metres away. The facilities here are a little more down to earth than the bling found at the university, and a tour, typically timed for the end of the school day, should take in a couple of classrooms and finish off with a song and dance routine by the school band. There are other secondary schools in Pyongyang and across the country that you may visit – they are all relatively similar in content so there should be no need to visit more than one, but a visit to one somewhere in the country is an interesting experience.

Kumsusan Palace of the Sun [89 F2]
Nestled between the increasingly bustling city and perpetually calm Mount Taesong, beside the sleepy Hapjang Stream, lies the holiest of holies, the Kumsusan Palace of the Sun – the mausoleum for Kim Il Sung and Kim Jong Il. Constructed in the 1970s, the building was the official residence of Kim Il Sung up until his passing in 1994, when it metamorphised within a year (at a cost estimated in the hundreds of millions of dollars) to become his mausoleum, the Kumsusan Memorial Palace. The palace became a monolith, a windowless mansion tomb from where the Eternal President could continue to rule the country from within his glass sarcophagus, with citizens by the thousand coming each day to pay their respects to the 'Benevolent Sun'. On Kim Jong Il's passing in 2011 the mausoleum was a chrysalis once more, re-emerging on 16 February 2012 (what would have been his 70th birthday), as the Kumsusan Palace of the Sun, the largest modern mausoleum in the world and far more impressive than the comparatively humble homes of the likes of Lenin and Mao. With the two leaders lying in state in their respective chambers, the highlight of a tour of this cavernous complex is to bow three times before the embalmed leaders, often surrounded by tearful locals.

Visiting this, undoubtedly the Mecca of Korea, is an honour in itself and one that many citizens can only dream of. While the Palace Square can normally be visited on any day for a quick photo opportunity, the mausoleum itself can only be visited by arrangement and is open for foreigners on Thursdays and Sunday mornings (but schedules can shift on and around public holidays). Kumsusan also closes for a couple of months each spring from early May to early July, but the exact dates are never known until the eleventh hour. Under 16s are prohibited from visiting.

While some locals may arrive by means of the VIP tram that ferries people from near Kim Il Sung University, tourists will almost certainly come by bus, arriving in the car park and being escorted to the waiting room for 'processing'. All visitors must be smartly dressed – locals will be sporting their *very* best. While no published dress code exists, men should at least be in long trousers with a shirt and tie and dark/leather shoes, while women should be in a smart dress or blouse with a knee-length (or longer) skirt (and no open toed/heeled shoes). Wearing jeans, trainers, T-shirts and the like would cause embarrassment and offence and a headache for all concerned – likely resulting in you being barred access, closing possibilities and damaging goodwill with your guides and travelling companions. Security is understandably tight: wallets, cameras, personal belongings – essentially all must be left in your transport or in the cloakroom, bar vital possessions such as medicines. There are no exceptions.

With security cleared, you will travel along a series of travellators, slowly entering a warren of marbled corridors and rooms, all well guarded and lined with a miscellany of photographs of the great leaders. The sombre mood deepens as the tour progresses, taking in statues of the leaders and countless medals, awards, titles and gifts presented to them, both in life and death. Highlights include Kim Il Sung's personal rail carriage, Kim Jong Il's motorboat, and diplomas and doctorates from the world over. The entire experience will last 2–3 hours and the crescendo is, of course, seeing father and son lying in state, a stirring, confusing and chilling experience aided by over-enthusiastic air conditioning. An entire book could cover this mausoleum (and one has, of course: published in Pyongyang), but rest assured – a visit here will stick with you for many years.

Mount Taesong and around

At the foot of Mount Taesong lies the **Pyongyang Central Zoo** [89 G2] and the **Central Botanical Gardens** [89 G2]. The zoo has been modernised under Kim Jong Un, and in 2016–17 transformed from a rather grim place to something more akin to a typical zoo elsewhere in the world – so still a rather grim place. The happiest little critters to be found here are the local children enjoying a family day out or school trip – it's a good spot for mingling with locals and the grounds are attractive enough, but that really is about it. The botanical gardens over the road opened in 1959 and occupy a 2.5km² plot; they're home to 2,500 species native to Korea and 4,000 from overseas. The sprawling area is often very quiet; run by botanists and largely aimed at botanists. This is not Kew Gardens – those looking to relax in scenic grounds would be better to look elsewhere, but the green fingered are of course very welcome. Nearby, the **Taesongsan Funfair** [89 H2] is a much more light-hearted affair. The tired grounds opened in 1977 and house over a dozen rides such as astro fighter, wonder wheel and the jet coaster. While the rides themselves are a little ramshackle and are often closed for repairs, the grounds, which include the restored Nam Gate of the Walls of Mount Taesong, are worth visiting on national holidays and warmer weekends for a spot of good old-fashioned people-watching.

Beyond the zoo, a dead-straight road leads for approximately 800m to the gate marking the entrance to the **Revolutionary Martyrs' Cemetery** [89 H1], with 530 steps (some of which can, thankfully, be avoided) leading up a gentle slope to the top of the cemetery, majestically located in front of Chujak Hill. The cemetery is a major site of pilgrimage in the country and the resting place of such notables as Kim Jong Suk (the first wife of Kim Il Sung and mother of Kim Jong Il), Kang Pan Sok (the mother of Kim Il Sung) and Kim Chaek (a general and high-ranking politician who even has a city named after him). The word 'martyr' is somewhat inaccurate; many of those that are buried here (over 150 and counting, with a few final plots remaining) were martyrs in the literal sense but many lived to a ripe old age. Most of those here are from Kim Il Sung's inner circle, the 'Guerrilla Faction' as it is often called – the ones that stuck with him and fought beside him against the Japanese in Manchuria; the ones that backed the right horse and stuck with him through and through, thus surviving the dark days and purges that wiped out all rivals and bestowed upon Kim absolute power. These greats, the builders of the DPRK as we know it, have been honoured with one of the most regal resting places in the land, a presiding view over Pyongyang in a tasteful, yet awe-inspiring, setting in what is just as much a monument as it is a cemetery.

It is customary and respectful for at least one person in your party to lay flowers, so your visit will normally start by driving to the florist's kiosk, which also allows you to bypass the first long bank of steps. While the flowers are typically of the plastic variety, all else that lies ahead is of the highest quality, with no expense spared. Fitting music piped from concealed speakers stirs through the grounds as you ascend, passing two stone and then bronze sculptures, all depicting the armed forces' struggle. The cemetery was inaugurated in 1975, with every gravestone having a stone bust atop it. A decade later, the stone busts were replaced with bronze, more befitting the importance of the souls within. Each gravestone is marked with four dates: the individual's date of birth, the date they commenced service in the revolution, the date of the greatest battle they fought in and, finally, their date of passing. Some of the fallen are interred with their spouses, and this is noted on the reverse of the tombs. The eight main rows of graves start with those that fell first, rising in age as you approach the focal point of the cemetery near the top of Chujak Hill: the graves of the most revered revolutionaries, with Kim Jong Suk at the very centre, a dominating stone sculpture of the red flag flying as a fitting backdrop. A bow here is expected, and the plastic flowers, somewhat incongruous with the gravitas of the location, should be placed before Jong Suk's grave. Respects paid, visitors normally descend the cemetery by road, as your transport will have crept up to the upper car park while you ascended on foot. Before departing, a quick view down the valley to the Taesongsan Funfair is worth taking in.

Besides all the fun in the foothills, **Mount Taesong** itself is really more of a hill at a paltry 272m above sea level; a densely wooded area that affords a little respite from the city when it all gets too much. A few narrow paths and access roads wind through the forested valley and slowly climb to the three peaks of Somun, Changsu and Guksa, all of which have pavilions and are ideal spots for a picnic and a spot of light hiking. The mountain was a major military fortification during the Koguryo Dynasty, and over 9km of the walls of **Taesong Fortress** [89 G1] exist in varying states of natural decay or over-exuberant renovation. To the south, and best seen from Somun Peak, traces of the **Anhak Palace** [89 H2], which existed from AD427 to 586, can be made out, but it is more of an archaeological dig than a tourist attraction.

Tucked away all alone on the northwestern slopes of Mount Taesong, the **Kwangbop Temple** [89 H1] dates to AD392, although the current buildings date to 1990, after a fire in 1700 and the Korean War destroyed the original, and its reincarnation. Better Buddhist temples can be found elsewhere in Korea, but few with such a long history and none so accessible.

RYONGSONG RESIDENCE

Also going by the name Central Luxury Mansion or Residence No 55, this 12km² complex is believed to be Kim Jong Un's preferred palace and main residence. Constructed in the early 1980s for his grandfather, Kim Il Sung, the complex, which is *never* openly discussed in polite Pyongyang society (any query as to where the leaders live is coyly answered with 'oh, we don't know about such things' and a quick change of subject), has all manner of facilities that most dictators can only dream of. Satellite imagery reveals numerous villas, lakes, sporting facilities, a private railway station and countless other decadent luxuries, but it's what's alleged to be underground that is more exciting – rumours of a private connection to the Pyongyang Metro and a subterranean wartime headquarters constantly surface, among other things. Extremely well hidden and well guarded, the palace is unsurprisingly out of view, but those heading towards Pyongsong will pass within 2km of the inner compound, totally oblivious of the residence's existence.

OUTER PYONGYANG While the highlights of Pyongyang are concentrated in a relatively small area, the city does have a scattering of sites in its outlying areas, as the administrative boundary of the capital stretches quite some way. While districts like Rangnang now have a degree of urban sprawl (although in a city of extreme centralised planning the word 'sprawl' seems unfair), some areas, such as Kangdong, are essentially rural, showing glimpses of country life. If you're spending extended time in Korea, or looking to really get under the skin of the capital, you would do well to consider visiting some of the city's peripheries.

North Pyongyang: Sunan (순안구역), Hyongjesan (형제산구역), Ryongsong (룡성구역) and Unjong (은정구역)

Almost all travellers will at least pass through north Pyongyang, for the Pyongyang Sunan International Airport is located – unsurprising given its name – in Sunan, the capital's northernmost district. **Sunan** town itself is essentially off-limits, although there has been talk for some years of an airport hotel being built in the area. Heading towards Pyongyang, which starts in earnest approximately 20km away, the **Pyongyang Ostrich Farm** occasionally materialises as a suggested place to visit when other plans go awry – plead ornithophobia and try to get your guide to hatch an alternative plan as this farm really is about as exciting as it sounds.

Bisected by the Potong River, **Hyongjesan** District is briefly passed through as one heads from the airport into Pyongyang – the only regular stop in this part of town is the **Korean Film Studio** [88 C2]. Inaugurated in 1947, the complex includes mock sets such as a Chinese, South Korean and Japanese street and all the technical facilities required to make the next local blockbuster. Though it is a popular request by tourists, unless you are particularly fortunate to witness a film being made (apparently at any given time they can be working on up to ten projects, but seeing any notable activity is rare), the studio can be something of a disappointment. The grounds are a little rundown and normally so sleepy that they would be the perfect set for a post-apocalyptic zombie film.

Neighbouring **Ryongsong** District also has a lack of places of interest, and is normally completely bypassed. Bar the final vestiges of urban sprawl and a few small satellite settlements scattered across Ryongsong, there is little in this hilly district and it is thus the ideal spot to secrete a couple of palaces, with the unmentionable

Ryongsong Residence (see box, page 127) and Changsuwon Residence both located here. One of the only things tourists may visit in Ryongsong at present is the **Oun Revolutionary Site**, but this large and rather sombre museum dedicated to Kim Jong Il's brief national service is only really suitable for the diehard fans of North Korea and political study groups. The main road through Ryongsong leads towards Pyongsong and passes through tiny **Unjong** District, which sadly has nothing to offer passing travellers.

South Pyongyang: Rangnang (락랑구역), Ryokpo (력포구역) and Sadong (사동구역)

The Taedong's south bank is far less populous than its north. While the central districts of Songyo, Tongdaewon and Taedonggang, located on a bend in the river, all have a degree of urban sprawl, the outlying southern areas of Rangnang (pronounced *Rakrang* and occasionally written as such), Ryokpo and Sadong are much thinner on the ground in both population and points of interest, but still serve up some must-see sights for those with time to explore Pyongyang in more depth.

Entering Rangnang via the Chungsong Bridge, the **Sci-Tech Complex** [88 C6] on Ssuk Islet was opened in 2015 and is one of Pyongyang's many white elephant projects constructed under Kim Jong Un. The complex, shaped like an atom, is promoted as a 'multi-functional diffusion centre of advanced science, technology and social education', and is of more interest for its fantastical architecture than the 20,000m² of floorspace, although the seemingly-to-scale model rocket in the main atrium is something to behold. **Turu Island** [88 C6], separated from Ssuk by a shallow channel is essentially a spot of agriculture in the heart of the city and *possibly* the location where the *General Sherman* was sunk (page 10).

Back on the Chungsong Bridge you may make out the **Rakrang Hotel** on the waterfront before you too arrive on the Taedong's south bank. This road eventually becomes the Pyongyang–Kaesong Highway (page 133), but before the city comes to a relatively abrupt stop you may catch a glimpse of the **25 April Film Studios** and the controversial **Pyongyang University of Science and Technology** (see box, below), both of which are typically off-limits to travellers. The main stop on this stretch of road is the **Monument to the Three-Point Charter for National Reunification** [88 C7], an oft-photographed stone arch straddling the road. The arch depicts two women, one from each side of the divided Korea, their outstretched arms jointly holding a map of a unified Korea. The base of the 62m-wide, 30m-tall structure has some revolutionary (in content, not design) bronze bas-reliefs that are worth a quick look after you have taken the near obligatory photograph of the monument from the middle of the road, likely to be devoid of traffic.

Bar the oft-empty Pyongyang–Kaesong Highway, the other main road in Rangnang is **Tongil Street** (Reunification Street) [88 D7], constructed in the early

---

PYONGYANG UNIVERSITY OF SCIENCE AND TECHNOLOGY (PUST)

Founded in 2010, this elite university is largely staffed and funded by evangelical Christians from overseas – Christians living and teaching in a country where proselytising is strictly forbidden. With all classes, save for languages, conducted in English, the university's ulterior motive, the cynics say, is to hit the ground running with its missionary work when the country finally opens up, striving to replace the worship of one idol for another. *Without You There Is No Us* by Suki Kim, published in 2014, is the Korean-American author's lonely account of her time spent teaching at the university.

THE THREE-POINT CHARTER FOR NATIONAL REUNIFICATION

The three charters for national reunification are the North's rather complex proposal on their vision for a reunified Korea, and consist of:

- The Three Principles for National Reunification (1972)
- The Proposal for Founding a Democratic Federal Republic of Koryo (1980)
- The 10-Point Programme for the Great Unity of the Whole Nation (1993)

While not succinct, the proposal, in sweeping summary, strives for a co-federal republic, achieved peacefully and independent of outside interference, respecting each other's ideas, ideals and systems. North and South would be represented equally; 'one nation, one state, two systems and two governments' to be known as the 'Democratic Federal Republic of Koryo', *Koryo* being the name of the first unified Korean state.

1990s. This major high-rise residential district is well worth driving along to soak up its brutalist architecture. Given the concentration of residents in this area, there is surprisingly little here for tourists (the Tongil Market sadly remains out of bounds), but a few restaurants, including the Pyongyang Duck BBQ (page 101), may lure carnivores this way. Just around the corner from the Pyongyang Dog Meat Restaurant, the **Hana Electronics Joint Venture Company** [88 D7] may be visited, but much like the dog meat restaurant, it is best avoided. Finally, if you really want to dash your hopes of joining the Workers' Party, you can request to attend a service at the **Jongbaek Church** [88 E7], the only Russian Orthodox church in the country. This Potemkin church opened in 2006 and also goes by the name Church of the Life-Giving Trinity.

Other than marking the beginning of the Pyongyang–Wonsan Highway (page 149), Ryokpo is largely farmland, scattered with an undisclosed number of unmentionable and out-of-sight bunkers and batteries, together with at least one underground missile complex – the last line of ground defence between Pyongyang and the South. Bypassing all of this as quickly as possible, the only stop in town is the **Tomb of King Tongmyong**, smack on the border with North Hwanghae. This oft-bypassed UNESCO World Heritage Site is just about worth a visit to those interested in such things. Tongmyong was the founder of the Koguryo Dynasty (277BC–AD668) and his tomb, together with the Jongrung Temple that lies within the grounds, was massively reconstructed in 1993, to mark, for some reason, the 2,291st birthday of King Tongmyong. While the heavy-handed works of the 1990s rendered the bulk of the area of little interest to most, the burial mounds behind the tomb, scattered in light forest on Mount Chaeryong, are largely untouched and arguably far more inspiring than the main tomb.

Sadong is normally approached via the Taedonggang District, but to add confusion the **Taedonggang Brewery** (see box, page 101) is firmly in Sadong and now generally closed to visitors, although it can't hurt to request a visit to, at the very least, down a couple of cold beers in the on-site bar/restaurant, as they do occasionally open their doors to thirsty travellers. Maintained by the Russian embassy but almost completely forgotten by everybody else, in Sadong there is a corner of a foreign field that is forever Russia in the **Cemetery of Soviet Servicemen** [89 G6], , where 745 Soviets were buried between 1945 and 1959. On 15 August each year the embassy holds a small event and lays wreaths here to commemorate Liberation Day.

Nearer to the Taedong, the modern facilities at the interconnected **Pyongyang Primary School for Orphans** and **Pyongyang Middle School for Orphans** [89 H5] showcase the comparatively excellent care that these unfortunate children are fortunate to be afforded, with state-of-the-art facilities including a swimming pool and artificially turfed sports pitches. Heading on about as far as one may go in the district, the **Mirim Riding Club** and attached **Mirim Aviation Club** [89 H5] provide entertainment to the local nouveau riche and occasional tourist, from horseback and the passenger seat of a microlight, respectively. The riding club, which opened in 2013, has a small museum, indoor training ground, race track and a staggering array of facilities of equine interest. Those with a disdain for health and safety may of course saddle up and hit the racetrack, but if you almost certainly want to invalidate your travel insurance policy, taking to the skies in a microlight may also be considered. The aviation club has struggled to get off the ground in more ways than one, with flights often being cancelled, confirmed and then cancelled again; if you are keen to take a leisure flight over the city it is worth checking to see if it is currently possible. When running, a range of options are available, from short take-off and landing experiences to 1-hour flights over Pyongyang. Microlight flights tend to route you over the city landmarks and are unlikely to take you over

KING TANGUN AND HIS TOMB

Tangun, or Tangun Wanggeom, was the legendary founder of the Ancient Joson Dynasty, the first Korean kingdom. His life is recorded in the 13th-century *Samguk Yusa* ('Memorabilia of the Three Kingdoms'), a collection of accounts, folktales and legends relating chiefly to the three Kingdoms of Korea. This tome is the earliest record of Tangun, who is said to have founded the Ancient Joson Dynasty all the way back in the 30th century BC. Given that over 4,000 years passed between Tangun's founding of Ancient Joson and the first written record of his being, his existence is highly questionable, to put it mildly – and that's before we look at his heritage, being the grandson of the 'Lord of Heaven', and the son of a bear. Despite this, in the early 1990s state archaeologists 'discovered' his tomb and through carbon dating 'proved' that these were indeed Tangun's remains, putting them at precisely 5,011 years old.

There are many reasons why Kim Il Sung and Kim Jong Il may have created this discovery and built the Tomb of King Tangun; drawing comparisons between the founder of the first Korean kingdom and the creator of Juche, between the Ancient Joson Dynasty and the great, modern socialist Korea is an obvious propaganda play. As for the location, where else could the remains of the founder of Korea's first kingdom have been discovered – it would have been unthinkable for the remains to have been found in South Korea, after all.

The tomb itself is a nine-tiered pyramid structure made of granite, with a flat top. Situated on a hillock in front of Taebak Hill, the structure is reached by ascending a fair few steps, 25m wide and lined with 12 statues depicting Tangun's sons and ministers. A stone tiger appears to lord over all from the base of the tomb. The site occupies 180ha and is as impressive from a distance as it is up close. Entering via the rear of the tomb, a small chamber houses the remains of King Tangun and his wife. *Possibly*. It is an impressive enough structure, but is more of a testament to modern political symbolism in the Kim Dynasty than to anything else.

a couple of points of interest near the airfield – the Mirim College for Electronic Warfare Research and the ruins of the replica of the Blue House (the South Korean presidential palace) are understandably not on the flight path.

East Pyongyang: Samsok (삼석구역) and Kangdong (강동군)

Eastern Pyongyang consists of rarely visited Samsok and Kangdong. There is not a great deal on offer in this rural area; you will be scraping the barrel a little by coming this way, but the mentioned sites here occasionally feature on tours – typically suggested when a sudden cancellation or change of plans frees up a couple of hours and your hosts are not quite sure how to occupy your time.

Travelling beyond Mount Taesong, a surprisingly good road will speed you through Samsok District so quickly that you will likely miss the turnoff to the **Samsok Residence**, one of Kim Jong Il's residential complexes that looks (via satellite mapping at least) to be rather plush. Other than the seemingly unvisitable Koguryo-era Homan-Ri Sasin Tomb, the only place of note in Samsok is the **Taedonggang Combined Fruit Farm**, a sprawling site that mostly comprises orchards and a terrapin farm. The terrapin farm looked a little disorganised on my last visit back in 2013; according to Western media reports the manager was shot the following year for mismanagement so I, for his replacement's sake, hope that things have improved somewhat. After visiting an observation point to view apple trees almost as far as the eye can see, you will be given a little background spiel on farming before being taken to the on-site shop that sells a range of apple-based products including shampoos, alcohol, crisps and, of course, apples.

Crossing the Taedong and arriving in Kangdong County, the road is still very good – this may be because it leads to the Tomb of King Tangun, but a more likely explanation is that it also leads to Kim Jong Un's **Kangdong Residence**, a 400ha compound alleged to be his main summer hangout. You may catch a fleeting glimpse here of Kangdong Airport, which seemingly only serves *you know who*, but at this juncture your guide may well try to avert wandering eyes by giving a brief background to the thankfully always-bypassed Ponghwa Revolutionary Site, and to your upcoming stop and the end of the line for you in East Pyongyang: The Tomb of King Tangun (see box, opposite).

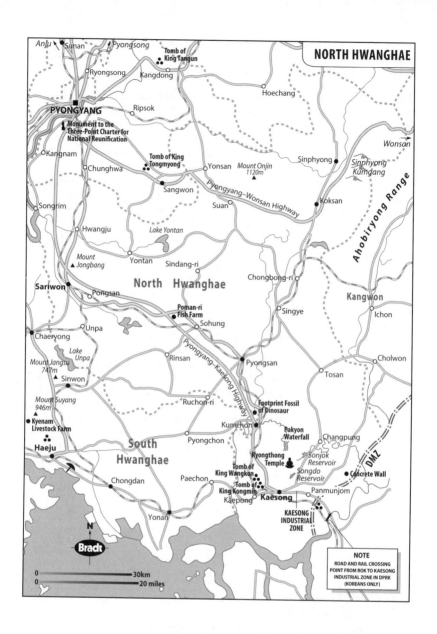

4

North Hwanghae
(황해북도)

Almost everybody coming to North Korea will visit North Hwanghae as it is the home of Panmunjom – arguably the nation's single most poignant reminder of a divided nation, and something upon which the majority of Koreans on either side of the divide don't like to dwell. In addition its 2.11 million inhabitants, an impressive (or alarming, depending on your outlook) yet undisclosed number of soldiers are based in North Hwanghae, so that, as almost anybody in the country will tell you, 'the aggressors will be defeated at a single stroke at anytime and anywhere they may attack'.

While mountainous in the east and northeast, the bulk of North Hwanghae is low hilly terrain with a good deal of agricultural land. Partially including territory south of the 38th parallel, territorial gains from the Korean War, North Hwanghae has no big industrial cities in comparison with most Korean provinces; Kaesong, Sariwon (and *presumably* off-limits Songrim) all feel quite parochial when compared with the big cities further up the food chain. The most developed light industrial site in this pocket of Korea is the Kaesong Industrial Zone (see box, page 143), a rare example of North–South co-operation.

After Panmunjom, the big draw for visitors is historical Kaesong, with its scattering of UNESCO World Heritage Sites, significant chunks of aesthetic pre-war housing and (comparatively) laidback atmosphere. Indeed, North Hwanghae is one of the most relaxed regions in the country to visit, due to the number of visitors that come here; somewhat ironic given that this is the only place where one may visit the DMZ, one of the most militarised places on earth. While the DMZ can be visited in a long and rushed day trip from Pyongyang, visitors could easily spend a few days touring North Hwanghae and all that it offers; after all, if you have come this far it would be a shame just to do so to look across a sad border that shouldn't be.

GETTING THERE AND AWAY

The Pyongyang–Kaesong Highway is one of the best roads in the country and can get you from the capital to the DMZ in as little as 2½ hours. The Pyongyang–Wonsan Highway also passes through North Hwanghae, and while not as fast as the Kaesong road it is still decent by local standards, at least until it reaches the mountains beyond Sinphyong. Once off the main roads, travel becomes drastically slower.

THE PYONGYANG–KAESONG HIGHWAY

Often referred to as the Reunification Highway as this road may, one day, be the link between Pyongyang and Seoul, this oft-deserted 170km-long dual carriageway bisects North Hwanghae as it ferries travellers across the province to the southernmost point one may visit – the DMZ. Completed on Kim Il Sung's 80th birthday (what do you give the man who has everything?), the highway is something of a prestige project – while such a road is convenient for tourists, it has little economic value. Often dead-straight with well-maintained hedgerows along the central reservation and cosmos flowers scattered along the side of the road, it is a surreal and scenic journey that flies by.

Heading south from Pyongyang, the Monument to the Three-Point Charter for National Reunification (page 128) is the first, or last, notable stop on the road, although you are still technically in Pyongyang until you leave Ryokpo District. Departing the capital there is normally no need to stop at the military checkpoint – you are, after all, leaving (it will be a different experience on your return). The small city of Songrim, which is brushed aside by guides as 'just another ferrous-metal production centre', is bypassed as you speed south, passing the turnoffs for Mount Jongbang (page 136) and Sariwon.

SARIWON (사리원시) The provincial capital of Sariwon is an agreeable little place, 62km and around 70 minutes' drive south of Pyongyang. This relatively flat and green city of 308,000 people on the plains of Chaeryong is an important road and rail junction for the southwest of the country, as well as having a navigable canal linking the city to the nearby Jaeryong River, a tributary of the Taedong. Sariwon is home to an impressive number of universities and colleges and has its own distinct atmosphere, quite different from most North Korean cities. Besides education, the economy is closely linked with agroindustry and textiles, with numerous plants such as the Sariwon Disabled Soldiers' Spinning Factory and the Sariwon Textile Factory helping to keep people looking busy and dressed smart. In a nation that has focused much of its development in heavy industry (and often struggled as a result), it is refreshing to see Sariwon succeed by keeping things simpler – life here appears to be more comfortable than in most cities.

Where to stay and eat *Map, opposite*

Sariwon March 8th Hotel (31 rooms) The only lodging in town is home to some comically garish furnishings, thanks to the bad taste of the South Korean investor who paid for its refurbishment. Once your eyes have had time to adjust to the décor (if they ever do), you will see that this is a relatively comfortable overnight option, with friendly staff, a bookshop & a small café. The restaurant, also the only option in town, save for snacks on Folk Customs St, serves up good food that keeps on coming. **$$–$$$**

What to see and do
The city starts in earnest when you pass the friendly welcome that is the **AK-47 Monument**. From here it's a couple of kilometres to the middle of town and the foot of Kyongam Hill. Much of the city centre, including the entire avenue that leads towards the twin statues of the late great leaders, is off-limits, but the leisure hub of Sariwon, a small semi-pedestrianised area in front of Kyongam Hill *is* open to tourists. This is **Folk Customs Street**, comprising half-a-dozen or so restaurants, two small boating lakes and a few small amusement halls. Visits here are normally brief, but tourists may generally stop for something to eat if they are *actual* customers (ie: not just coming in to gawp at locals tucking into their lunch), sampling local specialities such as sticky rice cakes or cold noodles. Those that don't fancy some of the more appetising dishes on offer could always opt for the perennially popular offal platter, but

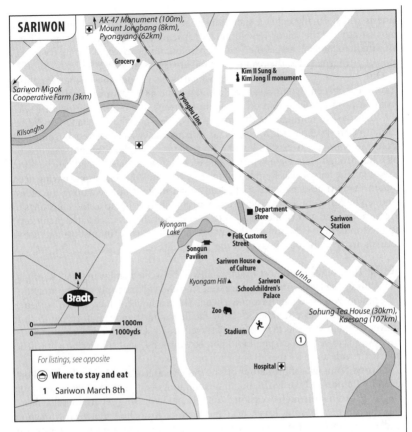

are recommended to make a polite departure at this juncture, and head to the **Kyongam Pavilion**, which dates to 1798, and from here head up one of the short and steep paths on **Kyongam Hill**, home to a number of pavilions that afford a partial panorama over Sariwon. From the uppermost viewpoint, Songun Pavilion, which is precariously attached to the rock with the support of a large concrete pillar, you will be able to make out Mount Jongbang to the north and the sprawling fields of the Sariwon Migok Co-operative Farm to the south and west, while below you the city passes by, locals come and go, and children splash about in rowboats on a small lake, just as they would the world over.

Heading southeast from Folk Customs Street, it's a short drive of just under 1.5km to the March 8th Hotel (see opposite) – you may be able to walk part way if your guides deem you ideologically sound and thus unlikely to 'misbehave'. The walk will take you via the exteriors of the **Sariwon House of Culture** and **Sariwon Schoolchildren's Palace**. Should you disobey your usually charming guides on this little jaunt you may well get the chance to visit the last building of note before the hotel, the North Hwanghae Provincial People's Security Bureau.

Farmland stretches almost as far as the eye can see immediately to the west and south of Sariwon, much of which comes under the jurisdiction of the **Sariwon Migok Co-operative Farm**, where you will be reliably informed that 'farming is implemented on a scientific and techonological basis'. This is a model farm, irrigated by Lake Sohung, which focuses on the cultivation of rice, maize and vegetables.

Guests will normally enjoy a short tour that takes in a farmer's home (which is interesting) and the Migok Revolutionary Museum (which really isn't), as well as a viewpoint to look out across the fields. Anybody coming to Korea should try to visit at least one farm, to see the realities of rural life (see box, page 197).

One last excursion from Sariwon, which is also a possible detour for those travelling between Pyongyang and Kaesong, is the 481m **Mount Jongbang**, 10km from Sariwon and just 3km off the main highway. The mountain, together with the Koguryo-era remnants of the Jongbang Fortress and the Jongbang Fort Walls, cannot be freely explored (for on its far side another walled fortress of some sort from the Kim epoch exists), but the draw here is **Songbul Temple**, reached by passing through Nam Gate, which is one of, if not *the*, largest walled gate pavilion in Korea. The temple was founded all the way back in 898 and, despite having been rebuilt many times since, the six buildings that make it up are among the oldest wooden buildings in Korea. The area is occasionally referred to as the Jongbangsan Pleasure Ground and is often busy with friendly yet slightly inebriated picnickers, so the monk here is happy for the change in setting when inquisitive and sober tourists arrive with questions about the area and its history.

SOUTH TO KAESONG Almost exactly halfway between Pyongyang and Kaesong, the **Sohung Tea House** makes an ideal rest stop and will probably be your jumping-off point as you head south from Sariwon. The tea house, which would be better described as a service station, has basic facilities and friendly staff trying to shift souvenirs and hot drinks to road-weary travellers. Upstairs, a hidden-away snooker room seems to be the focal point for kilometres around, while the restaurant will be able to provide a square meal if you have pre-booked.

Beyond Sohung, a short detour off the main road leads to the rarely visited but friendly **Poman-ri Fish Farm**, but almost all tours will push straight on towards Kaesong, driving through occasional tunnels and bypassing yet another fish farm, this one on the Ryesong River, near the town of Kumchon. Between Kumchon and Pyongsan (and best visited when returning to Pyongyang), the **Footprint Fossil of a Dinosaur** is housed inside a small building and levies an even smaller entrance fee to allow you to see these fossilised dinosaur footprints that were discovered during the road's construction. It really is a small site, but well worth dropping in as you pass. You will know that Kaesong is almost within sight as you pass through a number of military checkpoints, one of which is located smack on the 38th parallel (and thus the border from 1945–50); it won't be pointed out to you, but you may be able to spot an old milestone marking the border on the west side of the road.

KAESONG (개성시) South of the 38th parallel and synonymous with the Korean War, Kaesong is the only significant city that the North seized during the war – a war that they hail as a victory, despite their losing 3,900km^2 of territory. Largely spared from the conflict, relaxed Kaesong has an awful lot more on offer than just the infamous locations that highlight the results of a horrific three-year ideological war, with a wealth of historical interest near or within the city, much of which has been designated a UNESCO World Heritage Site. While most people just pass through to visit the border, it would be possible to comfortably spend a day or two exploring all on offer in this corner of Korea.

A well-appointed city of 308,000 people, its low-rise sprawl sits at the foot of 489m Mount Songak. With a significant portion of residents still living in traditional pre-war housing (likely the largest cluster of such in the country),

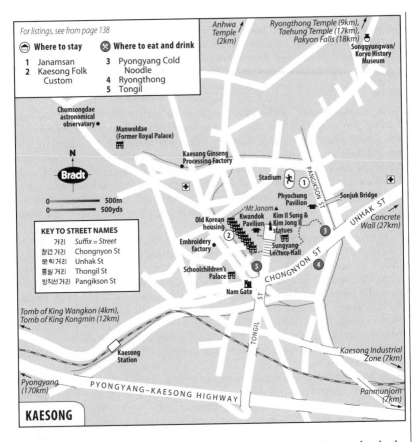

For listings, see from page 138

Where to stay
1 Janamsan
2 Kaesong Folk
   Custom

Where to eat and drink
3 Pyongyang Cold
   Noodle
4 Ryongthong
5 Tongil

Anhwa Temple (2km)
Ryongthong Temple (9km), Taehung Temple (17km), Pakyon Falls (18km)
Songgyungwan/ Koryo History Museum

Chomsongdae astronomical observatory
Manwoldae (Former Royal Palace)
Kaesong Ginseng Processing Factory
Stadium
Phyochung Pavilion
Sonjuk Bridge
Mt Janam
Kwandok Pavilion
Kim Il Sung & Kim Jong Il statues
Concrete Wall (27km)
Old Korean housing
Embroidery factory
Sungyang Lecture Hall
Schoolchildren's Palace
Nam Gate
PANGIKSON ST
UNHAK ST
CHONGNYON ST
TONGIL ST
Tomb of King Wangkon (4km), Tomb of King Kongmin (12km)
Kaesong Station
Kaesong Industrial Zone (7km)
Pyongyang (170km)
PYONGYANG–KAESONG HIGHWAY
Panmunjom (7km)

N
Bradt
0   500m
0   500yds

KEY TO STREET NAMES
거리   Suffix = Street
청년거리   Chongnyon St
문학거리   Unhak St
통일거리   Thongil St
방직선거리 Pangikson St

KAESONG

Kaesong has a very different look and feel from most Korean cities, and only the centre has any high-rise buildings. Largely walkable with wide boulevards and little traffic, you can *almost* feel like you're not in North Korea at times – if it wasn't for the statues of the leaders that preside over Kaesong from the top of Janamsan, a hillock in the centre of town.

History Kaesong was the capital of Korea during the Koryo Dynasty, from the beginning of the 10th to the late 14th century, although the Chosons moved it to Seoul (called Hanyang at that time) in 1392, where it stayed for over 550 years right up until the division of the peninsula in 1945. The Choson Dynasty largely ignored Kaesong because of its association with the regime they overthrew, so little of note happened in town until small-scale industrialisation arrived in the late 19th century. Only the university, founded in 992, continued to function under the Choson – and it still operates today.

In 1898, Isabelle Bird wrote in her book *Korea and her Neighbours*:

Kaesong is now the second city in the kingdom, but was the capital five centuries ago. The great gate is approached by an avenue of trees, and the road is lined with monuments to good governors and magistrates, faithful widows and pious sons.

Points of interest in a Korean city are few, and the ancient city is no exception to this rule. There is a fine bronze bell with curiously involved dragons in one of the gate towers, the Governor's Yamen, once handsome, now ruinous, a dismal temple to Confucius, and a showy one to the God of War. Outside the city are the lonely remains of the palace of the Kings who reigned in Korea prior to the dynasty of which the present sovereign is the representative. Even in their forlornness, they give impression that the Korean Kings were much statelier monarchs then than now.

With the introduction of the 38th parallel at the end of World War II, Kaesong became part of South Korea, due to the border falling to the north of the town. In the years leading up to the Korean War, there was much military activity in and around the town, with raids across the borders (in both directions) as each side tried to test the resolve of the other. Indeed, in May 1949, a full year before the full-scale war started, a four-day battle ensued, started by forces in the South and resulting in several hundred casualties. Nevertheless, Kaesong stood undefeated and remained in the South, although it did result in a number of genuine defections to the North from people living in the area.

Kaesong saw battle again on 25 June 1950, when the North Koreans attacked the border and captured the town; indeed, it was this attack that started the Korean War in full. Kaesong fell quickly, not only due to its proximity to the border, but because 60% of the South Korean troops were on leave during the time of the attack. From here, the North was able to reach Seoul quickly and almost unhindered, seizing it on 28 June. Armistice talks started in Kaesong on 10 July 1951, at the time in North Korean hands, although UN forces had seized it briefly in late 1950; these talks were broken off in August 1951, and when they restarted, it was at the village of Panmunjom. The two years between the summers of 1951 and 1953 were a time of constant bombing of all major North Korean cities, but Kaesong was spared from this, and today visitors can see a town little damaged by the war. It is the only town where control changed after the war from the South to the North because the ceasefire line did not exactly follow the 38th parallel.

Even today, the DPRK government continues to restore ancient buildings in Kaesong to give credence to the idea that Koreans, both racially and culturally, stem from areas that are now in the North. Tourism is a major beneficiary of this, particularly given that no other town in the North, or for that matter in the South, can display such a range of ancient buildings that remain undamaged by the war. The future of Kaesong will, however, very much depend on the success of the Kaesong Industrial Zone (see box, page 143): if 50,000 or more workers can again be employed there, the town's future is secure; if not, it will most likely return to being a quiet provincial backwater.

Where to stay *Map, page 137*

Shoddy plumbing, dodgy electrics and a warm welcome can be expected in Kaesong; you may have limited access to hot water, but don't count on it. The Yokjon Hotel opposite Kaesong Station appears not to accept foreigners these days, while the friendly sounding Foreigners' Hotel besides Pakyon Falls seems to have been forgotten completely.

Janamsan Hotel (43 rooms) A more conventional hotel with Western bedding, the Janamsan dates to 1984, with architecture more Orwellian than Choson. The charming staff, knowing that they are on the back foot as most visitors opt for the alternative option in town, really make an extra effort to keep guests content. A souvenir shop, bars, billiards & large restaurant will help you while away any free time. One of the best places in Korea for the open minded & empty stomached to sample *dangogiguk*, a spicy dog meat soup. $$–$$$

🏠 **Kaesong Folk Custom Hotel** (50 rooms) Comprising 19 single-storeyed Korean-style houses & often also going by the name Minsok Folk Hotel, this option in Kaesong's old quarter is about as traditional as it gets in the DPRK. While the hotel dates to 1989 the houses themselves date back to the Choson Dynasty, with each home having been divided into a number of rooms that share a small courtyard. The only catch, for some, is that guests sleep on traditional floor mattresses & typically dine on the floor also – a step too far for some. The 4 rooms in building 10 were recently renovated to an 'international standard' (at least through the eyes of locals) & are thus the most coveted. They are certainly the best rooms in the city, but don't be too disappointed if you don't manage to wrangle one. **$$–$$$**

✗ Where to eat and drink *Map, page 137*

Kaesong, being the home of ginseng (see box, page 140), has a number of speciality dishes that are offered by most hotels and restaurants, though do bear in mind that some dishes can take a while to prepare so may need to be pre-ordered. Some of the more famous dishes in the region include *pyeonsu* (dumplings), sinseollo and *insam takgom* (ginseng chicken), but they all pale in comparison to pansangi, which isn't commonly seen outside of Kaesong. Served to royals during the Koryo Dynasty, pansangi is presented in a number of small bronze bowls, each filled with various dishes that will include meats, tofu, vegetables, kimchi and acorn jelly. In case you are still hungry, a pansangi is normally always followed by rice and soup, as with most meals in Korea.

Besides dining in hotels, a surprising number of restaurants are available in Kaesong. They are mostly all identical in content and setting. Popular options include the **Ryongthong Restaurant** (**$$$**), the rather retro **Tongil Restaurant** (**$$$**) and the **Pyongyang Cold Noodle Restaurant** (**$$$**), a short walk from (and a good option for those staying at) the Janamsan.

What to see and do

Central Kaesong Coming into Kaesong from the highway, you will immediately enter Tongil Street, descending the wide avenue that leads to the city centre, passing notable buildings such as the Kaesong Kindergarten and Kaesong Cinema. The road descends to **Nam Gate**, one of the original seven citadel gates of the inner castle of Kaesong. Built between 1391 and 1393 and restored after the Korean War, the gate houses the 14-tonne Yonbok Bell, cast in 1346. Immediately to the west, the **Kaesong Schoolchildren's Palace** is a more bitesize (and less glitzy) version of the Pyongyang equivalent, and may open to larger groups, by appointment. To the north of Nam Gate, a steep road leads to the hillock of **Mount Janamansan**, atop which twin statues of the leaders can be found. Of more interest on Mount Janamansan is the **Kwandok Pavilion** that dates back to 1780, from where you will be afforded a good view over the old town.

Heading east, a little behind the Kaesong City House of Culture, the **Sungyang Lecture Hall** seems to have been dropped from tours in recent years. Constructed in 1753 to teach Confucianism, it is open to visitors (pre-arranged tours only), but is probably only worthwhile for those with plenty of time to spare. **Sonjuk Bridge**, near the Janamsan Hotel, is surrounded by historical remnants associated with it, such as the Phyochung Pavilion, all of which are UNESCO World Heritage Sites. The tiny bridge, which was built in 1216, is the spot where the Confucian scholar and statesman Jong Mong Ju was killed in 1392. A loyal advisor to the Koryo Dynasty, Jong was murdered by the orders of Ri Song Gye, who was striving (and succeeded that very year) to usher in a new dynasty. Jong's death came to symbolise unwavering loyalty (something well understood in the DPRK), and the additions to the site from the 18th and 19th centuries highlight that he is still highly regarded. Stone rails were added to the bridge in 1780 and somewhat detract from its appearance, but it is nevertheless a worthy stop on even the briefest tours of Kaesong.

Songgyungwan (Koryo History Museum) The biggest draw in Kaesong itself is Songgyungwan, often referred to as the Koryo History Museum, 3km from the centre of town near the foot of Mount Songak. Dating back to 992 and comprising over 20 buildings, this UNESCO World Heritage Site is one of the historical highlights of the entire country. The highest educational institute in the land during the Koryo and Choson dynasties and originally called Kukjagam, the site was renamed once more before settling in 1308 with its current name, when the Taesong Hall was constructed. Largely destroyed during the Imjin Wars, Songgyungwan was rebuilt in 1602–10, and most of what stands today dates to that time.

Entering through the outer gate, two 500-year-old ginkgo trees and a 900-year-old *Zelkova serrata* (also known as *keyaki* or Japanese *zelkova*) stand either side of a path leading to Myongrun Hall and the Inner Gate. Upon entering the main courtyard, the Memorial Services rooms to your east and west and the Taesong Hall in front of you constitute the Koryo History Museum, which opened back in 1987. These three small buildings include numerous models, photographs and historical relics, all giving a good insight into life during the Koryo era together with information on many remote and historical sights across the country. To the west of the museum, a small gift shop sells a plethora of ginseng products and traditional porcelain made by the Kaesong Pottery Factory – all at reasonable prices. By this stage in the tour your guides, who often have little interest in any history before 1912, may try to whisk you away, but outside the main west walls a number of monuments and pagodas, relocated from elsewhere, can be found and are well worth a look. These include the seven-storeyed pagoda of Hyonhwa Temple dating back to 1020 and the pagoda of Hungguk Temple from 1021.

GINSENG

Ginseng, or *insam* as it is known locally, has been cultivated in Korea for over a thousand years. While people the world over may disagree, *Panax ginseng* (also known as Korean ginseng) is generally considered as the finest variety of the plant, and should you ask a Korean, from North or South, exactly where the very best ginseng comes from they will almost certainly all agree – Kaesong.

The root of the ginseng plant is used in traditional medicine to treat a wide range of conditions and in Korea is hailed as a wonder tonic that cures all manner of complaints and conditions. While clinical research on the myriad health benefits that ginseng consumption affords is inconclusive, it is nevertheless a multibillion-dollar business that the North, home of the very best ginseng, hasn't tapped into, being responsible for less than 1% of international sales. Despite not making any real inroads into the global market, over 180 ginseng products are manufactured in the DPRK, from tablets and tonics to toothpastes and teas. If sanctions lift and marketeers can spin the mindset of shoppers into understanding that North Korea's Kaesong ginseng is the benchmark and the best, then business could really boom here – a rare North Korean success story might be just around the corner.

Once back in the car park you may want to pop into the excellent Stamp Shop, which has some unique postcards and a wide array of stamps, both for philatelists and postage, together with a comprehensive range of souvenirs – many of which you will be hard pressed to find elsewhere.

Other sites There are a few other sites in the city that have been overlooked by tourists for so many years that your guides may not even know that a visit is permissible, but you may want to investigate them if you have the time and more than a cursory interest in the Koryo Dynasty. Halfway up Mount Songak and 4km from central Kaesong, **Anhwa Temple** proffers a commanding view over the area. The temple was built in 930 and the road leading to it, given its condition, doesn't seem to be much newer – you may need to walk part way. In the northwest of town, just 2km from Nam Gate, **Manwoldae** dates from 919 and was the royal palace of the Koryo Dynasty. Destroyed in 1361 by a group the Koreans refer to as the 'Red Kerchiefed Rebel Army' (better known as the Red Turban Army), very little remains of it except for its stone foundations. To the northwest of Manwoldae's grounds, remnants of the astronomical observatory of **Chomsongdae**, which dates to the 10th century, still stand. The structure was destroyed at the end of the Koryo Dynasty and is regarded today as one of the oldest known examples of an observatory in the world.

Kaesong was a walled city in its Koryo Dynasty heyday, and 23km of the **Kaesong Walls** are still preserved today in some form. Walking the length of the wall is not a viable option just yet, but a little jaunt along short stretches of the fortifications, of which sections can be found near Nam Gate, Manwoldae and Songgyungwan, may help you picture how Kaesong appeared in its heyday.

Finally, if all the history is just a bit too much for you, you can fast-forward to the 21st century and tour the **Kaesong Ginseng Processing Factory** in the northwest of the city. There is big money in ginseng and many Koreans are obsessed with the stuff. An impressive array of products are made here, reputably the best ginseng manufacturer in the country. In 2010, when North Korea tried to settle 5% of its Cold War-era debt to the Czech Republic by offering them US$10 million worth of ginseng, the ginseng being offered was believed to have come from this very factory. The offer was politely declined.

AROUND KAESONG For those looking to linger in the area, up to a full day of touring (as always, as part of an escorted itinerary) can be enjoyed from Kaesong. While the sites mentioned can all be visited independently of each other, and the Tomb of King Kongmin should not be omitted on any account, they are described here as a circuitous day trip from the city, omitting the need for any significant backtracking along roads already travelled. Take a packed lunch.

The Tomb of King Kongmin Approximately 14km westnorthwest of Kaesong and normally reached by heading west through the city and skirting the edge of Kaepung, the Tomb of King Kongmin is undoubtedly the finest historic tomb in the country. Comprising two adjacent burial mounds (and slowly being renamed, to confuse things, as the Hyonjongrung Royal Tomb), the tomb contains the remains of King Kongmin, 31st king of the Koryo Dynasty, and his Mongolian wife, Queen Noguk. Construction began in 1365 after Noguk's death, and was completed in 1372, two years before Kongmin himself popped his clogs. Many tombs in the DPRK have been so 'restored' that most character has been lost, but not so here; the entire site is essentially untouched and in its original state. Consisting of a carved granite base topped with a hemispherical mound, each of which is surrounded by statues of sheep and tigers, which symbolise either fierceness and gentleness or Korea and Mongolia, depending on who you ask. Situated on a slope, the approach to the tomb is lined by statues of military and civil officials. Sadly, the tomb was looted by the Japanese in 1905 and cannot be entered, but a mock-up of the interior can be found at the Koryo History Museum (page 140). Interestingly, mention of Queen Noguk, a foreigner, seems to have been dropped in recent years from the local guide's official monologue; it seems the homogenous Koreans don't like to contemplate things such as mixed marriage. The hill facing the tomb, Acha Peak, literally meaning 'Oh my!', has a lovely legend surrounding it, a legend best heard on the spot from the raconteur groundskeeper, who must have delivered the tale thousands of times.

The Tomb of King Wangkon
Under 4km drive east of Kongmin's tomb, the Tomb of King Wangkon falls into the aforementioned 'overly restored' class of tombs. Wangkon, who lived from 877–943, was the founder of the Koryo Dynasty and the first king to unify the Korean Peninsula. Accordingly, his tomb really should have had a more cautious restoration. Sadly, heavy-handed works from 1994 have rendered this tomb into more of a film set than the major historical site it should be. Within the area of Wangkon's tomb, the Seven Tombs Cluster and three tombs of the Myongryung Cluster can also be visited, but these are of truly niche interest.

Pakyon Waterfall
From Wangkon, it's a 21km drive north-northeast to the Pakyon Waterfall. The journey is slow as the road narrows and winds over the Jongmyongsa Pass and through Pakyon-ri, but is nonetheless a scenic one. From the car park, which alludes to having facilities such as a hotel and restaurant, it is a short walk to the base of the 37m falls. Pakyon is not remotely as impressive as Kuryong Falls (page 205), but is still photogenic, particularly during the spring thaws and the rainy season; it is as good a spot as any to sit and soak up the tranquillity. The area around the falls is dotted with relics as this was the site of the Koryo-era **Taehungsan Fortress**, founded for the defence of nearby Kaesong. A short steep walk from the falls leads to the North Gate, while Kwanum Temple can be found around 1km away. While the North Gate really should be approached on foot for full dramatic effect, the points of interest beyond here, including the Taehung Temple, can now be reached by a new road, making the area far more accessible than it was in years gone by. Kwanum Temple was founded back in 970, and much of what stands today dates to the renovations of 1646. This was a beautifully tranquil little spot and is well worth a visit, but the new road does somehow detract from its serenity. Taehung dates to 921; originally a larger complex, the majority of it was destroyed by the various foreign invaders that came this way over the centuries, but the temple remains and is worth a quick look.

Ryongthong Temple
A new road from Pakyon leads south through mountains for 10km to Ryongthong Temple. Located in the Ogwan Valley near the Sachon River, this is a Koryo-era temple that was completely reconstructed (akin to the Tomb of King Wangkon), so is of limited interest to the casual visitor. Birthplace of the Chon Thae Jong school of Buddhism, Ryongthong was one of the most important temples in Korea until it was destroyed by a fire in the 16th century. The temple is a rare example of inter-Korean co-operation, with both North and South involved in its reconstruction from 2001–05. The grounds here are large, and include the tomb of Ui Chon, founder of Chon Thae Jong, so while it's not really worth a detour, should you be driving right past the temple a quick look around is worthwhile.

The Concrete Wall Saving what is, for many, the best until last, and normally possible only in the afternoons, the final spot on this circuit is 35km from Ryongthong and a good hour of driving away – the Concrete Wall. From Ryongthong, the road heads south, slowly descending as you skirt around Songdo and Sonjok reservoirs. Once past Sonjok, the mountains are essentially behind you and the DMZ lies ahead;

KAESONG INDUSTRIAL ZONE

In a rare example of North–South co-operation and optimism, the Kaesong Industrial Zone is a diminutive enclave of capitalism in the North, just a few kilometres from the border. Envisaged in 2003 during the years of the Sunshine Policy (page 30), the plan was to develop an industrial city for the mutual advantage of both Koreas; the South would have access to cheap labour while the North would see investment and the employment of hundreds of thousands of its citizens. Akin to how Mount Kumgang was operated (see box, page 206), with the land leased and heavily invested in by Hyundai Asan, the zone would be connected to the South by road and rail, allowing South Korean manufacturers to set up shop and employ North Korean labourers at salaries that were approximately 20% of the minimum wage back home. The project's final phase was optimistically expected to be completed by 2012 and was proposed to include residential areas, shopping centres and even a theme park.

The doors opened in 2004 and, at its peak, 123 South Korean companies employed 53,000 North Korean staff, whose wages, around US$160 per month, were paid directly to the North Korean government. The employment of 53,000 is nothing compared with the 700,000 target mooted by some, but there's the rub; history has taught us that doing business with North Korea is a dangerous game – the risk/reward ratio would send most investors running for cover. Dogged with setbacks from day one, the project's growth was hindered by sanctions imposed upon North Korea and disagreements over salaries and taxes.

After the Sunshine Policy was declared a failure, tensions between North and South were rekindled with events such as the sinking of the ROKS *Cheonan* and the shelling of Yeonpyeong Island. The grand optimism of 2003 turned to pessimism and the whole scheme faltered. In 2009 the zone was temporarily closed three times, but it was the political fallout from a nuclear test in the North and the US/South Korea military exercises of Key Resolve/Foal Eagle 2013 that caused a deepening war of words between the two Koreas, one that resulted in Pyongyang pulling its trump card – closing the zone entirely. Five months and an estimated US$944 million of losses later the South Koreans were allowed to return, but the excitement was to be short-lived. In 2016 further tensions closed the zone once more, as it remains today; talks on reopening repeatedly stumble and fall. In the meantime, Pyongyang has commandeered parts of the zone for its own use, in violation of all the agreements and much to the chagrin of the South. As Pyongyang ever so diplomatically puts it, 'it is nobody's business what we do in an industrial complex where our nation's sovereignty is exercised'. Much like in Mount Kumgang, quite what the South Korean investors will find, if and when they return, is causing many of them sleepless nights as they see their investments frittered away, as the buildings and infrastructure are, we all presume, slowly falling into disrepair.

the final portion of the journey is a mix of hills and farmland tinged with excitement and anticipation, as the border really is extremely close. The Concrete Wall, stretching across the southern boundary of the DMZ, is controversial as its very existence is questioned – the South and the US vehemently deny any such wall. The official line in the North is that the Concrete Wall was built by the South under the instigation of 'their masters', the USA, in order to create a permanent division between the two. Pyongyang claims that the wall varies in height from 5m to 8m and contains, along its entire length, near-countless pillboxes, lookouts and other such military instillations.

On arrival, a short walk up a trench pathway leads to a small building situated on the northern boundary of the DMZ. Here you will be met by a high-ranking military man with the gift of the gab; he will give an impassioned briefing on the Concrete Wall, which was built between 1977 and 1979, before leading you outside to see it all for yourself. Looking down from a slightly elevated vantage point on a clear day, across 4km of minefields through high-powered trench binoculars, one can definitely see … *something*. South Korean outposts and a barracks can be made out, as can the occasional vehicle in the distance (again, on a clear day), but fortifications of some form do also appear to exist. Real or not, fact or fiction, it is fascinating to get up close to the border at this seldom-visited spot – the only place where you can, for now, look out across the DMZ and take in the distant military installations of the 'puppet army'. After likely being commended, and possibly even saluted, for your bravery in visiting such a dangerous spot where, your military guide may tell you, 'a war may break out at any minute', it will be time to depart.

FROM KAESONG TO THE DMZ After Kaesong, the highway continues a further 8km to the border, and this last stretch is packed with interest, with views to your right of the Kaesong Industrial Zone (see box, page 143), the modern (and barely used) Sonha Station, together with an increasing number of simple road defences all reminding you that you have almost arrived at Panmunjom, the historic symbol of the long-drawn-out DPRK–US showdown. When you come to a large road sign informing you that Seoul is just 70km away you have indeed arrived at the northern boundary of the DMZ – this is as far as you can go without a military escort.

PANMUNJOM (판문점) AND THE DMZ (한반도 비무장 지대)

> The Korean people are a homogenous nation of the same blood that has lived for many centuries in the same territory, using one language.
>
> *The Democratic People's Republic of Korea*, Korean Pictorial, 1986.

While the above quote is true, nowhere so singly highlights this divided nation as Panmunjom, where, you will be told, the US forces, 'fell to their knees before the Korean people and signed the Armistice Agreement'. Panmunjom is actually a village just north of the border, but over the years it has come to be used as a metonym for what should more accurately be called the Demilitarised Zone (DMZ) and/or the Joint Security Area, the famous photographed spot where troops from each side glare and stare at each other, standing in the extreme reaches of their respective territory, the actual border: the Military Demarcation Line (MDL).

The three-year Korean War was one year of fierce fighting followed by two years of relative stalemate; though the fighting continued, little territory changed hands. By December 1950 the US was already discussing terms for an agreement to end the war, mooting at one point a 32km-wide demilitarised zone, but it was not until 10 July

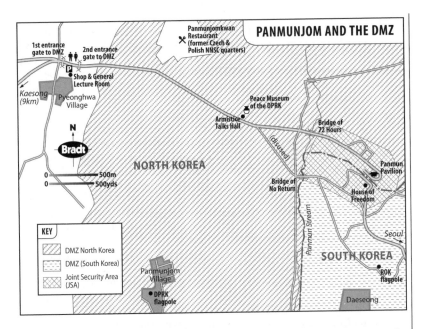

PANMUNJOM AND THE DMZ

1951 that armistice discussions started. Talks were originally held in Kaesong, in the possession of the North (page 138), but were moved shortly after to near Panmunjom, with the agreement that the protection of the area was shared by both powers.

The tense, painful and protracted meetings – 565 in total, comprising 227 liaison officer meetings, 179 subdelegate meetings and 159 plenary sessions – laboured over every point for a total of two years and 17 days, in which time the death toll continued to rise. The talks themselves were often a charade, with both sides engaging in time wasting and being deliberately obtuse, acerbic and venomous, such was the absolute aversion they had for each other. At last, on 27 July 1953 the armistice was signed. The North managed to paint the armistice as a victory, as while their original goal was to 'drive the enemy into the sea', in 1951 they quietly changed this slogan to 'drive the enemy to the 38th parallel', something they more or less achieved.

With the agreement signed, the Military Armistice Commission (MAC) was established to supervise the armistice, while the Neutral Nations Supervisory Commission (NNSC) was also set up to ensure both sides adhered to the finer points of two sub-paragraphs of an agreement that was understandably complex, to put it mildly. Both commissions still exist, but the passage of time has very much changed how things operate. Originally, an area called the Joint Security Area (JSA) was formed, a roughly circular enclave, approximately 800m in diameter, bisected by the Military Demarcation Line. This was envisaged as a neutral area, with free movement of both sides within the JSA; US and United Nations Command (UNC) troops could step into North Korean sovereign territory (and vice versa), as long as they stayed within the confines of the JSA. From 1953 to 1976 the JSA, despite perpetual tension, more or less functioned as a neutral zone, up until the Panmunjom Axe Incident (see box, page 149) resulted in the freedom of movement within the MDL ceasing. Since 1976 respective sides have stayed firmly on their own side of the border, save for when they have access to the huts that perfectly straddle the border, huts that are still in use to this day by both sides when they need to try and thrash out agreements on matters such as the 2018 Winter Olympics.

Today, in this sad place where, decades on, peace seems as far away as ever, crossing the border is impossible to all bar the very rarest of VIP delegations. No matter how small that little cement threshold appears, do not even think of trying to cross – it could well be the very last thing that you do; as the apt saying goes, 'the line between bravery and stupidity is so thin that you don't know you've crossed it until you're dead'.

WHAT TO SEE AND DO As you arrive at the entrance to the DMZ, a foreboding monolithic concrete gate spells out quite clearly that you have arrived somewhere rather serious. Your guides' typically affable and unflappable personas will likely shift to more stern and serious – from hereon in you are in the hands of the 'heroic Korean People's Army, the invincible revolutionary armed forces!'

Arriving in a quasi-courtyard, you will likely spend anything from 5 minutes to an hour waiting while paperwork is sifted through and cigarettes are smoked. Photography in the direction of the DMZ is prohibited from this point on – you will be told where and when you may take pictures.

Almost all visitors to the DPRK come to Panmunjom – anything from a handful to hundreds of visitors each day depending on the season – so, though it may sound odd, visiting Panmunjom is one of the most touristic things to do in the country and it can often feel overly busy with tourists. Groups are often pooled together depending on their nationality and status, but the system of deciding which group travels and when all seems rather arbitrary – often seeming to come down to the feminine whiles of your lady guide (so fingers crossed that you will have one), and her ability to flirt with the relevant male guards. While waiting, a bustling shop has a captive audience and plies a roaring trade in all manner of DMZ-related souvenirs – clearly the talons of capitalism have spread just a little north of the border.

After an indeterminate amount of time, you will all be rounded up and bundled into the small and often crowded **General Lecture Room** connected to the shop. Here, a dashing officer will give a brief introduction to the tour and the background of the DMZ – you may be sharing the room with various translators barking over his voice, so it pays to squeeze your way to the front and get up close, as nothing is repeated and there will be no time for questions, be it in this room or almost anywhere on the excursion. While all this is going on, the vehicles in the crowded courtyard will shuffle around in some form of carpark Tetris as they squeeze out of the courtyard and drive through the narrow entrance gate.

Back in the courtyard and lining up in strict single file, your party will be counted, checked and counted again, before being sent on, on foot, into the belly of the beast, where your vehicle awaits. Back on board you will be accompanied by a soldier 'for

POLES APART

Much like how Donald Trump boasted in 2018 that his nuclear button was bigger than Kim Jong Un's, back in the 1980s the South and North vied to outdo each other with something a little less threatening, but even more phallic – their flagpoles. When the South erected a 98m flagpole inside the DMZ, the North's 160m-tall rebuttal, also inside the DMZ, held the record as the world's tallest for over a decade until a 'flagpole war' erupted in the Islamic world and knocked them from their perch. At present, the North can only boast the fourth-tallest flagpole in the world, but still, Kim Jong Un has a much bigger one than Trump, with the US's tallest flagpole a paltry 120m.

OH CHONG SONG

In November 2017 Oh Chong Song, a driver in the Korean People's Army, defected from North to South by crossing the DMZ inside the JSA. In hair-raising publicly available surveillance footage, he can be seen speeding his jeep through the final checkpoints, along the very road that visitors here take, before grounding his vehicle and making a dash on foot into the South. Shot five times by his former comrades giving chase, Chong Song collapsed just metres inside South Korean territory, before a dramatic rescue whisked him away to safety. In what was an excellent public relations victory for Seoul, Chong Song was afforded the very best medical care possible, survived his ordeal and, by default, became a South Korean citizen.

your protection' and the anticipation and trepidation grows as you drive through an array of impressive and rustic defences, as you creep towards the MDL. Hawkeyed visitors may spot the old rusty sign warning you that you are entering the DMZ, together with the DPRK/ROK flags fluttering atop their respective flagpoles in the distance; close, but so far.

Your first stop will typically be at the **Armistice Talks Hall**, approximately 620m from the MDL. Here you will be taken into the small building – it can be a tight squeeze – where the armistice meetings were held. The table and chairs, which you may sit at, are said to be original and the officer in charge will be able to tell you who sat where, possibly peppering his discourse with the occasional jab at the 'arrogant yankee imperialists', who were, you will be informed, 'outsmarted at every step, both on the battlefield and in the negotiations'. Be quick, as before you have the chance to soak in the significance of this humble hut you will be moved onto the adjacent building, the **Peace Museum of the DPRK**, which used to be known as 'the Hall where the Armistice Agreement was Signed'. The less catchy name for this building says it all, and the table, chairs and flags here are also said to be the very ones used back in 1953. The military officer can once again be hard to hear on busier days; your time may be better spent looking at the back wall, which has a fantastic selection of photographs and, tucked away in a glass corner cabinet, an axe alleged to have been used in the Panmunjom Axe Incident (see box, page 149). Just being allotted a fraction of the time you would likely like to have here does hack most visitors off; before you have had the chance for a perfunctory glance of all there is to see you will be ordered to move on, back onto your bus for the final furlongs.

Back in your transport, at the Y junction in the road the right fork leads to the now essentially disused Bridge of No Return (see box, page 148), while you will take the left branch, crossing the Bridge of 72 Hours and driving over the Panmun Stream into the JSA, parking up behind the elevated Panmun Pavilion. Disembarking once more, you will be carefully reminded where you are, before being escorted, now under the watchful eyes and lenses of a fair few soldiers and cameras, as you walk anti-clockwise around the outside of Panmun Pavilion. Before coming to what you really want to see, you will be 'invited' to photograph a large stone slab engraved with the words and autograph of Kim Il Sung. The stone is littered with symbolism, with its height, length and the number of flowers, etc, all having meaning; but the greatest symbolism is in the text and the date – the words speak of reunification and the date, 7 July 1994, was the day before his passing – 'to the last breath President Kim Il Sung strived for reunification', you will be told.

Walking around the corner with a palpable tension in the air, even the most disorderly of groups somehow seem to march in rank and file by now as they arrive, at last, at **the MDL**. The famous huts stand metres in front of you, seven in all. The huts all straddle the border, with a door at each end – one opening to the North and one to the South. Behind the huts, the modern South Korean equivalent of the Panmun Pavilion, the House of Freedom looks back at you, as do a number of surveillance cameras. From left to right as you face them, the first, second and third huts are administered by the Korean People's Army (KPA), United Nations Command (UNC) and the Military Armistice Commission (MAC), with the final four interconnected huts under the jurisdiction of the Neutral Nations Supervisory Commission (NNSC). More often than not, the South is deserted (but you are always being watched), while at other times you may see ROK or US/UN soldiers standing on their side of the border; they may well photograph you, or trail you with binoculars.

Access to the huts cannot be guaranteed for obvious reasons, but the icing on the cake of a tour to Panmunjom is had by being granted access to the main hut, the **Military Armistice Commission Conference Hall**. Walking in, a table and chairs stand in the centre of the room, half in the North, half in the South. Even here the border is marked: microphone cables run across the centre of the table. Visitors may walk around the table, and thus step into the South, albeit by just a couple of metres. If you are truly fortunate, or worthy, you may be able to stand in the southern portion of the hut while being glared at through the window by a soldier of the 'puppet army', with just a pane of glass and a few inches separating you both. While it may be tantalising to try the door handle that opens onto Southern soil, it will be under guard by two very serious and burly Northerners – this really is not the time and place for any tomfoolery. If access has been granted to the MAC Hall, your time in it will be fleeting.

The final visit in the JSA is slightly more relaxed: the **Panmun Pavilion**. The building will be instantly recognisable as it features in the backdrop of all the

BRIDGE OF NO RETURN

The Bridge of No Return spans the Military Demarcation Line (MDL) and was North Korea's only road link with the JSA, albeit only its southern sector. When freedom of movement within the JSA was withdrawn in 1976 as a result of the Panmunjom Axe Incident (see box, opposite), the DPRK no longer had road access to their sector of the JSA and thus constructed the Bridge of 72 Hours, a direct link to bypass South Korean soil. In need of repair, the Bridge of No Return is now little more than a historical relic, but what a significant one; tens of thousands of prisoners of war crossed this bridge, in each direction, for repatriation between April and December 1953. As agreed, all prisoners had the option of staying where they were; nobody was to be forcibly repatriated. Those that decided to remain with the communists included 21 Americans and a Scottish Royal Marine, Andrew Condron. The majority of these men went directly to China and settled there for some years, but as the political climate evolved, both in China and back in the West, almost all of them had quietly returned home by the late 1950s. The last time the bridge was used for a major release of prisoners was in December 1968, when the 82 surviving crewmembers of the USS *Pueblo* walked, one by one, over the Bridge of No Return, ending their 11 months in captivity.

PANMUNJOM AXE INCIDENT

Also known as the Korean Axe Murder Incident, the Panmunjom Axe Incident of 1976 led to the JSA ceasing to exist in all but name. When US and ROK troops attempted to trim a poplar tree within the JSA, a tree that partially blocked the line of sight between a UNC checkpoint and observation post, the KPA took umbrage, arguing that any such activities with the JSA must be discussed and approved through the proper channels. With neither side backing down from the ensuing standoff, a brief and vicious fight ensued that resulted in the brutal deaths of two Americans, Captain Arthur Bonifas and First Lieutenant Mark Barrett, with Barrett being hacked to death with an axe. The US response came three days later with Operation Paul Bunyan – its aim being to cut down the tree through overwhelming force. Comprising numerous ground vehicles, heavily armed special forces, attack helicopters, fighter jets and more, the tree was felled in 42 tense minutes; 42 minutes in which hundreds of belligerents from the two sides faced each other, just one shot away from the likelihood of reigniting the Korean War. Ever since, both sides have stuck firmly to their own side of the now not so 'Joint' Security Area.

'watching them, watching us' photographs that the press loves to use when running stories on the 'hermit kingdom'. From the pavilion's balcony you will have a good view over the border huts and onto Freedom House, and here you can normally have a chat and photo opportunity with your military escorts, who by now are likely to be a little more relaxed. Returning to your transport there is none of the paperwork or delay in departing; it is time for goodbyes from the KPA and a salute, before you speed back towards Kaesong in no time.

One last possible detour in the DMZ is, however, possible by prearrangement. When the Czech and Polish NNSC were sent packing in the 1990s, the two main buildings they left behind no longer had any great purpose; one now functions as a restaurant serving traditional Kaesong cuisine. Given its location, the **Panmunjomkwan Restaurant** doesn't see many customers, and it only opens if you book ahead, but enjoying a meal inside the DMZ, in the abandoned headquarters for the Eastern-Bloc observers of the Korean Armistice, is a wonderfully surreal end to a bizarre morning.

THE PYONGYANG–WONSAN HIGHWAY

The Pyongyang–Wonsan Highway opened in 1978, travelling south through Pyongyang's Rangnang and Ryokpo districts before entering North Hwanghae a little beyond the Tomb of King Tongmyong (page 129). After the tomb there is essentially nothing tourists can visit on the road until you reach the Sinphyong Lake and Rest House, 94km away. The lack of sights doesn't mean that there is nothing to see, however, as the drive takes you over a highway strip (see box, page 67), affords views of Sangwon town and ever so slowly draws you into increasingly picturesque and rugged countryside, as the mountains ahead loom ever nearer.

SINPHYONG LAKE AND REST HOUSE Located on a lake above the Nam River's Sinphyong Dam, this rest house (7 rooms; **$$**) has an attractive setting, walled in by steep hills and crags known locally as Sinphyong Kumgang – a good indicator of things to come on the road ahead as from here it's up, up and away into the mountains towards the county border with Kangwon (page 191). Sinphyong is a logical stop for anybody heading east and can serve up a surprisingly good meal given its remote location. It is unlikely to be necessary, but foreigners can make use of the basic lodgings here and bunk down for the night. Bawdier Korean men talk proudly of their potent snake adder liquor and the special, *nudge nudge, wink wink* 'properties' that it affords them. The horrifically strong Sinphyong variety is considered as one of the best going – should you sample much more than a shot or two from the oversized jar in the restaurant here you may well be dragged to bed and horizontal within minutes, though you definitely will not be in the slightest state to 'excise your vigour'.

SINPHYONG KUMGANG A little detour from the rest house leads to Sinphyong Kumgang, a small area of short, steep and scenic walking paths that are vaguely reminiscent, if you *really* use your imagination, of the far more impressive Mount Kumgang. Keen hikers may want to consider a swift stretch of their legs here before moving onwards and upwards toward the real thing, but your time may be better spent elsewhere.

above   Pohyon Temple in North Pyongan is often referred to as a symbol of defence, having been destroyed and rebuilt many times during its history (K/S) page 177

right   The water at Rimyongsu Falls never freezes, despite its mountainous location (MT/S) page 229

below   Court officials and warriors are represented around the tomb of King Kongmin, near Kaesong (AI/S) page 141

left　A female employee at the Hungnam Fertiliser Complex in Hungnam (CM) page 217

below left　North Korea is outwardly secular, but a handful of Buddhist temples and monks preserve the traditions and beliefs of old (EL) page 41

below right　Tours often highlight many facets of society, including visits to factories and schools; pictured here, a worker at the Kangso Mineral Water Factory near Nampo (EL) page 161

bottom　New conscripts are drilled to perfection in preparation for a military parade (EL) page 75

above You're likely to see a handful of children's performances on a trip to North Korea, such as here at Sinuiju's Ponbu Kindergarten (j/S) page 184

right Young pioneer girls wave flowers at a celebration in Pyongyang (EL)

below On 15 April, the late Kim Il Sung's birthday, many locals go into the parks to dance and drink together (EL) page 74

above   Sunset over Sariwon, a relaxed and pleasant city in the agricultural heartland of the country (m/S) page 134

left   Typical propaganda posters, many of which are still hand painted, are found almost everywhere in the DPRK (AJ/S)

below   Up-and-coming Wonsan has a hint of Pyongyang-on-Sea about it (KG/AWL) page 191

above   Lake Chon, held within the volcanic caldera of Mount Paektu (EL) page 223

left   Kuryong ('Nine Dragon') Falls is a must-see on a trip to Kangwon province (SS) page 205

below   Tranquil Sea Kumgang, situated just a few kilometres from one of the most heavily fortified borders on earth (CM) page 210

above **Getting to Mount Chilbo isn't easy, but those who make the journey are rewarded with a spectacular variety of scenes** (KG/AWL) page 240

Specialists in tourism, cultural engagement and humanitarian projects
Channel 5 documentary Michael Palin in North Korea
Made in North Korea (Phaidon)
Game Of Their Lives (award-winning sports documentary)

Our expertise guarantees the best out of your trip | @koryotours f

We look forward to helping you travel to North Korea!

E.   info@koryotours.com
W.   koryotours.com
T.   + 86 10 6416 7544

KORYO
TOURS

North Korea travel experts since 1993

5

South Hwanghae
(황해남도)

In the southwestern corner of the DPRK, South Hwanghae is the smallest province in the country and largely overlooked by visitors, save for the occasional and brief transit before travelling onto the bigger and better things that lie elsewhere. Even the Pyongyang-based propagandists struggle to make the province, often considered as the breadbasket of North Korea, sound interesting: 'it has few mountains and abounds in wide and flat plains and hills. The feature of the terrain is fairly simple' – perhaps they never actually visited either.

The coastline is scattered with sandy bays and dotted with outlying islands, but proximity to the disputed maritime border with South Korea (see box, page 153) has kept all of this off-limits to the casual visitor and dissuaded the government from pouring too much money into significant industrial development. Instead, the powers that be have focused on South Hwanghae's agricultural development, to which the region is well suited. While those that live here are considered mere country bumpkins by many in North Korea, the local populace fared better than most during the lean years of the Arduous March, thanks to it being a rich agricultural heartland. Admittedly, there are better examples of cities and natural beauty elsewhere in the country, and South Hwanghae can be considered something of a rural backwater, but given both its proximity to Pyongyang and accessibility, those looking for a picture of pastoral life in the DPRK could happily spend a day or two exploring this overlooked corner of the country.

GETTING THERE AND AWAY

There are quite a few airports in South Hwanghae – unsurprising given its proximity to South Korea – but equally unsurprising is that they are not for civilian use. While the MiG-21 fighter jets at Kwail Airport are considered too modern and fast for you to see, the trains in South Hwanghae are considered too antiquated and slow for you to use – so your only means of transport in this part of the country is by road, most of which is unpaved, dusty, pot-holed and slow.

MOUNT KUWOL (구월산) AND THE NORTHERN COUNTIES

Immediately to the south of the Taedong River, and accessed by way of crossing the West Sea Barrage or coming via Sariwon, the north of South Hwanghae has a limited number of accessible sights, the majority of which are of niche interest. Still, a lovely day can be had trundling through this area, travelling from Nampo to either Sariwon or Haeju, or vice versa.

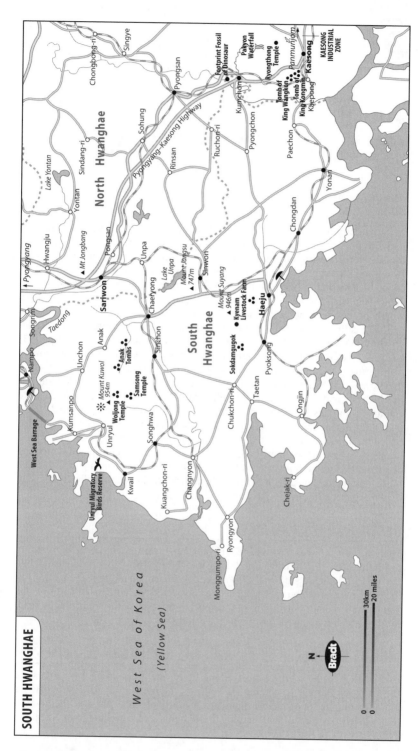

SOUTH HWANGHAE

THE NORTHERN LIMIT LINE (NLL)

Although the armistice in 1953 firmly fixed the land border between North and South Korea, the maritime demarcation of the two nations was not agreed upon at the time. The western seaboard of Korea, with its many bays, peninsulas and islands, would always be difficult to demark, and couldn't possibly be a straight line akin to the hastily concocted 38th parallel of 1945, particularly as some areas of the Five West Sea Isles, in possession of the South since the war, are as little as 12km from the North Korean mainland and are situated a fair way north.

In the immediate post-war years, the issue of delineating maritime borders was not high up on the list of urgent matters for either side to remedy, and while the Northern Line Limit (NLL) was alleged to have been drawn up by the United Nations Command (UNC) in 1953, records are almost as murky as the sea itself, with some accounts stating that it only came about in the 1960s. Regardless of when the NLL came into being, the North was not consulted and in 1973 lodged its first formal protest of the NLL, and continues to do so, taking the position that it is a 'bogus line unilaterally and illegally drawn by [the UNC] in the 1950s and our side, therefore, has never recognised it'. In response to the NLL, the North has drawn up its own interpretation of the line, the West Sea Military Demarcation Line – which is of course ignored by the South.

As time has gone by, agreeing upon a mutually acceptable maritime demarcation has become increasingly important for both Koreas, not just for their own security but also to ensure that each nation can safely fish the bountiful waters along the western seaboard. Commerce, too, has been hindered by this stalemate, with the North particularly suffering due to restricted access to its major port of Haeju – their ships currently having to make circuitous and costly detours in order to keep north of the NLL.

The North could argue its case at UN arbitration, as in a normal environment they would likely be ceded maritime territory under the UN Convention of the Law of the Sea (UNCLOS), but of course the situation is anything but normal, and the South is immovable and unprepared to discuss addressing any movement of their current line.

Frustrations turned to fury for the first time in 1999 during the First Battle of Yeonpyeong, when the two navies came head to head as they tried to exercise authority over their interpretation of the demarcation line, resulting in the loss of life to an undisclosed number of North Korea sailors. Three years later a very similar skirmish, the Second Battle of Yeonpyeong, resulted in fatalities on both sides. Lesser confrontations continued in the ensuing years, but the events of 2010 in the area, with the controversial sinking of the ROKS *Cheonan* and the Bombardment of Yeonpyeong (both page 33), highlighting that frank discussions between the two sides on this issue are desperately required before the death toll increases, as this disagreement has already bloodied the waters for too long.

WHERE TO STAY AND EAT At present there is no accommodation designated for the use of foreigners here, although by the time you read this a couple of basic options in Kwail and Unryul counties *may* have become available. Should you wish to see and do everything mentioned in this section, it's likely that a full day would not be enough – which means that until accommodation here is an option a good deal of backtracking will be required. Restaurants are few and far between – for now the best option is a prearranged packed lunch.

WHAT TO SEE AND DO

Mount Kuwol and around On entering Unryul County, shortly after crossing the West Sea Barrage, you will almost certainly start to head inland, skirting the Ido Reservoir as you head towards Mount Kuwol, or Kuwolsan. Mount Kuwol and its 99 peaks are the focal point of a 521.75km² UNESCO Biosphere Reserve; in addition to 110km² of heavily forested mountains, the reserve offers the potential for visitors to take in well-preserved coastal wetlands, lagoons and river estuaries. Within the wetlands, the **Unryul Migratory Birds Reserve** is an important habitat for northeast Asian migratory birds such as the red-crowned crane and black-faced spoonbill, and may be visited by ornithological groups. Sadly, few tourists come this way and even fewer show interest in much more than a brief picnic break in the area, so the relevant authorities have been reluctant to spend their efforts in developing the area and the plethora of ecotourism possibilities that could help protect the area for future generations.

The highest point on Mount Kuwol is 954m **Sahwang Peak**, partially encircled by 5km of walls, remnants of Kuwolsan Fort, built during the Koguryo era. The mountain is peppered with dramatic rocks and cliffs, with deep valleys rising up to rugged peaks – classic East Asian mountain scenery, so atypical of anything found in Europe. The area is densely forested with trees such as the Khingan fir and Jezo spruce. Unfortunately, trekking paths have not been developed to the extent that they have in areas such as Mount Myohyang and Mount Kumgang, and hiking is not really an option as yet, but those seeking natural beauty can strive to visit the Ryongyon Falls and other spots such as the Jonggok Valley. The peak can normally be reached by vehicle, with all but the largest buses able to make the journey over the picturesque mountain road that meanders from north to south, passing within a couple of kilometres of Kuwol's summit. Near the top of the pass, a narrow road for smaller vehicles (fair weather only) snakes west towards Sahwang Peak and the Sansong Revolutionary Site, a spot connected with the pseudo-historic activities of Kim Hjong Jik, Kim Il Sung's Father.

The main road south over the mountain descends, with just a short detour, to **Woljong Temple**. Located in Tanphung Valley, the temple is over 1,000 years old but was rebuilt in the early years of the Choson Dynasty. Remote Woljong consists of a scattering of pavilions and halls in a forest clearing to the east of Kuwol's Asa Peak; a tranquil little spot from where you may take a few moments to enjoy the scents, sounds and sights of the forest, ponder over the meaning of life with the resident monk and tuck into your supplies before getting back on the road. A number of other temples are scattered throughout Mount Kuwol, but most are hard to access and rather uninspiring to non-believers. Theologians may want to consider visiting **Samsong Temple**, but other than being a historical spot, the temple, which was completely rebuilt in 2000 after being destroyed during the Japanese colonial era, has little of merit to the casual visitor.

Sinchon Museum With the mountain behind you, it's just over 30km southeast through sleepy farmland to Sinchon, home of the harrowing and sombre Sinchon Museum, occasionally referred to as the Sinchon War Crimes Museum. Perhaps nowhere in the DPRK highlights that the Korean War is still unresolved and unforgiven more than here. The museum's disturbing photographs, relics and materials (2,800 in all) highlight the atrocities that took place during the 52-day

For some time, the powers that be have talked of offering up a few new places in Unryul and Kwail counties, which may be possible to visit by the time you read this. Spots such as the 4.6km **Long Distance Belt Conveyor of Unryul Mine**, which has helped reclaim over 47km² of tidelands to date, and the **Kwail County Combined Fruit Farm** are unlikely to be the most popular tourist spots in the country, but could well be worth a look. Should you be able to overnight in the area, you will likely be put up at the Ryongsupho Bathing Resort, where you will probably have the run of the resort and its beach to yourself, but don't stray too far – the north end of the beach is used by the Air Force for target practice. Cho Island is approximately 7km offshore from the beach and was in the control of the US Air Force (USAF) from January 1952 until the signing of the armistice. It is now home to a small naval base, so island-hopping boat trips are still some years off.

occupation of the area by UN/ROK forces, in which 35,383 residents (a quarter of the county's population) were killed, 900 of whom were locked in an air-raid shelter (found within the museum's grounds) and burnt alive. At the entrance to the museum, which was completely rebuilt in 2015, domestic visitors can attend the small outdoor auditorium, the 'Revenge Pledging Place', to, as suggested in the museum's own pamphlet, 'vow vengeance on the US imperialists and class enemies'.

Coming here is an unpleasant, unsettling experience, but helps tell the untold tales of war and gives a fascinating perspective into the mindset of contemporary North Koreans, for whom the war is neither over nor forgotten.

Anak Tomb No 3 From Sinchon it's a 35km drive northeast to Sariwon (page 134), or 62km south to Haeju (see below), although one last option is available to those looking for some dawdling discovery. Just 13km to the north of Sinchon, the splendid Anak Tomb No 3 is a Koguryo-era chamber tomb believed to be the mausoleum of King Kongukwon, which would date the tomb back to AD357. While its plunderable treasures are long missing, the mural paintings and tomb interior are in surprisingly good condition, depicting contemporary life and customs in the Koguryo era. This UNESCO World Heritage Site is so rarely visited that you will most likely have the entire place to yourself – ancient history buffs will be in their element. In case you were wondering, Anak Tombs No 1 and 2 do exist nearby, but they are not open to the hoi polloi.

HAEJU (해주시) AND THE SOUTHERN COUNTIES

The provincial capital of Haeju is an overlooked city of 273,000, well situated between the West Sea of Korea (Yellow Sea) and Mount Suyang. The area around Haeju has been inhabited since Neolithic times and over the last millennium it became a significant centre of Buddhist learning – something largely disregarded these days. The city has had over a hundred years of bad luck, never really recovering from the advent of both the modern age and a divided Korea. It was once a strategic transit point and trading port for goods being shipped along the west coast and onto China, but the birth of the railways in the region in 1905 saw an end to that, as they bypassed Haeju completely, while the ramifications of its southern environs being smack on the 38th parallel haven't really helped the city find its feet since

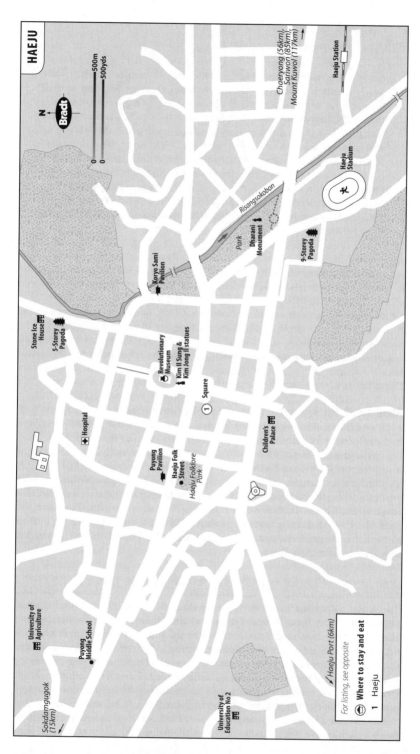

HAEJU

N

Bradt

0   500m
0   500yds

Chaeryong (56km), Sariwon (85km), Mount Kuwol (117km)

Haeju Station

Haeju Stadium

Risangsokobon

9-Storey Pagoda

Dharani Monument

Park

Koryo Sami Pavilion

Stone Ice House

5-Storey Pagoda

Revolutionary Museum

Kim Il Sung & Kim Jong Il statues

Hospital

Square

1

Puyong Pavilion

Haeju Folk Street

Haeju Folklore Park

Children's Palace

University of Agriculture

Puyong Middle School

Sokdamgugok (15km)

University of Education No 2

Haeju Port (6km)

For listing, see opposite

Where to stay and eat

1   Haeju

1945. South Korea's first president, Syngman Rhee, was born in Haeju in 1875, but he didn't spare his hometown during the Korean War. Syngman's attack on the city was aided on 3 July 1950 by British Seafire and Firefly aircraft that took off from the HMS *Triumph* aircraft carrier, striking an airfield in Haeju in the very first British shots of the war.

While the shipping business should be bigger here thanks to its ice-free port, restrictive shipping channels due to the Northern Limit Line (see box, page 153) have pushed a lot of business north to Nampo. It's not all bad news though; a fair few industrial sites such as the Haeju Steel Works and the Haeju Cement Factory help keep the city ticking over, with the intriguingly titled Youth Refinery showing that there may be hope yet for the future generations of Haeju.

As tourists may only approach Haeju by road from the north, a relative isolation has been imposed on the city, resulting in few foreigners coming this way. While Kaesong, for example, is only 90km away on rural backroads that are off-limits to tourists, the permitted road for foreigners is 180km, taking you all the way back via Sariwon. While obviously ridiculous, the chief benefit of this isolation is that very few people come here – if you want to see a provincial capital within a few hours' drive of Pyongyang that really does feel like the North Korea of old, then this is an obvious choice.

WHERE TO STAY AND EAT   *Map, opposite*
If coming this way, you will almost certainly need to spend the night in Haeju; there's only one option here. For now, the only reliable food option in the area is the Haeju Hotel but, with planning, a barbecue or picnic lunch may be arranged for you at some of the rural spots in the area. Otherwise, bring a packed lunch.

Haeju Hotel (48 rooms) In the heart of the city, the front-facing rooms here have a bonus view of the twin statues of you know who, a surreal backdrop to the window of local life that passes by in front of you. With acceptable facilities, this is a satisfactory stop for a night, particularly when you consider where you actually are. The spartan & somewhat clinical restaurant is welcoming enough & offers up a pretty standard selection of Korean dishes. Should you have an early start in the morning you may wish to set your alarm, but most guests are woken around sunrise by the air-raid sirens that boom out across the city from the hotel's rooftop. Thankfully the sirens turn to rousing music after a couple of minutes – in the unlikely event that the sirens continue you may want to locate your guides & the nearest bunker. $$–$$$

WHAT TO SEE AND DO
The road to Haeju Approaching Haeju from Chaeryong, roughly halfway between Sinchon and Sariwon, the road heads south through small towns, villages and relatively flat farmlands. The first possible stop on the journey is the perfectly pleasant yet somewhat overhyped **Mount Jangsu**, 19km from Chaeryong and just a short detour off the main road. This 747m peak is home to a mountain fort and the Myoum and Hyonan temples, but most visitors come for the scenery to the west of the mountain, enjoying a walk along the ravine floor to take in the natural beauty of an area that is hailed by slightly exaggerating, but rightly proud locals as the 'queen of valleys'. It is certainly an attractive spot with dramatic rock formations and thick forest, and the easy walk of a couple of kilometres is a pleasant diversion, although somewhat unnecessarily padded out by rather tiresome legends pertaining to seemingly every river, peak and point of interest.

Back on the road, prepossessing **Mount Suyang** rises to 946m and lies immediately to the north of Haeju. On the eastern flank of the mountain, the

128m-tall Suyangsan Falls are considered one of the eight wonders of Haeju – although quite what the other seven are is not clear. The waters fall down a rather polished cliff face, above which the Mount Suyang Mountain Fort Walls can be found. The 8km of walls, which date back to 1291, are an average of 6.5m in height and significant sections of the wall remain intact. Sure-footed travellers may ask about the possibility of scrambling along sections of wall before driving the last few kilometres to Haeju itself, entering from the east via the Hak Pass, where you may have to stop while your papers are checked.

In Haeju There is very little permitted to see in Haeju itself, but coming to this rarely visited city is an experience in its own right. Less than half a kilometre west from the Haeju Hotel, the **Puyong Pavilion** is the main draw in town, one that you may be allowed to access on foot from your hotel (of course, as always, with a guide). The pavilion dates to 1500 and partially sits atop a pond, but the structure today is of Korean Workers' Party heritage so is of limited interest, but worth a quick look nonetheless while you get your bearings. The shady pavilion is a popular haunt for Haeju's studious youth, many of whom can often be found sitting here, heads buried in their homework. You may be able to visit the small **Haeju Folklore Park** opposite the pavilion, but your guides will likely want to whisk you away quickly (the off-limits Haeju Market is too close for comfort). Occasionally, groups may visit the **Puyong Middle School**, a short drive west of the centre, but the facilities are tired and the tour on offer being far less interesting than similar options available elsewhere in the country. Other spots in the city that the persuasive may push to visit are the Koryo-era ice house, Haeju Sokbinggo, together with a number of 'national treasures' such as the Haeju Nine-Storey Pagoda, the Dharani Monument and the five-storeyed pagoda in the southern foothills of Mount Suyang.

By the time you read this, it may once more be possible to visit the **Hyongje Islets** in Haeju Bay. During the ebb tide a long stretch of beach is exposed on these uninhabited islands. Here, tourists may be able to enjoy sunbathing or taking a dip in the pools. The islands, approximately 7km southwest from Haeju Port, can only be accessed by chartered boat; the port is a rather dystopian one that may not be visited otherwise. The Hyongje Islets are around 30km from South Korea's Yeonpyeong Island, and thus the best place in the country to try and get one's head around the disputed maritime borders with the nightmare neighbours next door (see box, page 153).

Other sights around Haeju Once you have exhausted the options in Haeju it is, sadly, the case of returning towards Chaeryong, but the first portion of the journey can at least be on a different section of road. Heading northwest from the city, those who have requested it will skirt the southern fringe of Mount Suyang, being driven for 17km to **Sokdamgugok** on the Sokdam River. Translating as 'a stone pond and nine beautiful gorges', this is a picturesque and lightly forested spot sprinkled with historical relics such as the 16th-century Sohyon Academy and the Yogum Pavilion. Heading northeast, it's 14km from Sokdam to the **Kyenam Livestock Farm**, which focuses on breeding pigs, goats and rabbits. It really isn't the most exciting spot in South Hwanghae, but an interesting enough stop for half an hour or so. The highlight of your brief tour here may well be the methane production plant, with animal waste being used to partially power the village.

6

South Pyongan
(평안남도)

Bordering Pyongyang on three sides and appearing on the map like an amoeba about to envelop the capital, South Pyongan is the republic's most densely populated and populous province, with just over four million citizens calling it home.

Rising from the West Sea of Korea (Yellow Sea), the seaboard is largely tidal plains and farmland, with a peppering of salterns. Areas such as the Yoltusamcholli, Onchon and the Phyongwon Plains are considered to be the rice bowl of western North Korea, and great importance is placed upon them, especially due to their proximity to Pyongyang. Heading inland, the Taedong River – the second-longest waterway in the country – meanders upwards from the West Sea Barrage, through Pyongyang and up into the high and remote Rangrim Mountains in central North Korea. The river thins along with the population as it reaches the remote and very much off-limits Taehung County, home of the highest peak in South Pyongan, the 2,094m Mount Tongdae.

While agriculture in the lowlands of the province is of importance, state media proudly proclaim that South Pyongan is 'the number one base in the country for coal production' and that the well-developed province stands as a good example to the rest of the country. It is a shame, therefore, that only a small area of South Pyongan is open to visitors, particularly as it is so close to Pyongyang.

A significant portion of people coming this way will come just to visit the mammoth civil engineering project that is the West Sea Barrage, near Nampo. However, some more obscure sites cater to the inquisitive traveller, with the provincial capital of Pyongsong, under an hour's drive from Pyongyang, being an interesting and oft-overlooked city that feels like it is on the up, something that cannot be said of the whole country.

THE ROAD TO NAMPO

It's a 55km drive out of the capital to Nampo along the Youth Hero Highway, one of those fantastical 'only in Korea' developments: a motorway built by child volunteers during the late 1990s. Some Korean reports put the road's length as precisely 42.216km; 42 symbolising the year 1942 and the 216 as 16 February, thus 16 February 1942 – which, if you didn't know, was Kim Jong Il's birthday. It is the widest stretch of road in the country with five lanes in each direction – your driver (who will know the road intimately) will zigzag across all five, or even all ten, lanes to avoid any pot-holes as he attempts to break the North Korean land speed record.

Leaving Pyongyang, you will pass the **Chongsanri Cooperative Farm**, a famous model farm for the much-lauded (but now barely mentioned) 'Chongsanri Spirit

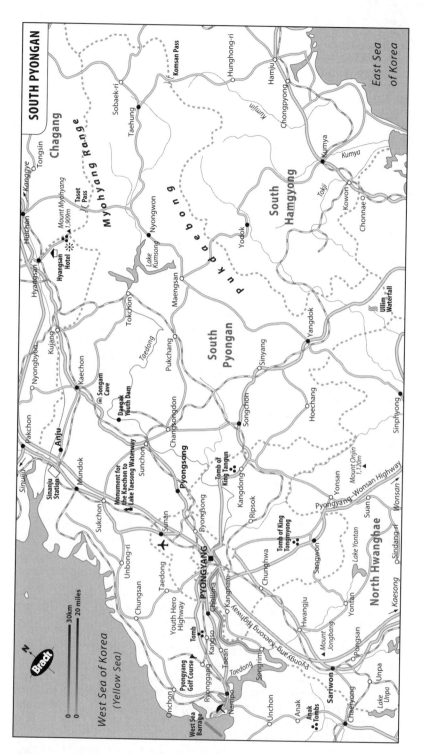

and Chongsanri Method' movement of the early 1960s, where superiors would assist and mix with their subordinates to find solutions to problems and consequently rouse the masses to 'conscious enthusiasm' by giving 'precedence to political work and work with people'. It's possible to tour the co-operative, with visits often taking in the kindergarten, a local home and certainly including their own revolutionary monument depicting – who else – Kim Il Sung. The on-site guides often seem quite hard line and unwelcoming when compared with their counterparts at other farms in the country (which are thus more enjoyable); possibly they feel that the rich revolutionary heritage of the area is too great for it to be a focal point for marauding capitalists. The staff at the nearby **Kangso Mineral Water Factory**, just a short detour off the highway, are generally much more welcoming, and visitors here will see the tapped spring and tour the bottling plant before almost certainly being sent packing with waves, smiles and a few complimentary bottles of water to quench your thirst as you head back off along the highway.

You may also wish to consider a round-trip detour of approximately 20km to visit the **Kangso Three Tombs** and the **Tokhung-ri Tombs**, two of the UNESCO World Heritage-registered 'Complex of Koguryo Tombs' that are scattered across 12 sites in the southeast of the country. While the sepulchres themselves cannot normally be entered, and there are admittedly more impressive tombs in the country, they are of interest to some, while others have likened them to 'a few mounds of earth'; you can decide for yourself.

One final 5km detour off the Youth Hero Highway is the 18-hole **Pyongyang Golf Course**, hidden from view in forest on the southwestern shore of Thaesong Reservoir, with well-maintained grounds and a dearth of visitors. The club house can, by appointment, provide meals to visitors passing through, while non-golfers can even whizz around the attractive grounds by hiring American-made golf buggies. Golf is of course available, as is equipment hire (of questionable quality and notable vintage). Prices for a round of golf are somewhat confusing as they jump around depending on the currency, exchange rate and arithmetical grasp of the staff, but expect US$150 per person to cover entry, club hire, access to the club house facilities and a snazzy electric buggy.

Back on the road, as you finally enter Nampo you will see to your right the entrance to the **Pyeonghwa Motors Plant**, the largest automotive factory in the country, which assembles a variety of models under licence from the likes of Fiat and the South Korean automaker SsangYong. Sadly, the factory is not open to tourists (it is alleged that the production line barely moves), but those interested in seeing a range of Pyeonghwa vehicles can always visit the Pyeonghwa Motors Showroom back in Pyongyang (page 122).

While almost all visitors travelling between Pyongyang and Nampo will head along the highway, the older road, which is also 55km long, is sporadically used. This route travels along the north bank of the Taedong River, entering South Pyongan in Nampo's Chollima District, home to the **Chollima Steel Complex**. This steel mill, one of the largest in Korea and certainly the most famous, was a Japanese colonial-era plant, the Kangson Steel Works, before it was adopted and renamed in the late 1950s as a symbol of the Chollima Movement (see box, page 18). The sprawling complex bellows a cocktail of pollutants as it produces millions of tonnes of steel and metal products annually in conditions that are reminiscent of a Pathé Newsreel from the 1940s. The site is occasionally open to visitors, but it is far easier to visit the nearby **Taean Friendship Glass Factory**. This factory opened in 2005 with heavy investment from China and was even visited by the then Chinese President Hu Jintao together with Kim Jong Il, as the Chinese government heralded it as 'a crystallisation of the traditional friendship between China and North Korea in the new period under new conditions'. Visitors today will see the modern production line from start to finish, but this really is of niche interest; there's no need to be too disappointed if a visit isn't on your schedule or is cancelled at the last minute.

NAMPO (남포시) AND AROUND

Nampo, designated a 'special city', is the prime port on the west coast (and thus the principal shipping link with China and much of East Asia) and a lifeline to nearby Pyongyang, with a good deal of freight passing through here thanks to decent road, rail and river connections with the capital.

It wasn't all that long ago that plans were in place to totally reimagine the city, with talks in the late 1970s and early 1980s of major development, regeneration and growth to build Nampo into a second city *almost* on a par with Pyongyang. A good deal of industry was developed in the boom years, with plants such as the Kum Song Tractor Plant and Taean General Heavy Machine Works being well known across the republic. Kim Il Sung placed great focus on the development of Nampo with a particular emphasis on foreign trade and shipping, with the aim (a problem that of course still exists to this day) of obtaining foreign currency – a factor in the construction of the West Sea Barrage (page 164). For a time, Kim pored over every aspect of Nampo's development, which became something of a pet project for him. Despite all the talk of developing Nampo, however, the city today certainly remains poorer than the capital, but a good deal of mutualism exists – Pyongyang needs Nampo just as Nampo needs Pyongyang. These days most tourists whizz through Nampo just to see the epic feat of engineering that is the West Sea Barrage, as other sights are a little thin on the ground. Regardless, the city does appear interesting – hopefully more will open up in time and, as Kim Il Sung had planned, it will one day rival Pyongyang.

WHERE TO STAY *Map, opposite*

While the key sights can be visited as a day trip from Pyongyang, a night or two in the area is worth considering by those wanting something a bit different. Any reference to the Waudo Rest Home and Waudo Hotel should be ignored – it appears they are currently so decayed that to admit foreign guests (and their cameras), would be a step too far. While a small and basic guesthouse in the Nampo Docks also exists, the Nampo Seaman's Club is for now only used by the handful of merchant sailors that come this way – those taking a river cruise down to the West Sea Barrage may pop in for a quick look. The toilet turned into a storeroom is just one of its less redeeming features.

Hanggu Hotel (104 rooms) A hotel of old that just about soldiers on, providing an authentic retro DPRK experience on Pyongyang's doorstep. A short drive from central Nampo, the Hanggu offers up cold water, broken lifts, good food & enough amusement to keep the open-minded entertained for the night. **$$**

Ryonggang Hot Spa Hotel (28 rooms) In a sleepy rural setting 27km northwest of Nampo, in Onchon County, this was once a VIP guesthouse for North Korean bigwigs (hence the saluting guard at the entrance), but since 2005 mere mortals have also been welcomed. A total of 28 rooms are scattered across 9 chalets, each room with its own hot tub providing piping-hot spring water that they claim treats all manner of ills. The whole place is starting to look a little tired, but gradual renovations are taking place. In autumn, the forested hill in the south of the grounds is normally covered by nesting egrets. **$$**

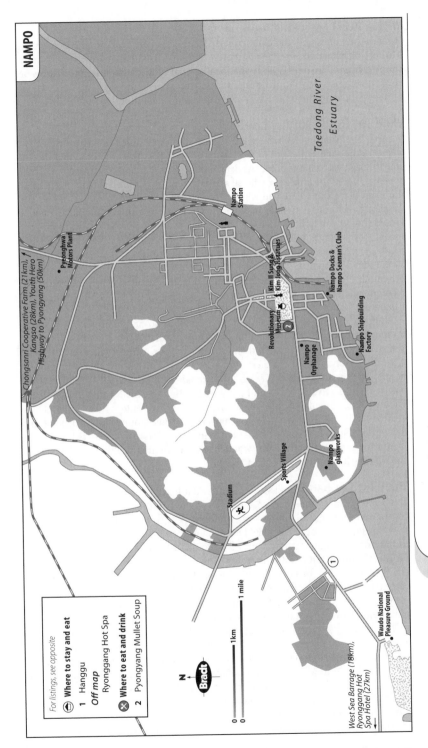

NAMPO

For listings, see opposite

Where to stay and eat
1 Hanggu
Off map
Ryonggang Hot Spa

Where to eat and drink
2 Pyonyang Mullet Soup

Taedong River Estuary

Chongsanri Cooperative Farm (21km), Kangso (28km), Youth Hero Highway to Pyongyang (50km)

Pyeonghwa Motors Plant

Nampo Station

Kim Il Sung & Kim Jong Il statues

Revolutionary Museum

Nampo Docks & Nampo Seaman's Club

Nampo Orphanage

Nampo Shipbuilding Factory

Nampo glassworks

Sports Village

Stadium

Waudo National Pleasure Ground

West Sea Barrage (18km), Ryonggang Hot Spa Hotel (27km)

N

Bradt

0   1km
0   1 mile

✖ WHERE TO EAT AND DRINK *Map, page 163*

Besides the hotels and golf club (page 161), options here are lean; the **Pyongyang Mullet Soup Restaurant ($$$)** in central Nampo can offer up more than just mullet soup (terrapin, anyone?), while the local speciality in Onchon is clam barbecue, cooked with petrol syphoned straight from your vehicle and eaten off the driveway of the Ryonggang Hot Spa Hotel – certainly an unusual experience.

WHAT TO SEE AND DO The number of open sites in central Nampo is thin on the ground. The **Nampo Orphanage** is a regular stop; a showcase facility providing the best care the state can afford to the infants and toddlers that would, should they be able to speak yet, call this home. As depressing as it may sound, the friendly staff here appear to adore the little kids, who all seem content. Your tour will likely finish off in the main playroom where you will be encouraged to partake in various games and singalongs before it is time to move on. The sprawling **Nampo Docks** can only be visited should you have chartered a leisure boat to transport you down the Taedong Estuary to the West Sea Barrage (although of course, this would need to be pre-arranged in advance through your tour operator), an enjoyable means of arriving at the barrage as you spend an hour or so cruising past the industrial sprawl and dockyards with the behemoth project slowly appearing on the horizon. (Should you arrive by boat, it is recommended that you return to Nampo by road, giving the best of both worlds as you will otherwise not be able to enjoy the drive across the bulk of the barrage.)

Stopping off on Nampo's main drag is normally a no-no unless you are breaking for lunch, so you will likely speed through town as you head west, passing the Sports Village, Hanggu Hotel and then the turnoff for the **Waudo National Pleasure Ground**, a somewhat dilapidated mini beach and leisure resort that is unlikely to be on the itinerary, such is its state of disrepair. A little beyond Waudo, roughly halfway between Nampo City and the West Sea Barrage, the **Nampo Shipbuilding Factory** was a regular feature on many tours until recently and may reopen to visitors in the future; it was always enjoyable to look around the workshops and dry docks, which had so much dated machinery and so many welders hot-footing it around the place that the scene would likely induce their health and safety officer, should they have one, with a heart attack.

The West Sea Barrage This 8km-long tidal barrage was constructed between 1981 and 1986 at the then cost of US$4 billion (although really, in a totally centralised economy where the bulk of the work is conducted by conscripts quite how this figure has been calculated is anyone's guess). The barrage is of great pride to the Korean people, as they, you will be told, achieved 'Kim Il Sung's grand plan for transforming nature into the reality'. This massive civil engineering project was chiefly constructed for flood defences, ease of shipping, irrigation, and to prevent the intrusion of seawater upstream. The barrage also acts, among many other things (as you will be told), as a road and rail link to the western coastal regions of South Hwanghae Province, south of the Taedong.

The impressive West Sea Barrage Construction Monuments bookend the road at each end of the barrage, while the three locks, fish leaps, sluices and all other excitement can be found sandwiched between Ok Islet, Pi Islet and the south bank. Pi Islet is home to a hilltop anchor-shaped lighthouse that masquerades by day as the Barrage Visitor's Centre. Here you will receive a detailed explanation on everything you ever wanted to know about the barrage, but only after watching a brief and dramatic documentary on the construction project. From the top of Pi you will have a near bird's-eye view down to the busy locks and control tower, seeing the barrage in all its glory, as all Nampo- and Pyongyang-bound ships pass through here. Pi Islet is also home to a small and stony beach; it's not the French Riviera but it is popular in the summer months with wealthy weekend day trippers from Pyongyang, and thus an interesting diversion at certain times of year for those with time to linger. Heading south from Pi Islet, over the locks, you will enter South Hwanghae, but do check in advance about coming this way as the road and rails are on a swing bridge that for many hours of the day will be closed to accommodate the up to 50,000-tonne ships that sail through here.

ANJU (안주시)

Comprising the two distinctly separate entities of Anju and Sinanju (New Anju), collectively known as Anju City, this rarely visited area is home to 240,000 people, many of whom are employed by the Namhung Youth Chemical Complex, a 1970s plant that is considered as the nation's premier petrochemicals processing complex. Since its construction, the site has been visited regularly by all three leaders, and in a country where many such sites appear to be in terminal decline, this complex has received significant investment and undergone substantial development and expansion of late.

GETTING THERE AND AWAY It is not possible to arrive or depart the area by train, but train travellers coming from or heading to China will enjoy a brief stop in Sinanju Station, where the bustling open-air platform will keep the inquisitive entertained for a few fleeting moments. Excluding any detours for sightseeing, Anju is 73km from Pyongyang and 82km from Mount Myohyang, all along comparatively good roads, making the city a logical spot to break the journey between the two.

 WHERE TO STAY AND EAT

 Chongchongang Hotel (30 rooms)
Somewhat bizarrely, Sinanju is home to a medium-sized hotel, the Chongchongang. This is a pretty basic place on a hillock overlooking farmland on the edge of town. On my last visit there was no electricity for the duration of my stay, so my heart goes out to those who were quarantined here during the Ebola panic of late 2014 & early 2015, when persons arriving in the country were sent to the Chongchongang for 3 weeks of strict monitoring. **$$**

WHAT TO SEE AND DO The **Namhung Youth Chemical Complex** is of course closed to 'normal' visitors, but you can just about see it in the distance from the only sight you can actually visit in town, the **Paeksang Pavilion**. Its name meaning 'one hundred scenes' because it 'commands a hundred beautiful scenes' (the anthracite gasification plant in the distance being just one of them), the pavilion was a command post of the Anju Fortress first mentioned in the 14th century, but was rebuilt in 1753 and once more after the Korean War. One of the few historical relics in Anju, this arresting pavilion, with its elevated floor and vibrant murals, is reached by heading through central Anju and ascending a hill in the main city park. Paeksang is considered a national treasure – having a packed lunch here is a relaxing diversion before getting back on the road.

PYONGSONG (평성시)

Capital of South Pyongan, Pyongsong is a mere 30km north-northeast from Pyongyang and was, for many years, considered little more than a sleepy satellite town. Thanks to its good rail connections with all corners of the country, however, this quiet town has grown over the last few decades to become a typical provincial industrial city and major transportation hub. Indeed, Pyongsong has fared better than many other cities in the post Kim Il Sung years; private enterprise, markets and the transit of all manner of goods has helped keep the city afloat, partly due to the comparative ease for traders to visit here when compared with Pyongyang (remember, freedom of movement in the country, particularly to the capital, does not exist).

Of late, Pyongsong has developed into something of a scientific centre – North Korea's answer to Silicon Valley, with a good deal of modern apartment blocks being constructed recently for the 284,000 people that call it home, many of whom are employed by organisations such as the Space Science Research Institute and the Atomic Energy Research Centre. The city is also alleged to be responsible

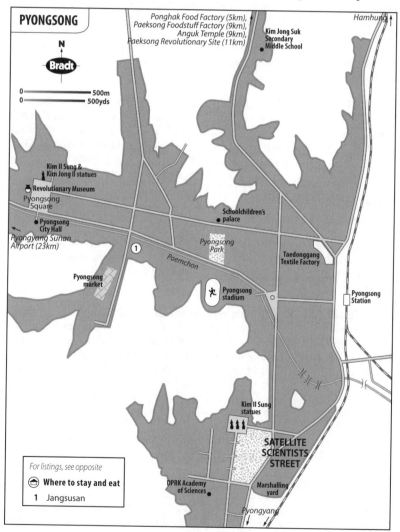

PYONGSONG

N

Bradt

0 ——— 500m
0 ——— 500yds

Ponghak Food Factory (5km),
Paeksong Foodstuff Factory (9km),
Anguk Temple (9km),
Paeksong Revolutionary Site (11km)

Hamhung

Kim Jong Suk
Secondary
Middle School

Kim Il Sung &
Kim Jong Il statues

Revolutionary Museum

Pyongsong
Square

Pyongsong
City Hall

Pyongyang Sunan
Airport (23km)

Schoolchildren's
palace

Pyongsong
Park

Paemchon

Pyongsong
market

Pyongsong
stadium

Taedonggang
Textile Factory

Pyongsong
Station

Kim Il Sung
statues

SATELLITE
SCIENTISTS
STREET

For listings, see opposite

Where to stay and eat
1 Jangsusan

DPRK Academy
of Sciences

Marshalling
yard

Pyongyang

for a significant portion of the methamphetamine produced in the country, but the good people at the Pyongsong College of Science, one of the institutions accused of being involved in this illicit manufacturing, would of course vehemently deny this.

For many years, all that most people knew of the city was that it was the home of Ponghak, one of the most famous beers in the country; it was only in 2012 when it opened to visitors that they discovered there was more to Pyongsong than the two varieties of pale lager produced by the Ponghak Food Factory. OK – the sights to visit are still a little thin on the ground and similar, or better, examples may be found elsewhere, but Pyongsong has enough to keep visitors busy for half a day or so and will give an insight into life in lesser North Korean cities. Those not venturing further afield to more interesting cities such as Chongjin, Hamhung and Wonsan should well consider a visit.

GETTING THERE AND AWAY From the statues of the Kims in the heart of Pyongyang to the statues of the Kims in central Pyongsong, it's a 32km drive on well-paved roads (assuming you don't make any detours to take in more statues). Beyond Pyongsong, Anju is as little as 59km away, depending on the route taken.

WHERE TO STAY AND EAT *Map, opposite*
For now the only option in town for both food and board is the **Jangsusan Hotel** (92 rooms; **$$–$$$**). The hotel is comfortable enough for a night or two and may be able to muster up hot water. The outdoor bar in the front courtyard affords good street views of the real world outside – so you can stare at the locals while they stare back at you. There is also a large banquet hall and a couple of smaller dining rooms should you be looking for a more private setting, but the food on offer is pretty standard Korean fare – nothing to write home about. Perhaps it's just as well then that they don't offer postal facilities either.

WHAT TO SEE AND DO Pyongsong starts in earnest as you pass the large modern **Satellite Scientists Street** estate in the south of the city, constructed, along with much else in the city, back in 2014 when significant chunks of Pyongsong resembled a building site while it underwent a beautification blitz. Your first visit in town will likely be to pay your respects to Messrs Kim and Kim in **Pyongsong Square**, with the imposing Pyongsong Revolutionary Museum and impregnable Pyongsong City Hall to your west and south respectively, which are both closed to tourists.

Necessary formalities taken care of, you may now visit what is for most the highlight in the area, around which your local sightseeing will be planned: the **Kim Jong Suk Secondary Middle School**. This prestigious seat of learning was named after Kim Jong Il's mother; only the most gifted in Pyongsong study here and your tour will likely start with a visit to the school's small museum room that exhibits the medals, honours and titles bestowed upon the school, its pupils and alumni over the decades. Pressing on as quickly as you can, the highlight of your visit will not be the moth-eaten sea turtle in the taxidermy exhibition room, but will undoubtedly be the grand finale, the chance to meet and interact with a classroom full of students. Depending on the size of your group and how long you spent admiring the stuffed deer and owls, you will have anything from 5 to 30 minutes to speak to students, either in the form of an informal chat with one or two schoolchildren or with you being given the temporary role of tutor to the entire class, a potentially daunting but certainly rewarding experience. If you want to try and get your head around how the schoolchildren are so intelligent, polite and disciplined, it's also worth requesting a visit to **Doksong Primary School**; here, in a dedicated classroom replete with model displays of the leader's birthplaces, you can see how the children start their education in political indoctrination – a setting that raises eyebrows but is little different from religious studies classes in the West.

It has been possible to visit a number of factories and light industrial sites in town since 2012, but with the recent changes of management they may or may not be willing to show you around. However, it cannot hurt to investigate the possibility of visiting the **Taedonggang Textile Factory**, which in its heyday manufactured clothing for export, including dress uniforms for higher-ranking members of the armed forces in a number of non-aligned countries. To the north of town, the **Paeksong Foodstuff Factory** and **Ponghak Food Factory** are two other sites that may, or may not, let you have a look around should they feel inclined.

Heading north from central Pyongsong, the modest **Anguk Temple** is approximately 13km from the centre of town on a road that will take you past a few colourful new buildings and sports pitches. The temple was founded back in AD503 during the Koguryo Dynasty, although all the present-day buildings are from the Joson Dynasty, having been rebuilt in 1419 and renovated in 1785. The small temple is registered as a national treasure, number 34 to be precise, but other than being used for the occasional film set Anguk is often overlooked and ignored. Of course, tour groups are very welcome to visit, but it was perhaps Kim Il Sung himself who best summed up the state's position on such things: 'If foreigners want to pray to Buddha, you must provide services for them. No-one in our country will be interested in Buddhist images or in praying to Buddha.'

The last possibility in Pyongsong is the **Paeksong Revolutionary Site**, approximately 2.5km from Anguk Temple as the crow flies (on the opposite side of Mount Pongrin), but a 12km drive via Ponghak. During the Korean War, Pyongyang's Kim Il Sung University relocated to tucked-away Paeksong, and the site now contains a museum, a monument to Kim Il Sung and a scattering of preserved buildings. Most people will likely find Paeksong even less exciting than it sounds, with the local guides here often being rather dour – not the best end to your tour of the area.

MOVING ON FROM PYONGSONG Leaving Pyongsong, Pyongyang Sunan Airport is only a 20km drive away, over a hilly road that takes you west. Owing to its proximity to the airport, those departing Pyongyang by air may consider spending the previous night in Pyongsong. This same road west from Pyongsong also leads to a junction of the main Pyongyang–Hyangsan dual carriageway. Heading north along this dual carriageway, Hyangsan-bound travellers rarely make any stops, but short detours are possible, such as in Anju (page 165). Once beyond the airport, the road is often elevated or tree lined, and at times your view is thus restricted, but the journey up to the county line with North Pyongan is essentially farmland all the way. If you want to stretch your legs for a few moments and take in the scenery from a slightly elevated position, a logical pitstop is the hilltop tower known as the **Monument for the Kaechon to Lake Taesong Waterway**, just one of Kim Jong Il's many architectural follies.

In addition to the aforementioned road heading west, another road bears north from Pyongsong, one which you would only likely travel on should you be heading to Mount Myohyang. This is a slower and bumpier route than taking the main Mount Myohyang-bound highway, but shows a lot more of rural and urban life as you really get off the beaten track, passing through farmland and the closed cities of **Sunchon** and **Kaechon** before you cross the Chongchon River and join the main Myohyang-bound road for the rest of the way. Sunchon is a large city near the confluence of the Taedong and Kumchon rivers that you will bypass with little information given. It was in the skies above here that the Battle of Sunchon took place in 1951, where the Royal Australian Air Force engaged (unofficially) in an air battle with the Soviet Union, the only direct engagement between Australia and the USSR during the Korean War. Before passing through Kaechon an optional detour east off the main road will take you to the **Daegak Youth Dam**, a tiny hydro-electric dam on the Taedong River, but you will really have to be a budding hydrologist to get much out of this. Finally, another detour before Kaechon, this time to the west, will lead to the rarely visited **Songam Cave**, a network of wonderfully garishly lit karst caves. The story goes that, one day in the mid 1990s, when the country was undergoing economic difficulties, Chairman Kim Jong Il was giving field guidance in a mountainous region. Surveying the topography of the area, he predicted that there might be a cave in the mountains – and the Songam Cave was duly discovered by the soldiers of the Korean People's Army. The cave is perfectly interesting but quite a detour – Ryongmun Cave in neighbouring North Pyongan is far more accessible (page 177).

HOECHANG COUNTY (회창읍)

Hoechang County quietly opened its doors to Western visitors as recently as 2015, after years of accepting occasional VIP and special-interest groups from China. The main reason why people come here is for Mao Anying, the son of Mao Zedong, as the main town in the area, also called Hoechang, is home to an important Chinese People's Volunteers Cemetery where Mao Anying is laid to rest.

Just 90km by road from Pyongyang (but 124km on the current permitted route), Hoechang County is truly a world away from the capital, and while not everybody may be particularly enthralled at the suggestion of spending a day or two making the round trip out here, the journey itself is a most scenic one that very few Western tourists make, taking you through mountains, towns, villages and seemingly almost the entire scope of inland Korean scenery as you snake and wind your way into Hoechang town itself.

Departing Pyongsong, the road and scenery starts off not too dissimilar from much of South Pyongan as you pass through relatively flat farmlands, heading along the north shore of the Paemchon River and crossing the Taedong at the Songchon Barrage. The journey gets more exciting beyond Songchon town, once the Songchon Knitting Factory is in your rear-view mirror. The next 45km is most scenic as the road skirts around, up and over three heavily forested mountains, one of which is home to a small molybdenum mine. Farmland all but disappears, save for times when you briefly travel along a valley floor before the next mountain emerges. During the final section of the journey the valley could *almost* be described as a gorge as the mountains around you become increasingly steep and craggy; so much so that it comes as a bit of a surprise when you suddenly arrive in Hoechang town itself.

WHERE TO STAY AND EAT Given the distance from Pyongyang and state of the roads, Hoechang is best visited as a day trip from Pyongsong. Unless the roads improve, trying to travel out and back from Pyongyang would be an overly long and ambitious day trip. Day trippers will be served up with a good meal at the guesthouse – otherwise it's a case of bringing a packed lunch, as the enticing-sounding Songhung Mine Workers' Club unfortunately doesn't cater to non-members.

🏠 **Hoechang Guesthouse** (5 rooms) Smaller groups can opt to overnight at this very basic option. If you want something completely different from the monumental hotels of Pyongyang & are happy to rough it a little for the night you'll have an experience to remember – expect cold water, coarse bedding & a rousing city-wide wake up, seemingly broadcast from a loudspeaker atop the nearby House of Culture. Jolly good fun! **$$**

WHAT TO SEE AND DO Surrounded by steep hills and mountains, Hoechang town appears on the map like the vines of a creeping plant, as the settlement snakes up into the deep valleys and tributaries of the Yongchon River. Entering from the southern end, it's a short drive through this curious little place, so different in layout from almost every other settlement in the country (where the grid plan is *de rigueur*), to the centre of town and the Hoechang Guesthouse, located a stone's throw from the Hoechang House of Culture and the Hoechang Middle School Number 1 (both off-limits to tourists). From the guesthouse it is a short walk up a rather steep set of stairs to the **Chinese People's Volunteers Cemetery**, the resting place of Mao Anying (see box, below) and a number of his fallen comrades, just a handful of the hundreds of thousands of Chinese soldiers who died in the Korean War. China's massive contribution in the war has, to all intents and purposes, been written out of North Korean history, but not so here: this small hilltop cemetery, in a picturesque little grove, is considered *the* principal Chinese war grave in North Korea. Even the locals, possibly learning from the trickle of Chinese visitors who pass through here, are aware of China's colossal involvement in the war, and may well appreciate (although they would never admit it) the inevitable outcome had China not assisted. The site underwent significant and tasteful renovation in 2012, and is often visited by top-level state delegations from China. The foreground of the cemetery includes a small pagoda and bas-relief, both depicting dramatic war scenes, together with a statue that may, or may not, be of Mao Anying, depending on who you ask.

A short drive up a narrow valley east of the town centre will pass the main plant of the town's prime employer and *raison d'être*, the **Songhung Mine**, as well as a variety of other buildings, all of which are packed tightly together like sardines in a tin, thinning out just slightly as you slowly wind upwards. From the numerous mine entrances located right beside the road, hard-hatted workers come and go – the entire scene could be imagined into a rather rousing example of a North Korean socialist-realist artwork. The **Songhung Revolutionary Site** is the last stop in town; this site was a major Chinese People's Volunteers Army headquarters during the Korean War and includes a small section of restored tunnels and a mess hall, as well as temporary billets used by Kim Il Sung and other senior North Korean and Chinese military figures. One or two of the rooms here have the air of the Führerbunker about them: windowless, spartanly furnished quarters not befitting the revered status of their wartime occupants. The atmosphere in these rooms and corridors, particularly in late 1950 when the North was really on the backfoot, could well have been like it was in the final days of the Third Reich – with no clear way out. Considering Kim Il Sung's position at the war's nadir, and how he then managed to get China on board, 'win' the war and go on to run North Korea for another four decades, it really was quite a feat. Kim Il Sung's frugal chamber, home to a single bed, field telephone and little else, is quite the contrast to the palaces he very quickly became accustomed to. This site may be one for military historians only (do note that the history you will imbibe here, much like anywhere in the country, will be somewhat skewered), but it is nonetheless a must visit when in Hoechang and, like at the cemetery, one of the few places in all of Korea where China's massive involvement and sacrifice in the Korean War is tacitly acknowledged.

UPDATES WEBSITE

You can post your comments and recommendations, and read feedback and updates from other readers online at w bradtupdates.com/northkorea.

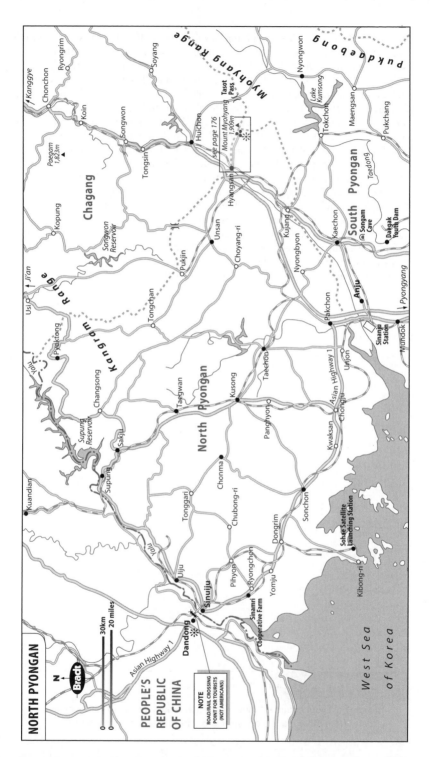

NORTH PYONGAN

N

Bradt

0 ___ 30km
0 ___ 20 miles

PEOPLE'S
REPUBLIC
OF CHINA

West Sea
of Korea

NOTE
ROAD/RAIL CROSSING
POINT FOR TOURISTS
(NOT AMERICANS)

Kanggye
Chonchon
Ryongrim
Soyang
Soyang
Ryongwon
Nyongwon
Pukdaebong
Koin
Songwon
Chonchon
Myohyang Range
Tasot Pass
Lake Kumsong
Tokchon
Maengsan
Pukchang
Huichon
Mount Myohyang 1,909m
see page 176
Hyangsan
Tongsin
Paegam 1,833m
Chagang
Songwon Reservoir
Unsan
Choyang-ri
Kujang
Nyongbyon
Kaechon
South Pyongan
Songam Cave
Daegak Youth Dam
Taedong
Pukjin
Kopung
Pyoktong
Usi
Ji'an
Kangdam Range
Tongchan
Tongchan
Pakchon
Anju
Pyongyang
Sinanju Station
Mundok
Yalu
Changsong
Sakju
Taegwan
Kusong
Taechon
Panghyong
Kwaksan
Chongju
Ujon
Asian Highway 1
Supung Reservoir
Supung
North Pyongan
Tonggari
Chonma
Chubong-ri
Dongrim
Sonchon
Sohae Satellite Launching Station
Kuandian
Yalu
Uiju
Pihyon
Ryongchon
Yomju
Kibong-ri
Sinuiju
Sinamri Cooperative Farm
Dandong
Asian Highway 1

7

North Pyongan (평안북도)

The principal gateway to China, the province of North Pyongan is primarily made up of low mountains and plains, bounded to the west by the West Sea of Korea (Yellow Sea). The northern perimeter of the province (and border with China) is the 790km-long Amnok River, known as the Yalu in China, its source being Lake Chon on Mount Paektu (page 223). While Korea has some spectacular coastline, it is sadly not to be found here; much of the seaboard is tidal plains, and land reclamation in the region is a never-ending business as the state pushes to obtain more agricultural lands. Consequently, this 12,680km² province is normally only visited for Mount Myohyang, an accessible and 'must see' region in the southeast of North Pyongan. The rest of the province is essentially closed, save for some limited sites in and around Sinuiju, the border city with China and the only city that can, for now, be visited in this domain of 2.73 million people.

Anybody entering or departing the country by rail from China will pass through North Pyongan, as the Pyongui Line, the main and most – nay, only – reliable rail line in the country and the principal overland corridor linking the two countries, passes through here on its 228km journey between Pyongyang and Dandong. Those rolling through will sadly not come within view of the Sohae Satellite Launching Station or North Pyongan's other infamous site, the Yongbyon Nuclear Scientific Research Centre, two oft-mentioned military facilities in the country that are, like all the other similar sites, very much off-limits to tourists.

MOUNT MYOHYANG (묘향산) AND AROUND

Mount Myohyang, one of the five celebrated mountains of Korea, is the most accessible mountain area in the country, at only 150km by road from Pyongyang. While just about manageable to visit in a long day trip from the capital, spending one or two nights in this area, which roughly translates as 'the mountain of fragrance', is recommended. Although Mounts Paektu and Kumgang are arguably more attractive, they are of course harder to get to, so if you cannot get to those far-flung corners of North Korea, then it's worth making time to fit in Myohyang.

Rising to 1,909m above sea level, the mountain sits near the confluence of the Chongchon River and the Myohyang Stream, with its long main ridgeline slowly rising from west to east. While the entire peak occupies 375km², the focus for visitors heading into the hills is on the four key valleys of Sangwon, Manpok, Chonthae and Chilsong, all of which are approached from the Myohyang Stream. Despite this, most visitors to the region will not explore the Myohyang massif in any depth, with the majority of those who venture here focusing on less arduous visits to sites such as the International Friendship Exhibition and the Pohyon Temple.

FLORA AND FAUNA The steep and craggy mountain is covered by mixed broadleaf and coniferous forest, with only the areas near the very summit being too high and windswept to support much significant foliage. Designated in 2009 by UNESCO as a World Biosphere Reserve, Myohyang is home to over 700 species of plants, including 16 globally threatened ones, and 12 species of endangered animal. Locals are particularly proud of the broad-billed roller and flying squirrel, not to mention the ever-elusive bear and Amur leopards, which may or may not still roam here, depending on who you ask.

GETTING THERE AND AWAY

By road Hyangsan County, the seat and base for Mount Myohyang, is well connected by road to Pyongyang, which, on the most direct route, is approximately 2½ hours away. The road, much of which is a comparatively quick dual carriageway, heads roughly north from Pyongyang into South Pyongan Province, bypassing Sukchon, Sinanju and Anju before crossing into North Pyongan. After Anju the road crosses the Chongchon River for the first time and then bears northeast through Yongbyon and Kujang counties. For the bulk of the journey beyond Anju, the road hugs the banks of the Chongchon as you ever so gradually ascend towards Hyangsan. The first major road junction once in Yongbyon (approximately 8km after you first cross the Chongchon) is the unsigned turnoff for the Yongbyon Nuclear Scientific Research Centre, which at its closest is only 6km away. As you push on, the concrete runway of Kaechon Airport may just come into view on the opposite riverbank before you enter Kujang County, but other than soaking up the scenery there is little to see on this stretch of road before the dual carriageway comes to a very abrupt stop 4km before coming into Hyangsan; the last little stretch being on a more 'typical' Korean road. As you approach the Hyangsan Barrage, keep an eye out for the Hyangsan Helipad, essentially a large 'H' painted on the side of the road. On crossing the barrage, you will come into Hyangsan town itself. All the sites of Mount Myohyang are within a short drive of Hyangsan, with most situated along the banks of the Myohyang Stream.

By air Besides travelling by road, it is also possible to charter a Mil Mi-17 helicopter, ferrying you from Pyongyang's Sunan Airport to the Hyangsan Helipad in style. While not cheap at around €3,000 for a return charter, if you can fill the aircraft (it can accommodate up to 12 people) it is a comparatively affordable and most memorable experience. Such charters are normally for quick day trips to take in the local highlights, but it is also possible to keep the helicopter waiting for you overnight while you explore the area – the height of Western decadence. Such complex logistics should, quite understandably, be pre-arranged long in advance of your arrival in the country.

By train A final option possible for special-interest groups or larger parties is to travel on a privately chartered train from Pyongyang to Myohyangsan Station. The 156km route travels on the Pyongui Line to Sinanju before branching off in Kaechon on to the Kaechon Line and then joining the Manpo Line for the final leg of the journey. The train normally comprises half-a-dozen old yet comfortable eastern European carriages, together with a fully staffed restaurant car, even if just ten or so people travel. The train will not run to a precise schedule and will likely take 4–5 hours as it slowly trundles through scenic countryside, so a recommended option is to arrange for the train to wait overnight in Hyangsan (not a problem) before you return to Pyongyang the following day. Like with flying in by chartered helicopter, coming by train isn't something that can be arranged at short notice – all must be requested weeks before arrival.

🏠 WHERE TO STAY *Map, page 176*

There are only really two options in the area now, since the Sangwon Hotel seems permanently mothballed. A tiny number of travellers each year do enjoy wild camping on the mountain, permitted as part of a fully organised hiking expedition with local mountain guides, through specialist operators. Mountaineers may also be able to stay in the very basic bothy at the bottom of the Chonthae and Chilsong Valley, though there is little reason to do so.

🏠 **Chongchon Hotel** (60 rooms) Located in Hyangsan, the Chongchon opened its doors back in 1987, but has had a gradual restoration of late. Given that most visitors in the region stay here, the steady stream of guests (& the money they bring in) helps keep the staff affable enough. With notice, the staff can rustle up a lovely barbecue at a secluded spot on the Myohyang Stream. Other than whiling away the evenings in the restaurant, a small shop & bar will help keep you occupied until the power cuts call time. **$$**

🏠 **Hyangsan Hotel** (134 rooms) Typically deserted, this 15-storey 'pyramid hotel' originally opened in 1986, but underwent such massive renovation that it is essentially a new hotel, opened in 2010. Situated on a bend of the Myohyang Stream, with the mountain directly behind it, it is an impressive building in an impressive spot, a short drive from the key sites in the area. Intended primarily for domestic VIPs, there's all manner of facilities here, including a theatre, swimming pool, dance hall, numerous bars & restaurants that can keep you busy long into the night. Most of the foreigners who come here tend to be day trippers having a look around, as the Hyangsan is a sight in itself, & thus briefly included in many tours of the area. **$$$$**

✖ WHERE TO EAT AND DRINK
Other than at the hotels themselves, there are no available places to eat in the area. Day trippers can always arrange for a picnic or barbecue at a suitable spot in the mountains. If you're heading into the hills, be sure to bring all supplies with you from Pyongyang or home – almost nothing suitable can be sourced locally.

WHAT TO SEE AND DO
Hyangsan town has little itself to offer, although it seems that fishing in the Chongchon River may be possible; at least it has been in the past. As you head southeast from town, along the north bank of the Myohyang Stream, the Hyangsan Hotel dominates the view ahead of you, so much so that you will likely miss the somewhat hidden and totally unmentionable airport and train station used by, well, you know who. Beyond the Hyangsan Hotel, the **Pyongyang Children's Union Camp** is the base for privileged children enjoying a week away from home, a week that will almost certainly include a visit to the major sight in the area, just up the road: the International Friendship Exhibition.

The International Friendship Exhibition
Hailed across the country as 'a symbol of greatness', this sprawling and cavernous museum complex first opened in 1978. With over 70,000m² of floor space, its two buildings were constructed to display gifts that Kim Il Sung and Kim Jong Il had been presented over the years from a near-endless list of international heads of state, political parties, public figures and a near-endless stream of sycophants from almost every nation on earth. The smaller western building comprises gifts to Kim Jong Il, while the larger

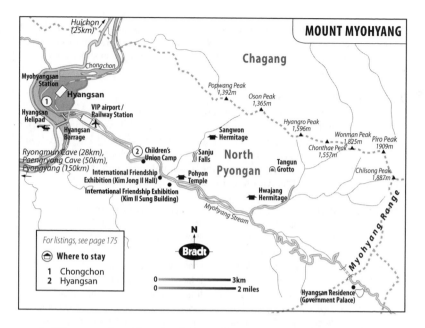

Huichon (25km)

Chagang

Myohyangsan Station

Chongchon

Hyangsan

Popwang Peak 1,392m

Oson Peak 1,365m

Hyangro Peak 1,596m

Wonman Peak 1,825m   Piro Peak 1909m

VIP airport / Railway Station

Hyangsan Helipad

Hyangsan Barrage

Sangwon Hermitage

Chonthae Peak 1,557m

Ryongmun Cave (28km), Paengnyong Cave (50km), Pyongyang (150km)

Children's Union Camp

Sanju Falls

North Pyongan

Tangun Grotto

Chilsong Peak 1,887m

International Friendship Exhibition (Kim Jong Il Hall)

Pohyon Temple

International Friendship Exhibition (Kim Il Sung Building)

Hwajang Hermitage

Myohyang Stream

Myohyang Range

For listings, see page 175

Where to stay

1 Chongchon
2 Hyangsan

N

Bradt

0 ___ 3km
0 ___ 2 miles

Hyangsan Residence (Government Palace)

east building contains gifts to his father; additional rooms have been constructed recently to accommodate gifts for Kim Jong Un. Built into the mountainside, the seemingly endless underground marble corridors lead to room after room, over 150 in total, each full of cabinets packed with gifts, some fantastic, some amusing and some downright awful – a grand total, they say, of over 220,000.

Owing to its sheer size, visitors will typically be shown the main western building and whisked around just some of the highlights. Each room typically consists of gifts from a specific country or region and the local guides will normally tailor the route depending on your nationality, although you may of course request to see whatever you wish: 'the room full of gifts to Kim Jong Il from Central America? Not a problem!'

On approaching each building, you will pass the honour guards, with their silver-plated Kalashnikovs, before entering; here the local guide will instruct you to leave cameras, bags, wallets and pretty much all your belongings in the cloakroom, before you are made to don cloth overshoes. Finally, you will be obliged to go through a metal detector and a possible pat down from bemused guards.

The next couple of hours will be a whirlwind tour through a James Bond villain-esque network of subterranean corridors and rooms, behind each door a plethora of surprises and shocks – a spotless Ilyushin 14 aircraft, gifted by Stalin; a railway carriage from Mao; a bearskin from Ceaușescu. The gifts have come from all and sundry, but it's a veritable who's who of infamous characters the world over, with presents from the likes of Gaddafi, Castro, Arafat, Mugabe and the Sandinistas. Of course, some of it is complete tat and couldn't be shifted in a car boot sale, so for every shock and smile you may smirk – just try to keep it hidden, especially when you are taken to the waxworks of the leaders, their respective rooms lined with some of the most valued gifts. Each building has a small gift shop and café that you can visit at the end of your tour, both of which have grand balconies affording pristine views of Mount Myohyang. Smarter-dressed guests may be asked to record their impressions in the faux leather-bound ledger – be nice as everything is translated, recorded and stored away in perpetuity.

Pohyon Temple A few hundred metres' drive farther up alongside the Myohyang Stream will bring you to the serene Pohyon Temple, arguably the best preserved in the country, named after the Bodhisattva of Samantabhadra (known as Pohyon Posal in Korea). Built in 1042, but subsequently repaired and reconstructed many times in the near thousand years since, the temple grounds originally consisted of 24 buildings and pagodas; sadly, many of these were destroyed in 1951 during the Korean War. In a nation where religion is frowned upon, these days the temple is often used as a symbol of national defence; during the Imjin Wars with Japan in the 16th century, Pohyon was a stronghold for thousands of Korean warrior monks, led by Seosan.

Pohyon, with its well-maintained grounds and mountain backdrop, is a tranquil spot and makes a pleasant contrast to the International Friendship Exhibition. Visitors will normally see the Bell House before passing through Haetal Gate, Chonwang Gate and Manse Pavilion, before coming to the 8.6m 13-storeyed octagonal Tabo Pagoda, in front of Taeung Hall, the main temple building. Respectful non-believers are welcome to enter Taeung after removing their shoes, and by this point in your tour a monk will likely materialise to give a detailed historical explanation of the site to anybody that may be looking for one. Moving on, you will come to Kwanum Temple, Ryongsan Hall and the Suchung Temple, which commemorates Seosan and others who were said to play a major part in routing the invaders in a battle near Pyongyang.

The last significant building only dates to 1974 and is home to the temple archive, which houses a copy of the *Tripitaka Koreana*, a UNESCO-designated cultural relic printed on 80,000 wooden blocks.

Ryongmun and Paengryong caves Possible to visit while on your way to or from Mount Myohyang, Ryongmun Cave is a round-trip detour of approximately 24km off the main Pyongyang–Hyangsan road. Alternatively, it can be visited as a standalone 56km round-trip excursion from Hyangsan, passing through Oryong and/or Kujang towns to get here. Ryongmun Cave has two main caverns up to 40m in height, and tens of smaller caverns including such wondrous sites as the 'Pool of Anti-Imperialist Struggle and speleothems resembling vaginas and penises'. The cave is rarely visited, but if you have time to do so it is an interesting diversion, even if it seems that almost every stalactite and stalagmite has a lengthy legend surrounding it that relates to various private parts of the human anatomy. Bring warm clothing and a torch. A little beyond the village of Taephung, a further 22km beyond Ryongmun Cave, is smaller Paengryong Cave – it is almost never visited and unlikely to be open without prior planning, but still, speleologists may want to consider requesting a visit.

Hiking Mount Myohyang is one of the best spots in the country for hiking, with the possibility of light walks of 2 to 3 hours up to serious treks of two to three days for keen and experienced hikers on this steep and densely forested mountain. From west to east, the key valleys of Sangwon, Manpok, Chonthae and Chilsong offer up a wealth of spectacular scenery, peppered with the occasional secluded hermitage, pavilion, temple and waterfall. The quality of paths varies significantly from valley to valley and year to year, and all visits, bar the very shortest foray, should be undertaken with a mountain guide from Hyangsan, which your main guides will source. This mountain is steep, and once beyond the lower slopes the crisscross network of paths can be almost impossible to follow, as they fall into decline and are slowly reclaimed by nature. Significant hikes here are relatively rarely undertaken and anybody heading out for anything more than a half day or so should pack supplies including water, which can be hard to come by once on the mountain, together with a first-aid kit. If visiting the upper reaches of Myohyang, heading along the ridgeline or planning to reach the mountain's true summit, Piro Peak, a safety rope is a must.

The following are the most popular hikes on Mount Myohyang and can be arranged through most tour operators, but the local guides, most of whom know the mountain like the back of their hands, will tweak any hike to suit the group and current conditions on the mountain.

Sangwon Valley Starting near the International Friendship Exhibition, just to the west of the Pohyon Temple, Sangwon offers up to 14km of main paths and, together with the Manpok Valley, is the most visited area for hiking on the mountain. Ascending to the top of Sangwon leads to 1,392m Popwang Peak, the westernmost peak on the mountain ridge, but this is a major undertaking. Most visitors will head just part of the way to take in sights such as the 29m-high Sanju Falls, diminutive Inho Pavilion, from where you will be afforded a good view back down the valley, and the Sangwon Hermitage, which dates back to 1580. Sangwon, at 585m above sea level, comprises the Su and Chilsong pavilions; drinking from the spring here, it is claimed, 'cures people of diseases and allows the drinker's wishes to come true'.

Manpok Valley Meaning the 'valley full of waterfalls', Manpok has 6km of main paths that lead to the nine-tiered Kuchung Falls. While most ascend and descend the same path, a somewhat circuitous hike allows trekkers to also take in the Hwajang Hermitage (which has a 17th-century mural depicting fairies) and Tangun Grotto where, legend has it, Tangun, founder of the first Korean kingdom, was born. The big draw in Manpok, however, is indeed the waterfalls, which become more impressive as you ascend, with Sogok, Murung, Unson and Yuson falls all leading to the 46m Pison Falls. Beyond Kuchung Falls a poor path leads to 1,596m Hyangro Peak, on the main mountain ridge.

A recommended day hike of 6–12 hours (depending on how far you want to ascend each valley) can take in the best of the Manpok Valley together with parts of Sangwon, linking the two by traversing the Munsu Valley.

Piro Peak Chontate and Chilsong, the easternmost valleys of Myohyang, are rarely visited, with the paths steeper and in far poorer condition than those found in Sangwon and Manpok. You will often find yourself climbing over and scrambling under fallen trees, while the fixed ladders and bridges that used to carry hikers up and over some of the more precarious rocks and rivers have nearly all been rusted or washed away since the paths last had any investment of note, back in the 1980s.

The prime reason to come here, however, is to get to the ridgeline and the very top of Mount Myohyang: the 1,909m Piro Peak. At the foot of these two valleys, the Pirobong Campers Lodging seems to be nearing a state of total disrepair, but staying in the basic bothy (which is, in the most literal sense, a fleapit) or, better yet, to just camp in your own tent, may be permitted for those looking for an early start in the morning. While getting to Piro Peak may be feasible in one extremely long midsummer's day, it should always be approached and planned as a two-day hike, with a night of wild camping. The hike would normally ascend the Chonthae Valley to the 1,825m Wonman Peak, before heading along the ridgeline via Jingwi Peak to the summit. Between Wonman and Piro it is best to stick close together and behind your guide as a small army post is tucked away just behind the ridgeline – a few somewhat bedraggled whistle-wielding conscripts may be found up here. Ask politely and they may oblige you with a refill of your water bottles from their supplies.

From the top you will, hopefully, be afforded the best views in all of Mount Myohyang; to your south and west you will look down on the steep and craggy valleys you have ascended, while to your north and east you can see far into Chagang and South Pyongan provinces. The Hyangsan Residence, a secret government palace far below on the valley floor, is sadly obstructed from view. Pushing on from Piro, the 1,887m Chilsong Peak is the last protuberance of note that you will reach before you commence the gruelling descent down to the Chilsong Valley, but note that the path to this is currently in terrible condition. At a suitable juncture your guide will no doubt find somewhere for you to camp and source water. The entire trek could be extended, for the hardy (or foolhardy), into a three-day trek taking in the complete ridge, but this is no mean feat to arrange or undertake.

SINUIJU (신의주시)

Sinuiju had been open and then closed to Western visitors on and off for so many years that it had, for many North Korea watchers, become an obsession. Travellers had to be content with fleeting glimpses of a city they were desperate to get to while passing through by train; the first, or typically last, thing they would see of North Korea before trundling over to China. This border city is now very much accessible to tourists, but for all the fuss and anticipation, there is not a great deal that visitors are permitted to see. Still, those with the time for a long tour of North Korea (two weeks or more) could always consider an overnight visit, but in my opinion the city is currently only worth including by those fixated with the DPRK. The majority of tourists coming to Sinuiju these days are Chinese day trippers; budget bus tours for poorer Chinese tourists often making their first trip onto foreign soil to eat, drink, shop and get a glimpse of a world that will be all too familiar to the older members of their group.

Set on the southern bank of the Amnok River, Sinuiju is poor in comparison to the bustling high-rise and flashing neon Chinese city of Dandong on the opposite riverbank – nowhere can North Koreans so easily see the contrast between their own lives and those in China than here, where just by looking across the river they can see how their Chinese brothers and sisters are, quite literally, decades ahead. Indeed, travelling from Sinuiju to Dandong by rail was one of the most poignant experiences I have ever encountered, one that left me quite affected after passing, it seems, from one universe to another. Still, Sinuiju is better off for having a wealthy neighbour on its doorstep, with a substantial portion of North Korea's international trade passing through here, allowing for a trickle of funds into the city and the pockets of its 359,000 citizens.

To develop the area, a special status, akin to Rason's (page 244), has been afforded to the city: the Sinuiju Special Administrative Region, although to date practically nothing has changed in an area that may be better to focus first on developing agriculture, given the amount of flat and fertile farmland that stretches right to the edge of the city. However, besides being a major transport hub, Sinuiju does have some light industry, including the Rakwon Machine Complex, the Sinuiju Chemical Fiber Complex and the fantastically titled Sinuiju Enamel Cast Iron Cookware Factory. The city is also home to an important munitions factory (that you won't see) and the countrywide-famous Sinuiju Cosmetics Factory (that you will).

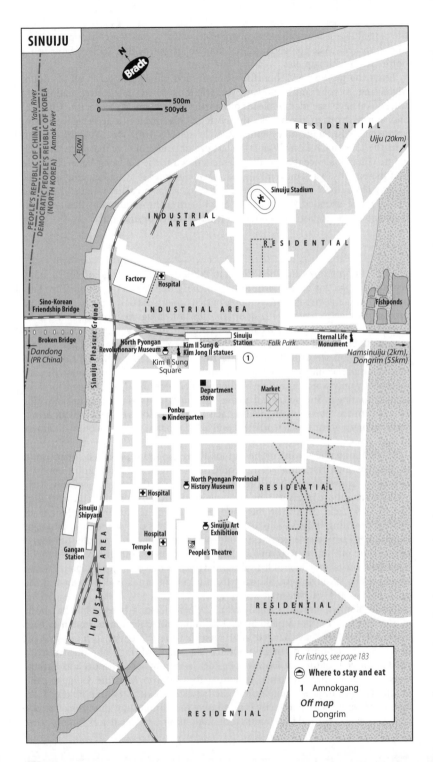

SINUIJU

N

PEOPLE'S REPUBLIC OF CHINA *Yalu River*
DEMOCRATIC PEOPLE'S REPUBLIC OF KOREA
(NORTH KOREA) *Amnok River*

FLOW

0 ──────── 500m
0 ──────── 500yds

RESIDENTIAL

Uiju (20km)

Sinuiju Stadium

INDUSTRIAL
AREA

RESIDENTIAL

Factory
Hospital

INDUSTRIAL AREA

Fishponds

Sino-Korean
Friendship Bridge

Broken Bridge

*Dandong
(PR China)*

Sinuiju Pleasure Ground

North Pyongan
Revolutionary Museum

Kim Il Sung &
Kim Jong Il statues

Sinuiju
Station

Folk Park

Eternal Life
Monument

*Namsinuiju (2km),
Dongrim (55km)*

1

Kim Il Sung
Square

Department
store

Market

Ponbu
Kindergarten

North Pyongan Provincial
History Museum

RESIDENTIAL

Hospital

Sinuiju
Shipyard

Sinuiju Art
Exhibition

Gangan
Station

Hospital

Temple

People's Theatre

INDUSTRIAL AREA

RESIDENTIAL

RESIDENTIAL

For listings, see page 183

Where to stay and eat

1   Amnokgang

Off map
Dongrim

180

HISTORY Very little is recorded on the history of Sinuiju prior to the 20th century, so we have to assume that the city had a role only as a border crossing, a minor industrial centre and perhaps as a fishing port. What we do know, however, is that Sinuiju has always played second fiddle to Dandong, though the city was probably most prosperous (not that it can ever openly be admitted) when Korea and northeast China were both under Japanese rule in the 1930s. The area was stable, well away from the fighting and ripe for agricultural and industrial development. With no border controls, in the winter, when the Amnok River usually froze, even skating across was possible for pleasure, and lorries could cross it with goods.

After the Japanese surrender in August 1945, it took two weeks before Soviet forces arrived in the town. The Soviets were extremely eager to have a smooth handover to a defined communist faction from political groupings best described as conservative and with considerable religious leanings, but this was not to transpire. There were many disparate forces active in the town that meant a clear handover of power could not take place, including the support for Korean activist Cho Man-sik, who had led guerrilla groups throughout the Japanese occupation. The Red Army, never known for tact, also had to deal with resentment over the quantity of grain they had seized, and parallels were immediately drawn between them and the behaviour of the Japanese forces a few years earlier. A further complication was the arrival of 2,000 communist Korean fighters from China on 24 October 1945, driven out of Andong as the town surrendered to the Guomindang (Chinese National forces under Chiang Kai-shek). Their aim was to take over their country, not to be subservient to the Red Army. In addition, Japanese civilians, who largely did not retreat with their army and who had many crucial administrative and educational roles, remained in the city. The Soviets had no plan for imposing their authority on such a diverse and largely hostile population, and language barriers greatly added to their woes. Local people spoke mainly Korean and Japanese, some presumably knowing Chinese as well, but very few were able to converse in Russian; in contrast, the Soviets had very few speakers for the three languages spoken by the city's residents.

The arrest of a middle-school headmaster at a school just outside Sinuiju was the catalyst for an uprising in the city on 23 November 1945. He had resisted attempts to totally change the curriculum to fit a Soviet mould. Students from across the town marched unarmed, except for a few stones and rocks, to the Communist Party headquarters that housed both Soviet forces and a small number of Korean sympathisers. With the inevitable overreaction by the Soviet troops, probably close to 100 students were killed by the soldiers and many more were injured. Kim Il Sung came to the town on 27 November and met with students in a way that would never happen again. Although officially the students agreed they 'had been misled by agitators', they were able to present their grievances directly to the newly appointed Supreme Leader. Upon speaking to them, Kim realised that he needed to strengthen the nationalism within his message, a tone that continued with equal intensity under his son and grandson.

Being on the Chinese border, the outbreak of the Korean War in June 1950 had little immediate effect on the town. In fact, Sinuiju appeared to be such a safe redoubt that the North Korean government moved here in the wake of the Inchon landings when they were forced to flee Pyongyang (page 16). However, this all changed on 7 and 8 November 1950 when Sinuiju was bombed by the US; the destruction was unprecedented, more than any North Korean town (or European town in World War II for that matter) had seen before. The US Joint Chiefs of Staff had wanted to ban any bombing within 8km of the Chinese border, despite the Chinese at this stage having joined the war. However, General MacArthur appealed against this decision to President Truman, who agreed with him (a very rare occurrence) – the devastation of Sinuiju was the result. Consequently, the North Korean government moved quickly to the mountains, realising that no urban area was safe anymore.

In the 1950s and '60s there was minimal contact between China and Sinuiju. Rebuilding the city took several years and the hostility to the Chinese Cultural Revolution in the 1960s prevented any cultural exchanges that might otherwise have taken place then. The railway and the road link with Dandong, across the Amnok River, did of course operate, but it was far more of a link between the two capitals, Beijing and Pyongyang, than between the two neighbours. Chinese tourists only started to cross over in the 1980s, usually just for the day, and local trade began at that time as well. China was by then openly running a market economy and the Koreans were keen to study this at a very local level. Many Koreans have been given the chance of living over the river in Dandong, where lots of small companies are now operated under Korean auspices. Over the last 30 years, Dandong has boomed -- with the Korean immigrants certainly contributing to this – and the contrast with Sinuiju becomes more glaring each year. UN sanctions on the DPRK have little effect here as the trade across the border is so local. It just has to be hoped that some of the wealth generated makes its way to the city, rather than going directly to Pyongyang or staying in Dandong.

GETTING THERE AND AWAY

By rail A daily train, service 51, leaves Pyongyang at 10.25, arriving into Sinuiju at 15.32. The train has a restaurant car that can offer up a meal, snacks and drinks to keep travellers fed and watered on the 225km journey. Heading north to China, this service typically departs Sinuiju at 17.13, arriving into Dandong at 16.23 (Chinese time). While it's possible to travel just as far as Dandong, the service continues all the way onto Beijing four times a week (on Mondays, Wednesdays, Thursdays and Saturdays), as train K28. It is therefore perfectly feasible to travel from Pyongyang to Sinuiju by domestic train, have a day or two in the area and then travel onto Dandong, or indeed Beijing by train. In reverse, train 52 departs Sinuiju at 13.09 each day, arriving into Pyongyang at 18.45.

It should go without saying, but trains can be delayed and schedules altered, although this is the most reliable service in the country. Also, you should not just get off, or on, a train without it being pre-arranged – as enticing as it may be to just get off in Sinuiju to explore, if you are not expected you will likely not have an enjoyable visit, to put it mildly.

By road While it is impossible for 'normal' visitors to travel by road between Pyongyang and Sinuiju, the road bridge between Sinuiju and Dandong is open for tourists in each direction. Assuming all paperwork is in place, you can be transported across the border by bus – a cheaper, quicker, more flexible (but less interesting) way of crossing the border than by train.

By air Air Koryo repeatedly toy with trying to get a scheduled domestic flight to Uiju, home of the Air Force's 24th Bomber Regiment, off the ground, but these 'scheduled flights' always seemed to be cancelled at the eleventh hour due to a lack of demand. Still, as North Koreans become increasingly mobile, the proposed flights into Uiji Airfield, a 10km drive out of town, may become viable. Groups can charter aircraft into this airport should they wish; a multi-day charter flight could incorporate other areas that are hard to reach, such as Ryanggang and North Hamgyong provinces.

WHERE TO STAY *Map, page 180*

The city advertises two options available to tourists, but be warned: most are normally obliged to stay in the Dongrim Hotel, a staggering 55km from Sinuiju, which, given the road, can take a couple of hours to reach. Owing to this sheer distance from Sinuiju, local authorities claim that, by appointment, the train can make an unscheduled stop in nearby Dongrim town for passengers staying at this hotel to board or disembark.

Amnokgang Hotel (53 rooms) In the centre of town, the Amnokgang would be the logical place to stay for those spending the night in Sinuiju. It is admittedly tired, but undergoing a gradual refurbishment at the time of writing. **$$**

Dongrim Hotel (63 rooms) Opened in 2014, the rural & out-of-the-way Dongrim Hotel feels more like China than North Korea, with a bit of a shoddy finish. The surly staff, almost unheard of elsewhere in the country, leave guests feeling a bit disappointed by the whole experience. Still, the hotel does have facilities to try & keep you entertained, including a surprisingly large swimming pool. If you have time, a walk into the forests to the north of the hotel leads to the small Dongrim Falls, an enjoyable enough little jaunt for the early riser. **$$$**

WHERE TO EAT AND DRINK While the local authorities deliberate on quite how they want to handle the trickle of tourists that pass through the city, they will most likely decide for you where you may eat and drink, typically assigning visitors to the confines of their hotel or one of the restaurants near the Sinuiju waterfront, such as the Myohyangsan International Travel Company Restaurant.

WHAT TO SEE AND DO

In Sinuiju Exiting the train station (train being your most likely means of arriving in Sinuiju) you will immediately step into the main square and see the twin statues of Kim Il Sung and Kim Jong Il to your right; the quasi-obligatory bow here will be a good ice-breaker to appease the Sinuiju-based guides you will have just met. In the city itself, a significant portion of local sights are of the revolutionary nature – if you haven't seen a similar example of such sites elsewhere in the country, well fine, but if you have already been to one you may not find the **North Pyongan Revolutionary Museum** or the **North Pyongan Provincial History Museum** totally enthralling; still they are common visits that 'you *will* enjoy' for 30 minutes or so.

Of more interest for most visitors are the parts of town that allow one to see what could have been, rubbernecking over the river to understand how far things have

---

ASIAN HIGHWAY 1 (AH1)

Stretching from Tokyo to Istanbul and passing through Sinuiju, the Asian Highway 1 is a 20,557km road that takes in 14 countries (and one special administrative region) before joining the Trans-European Motorway, which itself continues over 6,000km to Lisbon. Part of a co-operative project between the countries themselves, the UN's ESCAP, and others, to improve transportation and roads in Asia, travelling the length of the AH1 would be an epic journey. Sadly, undertaking such an expedition remains a pipe dream for anybody considering it; closed borders, war zones and nigh on impossible logistics make this a route that can exist only in the minds of the UN staffers and others who dreamt it up. One day, perhaps.

China's largest border city, with a population that will soon nudge the one million mark, Dandong is a world apart from Sinuiju, its neighbour on the opposite bank of the Amnok River (or the Yalu, as it is called in China). Chairman Mao once proclaimed that China and North Korea were 'as close as lips and teeth' but these days, aside from its physical proximity, Sinuiju – or any North Korean city for that matter – may as well be another planet. With bustling streets, international fast-food chains like KFC and McDonald's, and even a Tesco, Dandong isn't just the frontier of China – it's where the life as we know it ends and otherworldly North Korea begins.

As the principal overland gateway to North Korea, Dandong is passed through by a fair few travellers on their way south, particularly now that a daily train operates between the city and Pyongyang (page 182). Many of the sights on offer in Dandong are of the 'stare into North Korea' ilk – perfectly interesting for those not visiting the country, but not essential to anyone who has actually been to, or is going to the DPRK.

Dandong has a small international airport, a thrice-weekly ferry to South Korea and high-speed rail links connecting it with major cities such as Shenyang and Beijing – it's unsurprising, then, that Dandong also offers all manner of accommodation and dining, from basic options to comfortable international chains. While visitors will almost certainly find the secretive cities of North Korea far more interesting than modern Dandong, a day or two here to explore is worth considering by those with plenty of time and a more in-depth interest in the DPRK. Of course, more conventional Sino-centric sights exist in addition to those listed in this box, but we have covered the ones most relevant to North Korea here.

developed in Dandong, which just a few generations ago was the poorer of the two cities. A short drive from the train station leads to the **Sino-Korean Friendship Bridge**, the road and rail bridge connecting these two very different worlds. At the right time of day trucks and trains may rumble overhead, while you will likely see Chinese tour boats approach, as far as they dare, to gawp into North Korea and at you. This is also the closest point (other than by visiting China) that one can get to the **Broken Bridge**, which succumbed to US bombing during the Korean War. When this bridge was built in 1911, Korea was for the first time connected with the Eurasian rail network. On the Chinese side the bridge is restored almost to the midpoint of the river, while on the North Korean side only the foundations remain. The waterfront area here has been spruced up of late with a small open-air swimming pool and water slides (for locals only, it seems) and a few often-empty restaurants, where you will likely have a meal.

Moving inland, the **Ponbu Kindergarten** is famous within the DPRK and a tour here will typically include an impressive song and dance routine. It is, much like any kindergarten in the country, a remarkable spectacle, but many of the performances at Ponbu are geared towards Chinese tourists; a good portion of the routines are likely to go over the head of Western visitors. Not far from here, the **Sinuiju Art Exhibition** has one of the largest selections of socialist-realist art for sale anywhere in the country, and prices seem a little lower than in Pyongyang – if you see something you like, buy it, as you will never see it again (as I have sadly discovered!).

Stretching southeast from the train station for around 500m, the **Folk Park** is a little wedge of tranquillity in central Sinuiju that runs all the way to a stelae known

In the city itself, the excellent **Memorial of the War to Resist US Aggression and Aid Korea** is the only official museum in China that memorialises the Korean War, and well worth a visit for military and history buffs. Along the riverfront, the **Broken Bridge** (see opposite) can be visited and a number of **boats and speedboats** ply their trade, ferrying passengers as close as they dare to the southern shore. A little way out of Dandong, the **Hushan Great Wall** at Tiger Mountain is the eastern end of the Great Wall of China, terminating atop a hill overlooking North Korea. A walk along the restored wall, which in places is particularly steep, is nonetheless manageable at just 1.25km in length. As you will have no minders with you, you may of course set your own pace. A number of restaurants operated and staffed by North Koreans can be found across the city and a meal in one of them is a recommended and somewhat bizarre experience, feeling as if one is dining within a North Korean enclave, with the service and surroundings often more memorable than the food.

With more time to play with, you may want to consider a day trip out of Dandong to drive northeast along the 319 Provincial Road. The journey often hugs the north bank of the river and affords good views into North Korea as you head upstream to locations such as the **Taipingwan Dam** and **Sup'ung Dam**, hydro-electric plants operating for the mutual benefit of both nations. Return boat trips along the Amnok River, aimed at Chinese tourists wanting to look into North Korea, can be taken from various spots on the river – but one such tour is enough for most. Finally, those with an interest in the war should visit the **Hekou Broken Bridge**, around a 55km drive from central Dandong, which was crossed by **Mao Anying** (see box, page 170) in 1950. Like many others in the People's Volunteer Army, he never returned.

as the Eternal Life Monument, one of countless such monoliths in the country built to honour the Kims. The friendly park is often full of children, picnicking families and young couples – the ideal place to strive for a spot of local fraternising. A few basic food and entertainment stalls pop up in the warmer months, while braver visitors may want to try out the traditional Korean swings – so high that you would be remiss not to check the small print of your travel insurance first.

Around Sinuiju
Heading southeast along the main road out of town along Asian Highway 1 (see box, page 183), the city comes to an abrupt stop, with the apartment blocks suddenly turning to farmland; a 2km agricultural buffer divides the main city from Namsinuiju (South Sinuiju). A brief photo stop can take in the curious and conspicuous **Three Tigers of Mount Paektu**: three large mosaics of Kim Il Sung, Kim Jong Il and Kim Jong Suk, with a nine-storey apartment providing a backdrop – an interesting 5-minute interlude before visiting the **Sinuiju Cosmetics Factory**, which makes a variety of products from soap and toothpaste to washing powder and shampoo. During a tour, you will see the production line and can even stock up on supplies for your washbag and loved ones back home from the small factory shop.

While Sinuiju – which literally means 'New Uiju' – is a modern city, **Uiju**, 20km away, is a much older settlement altogether. Here you'll find some genuine historical sites, such as the well-preserved **Uiju South Gate**, topped with a two-tiered pavilion, and the humbler **Thonggun Pavilion**, which dates all the way back to 1117. Thonggun, on Mount Samgak, affords views over the floodplains and the

Amnok River into China – farmers toiling on the Korean side, urban sprawl on the Chinese side. The area has a number of other almost never-visited sites, including the dreary **Uiju Revolutionary Museum** and, perhaps more interesting, a small pleasure ground. Surprisingly, a couple of restaurants in Uiju will welcome tourists, with the Nammun Restaurant and Thonggunjong Restaurant being the only, and thus best, options in town.

South of Sinuiju, the **Sinamri Cooperative Farm** is 13km from town. Local tour guides seem to struggle to give much explanation of what types of farming actually take place here, but the visit is typically a brief one – you are brought here for the elevated vantage point and vista into China, one that affords views of the **New Yalu River Bridge**, a 3km-long, US$350 million project built and paid for by the Chinese. The four-lane bridge that was constructed in 2014 remains closed; it comes to an abrupt stop in the middle of farmland a few hundred metres inside Korean territory – disconnected from Korean roads and completely closed while the two sides argue out the fine detail.

Beyond Sinamri, it's 42 bumpy and dusty kilometres of driving to the **Dongrim Hotel** (page 183), a journey which will take you through a couple of checkpoints as you pass through the towns of Ryongchon, Yomju and Dongrim itself. The modern shiny railway track that you may notice as you pass through Dongrim is the new 27km branch line leading to the controversial **Sohae Satellite Launching Station** (which is very much off-limits to tourists). The southbound road from Dongrim remains, for now, off-limits – presumably there is something on the hundred or so kilometre stretch of road between here and the 'open' areas further south that you are not supposed to see. Watch this space ...

8

Chagang
(자강도)

Despite its long border with China, isolated Chagang is essentially closed to foreign visitors: the only province in the DPRK that can claim this sad fact. Being 98% mountainous, this remote and sparsely populated backwater, far beyond the prying eyes of most Koreans and foreigners alike, is a prime spot from which the government can operate some of its more questionable activities. With rich mineral wealth and an abundance of timber, the county is ripe for much-needed economic development, yet this is hindered by the government itself; with many of the DPRK's secretive military facilities and operations based in Chagang the ever-suspicious authorities do not want too many people passing through the province – for obvious reasons. The only foreigners likely to be permitted to visit Chagang at present are not likely to be tourists and not likely to want to openly discuss their reason for being there.

HUICHON (희천)

According to the *Panorama Of Korea*, Huichon was 'merely a dirty town in the mountainous area before liberation'. Three-quarters of a century on and the place has thankfully developed somewhat since those days, but with nothing permitted to see in this industrial city of approximately 168,000 people, the only reason you are likely to come here at present is to spend the night in the Huichon Hotel. The only nearby sites of interest are the stunning Mount Myohyang and the town of Hyangsan, both back in North Pyongan, so you'll only stay here if you request it specifically, or if the hotels back in Myohyang and Hyangsan are

> **FUTURE POSSIBILITIES?**
>
> If and when Chagang opens up to tourists, those fortunate to visit will find it an adventure playground, with an untapped wealth of possibilities such as trekking, rafting and other low-impact/ecotourism options in this densely forested mountainous region. The opening up of existing roads and rail lines would also provide an alternative access point to the east coast and north of the country, giving overland access from Pyongyang to South Hamgyong and Ryanggang provinces and also to China. Should this become a reality, the need to backtrack over the same roads to reach the north and east could be avoided; much-needed and potentially very exciting circuitous routes would bring about a plethora of new possibilities in the DPRK. Watch this space…

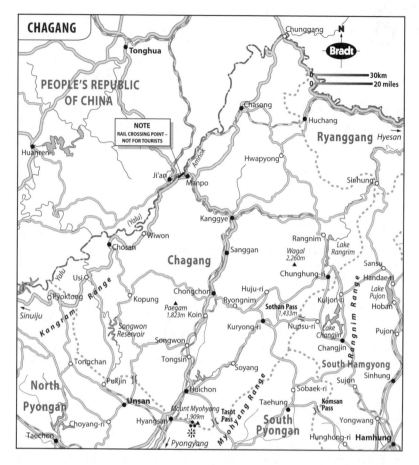

not available for any reason. Both scenarios are unlikely. Should any sites open in Huichon, they will likely, for now, showcase the city's industry, as Huichon is an important centre within the country for electronics and machinery. For those with a yearning to see a spot of industry, it would not hurt to ask of the possibility of visiting sprawling workshops such as the Huichon General Machine Tool Factory, the Huichon Silk Mill or the Huichon Hard Glassware Factory.

GETTING THERE AND AWAY For now, the only permitted way to enter Chagang is by road from the southwest, pressing on after travelling the main Pyongyang–Hyangsan dual carriageway. From Hyangsan, the last town in North Pyongan, Huichon is a drive of only 25km (approximately 40 minutes) on a scenic road that often hugs the west bank of the Chongchon River. If travelling this way, expect to be held up for a few moments at the county border checkpoint while your guides explain your reason to be here. Although passenger trains do operate from Pyongyang to Huichon and beyond, these are still designated for local use only.

 WHERE TO STAY AND EAT For now, Huichon is the only place in the province where 'normal' visitors may stay, with the excitingly named Huichon Hotel the only option. While Huichon is an attractive enough city by local standards and has a few places to eat, visitors are encouraged to take all their meals at the Huichon Hotel – best to do as you are told!

Huichon Hotel (43 rooms) This is an acceptable & comfortable enough hotel to spend a night or 2 in, but an inferior option to those available back in Mount Myohyang & Hyangsan. Plumbing can be a little iffy, but hot water is normally available for a limited time in the mornings & evenings. Given the lack of visitors the restaurant provides surprisingly good food & service. Those lucky enough to stay in room 303 will discover a very large (& noisy) refrigerator in their room – a gift to the hotel from Kim Jong Il. Don't even think about unplugging it! **$$**

NORTH KOREA ONLINE

For additional online content, articles, photos and more on North Korea, why not visit **w** bradtguides.com/nkorea?

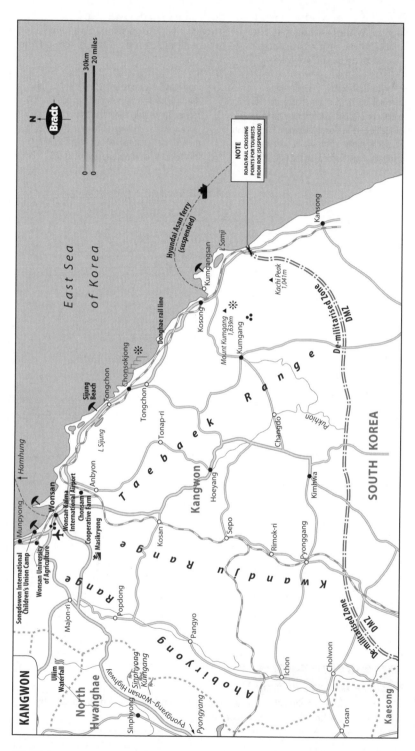

9

Kangwon
(강원도)

This southeastern corner of the DPRK offers plenty to the traveller with the time to invest in getting here. Spanning an area of 11,755km², it is home to the coastal city of Wonsan, the beautifully pristine and jagged Mount Kumgang, and the modern, much-lauded, Masikryong Ski Resort. The region offers year-round potential with an emphasis on natural beauty and the outdoors; beaches, hiking and skiing are all on the menu. There is more than enough here to occupy a few very enjoyable days, as active or lethargic as you desire. The area is well suited to visit in combination with neighbouring South Hamgyong Province.

WONSAN (원산)

> There is nothing sensational about Wonsan; it has had no booms in trade or land, but keeps the even tenor of its ways. It is the most attractive of the Treaty Ports, a place where it is always afternoon. Its future should be that of a salubrious and popular sanatorium.
>
> Isabella Bird, *Korea and Her Neighbours* (1898)

The capital of Kangwon Province, this pleasant port city of 363,000 people is arguably the most affluent city on the east coast of the DPRK and has a hint of Pyongyang-on-Sea about it, with yellow sandy beaches and a good (for North Korea) infrastructure. On summer days Wonsan Bay seems awash with people of all ages strolling along the harbour, fishing from Jangdok Islet or enjoying a barbecue from one of the many makeshift stalls that pop up along the waterfront. In easier times this port traded a great deal with Russia and Japan, but in the West its most famous import was the USS *Pueblo*, a US Navy intelligence ship captured in January 1968 (page 23). Owing to the benefit of hydro-electric power in the region, energy shortages are not such an issue here in Wonsan – when looking back at the city from Jandok Islet in the early evening, the well-lit high-rise tower blocks can, just for a moment, make you feel like you could be in the South.

Mooted as a possible hub for investment, relaxed Wonsan has plenty of business potential; those staying here could well be rubbing shoulders in the hotel bar with resident Chinese businessmen involved in processed seafood and a host of other unspecified 'import/exports', whatever that may mean. There's plenty of scope for tourism, too, with the new Wonsan Air Festival encouraging visitors to the city. Wonsan is also the natural gateway to Hamhung in the north and Mount Kumgang in the south, as well as a possible spot to pass through if travelling to or from the Masikryong Ski Resort. Conventional sightseeing in Wonsan itself is limited, but

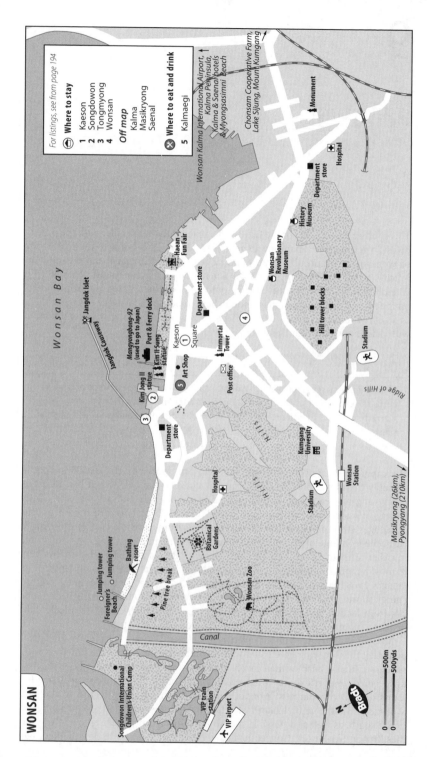

WONSAN

Wonsan Bay

Jangdok Islet

Jangdok Causeway

Jumping tower
Jumping tower
Bathing resort
Foreigner's Beach
Pine tree break
Botanical Gardens
Wonsan Zoo

Songdowon International
Children's Union Camp

VIP train station
VIP airport

Canal

HILLS
HILLS

Hospital
Department store
Stadium
Kumgang University
Wonsan Station

Ridge of Hills

Masikryong (26km),
Pyongyang (210km)

Kim Jong Il statue
Kim Il Sung statue
Mangyongbong-92
(used to go to Japan)
Port & Ferry dock

Art Shop
Kaeson Square
Immortal Tower
Post office

Haean Fun Fair
Department store

Wonsan Revolutionary Museum
History Museum
Hill tower blocks
Department store
Hospital
Monument
Stadium

Wonsan Kalma International Airport,
Kalma Peninsula,
Kalma & Saenal hotels
& Myongsasimni Beach

Chonsam Cooperative Farm,
Lake Sijung, Mount Kumgang

For listings, see from page 194

Where to stay
1 Kaeson
2 Songdowon
3 Tongmyong
4 Wonsan

Off map
Kalma
Masikryong
Saenal

Where to eat and drink
5 Kalmaegi

N

0   500m
0   500yds

Bradt

you can spend at least half a day exploring the city, as you will almost certainly need to pass through here should you be visiting anywhere in the southeast of the country.

HISTORY It is Japan that made Wonsan prosperous and it will be Japan on which any future prosperity depends. With Korea being deliberately isolated until the late 19th century, Wonsan could not develop as a port with an industrial hinterland, as so many other port towns did earlier in the 19th century all over the world. However, the Japanese realised the industrial potential for the area during their occupation between 1910 and 1945 and exploited it to the full, developing the port as a major outlet to Japan; railway lines soon linked it to both Pyongyang and Seoul. During the Korean War, the town was both bombed and blockaded for two years as UN forces could not hold it against the Chinese, but wanted to prevent its use as a port. The blockade lasted until the day the armistice was signed in July 1953. With the town 80% destroyed, building had to start from scratch.

South Korean media reported in 2013 that Kim Jong Un had given instructions to develop Wonsan as a full-scale resort and the extensive building programme of the last few years bears this out; Kim also referred to this project in his 2018 New Year speech. The local airport, previously only used by the military, has been developed to take long-haul flights; however, as with so much in North Korea, no plans have been published, so one can only speculate on what might arise here.

GETTING THERE AND AWAY

By road Heading northeast from Sinphyong (page 149), the last stop of note in North Hwanghae, the road deteriorates as it slowly winds up across steep, attractive mountains, passing through numerous dank tunnels. After 32km you'll pass the county line in to Kangwon before ascending for a further 5km to the 876m Ahobi Pass where, time permitting, you can visit the **700-Ridge Pavilion** to take in the vista from this remote spot deep and high in the mountains – as good a spot as any on the journey to stretch your legs. From here the road slowly descends for 21km to the first permissible junction, which leads to the Ullim Waterfall (page 200). Continuing eastwards along the main road, it's another 16km to Masikryong, beyond which you will drive through the impressive 4km-long **Mujigae (Rainbow)**

WONSAN KALMA INTERNATIONAL AIRPORT

Somewhat typical of the DPRK's disjointed infrastructural development, this airport has undergone massive development in recent years, reopening in 2015 to much fanfare. Opened just a few months after Pyongyang's much-delayed new international terminal, at a reported cost of US$200 million, quite why Wonsan needs such an impressive airport is beyond almost everybody – there aren't even regular scheduled flights to the capital, let alone to international destinations. Arguably, this money could have been better spent in improving the road between Pyongyang and Wonsan, but trying to understand why the North Korean government does what it does is no easy task. One upshot of this new airport was the Wonsan Air Festival. Held in September 2016, it was hoped to become an annual aviation event where enthusiasts would be able to enjoy leisure flights in a variety of Soviet-era aircraft, enjoy aerobatic displays from both the Korean People's Army Air Force and Air Koryo, try their hand at skydiving and much more, but geopolitical factors have scuppered subsequent festivals.

Tunnel, 20km from Wonsan. The entire drive from Pyongyang to Wonsan is 210km on what was, many years ago, a good road. Until the much-needed renovations of this pot-holed highway are carried out, expect the journey to take around 3½–4 hours, excluding any sightseeing en route.

Departing Wonsan by road, there are three possibilities: to return west on the main highway towards Pyongyang, north towards Hamhung or south to Sijung and the famous Mount Kumgang region.

By train and air   While trains do serve Wonsan, for now tourists can usually only arrive here by chartered train – an incredibly expensive ticket indeed. Similarly, flights from Pyongyang to Wonsan Kalma International Airport are normally by charter only, so unless you are an aviation enthusiast you almost certainly have to stick to the road.

 WHERE TO STAY   *Map, page 192*

Wonsan offers a variety of accommodation options, with the majority of the hotels falling in to the 'it may be possible' category. Most visitors are likely to stay in either of the hotels listed here; however, when Wonsan is busy some of the other establishments in town may open their doors to travellers, including the budget **Kaeson** and **Wonsan** hotels located in the city centre. On the Kalma Peninsula,

---

COMING SOON: THE WONSAN–KALMA COASTAL TOURIST AREA

At the time of writing, Wonsan's Kalma Peninsula is a massive construction site, with the 4km-long Myongsasimni beach being transformed from a sleepy strip of yellow sandy beach into the 'Wonsan-Kalma Coastal Tourist Area' - North Korea's answer to Benidorm. With construction proposed to be complete by October 2019, a reported 140,000 workers are building a number of ostentatious hotels and all manner of tourism-related facilities in a complex that will have, Pyongyangites claim, up to 10,000 hotel rooms. With the US$200 million Wonsan Kalma International Airport a stone's throw from this development, the Korean government clearly has ambitious plans, but quite how they are going to fill these hotels is anybody's guess, particularly as Wonsan's current lodgings are largely bereft of guests at the best of times.

This development is the latest in a run of somewhat nonsensical tourism development projects that the government has spearheaded over the last few years, with the authorities aiming to have two million incoming tourists per year by 2020. Although not public knowledge per se, the number of current visitors per annum is believed to be around 5% of this figure, and primarily comprises Chinese tourists on short, budget group tours – certainly not the type of traveller that would want to linger in a 'luxury' hotel for a fortnight. If this resort is a success – and that's a very big if – Wonsan will likely change beyond recognition, but most observers are extremely sceptical. Major questions remain unanswered, such as how people will get to Wonsan (the 'international airport' still doesn't have scheduled domestic flights, let alone international), and if visitors will be allowed to roam freely around the resort (which seems highly unlikely at current). Nevertheless, one thing that North Korea has successfully managed to do over the decades is surprise people, so you never know – Wonsan could well become North Korea's answer to South Korea's ever-popular Jeju. Just don't hold your breath.

---

near the airport, the beachfront **Kalma Hotel** and **Saenal Hotel** are upmarket options normally reserved for government and military bigwigs, but it cannot hurt to ask about staying here. Occasionally, when Wonsan is really full to the brim, people have been known to stay at the Songdowon International Children's Union Camp (see below). With Masikryong just 25km away, the Masikryong Hotel (page 199) is another possible base for the city.

🏠 **Songdowon Hotel** (180 rooms) With a good location next door to the Tongmyong Hotel, the Songdowon is getting a little tired these days, but is acceptable enough for an overnight stay. This hotel, too, has all you would expect in a Korean hotel of its size, including a café, numerous bars, restaurants & a bookshop. **$$**

🏠 **Tongmyong Hotel** (42 rooms) This hotel, situated next to the causeway leading to Jangdok Islet, was built in 1992 & despite undergoing occasional renovations looks much older. Although rooms are looking a little dated, the hotel is comfortable enough & given its size has an impressive array of facilities, with a good bookshop & numerous bars/restaurants – there's even an affable barber. Sadly, the Mount Paektu forest-themed bar did not survive the latest renovation. **$$**

✖ WHERE TO EAT AND DRINK *Map, page 192*

There is an ever-increasing number of places to eat in Wonsan, with the majority near the waterfront. Being a coastal city, nearly all eateries specialise in a weird and wonderful array of seafood, much of which will be unfamiliar to those new to this part of the world. While the **Kalmaegi Restaurant** is the most popular dining spot for those on a tour, arguably the best seat in town is a plastic stool at one of the many unnamed stalls that pop up along the causeway leading to Jangdok Islet, where you can rub shoulders with locals while tucking in to all manner of freshly caught seafood, washed down with a glass or two of soju.

WHAT TO SEE AND DO

In Wonsan In the northwest of the city, the 500ha Songdowon area boasts a sandy strip of beach at the **Songdowon Sea Bathing Resort**. Popular with locals and often packed on summer weekends, it's an enjoyable place to spend an afternoon doing very little, enjoying grilled fish and cold drinks in between paddling in the sea. Likely far less enjoyable would be the nearby **Wonsan Zoo**, rarely visited by tourists. The **Botanical Gardens**, next door to the zoo, are far less depressing, but those with an interest in botany would be better to visit the sprawling Central Botanical Gardens in Pyongyang (page 125).

The big draw in this part of the city is the **Songdowon International Children's Union Camp**, one of the country's most famous summer camps, which hosts up to 1,200 children at any given time. After a massive renovation in 2014 the camp now boasts 12,000m² of grounds, including an aquarium, indoor and outdoor swimming pools, sports fields and an aviary. This site is most impressive – a vast improvement on the British summer camps from this author's youth, and the children here seem delighted to be selected to come on these coveted holidays. The camp is open from April to October and once or twice a year opens to children from around the world, hence the 'international' in the name; it's a long way from home but I know I would have loved it! Hidden out of sight behind the camp is a small paved runway and train station – depending on who you ask (but it's best not to ask) it is either for the children themselves or for those staying in the VIP compound just a few hundred metres away.

Back towards the city centre, a walk along the causeway to **Jangdok Islet** is a delightful way to while away a couple of hours, particularly if you can time your visit with a weekend or busy afternoon, when it's lined with pop-up stalls, picnicking families and fishermen. On reaching Jangdok itself you will be afforded a good view across the water back to central Wonsan and its high-rise buildings. Should you politely ask the lighthouse keeper, you may be permitted to climb to the top of the small lighthouse, from where you may be able to make out the buildings of the Wonsan Kalma International Airport, along with the Kalma and Saenal hotels, all due east.

On firmer land, the walk from the Tongmyong Hotel towards Kaeson Square will take you past the Kalmaegi Restaurant and a small, yet excellent state-run **Art Shop** – one of the best spots in the entire country for picking up socialist-realist artworks. A couple of hundred metres further, **Kaeson Square**, the main square in the city, is just about worthy for a quick photo stop, but the small strip of land between the leaders' statues and **Haean Fun Fair** is of much more interest. Like Jangdok Islet, come at the right time of day and this area can be busy with locals, with kids of all ages enjoying the pop-up funfair games and stalls. The *Mangyongbong-92* (see box, below) cargo-passenger ship is moored here and unless there are any significant changes in the DPRK's international relations, you should still be able to see it when you visit. There are a few smaller leisure boats here, too, occasionally running short sunset cruises around the bay – a perfect way to end the day.

MANGYONGBONG-92

This cargo-passenger ship has been moored in Wonsan for so long now that it feels like a fixed structure. Despite the rare sailing, it has always been present during this author's many visits to the city. Built in 1992 by Chongryon (also known as the General Association of Korean Residents in Japan), a Japanese organisation affiliated with the North that supports ethnic Koreans living in Japan, the ship was primarily constructed to transport passengers and cargo between Wonsan and Niigata, Japan. Making the 28-hour voyage once or twice a month, the *Mangyongbong-92* could carry up to 218 paying passengers and 1,000 tonnes of cargo.

As international relations between Japan and the DPRK soured in 2002, when the North admitted to abducting Japanese citizens in the late 1970s and early 1980s, the spotlight turned to the *Mangyongbong-92*, with the allegation that it was used by the Koreans as a smuggling route between the two countries. Little hard proof, if any, exists, but it has been suggested that the ship was used to transport all manner of things, ranging from drugs and cash to missile parts. With Japanese suspicions running high, they tightened their regulations on North Korean vessels entering Japanese waters. The *Manyongbong-92* continued to run, but in 2006, after North Korean missile tests in June and a nuclear test in October, Japan banned all North Korean ships from entering their waters, a ban that still exists today.

Losing its *raison d'être*, the ship has barely moved since 2006, with the government seemingly unsure quite what do with it. Pyongyang talks of resuming the service to Japan 'soon', but given relations with the country this seems unlikely. In 2011, a lacklustre effort at commencing cruises from Rajin to Kumgang seemed doomed to failure before the venture had even started, as did the trial cruise between Rajin and Vladivostok, Russia, in 2017. The biggest losers from the situation are the Chongryon members themselves, as a direct lifeline between them and their homeland and family members has been lost. In a world of globalisation they are now further away from the DPRK than ever before.

DOWN ON THE FARM

All farming in North Korea had been collectivised by the late 1950s and farms today can be divided into two main categories: co-operative farms and state farms. A farm in North Korea is not a quaint little homestead, and 'villages' essentially do not exist in the county; agriculture is implemented *en masse*, with typical farms being worked by hundreds of families and thousands of workers. Accordingly, a farm is more akin to a scattering of collective settlements within walking or cycling distance of a communal centre, which is likely to home the integral facilities of the farm together with a scattering of public buildings such as community dining halls, elementary schools, health clinics and a shop or two.

Within the more common co-operative farm system, the farm is technically owned by the workers and the workers normally have a target to strive for, selling their agreed quota to the state (albeit at a price set by the state). Any excess production can be sold on or bartered/traded as the farm sees fit, to the benefit of all. Given that many farms are monocultural, the ability to barter and trade with other farms (which is implemented both formally and informally) is imperative. As a reaction to the agricultural chaos and famine of the 1990s, families living on co-operative farms were all allocated additional private family plots of land of 100–170m^2, with which they could do what they wish, allowing the savvier to supplement their income with a spot of private enterprise.

State farms, considered the more ideologically advanced method of agricultural management, are few and far between in contemporary North Korea, only making up around 10% of cultivated land. Within the state farm system, employees receive a wage and nominally work fixed hours. The state owns the farm and all produce goes directly to the state. Other than being lambasted for their failures or congratulated for bumper yields, employees therefore gain no material benefit for going the extra mile, but going that extra mile will almost certainly be expected. In a country where many require alternative income streams to stay afloat, the prospect of working on a state farm in the country is low risk, yet low reward, and far less attractive than working on a co-operative farm, which allows the harder workers to make just a little more hay when the sun shines.

Away from the water, the **Wonsan Revolutionary Museum** confusingly seems to go by several names such as the 'Train Museum', 'Railway Museum' and similar variants. You'll need to take off your shoes to tour this small guesthouse-turned-museum, the very place that Kim Il Sung stayed on 19 September 1945, his first night back in the country as a free man after 26 years of exile. It will likely only be after you have toured the spotless guesthouse and ticket office that your guide will, grudgingly, tell you that this is all a complete reconstruction from the 1970s. Behind the fabricated ticket hall, however, there is something that is well worth seeing – a beautifully restored colonial Japanese-era steam locomotive, complete with a period third-class carriage – allegedly the very carriage in which Kim Il Sung travelled during his historic journey to Pyongyang. It must have been a memorable journey indeed, as decades later Kim Il Sung recalled the very seat in which he sat, now clearly marked.

The Kalma Peninsula on the eastern end of Wonsan Harbour is home to **Myongsasimni**, a 4km stretch of beach that you *may* be able to visit, but it could well depend on who is staying in the VIP Kalma and Saenal hotels. The **Wonsan Kalma International Airport** (see box, page 193) can also be found here, but don't expect to be able to look around unless you have an air ticket.

AROUND WONSAN Approximately 7km north of Wonsan, on the road to Hamhung, the **Wonsan Agricultural University** is an occasional feature on tours. Formerly the Territorial Abbey of Tokwon, established by German Benedictine monks in 1928 with the monastery and church added shortly after, the university incorporated the building in 1949 when the abbey was dissolved. Today, it's the largest university of its kind in the country and its buildings are a rare example of both pre-Korean War and Western styles. Architectural history aside though, visits here can be a little dreary, with the facilities a stark contrast to some of the gleaming university buildings found back in Pyongyang.

Heading south on the main road out of Wonsan, a long and steep flight of steps leads to an overlooked war memorial, and the city abruptly ends shortly after you pass Kalma Market and Kalma Station, just out of sight from the main road. No visit to the DPRK would be complete without a trip to one of the country's many model farms (see box, page 197), and the **Chonsam Cooperative Farm**, around 11km south of the city, is one of the friendliest in the country. While touring the arable farm and its central village you may have the opportunity to visit a 'normal' home and shop, together with a barbers and kindergarten. Don't be embarrassed if you can't guess the exact number of persimmon hanging from the historical tree west of the main square – to date only Kim Il Sung has managed this feat.

MASIKRYONG SKI RESORT (마식령 스키장)

A symbol of Kim Jong Un's era, the Masikryong Ski Resort was built in 2013 at breakneck speed, allegedly after the Supreme Leader decided that the country needed a modern ski resort. The timing of the construction, with South Korea having been chosen in 2011 as the host nation for the 2018 Winter Olympics, was surely not a coincidence. Built by the Korean People's Army in just ten months, the resort opened in December 2013 under much scrutiny and scorn from the Western media.

Masikryong is open year-round to visitors, and while the ski season is advertised as being November to March, January and February are the best times to visit for a chance of good snow. With a base elevation of 768m, the resort rises to the 1,363m **Taehwa Peak** from where, on a clear day, the coast can be seen. Atop Taehwa, an expensive restaurant/café claims to offer cocktails and is well worth a look in before you set off downhill. The resort has a total of ten runs, ranging from 682m to just over 5km in length. With just one gondola and three rather slow ski lifts (as well as a short tow rope on the nursery slope), it will hardly be a rival to the Alps or Rockies, but one could enjoy a very surreal couple of days here. Out of season the resort still functions, and a stop in Masikryong to soak up the bizarreness of it all mixed with some walking in the hills is recommended, particularly as you will drive straight past the resort if travelling from Pyongyang to Wonsan.

Although they are aware that a ski resort doesn't have many visitors outside of the short winter season, the DPRK authorities haven't really tapped in to offering summer activities such as light trekking and mountain biking. However, in September 2016 the resort hosted the inaugural Masikryong 10km race with just 25 competitors, with the hope that in time an annual event will follow, including both a half and full marathon (see box, opposite).

GETTING THERE AND AWAY Besides arriving by road, it's possible to arrive in style by your own chartered helicopter (see box, page 56), as the resort has its own helipad. However, unless you have money to burn or broke a limb on the giant slalom, it's best to take the road.

🏠 WHERE TO STAY AND EAT *Map, page 200*

For now the Masikryong Hotel is the centre of the resort and the only place to stay. However, at the time of writing, a new hotel, a few hundred metres to the northwest of the existing one, is under construction. It is 'scheduled' to be up and running in time for the 2019–20 ski season, but note that building projects in North Korea can often grind to a halt without explanation as to why.

🏠 **Masikryong Hotel** (120 rooms) This impressive hotel is one of the best in the country, & despite its relatively small number of rooms there is a bewildering range of facilities on offer, with a swimming pool, health centre, business centre & bookshop, not to mention the seemingly countless number of bars & restaurants. There's an alpine lodge meets 'Pyongyang chic' feel to the place, & an hour or so just exploring the hotel is an experience in itself. Together with the more conventional facilities, the hotel has a ski shop (the only one in the resort) where you can hire all necessary equipment, but keen skiers coming all this way may prefer to bring their own gear as

---

MASIKRYONG 10K *Hilary Bradt*

If there's one regret that I have about my 2016 trip to the DPRK it's that I didn't bring my running gear because I would have dearly loved to enter – and even complete – the Masikryong 10k race. It would have made my trip to that extraordinary place even more surreal and, more importantly, I would have been presented with a certificate as well as a medal and T-shirt. None of the British 10ks that I have struggled through can match that.

Two people from our group competed, although neither admitted to running any sort of race before, and one was our English guide, Carl Meadows, who had the most to lose in face-saving. Our male local guide also ran valiantly with them, meaning I was left unattended to watch the race at strategic parts of the route and enjoy the gorgeous mountain scenery and sunshine. Admittedly, I did feel rather relieved that I wasn't toiling up half way up the mountain to an altitude of 1,000m, nor slithering down it on gravel.

It wasn't a big field. I'm writing this a few days before the 2018 Great North Run, where 65,000 runners will pound the roads of Newcastle. On Masikryong's mountain tracks, however, there were just 25 individuals, and our Carl came 5th. Part of the fun was speculating on what North Korea's first Masikryong 10k would be like for the participants. For instance, the pre-race information said that a vehicle would transport runners across a river, so we wondered if it would wait until there were enough passengers to make it worthwhile driving across. Then there were the bananas offered as sustenance. Would the usual North Korean system apply, where first the fruit must be weighed, then the price agreed on, then the currency decided? Of course none of this happened; the runners splashed across the shallow stream, bananas were offered gratis at the end, and the medal-giving ceremony was splendid. A memory the runners will keep forever, however often they do more conventional and perhaps faster runs. Actually, neither has run a step since, but never say never …

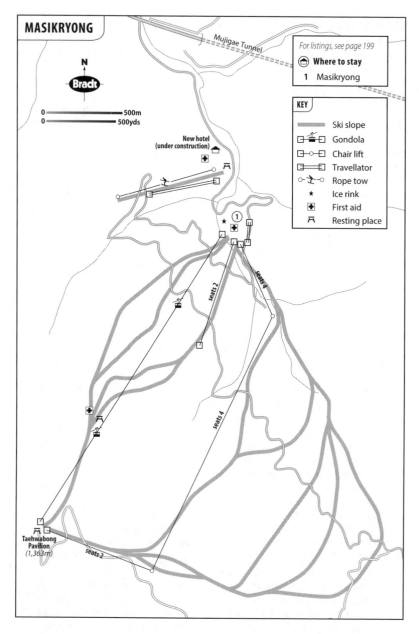

MASIKRYONG

N
Bradt

0 ————— 500m
0 ————— 500yds

New hotel
(under construction)

For listings, see page 199

Where to stay
1 Masikryong

KEY

	Ski slope
	Gondola
	Chair lift
	Travellator
	Rope tow
★	Ice rink
✚	First aid
ㄒ	Resting place

seats 2
seats 4

seats 4

seats 2

Taehwabong
Pavilion
(1,363m)

the equipment, while newly purchased, doesn't appear to be well serviced. The main ski lifts are based just behind the hotel, as is an outdoor ice rink. **$$$$**

AROUND MASIKRYONG Some 25km from Masikryong, a short cut for those travelling from Pyongyang or Masikryong to Hamhung will lead along a slow and winding mountain road to the attractive **Ullim Waterfall**. Meaning 'echo', Ullim is one of the most accessible waterfalls in the country, and the 63m-high falls and adjoining rockpool are a truly beautiful sight. To reach the falls, take the well-paved path that leads up from the lower car park, past a small café, for around 800m. The café may be able to rustle up a hot drink or two (although don't count on food being available), but it's a good a spot as any to stop for a packed lunch. Several walks are possible from the falls, but most visitors just come for the impressive views.

Continuing from Ullim along this short cut towards Hamhung, it is a further 28km, chiefly downhill, before the road joins the main Wonsan–Hamhung Highway. From this junction, it is 30km along a relatively flat road heading southeast back to Wonsan or, heading north, 44km to the Ko Song Ryong Tea House (page 215), the first 'stop' in South Hamgyong.

MOUNT KUMGANG (금강산)

Two days of perfect heavenliness. The Great Rock Peak compels senseless admiration, the air was an elixir. A description can only be a catalogue: the actuality was intoxicating, the canyon on the grandest scale with every element of beauty present.

Isabella Bird, *Korea and Her Neighbours* (1898)

Running along the eastern edge of the Korean Peninsula, the Taebaek Mountains stretch for 500km from Wonsan in the North all the way to the port city of Busan in the South. While South Korea may lay claim to having the greatest infrastructure for those heading in to the hills (thanks to the 2018 Winter Olympics taking place in Pyeongchang in the South) and boast the highest peak in the range with Seoraksan's Daechongbong (1,708m), the North can argue that they have the most pristine and best-preserved stretch of mountains on their soil in Mount Kumgang.

Revered by all Koreans, Mount Kumgang (meaning 'Diamond Mountain') has been a site of near-mythical status since at least the 7th century, with many writers, poets, artists and clergymen making pilgrimages to this beautiful corner of Asia. Like some other regions in Korea the mountain has four names, one for each season ('Kumgang' in spring, 'Pongnae' in summer, 'Phungak' in autumn and 'Kaegol' in winter), but over time Kumgang has become the most used. According to local cartographers, Kumgang has over 100 principal peaks, and a grand total of 12,000 lesser peaks; while few may have verified this subsequently, after a walk in Manmulsang, or almost anywhere in the region, most will hopefully accept this figure as just a slight exaggeration and dispel any need for thoughts of independent verification.

The mountain is loosely divided into three regions, from the attractive lakes and coastline of the **Sea Kumgang** to the stunning scenery of Kuryong and Manmulsang in **Outer Kumgang**, before it rises all the way up to the 1,639m Piro Peak (not to be confused with the other Piro Peak in North Pyongan) in **Inner Kumgang**. Covering an area of 530km², the region was previously a part of Kangwon Province until becoming the Kumgangsan Tourist Region in 2002, a result of the deal made between Hyundai Asan (a branch of Hyundai, the South Korean conglomerate) and the North. Somewhat confusingly, the region is still occasionally included as part of Kangwon Province (as it is in this book), now that Hyundai Asan has no control in the region (see box, page 206).

FLORA AND FAUNA Mount Kumgang boasts over 1,000 plant species, including more than 100 indigenous varieties such as the demure *Stephanandra* shrub and the rich violet diamond bluebell, *Hanabusaya asiatica*. Much of the mountains are covered in broadleaf and coniferous forest and, should you be fortunate to catch the autumn leaf

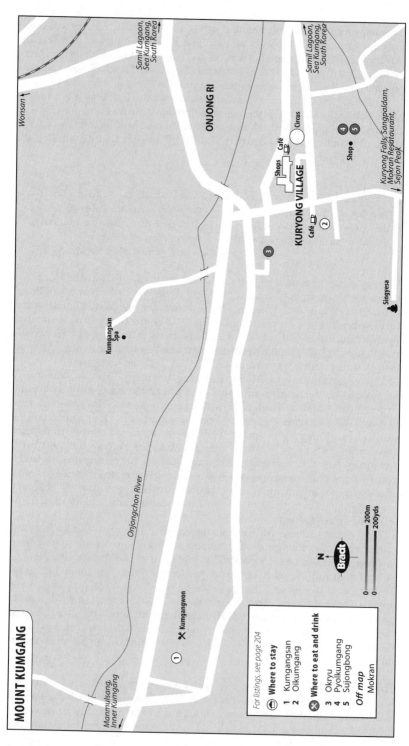

MOUNT KUMGANG

Wonsan

Samil Lagoon, Sea Kumgang, South Korea

ONJONG RI

Café

Shops

Circus

KURYONG VILLAGE

Café 2

Samil Lagoon, Sea Kumgang, South Korea

4
5

Shop

Kuryong Falls, Sangpaldam, Mokran Restaurant, Sejon Peak

3

Singyesa

Kumgangsan Spa

Onjongchon River

Manmulsang, Inner Kumgang

✕ Kumgangwon

1

N
Bradt

0   200m
0   200yds

For listings, see page 204

🏠 Where to stay
1 Kumgangsan
2 Oikumgang

✕ Where to eat and drink
3 Okryu
4 Pyolkumgang
5 Sujongbong

Off map
Mokran

202

colours, typically in mid to late October, the scenery is simply breathtaking. The rich flora has led to a burgeoning cottage industry in the region with a variety of medicines, fruit honeys, liquors and such available for purchase – some of the alcoholic drinks are promoted as being so pure they will help treat or even cure a plethora of illnesses and ailments, not to mention being 'guaranteed' not to induce a hangover!

The mountains are allegedly rich in larger wildlife, which is said to include musk deer, brown bear, ferret and the long-tailed whiskered bat, but despite hunting being strictly banned here visitors will need an eagle eye to spot any. Birdlife, which is also hard to spot, is reported to include 130 species, including the white-throated needletail, swift, kingfisher, eagle owl and cuckoo. At your feet you may be lucky to spot one of the ten species of anurans or nine species of reptile, while the rivers are home to fish such as carp, eel, catfish, trout and salmon, together with lesser-known indigenous species such as the Kumgang fat minnow or the endangered Korean doty barbel. Over 400 types of insects can be found in the region, including a whole host of butterfly species.

GETTING THERE AND AWAY Despite outdated websites alluding to cruise ships such as the *Mangyongbong-92* serving the area (see box, page 196) and even visiting from the South, the only way to reach Mount Kumgang at the time of writing is by road from Wonsan, a journey of about 110km that normally takes around 3 hours, allowing for a brief stop. Talks of permitting tourists to travel by train from Pyongyang or Wonsan to Mount Kumgang remain just that, despite a functioning track being in place.

Departing Wonsan, the road heads through the Kalma District, with the impressive but not yet quite 'international' Wonsan Kalma International Airport just out of sight to the north (see box, page 193). Approximately 15km beyond the suburbs of Wonsan the road meets the coast for the first time, and much of the journey from hereon to Mount Kumgang hugs the East Sea of Korea as you trundle past deserted beaches and small fishing villages. Despite an electric fence running along much of the coast, this journey arguably provides the most stunning coastal scenery in the entire DPRK.

After 45km and around 1¼ hours of driving you'll arrive at **Sijung Beach**, a perfect spot to break the journey and go for a dip in the sea. Here, a resort building has a café, changing rooms, showers with towels and a small shop selling a rather uninspiring selection of goods. Prices are very reasonable, and if you ask politely staff will likely allow you to tuck in to your own packed lunch in their café. Until Mount Kumgang became possible to visit in 2010, the nearby **Sijung Lakeside Guesthouse** was the southernmost permissible lodging on the east coast, but despite the accommodating staff, this basic guesthouse is really only worth considering for those on a tight budget or with time constraints, as options in both Wonsan and Mount Kumgang are far superior. Some tour operators have used the Sijung Lakeside Guesthouse, which is well known in the country as a centre for mud treatments, as a hub for rare surfing tours.

As you are escorted further south you'll arrive in **Tongchon**, where an abrupt right turn leads away from the coast. From here it is a detour of only a couple of kilometres to the geodesic rocks of **Chonsokjong** – a large sign in English will tell you so – yet sadly the DPRK's answer to Giant's Causeway is currently off-limits. From Tongchon it is 36km to the main checkpoint (the first of three) that marks your entrance to Mount Kumgang; a special permit is required to enter the area (pre-arranged by your guide). For this last stretch of the journey the scenery becomes unremarkable, as the road moves away from the coast and floodplain. On clearing the initial checkpoint in to Kumgang, another 11km will bring you to the Kuryong Village area.

🏠 WHERE TO STAY   *Map, page 202*

Hyundai Asan built all manner of accommodation options in the area for a variety of budgets, but now that the resort is firmly in the control of the North most options are temporarily closed due to a lack of visitors, including the floating **Haekumgang Hotel** and nearby **Kumgang Family Beach Hotel**.

🏠 **Kumgangsan Hotel** (215 rooms) The DPRK's flagship hotel of old in the region, the Kumgangsan was refurbished to a high standard during the boom years of the early 2000s. Facilities include a pleasant top-floor bar & balcony, complete with a woefully out-of-tune grand piano, a small souvenir stall & a ground-floor lounge that may be able to rustle up a cold beer from the on-site micro-brewery. **$$$$**

🏠 **Oikumgang Hotel** (179 rooms) Opened in 2006, the Oikumgang is similar in quality & facilities to the Kumgangsan but benefits over the Kumgangsan by being connected to the resort centre, allowing guests to leave the hotel & explore the shops & restaurants unchaperoned. **$$$$**

🍴 WHERE TO EAT AND DRINK   *Map, page 202*

The functioning hotels will of course cater to visitors and can, with notice, normally prepare a light packed lunch should you be heading out into the hills. However, an increasing number of restaurants have started to operate from the old Hyundai buildings. Three or four small basic outlets have also popped up of late in the abandoned cafés in and around Kuryong Village. Sporadically open, they could likely rustle up a round of drinks or snacks without notice, but may struggle to offer much more. Should you have time they are still worth a visit for a quick drink and to soak up their bizarre novelty. Sadly, the **Tanpung**, **Konsung Seafood Restaurant** and **Kumgangwon** were closed at the time of writing.

🍴 **Mokran Restaurant** Located near the car park at the bottom of the path leading to the Kuryong Falls, this spot is a logical lunch stop for those hiking to Kuryong &/or Sangpaldam (see opposite). During busier months, a couple of outdoor stalls pop up offering a selection of snacks together with hot & cold drinks, including refreshing draught beer. **$$$**

🍴 **Okryu Restaurant** Across from the car park of the Oikumgang Hotel, this attractive restaurant specialises in cold noodles, but also offers a variety of Korean dishes. **$$$$**

🍴 **Pyolkumgang Restaurant** Located on the ground floor of a building in Kuryong Village, this is a good dinner option within walking distance of the Oikumgang Hotel. As the staff typically have a lot of time on their hands, meals often end with a rather polished song & dance routine. **$$$**

🍴 **Sujongbong Restaurant** Directly above the Pyolkumgang, staff here try even harder to entertain guests, with meals often finishing not just with a song & dance but with a conga line as well. **$$$**

WHAT TO SEE AND DO

Outer Kumgang   Visitors today are likely to be drawn chiefly to Outer Kumgang, which is home to the bulk of the tourist infrastructure, situated in and around the small town of Onjongri and the segregated tourist centre of Kuryong Village, the logical base while exploring Mount Kumgang.

Kuryong Village and around   Kuryong Village is the centre of the resort built by Hyundai Asan, and while you will likely have a meal here, it is well worth spending an hour or so exploring what is not far off from being a ghost town. Some of the shops and cafés sporadically function, but the dearth of visitors makes this a surreal spot. A fading sign displays bus times around the resort (long ceased), a long-closed circus shows performance times and the restaurants, when

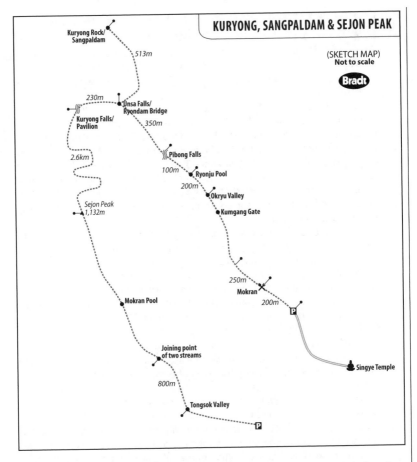

(SKETCH MAP)
Not to scale

Kuryong Rock/
Sangpaldam

513m

230m

Unsa Falls/
Ryondam Bridge

Kuryong Falls/
Pavilion

350m

2.6km

Pibong Falls

100m   Ryonju Pool

200m

Okryu Valley

Sejon Peak
1,132m

Kumgang Gate

250m

Mokran

200m

P

Mokran Pool

Singye Temple

Joining point
of two streams

800m

Tongsok Valley

P

they do function, will likely serve you with South Korean crockery and cutlery and pour your drinks into South Korean-branded glassware, all left behind when the South Koreans departed. A few hundred metres from the Kumgangsan Hotel, the convivial **Kumgangsan Spa** offers a welcome respite after a walk in the mountains, with the waters bubbling up at 37–44°C. A range of massages and other treatments are available here, but it's best to get your guide to call ahead to make sure they will be open. The **Kumgangsan Revolutionary Museum** is also near the Kumgangsan Hotel, but is unlikely to be open – if it is, it is only worth visiting if you have an intense dislike of stunning natural scenery and a burning desire for a dose of revolutionary history. A couple of hundred metres southwest of the Oikumgang Hotel are the crumbling remains of the **Singyesa Temple**. Dating back to the Silla Dynasty, it was firebombed in 1951 and although restoration took place in 2006, the damage was so great it has lost most of its appeal.

Kuryong Falls and Sangpaldam Should you only have half a day for sightseeing in the area, a visit to **Kuryong ('Nine Dragon') Falls** is a must. Departing from Kuryong Village, a short drive south will bring you to the Singye Valley, from where you bear west along the north bank of the river, passing the **Pogwang Hermitage**,

THE RISE AND FALL OF THE MOUNT KUMGANG TOURIST REGION

The Kumgang Mountains, revered by Koreans on both sides of the divide, provide an excellent case study of the trials and tribulations of inter-Korean exchanges, telling a sad story of what could have been if 20th-century history had taken a different path.

With a divided Korea, Mount Kumgang was naturally accessible only from the North, and the area was developed slowly for domestic tourism, with North Korean citizens visiting alongside occasional foreign tourists, chiefly from the communist bloc. Those from south of the DMZ were not permitted to visit Kumgang. This status quo remained until 1998, when the Sunshine Policy (page 30) helped bring about change, albeit short-lived. A term coined for the South's foreign policy towards the North, it was kick-started by South Korean President Kim Dae Jung and based on the traditional Korean custom of dealing with perceived enemies by engaging them with gifts.

In 1998, with both countries celebrating their golden anniversaries, the North and South respectively looked to each other for some interchange, seeking an improvement on half a century of stalemate. The DPRK of the late 1990s was in a dire financial situation, coming to the end of a decade that saw the collapse of most of the communist bloc and the death of Kim Il Sung, plus drought, flood and famine. So when the South's Hyundai Asan, an arm of the Hyundai Group, approached the North with a proposed investment of hundreds of millions of dollars, they couldn't refuse.

The proposal was for the development of the Mount Kumgang Tourist Region, a special tourist zone that would, crucially, be accessible exclusively to visitors from the South, with Hyundai having the sole rights to developing the infrastructure and selling tours in the area. With the deal signed off, the 530km^2 area underwent massive development, with Hyundai bankrolling the construction of everything associated with a sprawling tourist resort: an entire town was built, with hotels, restaurants, roads, a golf course, resort buses and mountain walkways constructed from scratch. As development was implemented by the South, everything was much more lavish and luxurious than one would have found almost anywhere else in the DPRK.

With the massive investment from Hyundai, the seemingly insurmountable bureaucratic hurdles were overcome and the first South Koreans, who until that time could only dream of visiting the North, arrived in November 1998. The tours, considered quite costly, initially allowed visitors to arrive by ship from the South, with further developments opening a road link between the two countries in 2003. From 2000 restrictions were eased, and other nationalities could join these tours, and so at the start of the 21st century Mount Kumgang enjoyed a renaissance, bringing in hundreds of thousands of visitors a year.

A variety of tours for a range of budgets was available, and the surge in visitors was a welcome boost for the North's economy: while the infrastructure was all

a Buddhist site that is normally not included in tours of the area, but possible to visit if requested in advance. After a journey of 10–15 minutes you'll arrive at a car park just a couple of hundred metres' walk from the Mokran Restaurant, the base for this rewarding hike, which is a round trip of approximately 7km. It would be difficult to get lost on this route, but a slowly fading map in the car park (in Korean and English) will help explain the way, just in case.

paid for by the South, it was the North that sold them the bulk of the construction materials and supplied workers to build the infrastructure, staff the hotels, supply the restaurants and, ultimately, count the profits. Besides the obvious employment benefits, visitors spent a small fortune on all manner of things, from tickets to see acrobatic performances in the custom-built circus to paying top dollar for mineral water hand-winched from the rockpools of Sangpaldam. Business boomed.

However, once Mount Kumgang opened to visitors coming from the South, the possibility of visiting from the North ceased. Mixing 'normal' foreign tourists (who had come via Pyongyang) in this luxurious tourist enclave with 'special' foreign visitors (who had come by way of the South) was one step too far for the authorities in Pyongyang.

Tours in Mount Kumgang at this time were very different from the rest of the DPRK; politics, history, war – all was toned down or indeed ignored totally. Visitors at that time would have found their experiences totally alien compared with anywhere else in the country.

In February 2008, after nearly a decade of comparatively good inter-Korean relations, things began to fall apart when Lee Myung Bak became president of the South, ushering in a new and far more hostile approach to the North. For Mount Kumgang, though, the shooting of South Korean holidaymaker Park Wang Ja in July 2008 was the straw that broke the camel's back. Over a decade since her death, the story remains murky as to what exactly happened, and precisely where the incident took place. Pyongyang maintains Park had ignored a warning and entered a military area, but a whole host of questions remain unanswered, with the South unable to investigate the killing to their satisfaction. The shooting resulted in a major fall out between the two Koreas and the suspension of tours. Suddenly Mount Kumgang was essentially deserted, as tourism ground to a complete halt. The few South Koreans employed in Mount Kumgang had to leave, and for almost two years essentially nobody could visit from either side.

In summer 2010 the North seemed to give up on the hope of the resumption of tours from the South and opened access to Mount Kumgang from their side. At first visitors could come only for day trips, but by the end of the year the North permitted tourists to stay in the area, much to the chagrin of the South. Although inheriting a world-class tourist resort, Pyongyang does not have the ability to draw in the vast numbers of visitors that Hyundai did, and much of the area has become mothballed. The once-bustling resort centre at times feels like a ghost town, and the hotels and infrastructure, although among the very best in the country, are in a slow decline due to lack of maintenance and investment. Mount Kumgang could be an ideal hub for the North to promote hiking and more conventional leisure tourism, but, for now, they seem reluctant to foot the bill. If and when Hyundai ever get back into Mount Kumgang, their investments could well be near worthless.

Departing Mokran the well-maintained path heads roughly west, initially away from the river through dense forest. On passing the Kumgang Gate you'll leave the Singye Valley behind and enter the Okryu Valley, with the path now leading you southwest. From here onwards the path mostly hugs the course of the Samnok Stream, as you crisscross from one bank to the next over a series of footbridges. Ascending the valley, the views seems to get more impressive the further you go as the crystal-clear pools get deeper and steeper and the valley slowly closes, becoming more of a gorge as you pass the Ryonju Pool, Pibong Falls and Unsa Falls. If travelling with a local guide, he or she will likely strive to impart dozens of stories and legends as you ascend towards the Kuryong Falls; interesting enough as they are, if you stopped to listen to all of them the hike would take all day, as opposed to the leisurely 75–90 minutes each way that is normal.

Just before the Kuryong Pavilion you'll come to a fork in the route. The main path continues up along the south bank of the stream while a right turn over the Ryondam Bridge leads towards Sangpaldam. Ignoring this fork, head straight on and after a couple of hundred metres' more walking you'll see the **Kuryong Pavilion**, from where you will be afforded a spectacular view of the 74m **Kuryong Falls**. From the pavilion it *may* be possible to approach the base of the falls and the 13m-deep Kuryong Pool, but it is not advised – not only is the rock extremely slippery, but legend has it that nine dragons have been known to defend the falls from this very spot. As you ascend along the route there are a couple of spots from where you can drink spring water, but at the pavilion itself you can often find a waitress or two from the Mokran Restaurant selling drinks that they carry up the mountain day in, day out, to sell at slightly inflated, but all things considered, reasonable prices. After time to soak in the spectacular scenery of Kuryong it's the case of returning back on the same route you came, unless you feel inclined to take the detour to view Sangpaldam or, by prior arrangement, attempt the taxing full-day hike to Sejon Peak (see below).

From the aforementioned fork in the path at the Ryondam Bridge it is possible to ascend **Kuryong Rock** for views of the pools of Sangpaldam. It's a short, steep path, including 14 safety ladders and sections of manmade steps – allow a good hour for the 1.4km round trip. Keen walkers will be absolutely fine, but this route is not suitable for the faint hearted or for those that suffer vertigo. On reaching Kuryong Rock the panoramas over the spectacular Kuryong area are arguably better than those of the Kuryong Falls, looking down on the eight rock pools that feed the waterfall. Legend has it that many years ago fairies would descend from heaven to bathe in these very pools. One was so enchanted by the beauty of the area and its men that she got married and settled down in a nearby village, becoming 'a resourceful woman of this land and a hard-working and dutiful wife'.

Sejon Peak This circular route is one of the finest permitted full-day hikes in the country, including Kuryong Falls, views of both Piro Peak and the sea from the craggy summit of Sejon, together with a foray into the rarely visited Tongsok Valley. Seldom undertaken, a local guide is a must, as is prior investigation as to the current conditions of the paths.

As with the trek to Kuryong Falls and Sangpaldam, the hike starts from the Mokran Restaurant. From the Kuryong Pavilion a steep and overgrown 'path' leads east for 2.6km to the summit of Sejon. The path here can be so vertiginous that occasional safety ladders are installed along the ascent, all in varying states of decay. Accordingly, the 2.6km from the pavilion to the summit could well take a couple of hours or more. When not ascending rickety ladders, the path can be so overgrown that you may not know if you are on it or not, hence the necessity for a local guide. Part way along this ascent a very rough 10km spur would potentially lead you all the way to Piro Peak, the highest point in Kumgang, but this route is off-limits and appears in terrible condition. Still, this could potentially be an adventurous multi-day hike, and it cannot hurt to ask – should enough people show an interest the government may relent.

The climb gets steeper the closer you get to Sejon Peak. Once on the peak, Piro can be seen in the distance, as can the East Sea of Korea. From this remote spot a long ladder affixed to the rockface will help ferry you down into the Tongsok Valley. From here on the hike eases off, but a good couple of hours or more will still be needed to get you back to the road in the Singye Valley. Although swimming is technically not permitted in any rivers in Kumgang, a refreshing mid-afternoon dip is most refreshing after 6 or so sweaty hours on the go. On arrival at the road you are more or less equidistant between the car park near the Mokran Restaurant and Kuryong Village, so make sure that your guide liaises with your driver as to the precise spot where you should be picked up. Allow 8–10 hours for the entire hike, and another hour should you wish to visit Sangpaldam – start early!

Manmulsang While Kuryong is the most popular excursion in all of Kumgang, a half-day jaunt in Manmulsang is a must for keen walkers. However, like Sangpaldam, it's only recommended for those with a head for heights. The trailhead for the hike lies 12km west of Kuryong Village at the Mansang Pavilion. As you draw nearer to Mansang the road narrows, so those travelling in larger buses should ensure that their guide has sourced suitable transport in Kuryong village before setting off.

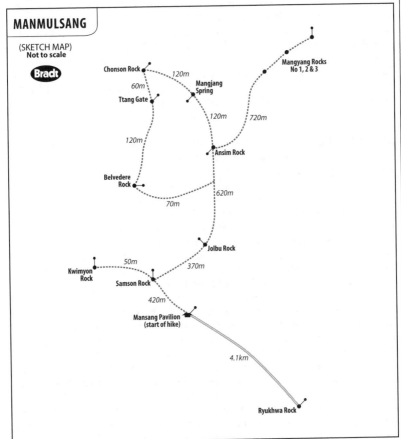

While hiking in Kuryong affords river views as you ascend a valley, Manmulsang takes the scenery to a whole other level, with dramatic vistas of the spectacular peaks and rocks of the Kumgang Mountains. Departing from Mansang Pavilion the path is initially quite easy going as you come to Samson Rock. A steep 50m spur to **Kwimyon Rock**, from where you will have the first breathtaking views of the craggy rocks and peaks of the area, will give you a hint of the fine views and daunting gradients to come. From here, the path slowly steepens as you approach **Jolbu Rock**. The worst of the hike lies in the next stretch, as the short gruelling ascent between Jolbu and Ansim Rock offers little aesthetic respite to make you feel like it is all worthwhile. But please – do push on, as the best is to come. On coming to a fork in the path as you ascend, this spot is as good a place as any for a quick breather before your guide escorts you up and along the left fork. Presently you'll encounter the first fixed ladders of the hike at **Belvedere Rock**. These dramatic exposed ladders and walkways, affixed to the rockface, will ferry you onwards and upwards, passing Ttang Gate and bringing you to the uppermost point of the trek, **Chonson Rock**. The views from here are truly something to behold, with seemingly countless jagged peaks around you and a dense carpet of forest below.

After taking the obligatory photographs, the alternative descent route from Chonson Rock leads to the **Mangjang Spring**, where the water is so clear that legend has it 'an elderly couple once drank it and recovered their looks from when they first married'. Assuming your mountain guide still recognises you after imbibing these waters, you may with your renewed vigour wish to make the 1.5km detour to the Mangyang Rocks, which starts near here. Assuming you just don't have the energy and continue downhill on the main path, you will eventually arrive back at Ansim Rock, from here returning on the same path travelled earlier. The entire hike is a round trip of around 3.5km (excluding Mangyang Rocks), but given the breathtaking scenery and steepness of the paths allow a good 3 hours.

Sea Kumgang

With weary legs from hiking in Outer Kumgang, a visit to Sea Kumgang, a picturesque coastal area comprising fertile farmland intertwined with rocky outcrops and bays, provides gentle respite for a few leisurely hours. Heading east from Kuryong Village, the road heads towards the DMZ for approximately 10km, before making a left turn, crossing the Puk River and the disused section of railway that also leads south. From here, the road continues for another 1.5km to the alluring **Samil ('Three Day') Lagoon**. From the car park just before the lagoon a short walk will bring you to the Chungsong Pavilion, from where you will have good views of the lake and Wau Islet. The legend here is that a king who once visited the lagoon was so enthralled by its scenery that he stayed for three days – hence the name. Should you choose to descend from the pavilion and cross the suspension bridge, a handful of paths will branch out, leading you towards the shoreline and Tanphung Restaurant via Bongnae Rock and Ryonhwa Rock, or on an alternative route that will spit you out back near the car park. Those who have prearranged the requisite permission can head east for a further 6.5km to visit Sea Kumgang. Approximately 5km from Samil Lagoon, you'll arrive at the impressive entry checkpoint for Sea Kumgang, replete with raked sand, barbed wire, goose-stepping guards and electric fences – you are, after all, very close to the border. Once permits have been checked, the last stretch of the journey brings you close to a lovely patch of coastline – a nice spot to scramble around on the rocks, take a dip (if nobody is looking), barter with fishermen or, if you are really sure nobody is looking, use the weak South Korean mobile telephone signal to make a quick call home.

Inner Kumgang Sadly, at the time of writing, Inner Kumgang seems completely off-limits to visitors, despite offering a wealth of cultural treasures and spectacular potential for hiking. The route from Kuryong to Piro Peak could be a fantastic and challenging multi-day trek, but sadly it was closed at the time of writing and poorly maintained. Should restrictions be lifted, or you are lucky enough to be granted access to this remote pocket of the DPRK, you will be rewarded with pristine mountain scenery and some of the best Buddhist sights in the country.

Heading west out of Kuryong Village along the same road to Manmulsang (remember, this road is not suitable for larger vehicles – your guide may need to source suitable transport locally), after 15km you'll come to the Onjong Pass, where you'll head through a tunnel that marks the boundary of Outer and Inner Kumgang. On exiting the tunnel, you will come to the first military checkpoint, for which you will require a permit to pass through. On this author's last visit to Inner Kumgang, this was the first of six checkpoints encountered, each way. A contrast to the more visitor-friendly Outer and Sea Kumgang, this entire area has a heavy military presence. Descending into a picturesque valley, the road continues in a southwesterly direction for 5km, before you arrive at the road junction for Piro Peak. If you have friends in very high places you may be permitted to drive the 15km jeep track that leads to the 1,639m summit, where a pavilion *should* afford commanding views of the entire area – if you do manage to visit please get in touch to tell us of your experience! From the summit an alternative 21km track can be taken down the mountain back into the valley, bringing you out approximately 4km southwest of the aforementioned road. Even during the days of Hyundai's tours in Inner Kumgang, visits to Piro Peak were very much off-limits, so most information on this area is over 20 years old. At one time, a whole network of trekking paths to the peak were open, but for now they all remain closed to 'normal' visitors.

Assuming you aren't allowed to drive to Piro Peak, you'll continue on the main road for 24km along the floodplain of the Kumgang Stream through timeless rural scenery, stopping for the occasional salute at a military checkpoint. The road leads south through Kumgang town, before heading east, bringing visitors to the foot of a gentle 7km hiking path through the Manpok Valley – likely to be the only place you'll be allowed to visit in Inner Kumgang, should you be granted a permit to visit at all. The trail begins at the 7th-century Pyohunsa Temple, which retains a certain charm having survived numerous wars, including the Korean War, unscathed. Heading northeast the path often hugs the river as it leads up past a series of rock pools and patches of forest. A short steep detour leads to the small picture-postcard **Podok Hermitage**, which dates to the Koguryo era. The single-roomed hermitage is perched precipitously on a 20m-high cliff, supported by a large pole.

If you are fortunate to visit this pocket of Korea the likely terminus of your hike will bring you to what is arguably the cultural jewel of the Kumgang region: the 15m-high, 9.4m-wide **Myogilsang Buddhist Statue**, which dates back to the Koryo Dynasty. Carved into the rock, Myogilsang is allegedly the largest stone Buddha in the country, but in a predominantly atheist country it is somewhat disregarded. A viable footpath allegedly leads from here all the way to the summit of Piro Peak, but trekking this route remains a pipe dream.

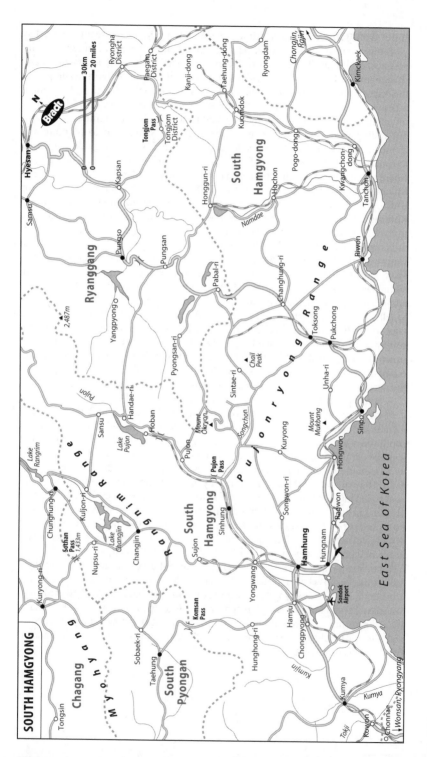

SOUTH HAMGYONG

10

South Hamgyong (함경남도)

At 18,970km², South Hamgyong is North Korea's largest province. Its name is a combination of the 'Ham' of Hamhung, present-day capital of the province, with the 'gyong' of Gyongsong (now Kyongsong), a small town in North Hamgyong, near Chongjin. Despite being home to just over three million people, South Hamgyong only truly started to open to foreign visitors in 2010, and although the majority of the province remains closed, those planning on visiting Kangwon should well consider spending at least one night here, to take in the city of Hamhung, enjoy a spot of downtime on the beach in Majon or to head to remote and rarely visited Pujon.

With forests covering more than 80% of the province, the majority of the residents live in the southeastern lowlands and along the coastal plains. While farming is, as ever in Korea, important, the bulk of the economy here is tied with heavy industry and the exploitation of mineral resources that include rich deposits of magnesite, lead and zinc. Hamhung, the second-largest city in the DPRK, is quite a contrast to comparatively utopian Pyongyang and, despite not offering a great deal to see, is currently the sole base for exploring the province.

HAMHUNG (함흥시)

Hamhung is North Korea's second city, but is very different from impressive Pyongyang. With a population of approximately 769,000 people, this industrial city seems to be somewhat ignored by the capital, with its infrastructure and large factories seemingly struggling to operate. While Pyongyang has seen a wide array of showcase developments in recent years, Hamhung seems little changed since the 1980s. Heavily damaged during the Korean War, assistance from East Germany from 1955–62 helped to rebuild the city, which does have a few interesting sites that alone can occupy half a day. Those visiting in warmer months may wish to factor in some downtime and enjoy a few hours relaxing on the beach or paddling in the sea at Majon, home to two of the city's three hotel options.

GETTING THERE AND AWAY

By road The most common means of arriving in South Hamgyong is by road from Kangwon Province. Hamhung can be reached in one *long* 6–8- (or more) hour drive from Pyongyang, Nampo or Sariwon. With the drive from Pyongyang alone being 300km via the Ullim Waterfall or 330km if travelling via Wonsan, it is often better to break the journey with an overnight stay en route, at least in one direction, with the logical place being Masikryong or Wonsan. From Masikryong it is 135km (3 hours) to Hamhung, whereas from Wonsan it is 115km (2½ hours).

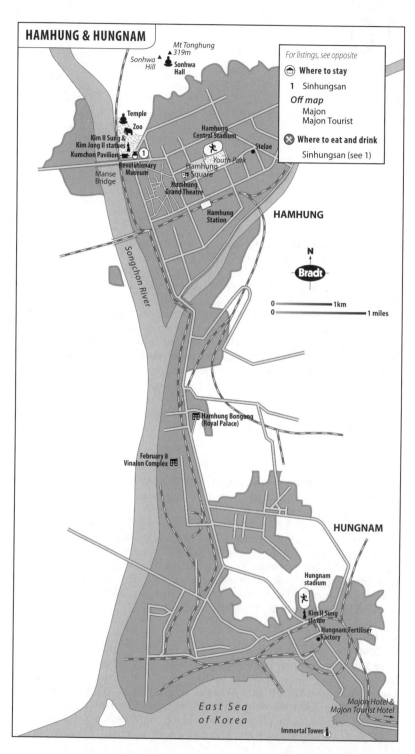

HAMHUNG & HUNGNAM

Mt Tonghung
319m

Sonhwa
Hill

Sonhwa
Hall

For listings, see opposite

Where to stay

1 Sinhungsan

Off map
Majon
Majon Tourist

Where to eat and drink

Sinhungsan (see 1)

Temple
Zoo

Kim Il Sung &
Kim Jong Il statues
Kumchon Pavilion

Hamhung
Central Stadium

Stelae

Manse
Bridge

Revolutionary
Museum

Youth Park

Hamhung
Square

Hamhung
Grand Theatre

Hamhung
Station

HAMHUNG

Songchon River

N

Bradt

0 ———— 1km
0 ———— 1 miles

Hamhung Bongung
(Royal Palace)

February 8
Vinalon Complex

HUNGNAM

Hungnam
stadium

Kim Il Sung
Statue

Hungnam Fertiliser
Factory

East Sea
of Korea

Majon Hotel &
Majon Tourist Hotel

Immortal Tower

The road leading north from Wonsan to Hamhung was partially renovated in 2011 and is acceptable enough as local roads go, but is single lane all the way. Arriving in South Hamgyong, you will pass through the small towns of Kowon and Kumya before arriving at the **Ko Song Ryong Tea House**, 102km from Masikryong and 80km from Wonsan. The tea house has a basic shop and smoky café on the ground floor, with some additional seating upstairs. In warmer months, a couple of outdoor stalls may well sell cold drinks, including refreshing homemade *makgeolli*, a mildly alcoholic drink made from rice or wheat. Back on the road, you'll continue north-northeast for 35km, passing through Hamju before crossing the Songchon River and arriving in Hamhung.

For now, travelling to South Hamgyong by road is only possible if coming from Kangwon Province; travelling on to other provinces is not yet permitted.

By rail While domestic trains regularly serve Hamhung, tourists are generally only permitted to come by train to/from Hamhung if travelling on either an *extremely* costly privately chartered train, or on a scheduled international train (ie: one ultimately heading to or coming from Russia). Both options are somewhat complicated to arrange, but with proper planning the 314km Pyongyang–Hamhung rail journey is something of an adventure, travelling for approximately 9 hours (assuming all is on schedule) through sleepy rural countryside on a rickety train that for the most part travels a different route from the road.

By air Sondok Airport, a 30km drive to the southwest of Hamhung, is generally only served by chartered aircraft, but groups could well opt to arrive or depart Hamhung by air, possibly as part of an aircraft charter tour that includes the more far-flung parts of the country further north.

🏠 WHERE TO STAY *Map, opposite*

Hamhung has three viable accommodation options, conveniently falling into the budget, mid-range and superior categories. City lovers should note that only the Sinhungsan Hotel is in central Hamhung; the other two options are both beside the beach in the city's Majon suburb, approximately 20km away.

🏠 **Majon Hotel** (108 rooms) The Majon Hotel (not to be confused with the Majon Tourist Hotel, a few hundred metres north) was built in 2009 & originally intended for domestic VIPs only, which explains the armed guard at the entry gate & walls surrounding the grounds. This hotel, located on a private beach, is one of the best options in the entire country, offering all sorts of facilities, such as a swimming pool, sauna, massage, games room & bowling alley. Spending a few hours relaxing here part way through a tour of the country is highly recommended. Keen swimmers should be careful not to swim out of sight – beyond the rocky outcrop at the south of the hotel's beach lies a secluded cove & VIP mansion, where your arrival would, to put it mildly, be most unwelcome. **$$$$**

🏠 **Majon Tourist Hotel** (77 rooms) Located on a private beach in the Majon suburb of the city, the rooms here, split up into a number of villas, have seen better days. The main building has perfectly acceptable facilities including billiards, karaoke & restaurants, but this option is only worth considering if on a very tight budget. From time to time the hotel confusingly seems to go by the name of Majon Bathing Resort. **$–$$**

🏠 **Sinhungsan Hotel** (77 rooms) Located in central Hamhung, this hotel was built in 1986, yet feels much older. Hot water may be provided here & rooms are rather basic, but a good bookshop, hotel bar & table-tennis room will hopefully keep you occupied. For those with limited time in Hamhung, or visiting in winter when swimming will definitely be off the cards, this is a logical choice. **$$**

✕ WHERE TO EAT AND DRINK *Map, page 214*

For now, besides eating in your hotel, the only option in Hamhung is the **Sinhunsang Restaurant ($$$$)**, a large traditional noodle-house a short walk from the Sinhunsang Hotel. While the hotels offer typical Korean dishes, both accommodation options in Majon should, with enough notice, also be able to arrange a lamb or seafood barbecue on the beach.

WHAT TO SEE AND DO

The road to Hamhung Approaching Hamhung from the south, a 2km detour from the small town of Hamju will lead to the **Tongbong Cooperative Farm**. As mentioned elsewhere in this book, a visit to at least one farm is recommend on any tour to North Korea, and Tongbong is this author's favourite. Tongbong is home to around 1,000 farmers and their families, and you will likely be obliged to visit the tiny farm museum before having the opportunity to visit the kindergarten, tractor yard and local shop. The shop has a limited yet rather eclectic mix of goods available, from inflatable toy animals to notepads and matches – it is interesting to see just what is available to the locals with their small disposable income. If you are polite and respectful your local guide may suggest popping into a family home for a few minutes – you should jump at the chance as it will give an insight into how people really live in the provinces.

Hamhung City Returning to Hamju, a drive of 8km will bring you into the suburban fringes of Hamhung on the west bank of the Songchon River, but the city starts in earnest on the east bank, the moment you cross the conspicuous concrete **Manse Bridge**. Immediately on spanning the bridge, the statues of Kim Il Sung and Kim Jong Il will loom above you from a nearby hill. While a visit here is not obligatory, the nearby pavilion affords a commanding view over central Hamhung. These statues and gardens are part of the 319m **Mount Tonghung**, and although not the most interesting sites, those with the time and inclination may here wish to visit the well-preserved **Kumchon Pavilion** and associated old city **walls**, which date back to 1108. Finally, a typical example of Ri-Dynasty architecture exists with nearby Sonhwa Hall, a 15th-century government office which was rebuilt in the 18th century.

On the main road you will also find the Revolutionary Museum – but this is best avoided unless you are a real glutton for punishment. Arguably the most impressive spectacle in central Hamhung is the **Hamhung Grand Theatre**, the largest in the country and built in 1984. The building is sadly not open to visitors unless you are fortunate to arrive when a rare performance (typically a Revolutionary Opera) is taking place. The truly spectacular interiors (you will have to take our word for it) are archetypical North Korean grandiose architecture and really should be preserved as a listed building. Sadly, it seems plans are afoot for a comprehensive refurbishment of the entire theatre. The theatre is located on **Hamhung Square**, and this is normally a good spot for people-watching and mingling with the bemused locals who congregate here. Directly behind the square lies Hamhung Youth Park and Hamhung City Stadium, both of which are generally off-limits. The main railway station lies a few hundred metres southwest of the main square, but you cannot normally visit unless you are arriving or departing by train.

Hungnam Most of the high-rise buildings in Hamhung are along the tree-lined stretch of road that leads south towards Hungnam District, where you will likely see the **narrow-gauge railway** that transports passengers between Hamhung and

Vinalon, known as Vinylon in the West, is a synthetic fibre made from polyvinyl alcohol produced with anthracite and limestone (both of which are abundant in North Korea). Invented in 1939, it is said to be the world's second artificial textile, arriving two years after nylon. This durable material has good resistance to heat and chemicals but is let down by being hard to dye, stiff and expensive to manufacture. Notwithstanding all of this, Vinalon is much lauded in the DPRK as a *juche fiber*, and is an important textile in the country, being used in clothing, shoes and rope, for example.

Despite being considered a near miracle fabric, the February 8 Vinalon Complex closed its doors during the difficult period of the 1990s, only reopening in 2010. Passing the steam, smoke and fire belching factory today, it is amazing to think that so much effort goes into the manufacture of this synthetic fibre – can this be remotely economically viable? Probably not.

Hungnam. The authorities have talked for some years of offering tours of Hamhung that incorporate this commuter railway, which would be a fun way of exploring the city – while still not possible it can't hurt to ask, as whoever decides on such matters may eventually bow to pressure. As the apartment blocks start to thin out, a short detour will bring you to the historical sites of **Hamhung Bongung**. Once the royal palace of Ri Song Gye, founder of the Choson (Yi) Dynasty, it was settled by Song Gye in 1400 after he abdicated the throne to his son. The buildings, despite being restored and rebuilt over the years, retain an air of authenticity and this little island of tranquillity in a sea of urbanity is a relaxing diversion well worth 30 minutes or so of your time. Included in the small grounds are a few museum pieces in the poorly lit main building (take a torch), and a centuries-old tree that seems to terribly excite domestic visitors. The amicable local guides have a lot of time on their hands and have used this to perfect some rather amusing and fruity historical anecdotes.

As you are driven onwards, with Hamhung now behind you, enter Hungnam. Industrial Hungnam was a city in its own right until being incorporated into Hamhung in 2005 and is home to the sprawling satanic mills that make up, among others, the February 8 Vinalon Complex and the Hungnam Fertiliser Complex. Despite the Vinalon Complex being closed to visitors, the Hungnam Fertiliser Complex is bizarrely promoted on tours of the area, and while most would not consider visiting a fertiliser plant when touring a city, it is, for some, rather interesting!

With its colonial Japanese-era history slightly brushed over, the **Hungnam Fertiliser Complex** is famous throughout the DPRK as a major industrial powerhouse and produces, they say, over 40% of the fertiliser in the country. Your factory escort will explain in acute detail that before 1945 the factory produced only ammonium sulphate, but they now proudly manufacture a panoply of chemicals such as urea fertiliser, superphosphate of lime and microelement fertiliser. The subject of chemical weapons, which has been alleged are also made here, will, quite understandably, not be touched upon. A tour of the sprawling fertiliser complex normally focuses on a visit to the generator hall (where you could well get a little teary eyed thanks not to the impassioned speech from the local guide, but due to the occasional strong whiff of ammonia), before moving on to the control room and distribution/packing hall. Tours can also include a visit to the museum, although this is only likely to be arranged for those with a deep-seated interest in fertiliser production or the famous 'Rice is Socialism!' speech that Kim Il Sung gave in 1956. Unlikely. Much of the plant appears dilapidated and it seems, to the untrained eye at least, that keeping everything up and running is a daily struggle for the thousands who work here; it is somewhat incongruous to see cabbage and other vegetable allotments growing beside a rundown building that *could* be manufacturing lithium-6, a material used in the production of hydrogen bombs.

The heavy industry thins out as you head southeast from the Hungnam Fertiliser Complex, and after around 5km the coast comes into view. Here lies the Majon Tourist Hotel and Majon Hotel (page 215), and if visiting in warmer months, a few hours to relax on the beach here, doing very little, can be most appealing. Dozing on this beach as the waves gently lap against the shore you can quite easily forget where you are; literally sandwiched between a major chemical plant and the headquarters of the East Sea Fleet, which is just 12km further up the road.

PUJON AND MOUNT OKRYON

A tiring yet rewarding full-day trip from Hamhung, a visit to Pujon and Mount Okryon is worth considering for those who really want to get off the beaten track to see a rarely visited part of the county and country. The road to Pujon is unpaved and mountainous; while technically open year-round, tourists are normally only permitted to visit from mid-May through to late September due to poor conditions. Despite this, visits can still be cancelled at any time of year due to heavy rains, which can turn the road into something of a quagmire. The round-trip journey today is approximately 210km of driving – expect the journey to be 3½ hours of driving each way so set off early. The local guides at Mount Okryon may be able to rustle up a basic potato barbecue if you are expected, but with poor communications in the area it is wise to take a packed lunch and all supplies with you, as there is nowhere else to eat in the area and any options in Pujon town are not available to foreigners.

PUJON PLATEAU From central Hamhung, the road heads north along the eastern bank of the Songchon River, passing a relatively new yet rarely functioning waterpark. For the next 40km or so the road continues as you slowly ascend on the river floodplain, passing through small settlements and towns such as Yonggwang. The floodplain narrows and the soil becomes evidently rockier as the mountain pass looms ahead to the north. Approximately 10km beyond the town of Sinhung, a left turn at a fork in the road takes you across the Songchon River. Here your ascent starts in earnest, as the next 25km leads to the top of the Pujon Pass and the entrance to the Pujon Plateau. The last 13km leading to the pass becomes an increasingly steep series of mountain switchbacks with some rather precipitous drops – very slow going in any vehicle. A viewing pavilion at the top of the pass is a logical place for a quick break and photo stop – you will have been on the road for at least 2 hours, but will only be 70km from Hamhung. Pressing on, a short gradual descent brings you into the Pujon Plateau and the small town of Pujon, 15km beyond the pavilion.

The Pujon Plateau is an oddity in North Korea; one of the few plateau areas in the country, the landscape here is more akin to Siberia or Mongolia than it is Korea. Housing is mostly log cabins and visitors will likely see horses, pigs and sheep – almost impossible to spot elsewhere in the country. While you will not be able to stop in Pujon itself the town looks interesting enough, with something of an outpost feel to it. In the future, it may be possible to stay here in basic lodgings –

Pujon would be a sensible overnight spot for those travelling overland to Ryanggang Province, if this is ever permitted. From Pujon town, a drive of 15km leads to the two main attractions in the area, the Stone River and Mount Okryon.

THE STONE RIVER From the T-junction at the entrance to Mount Okryon, a short 5-minute walk north leads to the Stone River or 'River of Rocks' as it is sometimes called. The Stone River is an 800m-long, 60m-wide boulder field, similar to the more famous example found at Hawk Mountain in the Appalachian Mountains. This boulder field, formed by periglacial processes in the ice age, is a site of scientific interest and has attracted a handful of domestic and foreign geological expeditions over the years. For those without an understanding or interest in the geological processes that created this natural wonder, it still remains an attractive site, set in these densely forested mountains. Should you happen to venture 100m or so up the footpath beyond the stone river, what you discover is not a secret revolutionary site that nobody has discovered; the dilapidated log cabins here were built as a part of a set for a long-forgotten movie.

MOUNT OKRYON Back at the T-junction, the other fork is a 5km-long dirt track that leads to the top of Mount Okryon. While not particularly steep, vehicles may struggle in muddy conditions along this dirt road, and your local guide may suggest walking to the peak. From the viewing pavilion near the top of Mount Okryon a sea of dense forest stretches as far as the eye can see. A 5-minute walk from the pavilion leads to the rocky peak of Mount Okryon; on the path two revolutionary sites relating to Kim Jong Suk can be seen, but most will be more impressed with the view of seemingly endless forest.

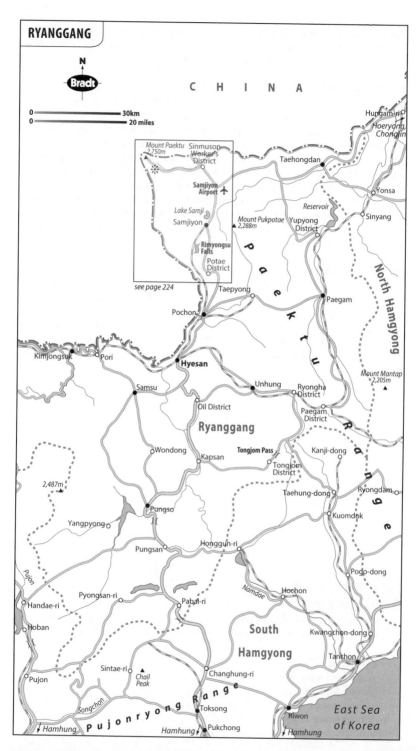

RYANGGANG

N

Bradt

0 ———————— 30km
0 ———————— 20 miles

C H I N A

Hungam-ri
Hoeryong,
Chongjin

Mount Paektu
2,750m

Sinmuson
Worker's
District

Taehongdan

Yonsa

**Samjiyon
Airport** ✈

Sinyang

Reservoir

Lake Samji
Samjiyon

▲ *Mount Pukpotae*
2,288m

Yupyong
District

**Rimyongsu
Falls**
Potae
District

see page 224

Taepyong

Paegam

P
a
e
k
t
u

Pochon

Mount Mantap
▲ 2,205m

Kimjongsuk

Pori

Hyesan

Samsu

Unhung

Ryongha
District

Oil District

Paegam
District

Ryanggang

R
a
n
g
e

Wondong

Kapsan

Tongjom Pass

Kanji-dong

Tongjom
District

▲ 2,487m

Taehung-dong

Ryongdam

Yangpyong

Pungso

Kuomdok

Pungsan

Honggun-ri

Podo-dong

Pyongsan-ri

Pabal-ri

Namdae

Hochon

Kwangchon-dong

Handae-ri

Hoban

Tanchon

Pujon

Sintae-ri

▲ *Chail
Peak*

Changhung-ri

South

Hamgyong

Songchon

Toksong

Riwon

*East Sea
of Korea*

↗ *Hamhung*

P u j o n r y o n g   R a n g e

Hamhung ↗

Pukchong

Hamhung ↗

North Hamgyong

11

Ryanggang
(량강도)

The remote and landlocked border region of Ryanggang Province sits at an average altitude of 1,300m above sea level and consists mainly of highland plains and plateaus. Ryanggang, meaning 'province of two rivers', is so named for being the source of both the Amnok and Tuman rivers, with the Amnok (Yalu in China) heading to the West Sea and marking the Chinese border, while the Tuman courses to the East Sea, delineating the border with China and then Russia. The source of both these rivers is the semi-mythical Mount Paektu, a 2,750m-high active volcano that straddles the border with China.

With a harsh Siberian-esque climate, Ryanggang has the lowest population density of all the nation's provinces, hovering at around 50 people per km², and is home to just one city, Hyesan, which for now remains closed. The economically depressed province is only normally visited by foreign tourists for Mount Paektu, but a staggering number of pseudo-historical revolutionary sights drag domestic travellers here, quite literally, by the truckload. With a climate unsuitable for intensive agriculture, bleak winters and no coastline, life here is admittedly tough.

While this may sound a little bleak, visiting jaw-droppingly spectacular Mount Paektu is a highlight for many visitors to the country, with the journey being an adventure in itself as you fly into Samjiyon Airport in an ageing Soviet-era aircraft. For those visiting at the right time of year, typically mid-June to mid-September, and with the time to spare, one or two nights in Ryanggang will be an experience to remember. The itinerary of any trip to the region will vary significantly according to the weather and time available. At 2,750m, Mount Paektu is a considerable peak with very changeable weather. Your guides will be well aware that a visit to the mountain, ideally in good weather, is the main reason for most visits to Ryanggang, so they will likely alter the order of your itinerary on the spot to maximise your chance of seeing the peak at its best. While it has been known for groups to fly in just for a day trip, this is extremely rushed and would only likely afford a fleeting visit to Mount Paektu, with little time for anything else. Spending one, or even two nights in the area is recommended, allowing to see more of the province.

GETTING THERE AND AWAY

The sole means of getting to Ryanggang is by air, flying into Samjiyon on a chartered Air Koryo flight. Air Koryo have talked for years of starting a scheduled seasonal service of some kind between Pyongyang and Samjiyon, but this remains just talk. So here lies the rub – chartered aircraft don't come cheap, with the smallest aeroplane available being an Antonov An-24 that can accommodate approximately

40 passengers. Unless you are prepared to pay through the nose, the only way to get to this far-flung corner of Korea will be to find a tour operator operating a charter, with the larger operators typically arranging a few flights each year, from mid-June to mid-September. While the majority of people coming to the area will therefore be part of a larger group tour, some tour operators sell on spare seats on their flights to those arranging a tailor-made trip with them.

The flight from Pyongyang into Samjiyon in an An-24 takes approximately 80 minutes, whereas some of the larger aircraft available can cut this time almost in half. The aircraft flown (see box, page 56) will likely depend on the ultimate number of passengers on the flight and economies of scale, although for the right sum aviation enthusiasts can charter essentially whichever craft in the Air Koryo fleet that they wish. After your time in Samjiyon you will need to exit by air, either flying back to Pyongyang, or on to another remote corner of Korea as part of a multi-day aircraft charter.

WHERE TO STAY AND EAT *Map, page 224*

While some information out there alludes to a variety of options, including the Hyesan and Onsupyong hotels, together with the existence of a number of mountain refuges on and around Mount Paektu, the only true option for now is the Pegaebong in Samjiyon. Campers may, with enough planning, be able to convince the authorities to allow them to camp in the mountains.

For now, all breakfasts and dinners are likely to be had in the hotel, which can arrange packed lunches and also offer up a rustic potato barbecue without much notice. If heading out to Mount Paektu, make sure you take all your food and supplies with you for the trip. Those venturing to rarely visited Taheongdan or Pochon counties may have the pleasure of eating in a local restaurant, but always get your guide to check in advance.

Pegaebong Hotel (122 rooms) The only option in all of Ryanggang is the Pegaebong situated a couple of km northwest of Samjiyon town centre. First opened in 1986 but subsequently extended, the staff try their best, but shocking plumbing & electrical problems are to be expected, & the large dining hall & public areas can be chilly, even in the height of summer. A couple of bars, which bizarrely seem to move around the hotel from one year to the next, help keep guests entertained on the cold nights. **$$**

SAMJIYON (삼지연군)

The small town of Samjiyon is the gateway to the region as its airport remains, for now, the only permitted entry and exit point for us foreign devils. As the home of the main airfield in the region, and thanks to its proximity to sacred Mount Paektu, it would not be proper for the area to appear too shabby and the town is attractive enough in its own way. While there is nothing of great interest in Samjiyon itself, spending an hour or so pootling around the place is a pleasant diversion after what will inevitably have been a busy day or two.

Arriving into the perpetually deserted Samjiyon Airport, an 11km drive southwest will bring you to the **Samjiyon Grand Monument**. Built in May 1979 to commemorate the 40th anniversary of a nearby battle with Japanese forces, this monument, even for those who don't go in for the socialist-realist style, is nothing but impressive. With Lake Samji and Mount Paektu providing a natural backdrop, the centrepiece is a 15m-tall bronze statue of a 20-something Kim Il Sung. To Kim's right stands a 50m-tall 'torch tower', and he is flanked on both sides with bronze and stone statues, primarily depicting the war. After the obligatory bow at the foot of the statue and a chance for photographs, it is worth visiting the lakeshore, where a few smaller statues of guerrillas can be spotted, tastefully positioned atop rocky outcrops in the shallows of the lake.

Another 3km of driving on the same road southwest brings you into Samjiyon itself. Those on longer tours may have the opportunity to stroll, with your guide, around this sleepy town, but conventional sights are thin on the ground. It is possible, by prior arrangement, to visit buildings such as the Samjiyon Military Palace of Culture and the Samjiyon Schoolchildren's Palace, but unless you have plenty of time on your hands other sights in the area should take precedence.

MOUNT PAEKTU (백두산)

The prime reason for visiting the region is to come to Mount Paektu, or Paektusan as it is known to all Koreans. The importance of Mount Paektu in the DPRK cannot be emphasised enough, and local texts perhaps summarise it best: 'It is said that if one is to know Korea one must see Mount Paektu.'

The mountain, which rises up to 2,750m above sea level, is an active volcano and the highest peak in not just the Korean Peninsula but Manchuria also, as it sits on the border of both, with the summit, Janggun Peak, situated in and accessible only from the Korean side. The crater lake of Lake Chon, formed in AD946, lies in the caldera atop the mountain at an altitude of 2,190m. Further eruptions, the last in 1903, have occurred over the centuries and the mountain is studied by both domestic and foreign volcanologists, all trying to predict when the mountain may next blow its top. Alleged to hide in the depths of the lake, the Nessie-esque 'Lake Tianchi Monster' ('Tianchi' being the Chinese name for the lake) is believed by some to surface from time to time, but the jury is still out on that one. Still, with an area of just over 9km^2 and a maximum depth of 384m, the lake is as good a place as any for a cryptid trying to keep a low profile.

Geography aside, the mountain is considered a place of Korean ancestral origin and the birthplace of the legendary founder of the Ancient Joson Dynasty, Tangun Wanggeom, the grandson of heaven and son of a bear. While proof of his existence is *very* questionable, Tangun's 5,000-year-old bones and relics were *discovered* (yes really!) in 1993, in Pyongyang's Kangdong District (see box, page 130). Fast forward 5,000 years or so, and the mountain has been used as the backdrop for more legends, with Paektu so steeped in revolutionary history that it is quite possible Korean People's Army divers will soon discover an Excalibur weapon of some kind, à la King Arthur, that Kim Il Sung carried in the vanguard of some campaign against the Japanese.

While accurate Soviet records will tell you that Kim Jong Il was born in Vyatskoye, near Khabarovsk in Russia, on 16 February 1941, all North Koreans will tell you otherwise – Kim Jong Il was born one year later on the southern slopes of Mount Paektu, in the Paektu Secret Camp.

For the Korean people his birth was a great occasion and heralded as the happiest and proudest event. His childhood was replete with ordeals. The Secret Camp of the Korean People's Revolutionary Army in the primeval forest was his home, and ammunition belts and magazines were his playthings. The raging blizzards and ceaseless gunshots were the first sounds to which he became accustomed.

Kim Jong Il In His Young Days, Kum Song Youth Publishing House, 1990.
(No author credited to book.)

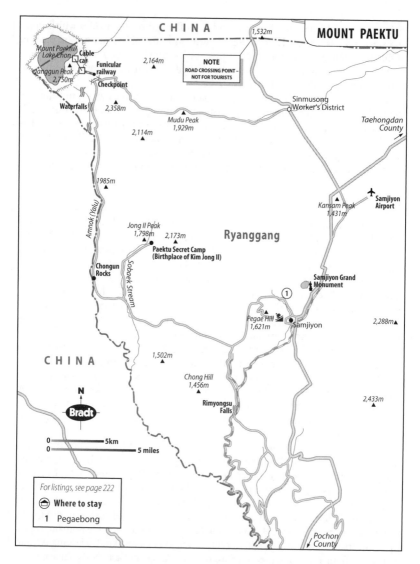

The region is littered with numerous 'secret camps'; formerly hidden military camps deep in the forest and mountains. It was at the camp, you will be told, that Kim Il Sung was headquartered from 1936 through to 1943, and also from where Kim Il Sung and his band of merry men frequently came out of hiding to deal repeated blows in hundreds of 'battles' against the Japanese who, despite their superior strength, lived in great fear of Kim Il Sung. The seeds of independence were literally sown on the legendary Paektu.

Endless tomes have been published in Pyongyang on the 'history' of the revolutionary struggle and anti-Japanese activities during the Japanese colonial war, and while the majority of it seems *totally* fabricated, some is indeed true. The Korean government, with total control over all facets of media in the country, has concocted such a fantastical tale that it has become, locally, undisputable fact. The region is therefore not just an area of outstanding natural beauty; it is the birthplace of the Korean people, of North Korea and of its former Dear Leader, Kim Jong Il. Mount Paektu is renowned locally as the sacred mountain of the Korean Revolution, and as such has become the Mecca of the DPRK.

FLORA AND FAUNA The entire region is heavily wooded to approximately 2,000m, being a mix of typical temperate needleleaf and broadleaf forest; predominantly pine at lower climes with larch and birch, including Erman's birch, nearer the treeline. There are more than 200 species of plants growing around Mount Paektu alone, including mountain cranberry, blueberries, yellow day lilies, bracken, bellflower and thyme. A plethora of tonics, lotions and potions manufactured from these natural ingredients can be found in shops across the country.

Koreans will inform you that the region is a habitat for a wide range of animals including Siberian tigers, brown bears, sable, yellow-throated marten, Mount Paektu roe, long-tailed goral, musk deer and wild boar. Given, however, the propensity for taxidermy in North Korea, with wild animals being seen in dusty exhibits across the country, your chance of seeing any significant wildlife will be slim to none. Birdlife, which is also a popular branch of taxidermy in the country, includes the Mount Paektu hawk owl, woodpecker and hazel grouse, although you will need an eagle eye to spot anything. A small variety of cold-water fish can be found in the streams and rivers, including in Lake Chon itself, after they were introduced in 1984.

THE HIKING ROUTE Mount Paektu is best visited as a circular day trip that will most likely start from the Pegaebong Hotel or the airport, depending on your

---

A WORD OF WARNING

While visiting Mount Paektu is not particularly challenging, the mountain should not be underestimated. The weather on the summit will be much cooler than down in Samjiyon, and conditions can change quickly. Visitors should have suitable footwear and outdoor clothing. A day bag with supplies, including liquids and any snacks, is a must. Even in summer the temperature can drop below zero, and winds can be strong. With no accurate accessible weather forecasting, you should be prepared for all conditions and pack accordingly.

Weather aside, your hosts on the mountain are likely to be your tour guides from Pyongyang and *not* local mountain guides. While your guides, and any locals you encounter, may seem relaxed and woefully ill-prepared for a day out on the mountain, do not follow suit. Korean guides, who are elsewhere generally excellent, often struggle in their organisational skills once they arrive on the mountain, as invariably some people want to relax at the crater rim, some want to visit the summit, some want to head to Lake Chon and some want to try to squeeze in everything. It seems obvious, but when arriving at the mountain it is a basic safety precaution for any group to take a few moments to check who wants to do what and, if needs be, to split up into separate parties. Ensure that everybody is accounted for and agree a schedule. Bear in mind that Mount Paektu, which reaches to 2,750m in height, is at an altitude where acute mountain sickness (AMS) could occur. At such elevations this should only present itself in some as light breathlessness; take it easy and enjoy the views.

schedule. The entire trip summarised here can be done in reverse, but as the highlight of the day will almost certainly be Mount Paektu, we recommend the route as follows, with the lesser sites in the afternoon. Accordingly, should the group want to linger on the mountain, some of the sites in the afternoon can be curtailed or omitted altogether.

Getting to Mount Paektu From your hotel, as early a departure as possible is recommended so push your driver and guide for a spritely start. Departing Samjiyon, you will head northeast on the road towards the airport, passing the airport turnoff and continuing onwards. After 15km of driving from Samjiyon you will branch left and continue through dense forest for another 8km to the Sinmusong Worker's District, the last settlement before the mountain. Here the road heads west and for the next 22km you ascend, slowly at first, to the base of Mount Paektu. The dense forest starts to thin as you climb, before you finally come out above the treeline altogether at approximately 2,000m above sea level and the mountain starts to come into view. Your local driver will likely be keen to get you to the mountain, but one or two quick photo stops of the lunar landscape cannot hurt; do bear in mind that you will not return on this road.

After a total of 45km, and around 75–90 minutes of driving from your hotel, you will arrive at the end of the main road, at approximately 2,330m above sea level. This is a military checkpoint and you will likely be held up here for around 15 minutes while the relevant checks are made and simple questions turn into protracted three-party discussions between your guide, driver and the army guards (as the United Nations are well aware, discussing anything with a North Korean is normally a complicated affair). The issue is in terms of access to the crater rim, as from this spot there are three ways to the main area atop the crater rim: by funicular railway, by car or on foot. Your driver, depending on the size of your vehicle and the weather, may be happy to drive up to the rim on the narrow 3km cobbled track, but if the funicular is working this road may be closed to 'non-essential' traffic, ie: you. The funicular railway struggles to operate but, if in luck, this is the most novel way up the mountain. While a ticket booth exists, it does not appear to have been regularly staffed in decades and the question of ticket cost is normally another protracted discussion, but expect it to be around €5 for a return journey, with your guide haggling and handling everything on the spot. Finally, if the funicular is closed and should your vehicle for any reason not be able to drive up to the rim, you can always walk the 3km, but there is normally some means of avoiding the need to do so, even if it involves hitchhiking on the back of a small vehicle that *is* permitted to pass.

Ascending to Janggun Peak and the descent to Lake Chon Once at the crater rim, the track and funicular converge at the top station of the funicular, which can double in poor weather as a shelter. Here, at around 2,620m above sea level, Lake Chon – occasionally tranquil, often tempestuous but always enthralling – will, weather permitting, be seen in all its glory. Looking towards the lake, the far side of the mountain is Chinese territory; if lucky you may even spot the silhouette of Chinese tourists waving at you – presumably semaphore at this juncture is not permitted. Other than soaking up the spectacular scenery of this picture-postcard mountain, replete with dramatic crags, unforgiving cliffs and Lake Chon (which, as the weather changes, can rapidly transform in colour from a welcoming azure to threatening grey), there are now two options: taking the short hike to Janggun Peak, the very summit of Paektu, or down to Lake Chon.

From the top station of the funicular it is a walk of around 600m to **Janggun Peak**, a journey of around 20 minutes each way that will likely take double this time should you make photography stops. With the lake on your right-hand side, ascend around the crater, heading west-southwest up along the scree-strewn footpath, keeping to the left of a low barrier fence. The view from anywhere along the crater rim is impressive, so those with weak will, lungs or legs need not push all the way to the summit – at any point dramatic views of the craggy crater rim, with Lake Chon far beneath, will be present. Looking back to Korea and the road along which you will have travelled, the vast panorama is one of undulating treeless slopes slowly descending into a distant blanket of forest, stretching as far as the eye can see. Eventually the gradient will level off and a large metallic trig point will come into view. You are now essentially at the summit; congratulations! Well, almost. The very summit, just a couple of metres higher, is within view, behind the low barrier fence that keeps people away from the precipitous drop down to Lake Chon. For now, nobody will stop those who step over the fence (which is there for a reason) and climb the craggy outcrop to the top of Korea, but this involves a few metres of easy scrambling on very exposed rock with a long drop on three sides – proceed with caution. Presumably one day somebody will slip and fall to their death and then the summit really will be closed to casual visitors; try to make sure it isn't you. From the top of Korea there is only one way down (other than falling) – back the same way you came to the top station of the funicular.

With the summit bagged, the next thing to consider is **Lake Chon**, a beautiful textbook example of a volcanic crater lake. Chon, which is approximately 9.2km^2 in area, can be accessed in two ways. A cable car does operate, but, like the funicular, this can be temperamental. When it does operate a return journey will likely cost €10 per person, with this transaction also being an overly complicated procedure akin to the funicular. Those keen to follow in the footsteps of the great may argue it out among themselves on who gets to travel in the much-coveted cabin that Kim Jong Il travelled in, which is marked with a small commemorative plaque. While paying €10 may sound steep, it is not as steep as the alternative option – on foot. Do bear in mind though that the rickety cable car does shudder somewhat; those who suffer from vertigo may be best to give this a miss. The walk to Lake Chon is allegedly made up of 2,160 steps, symbolising 2.16, 16 February, Kim Jong Il's birthday. While I have not independently verified this number, the figure seems about right, as it is a descent (and gruelling return ascent) of around 430m in elevation. This is a tiring, but rewarding, challenge. While these days more often than not the cable car does work, there is always the concern that it may be able to take you down to the lake, but not function when you want to return back up. While not aware of this having happened, yet, those who know they could not even begin to contemplate hiking up over 2,000 steps may be better off waiting at the rim, where the views are arguably better.

Down at the lakeshore you may want to dip your toes in the chilly waters, just for the novelty, but after a few photographs, possibly taken together with amused local holidaymakers, there is little reason for you to linger in the water, or on the shore. The small army post/weather station has a couple of little outboard motor boats and they seem to occasionally offer quick trips out onto the lake, with no lifejackets and zero concern for any health and safety. However, for now they seem reluctant to take foreigners out, which is probably a good thing.

You must now return up to the crater rim, and then down to the main road, by whichever viable means you wish, as aforementioned, albeit in reverse. Depending on a variety of factors, including your own inclination, once back at the main road you will have been on the mountain for anything from 2 to 6 hours.

Return to Samjiyon   Back inside your vehicle, an alternative route will take you back to Samjiyon, arguably more impressive than the road taken on your way up. Descending on a narrow rollercoaster of a road that often hugs the Chinese border, you will pass a few small waterfalls such as **Sagimun** and **Hyongje** falls before the gradient starts to ease off. Approximately 22km from Mount Paektu, the viewing platform at **Chongun Rocks** proffers a view about as close as one can get to China, and this is a logical spot to stop for a bite to eat; sheltered below the treeline the weather will be noticeably warmer already. The rocks themselves, weathered into curious shapes through erosion, cling to and jut out from a small sliver of land that is yet to be ground down by the passage of time. A Chinese backroad on the opposite riverbank is just 200m away and clearly visible, but normally devoid of traffic.

Leaving the border behind as you slowly head inland, the day now turns from mountain adventure to, what is for locals, a near-spiritual journey, as you press on to the birthplace of Kim Jong Il, the **Paektu Secret Camp**, around 8km beyond the Chongun Rocks. Here you will meet with a local guide, dressed in period military uniform of the time, who will escort you around the now not so 'secret' camp. It is all a bit of a hoot for many foreign visitors here, as almost all are well aware of the truth, but it is important not to question or insult your hosts, who have almost certainly heard these Western rumours surrounding the Dear Leader's true origins from previous, less sensitive, travellers. Instead, smile and try to think of suitable questions as you spend around 30 minutes touring the area. You will be shown Kim Jong Il Peak, see the mosaic mural of a young Kim Jong Il with his parents, and be offered the chance to drink waters from Sobaek Stream, the very spring waters young Jong Il drank from, before being taken to the *actual*, and very humble, log cabin that he was born in. Besides these key sights of interest there are countless slogan-bearing trees (see box, below) in the area and a few other sites relevant in Korea's revolutionary folklore, but it is best not to ask too much about these unless you want an extended monologue on something that may never have happened.

Back on the road, a further 18km of driving through forest leads to a junction; turn left here and it is just 8km back to Samjiyon and the relative comforts of the Pegaebong Hotel. Unless you are in a rush to get back to your room, it is better

---

SLOGAN TREES

Slogan trees are trees that have had political slogans and messages carved into their trunks. Though found throughout the country, they are particularly common in Ryanggang Province and are chiefly associated with the era of Japanese occupation, bearing slogans praising Kim Il Sung, socialism, independence and the like, such as 'Birth in Mount Paektu of the bright star, heir to General Kim Il Sung'. These trees, once discovered, are preserved in reinforced glass and often surrounded by protective fencing for posterity. The problem is that, bizarrely, more and more of these trees seem to be 'discovered' all the time – there are allegedly now over 1,800 in the country, bringing serious questions as to their authenticity in the first place. It may or may not be true, but all Koreans seem to know the awful story of the 17 young soldiers who died protecting such trees from a forest fire, highlighting just how important even a tree is in North Korea when it has a connection with revolutionary history and the Kim family.

to instead request your driver hangs a right and ferries you to the village or Rimyongsu, 7km away. The draw here is scenic **Rimyongsu Falls**, where water gushes out from crevices in the basalt rock. With thermal water still holding a little heat from further up in the mountains, the falls never freeze and in winter are said to appear like frosted flowers in full bloom. A short walk leads to a pavilion above these small falls and is worth a visit, if anything, just to mingle with the local tourists who will likely also be here. After 20 minutes or so in Rimyongsu it will definitely be time to head back to the hotel and rest up those weary legs. You will most likely do a U-turn and head back to the aforementioned T-junction, but an alternative and slightly longer drive of 21km will take you back to the Pegaebong on a different road altogether, which approaches Samjiyon from the south – ask your driver politely and there is no reason why you cannot take this route; after all, variety is the spice of life.

TAEHONGDAN (대홍단군) AND POCHON COUNTIES (보천군)

Those on a longer tour of the region may want to consider a visit to Taehongdan and Pochon counties (if all the aforementioned places in this chapter have been seen), both of which can be visited in half-day excursions from Samjiyon town.

TAEHONGDAN COUNTY A visit to Taehongdan starts with a drive 48km northeast from Samjiyon or the Pegaebong Hotel, passing the airport and turnoff to the Sinmusong Worker's District as you travel, partly on the Japanese-built Kapsan– Musan Military Road to your first stop, the **Monument to the Victorious Battle in the Musan Area**. This is another impressive statue of, who else, Kim Il Sung. The statue, built in 2002, replaced an earlier monument and depicts a powerful-looking Kim Il Sung facing south, arm outstretched (albeit his left), in something akin to a Nazi salute. Kim holds in his right hand a pair of binoculars and to his right stands a tower in the form of a rifle with bayonet. You will likely have a local guide tell you about the history of the region, and almost certainly be met here by your local government minders from Taehongdan.

Pressing on, the itinerary for the next couple of hours will be up to your friendly local chaperones, who will want to show you the best of the county. Your tour should take you on to **Taheongdan town**, a further 20km beyond the monument, and include a visit to the potato fields and the potato processing plant where all manner of products are made, including copious amounts of vodka to help get the locals through the hard winters. After seeing all that is permitted, you may have the chance of a bite to eat in the local potato noodle house before setting off back to Samjiyon on the same road. The roads in this area are, while unpaved, normally relatively good and flat; expect the driving time from Samjiyon to Taehongdan town to be around 90 minutes each way, excluding any stops.

POCHON COUNTY A final option in the area is a journey south from Samjiyon to visit Pochon County, a drive of 46–55km each way depending on which route your driver wishes to take. Regardless, expect the journey to take around 75 minutes each way. Other than taking in the local scenery, there is nothing to see en route save for Rimyongsu Falls (see above), if you have not yet visited.

Pochon town is a sleepy little place, only around 1km from the Amnok River and thus, the Chinese border. This unassuming settlement is famous for being the site of the Battle of Pochonbo (see box, page 230), where, on 4 June 1937 the first battle

THE BATTLE OF POCHONBO

The battle of Pochonbo is an important event in the country's historical narrative. By local accounts, an expeditionary force of over 150 men, commanded by Kim Il Sung, attacked the Japanese garrison here, the very first of many strikes on Korean soil. In Kim Il Sung's own words:

> At 10pm sharp, I raised my pistol high and pulled the trigger. Everything I had ever wanted to say to my fellow countrymen back in the homeland for over 10 years was packed into that one shot reverberating through the street that night. The gunshot, as our poets described, was both a greeting to our motherland and a challenge to the Japanese imperialist robbers whom we were about to punish.
>
> *Reminiscences: With The Century (Volume 6)*, Kim Il Sung

The battle, essentially an attack on a small garrison followed by a hasty retreat, was all over in a few minutes and dealt 'a telling blow at the Japanese Imperialists who had been strutting around Korea and Manchuria as if they were the lords of Asia'. History is blurred by time, and this is likely more true in the DPRK than anywhere else, but a battle did take place in Pochonbo, a battle that while minor, was significant in the region. However, when the Japanese did finally leave Korea in August 1945, it was, most would agree, the end result of something they themselves had instigated in Hawaii in 1941 and most certainly not a result, which the Pyongyang propagandists will tell you, of something Kim Il Sung started here in this sleepy town in 1937.

on Korean soil between anti-Japanese guerrillas and the Japanese armed forces took place. Given Pochon's importance, the statue here of Kim Il Sung is, by North Korean standards, rather uninspiring, and visitors will normally be whisked away rather quickly to see the Japanese-run Police Substation and Administrative Office (two of the main buildings attacked in the battle), together with the Pochonbo Revolutionary Museum. You will be unlikely to occupy yourself for more than an hour or so in Pochon before it is time to return to Samjiyon, so it really is only worth a visit if you do have the time to spare, or should you be allowed to travel onto the currently closed city of Hyesan, only 22km further down the road.

12

North Hamgyong
(함경북도)

Life in the nation's northernmost province, North Hamgyong, is rather well documented in the West. A lot of the country's defectors originally stem from this region – thanks in part to a range of serendipitous geographical factors, such as the largely narrow (and thus fordable) Tuman River, making illegal crossings from here into China easier than in other parts of DPRK. Considered within the DPRK as a bit of a backwater, the 15,980km^2 region is home to 2.33 million people and encompasses everything from sleepy fishing villages to heavy industrial cities, and from timeless coastal scenes to the high Hamgyong Mountains. Owing to its relative distance from Pyongyang, the collapse of the centrally planned economy in the 1990s was particularly acute in North Hamgyong. Today, while Pyongyang somehow enjoys its own little economic boom, the money seems a long way from trickling all the way down to North Hamgyong; in places the province reminds seasoned visitors to the DPRK of what Pyongyang was like 15 years ago – dim lights, little traffic, suspicious locals and neurotic guides. Is it the 'real' North Korea? Perhaps.

GETTING THERE AND AWAY

BY AIR The majority of visitors coming to North Hamgyong will be flying into Orang Airport from Pyongyang, a journey of 80 minutes or less, dependent on the aircraft. Orang is a military airfield approximately 50km south of Chongjin and while it is occassionaly served by scheduled flights, the only reliable means of flying in, for now, is by chartered aircraft, with the same setup as flights to Samjiyon (see box, page 56). After your time in North Hamgyong you may then fly onto other airfields in the country by your pre-arranged charter, or exit overland to China or Russia, as below.

BY RAIL Tourists are now able to arrive in Chongjin if travelling on an infrequent international train, ie: a Russia-bound service from Pyongyang, or a Pyongyang-bound train from Russia. Such a trip is a little complicated to arrange, but rewarding. The 720km journey from Pyongyang to Chongjin is scheduled to take just under 22 hours, and you will be accommodated in four-berth shared sleeping compartments. Delays are to be expected and, with no restaurant car, this journey is not the most comfortable, but an adventure nonetheless.

BY ROAD While it is not permitted to drive from North Hamgyong to Ryanggang or South Hamgyong provinces, it is possible with prior arrangement to arrive/depart the region by way of China, one of the few border crossings approved for tourist use. The land border in Namyang, in Hoeryong County, is now a fully open

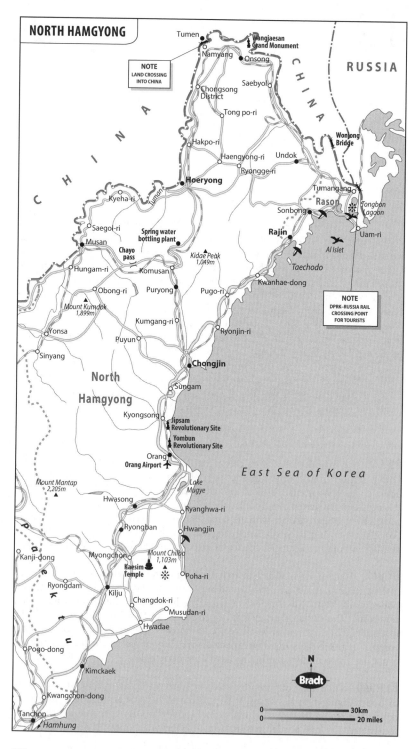

NORTH HAMGYONG

RUSSIA

CHINA

Tumen
Namyang
Wangjaesan Grand Monument
Onsong
Saebyol

NOTE
LAND CROSSING INTO CHINA

Chongsong District
Tong po-ri

Hakpo-ri
Haengyong-ri
Undok
Ryongge-ri
Wonjong Bridge

Hoeryong
Kyeha-ri

Tumangang
Rason
Sonbong
Tongbon Lagoon
Uam-ri

Saegol-ri
Musan
Spring water bottling plant
Rajin

Chayo pass
Kidae Peak 1,049m

Hungam-ri
Komusan
Al Islet
Taechodo

Obong-ri
Puryong
Pugo-ri
Kwanhae-dong

Mount Kumdok 1,899m

NOTE
DPRK–RUSSIA RAIL CROSSING POINT FOR TOURISTS

Yonsa
Kumgang-ri
Ryonjin-ri

Sinyang
Puyun

North Hamgyong
Chongjin

Sungam

Kyongsong
Jipsam Revolutionary Site
Yombun Revolutionary Site

Orang
Orang Airport

Mount Mantap 2,205m
Lake Mugye

Hwasong
Ryanghwa-ri

Ryongban
Hwangjin

Myongchon
Mount Chilbo 1,103m

Kaesim Temple
Poha-ri

Kanji-dong

Ryongdam
Kilju
Changdok-ri
Musudan-ri

Hwadae

Pogo-dong

Kimckaek

Kwangchon-dong

Tanchon
Hamhung

East Sea of Korea

N

Bradt

0 — 30km
0 — 20 miles

border on the southern bank of the Tuman River, opposite the small Chinese city of Tumen. Nevertheless, this border is rarely used and, like anything in the country, all must be meticulously arranged in advance. Expect bemused immigration officials on both sides of the river.

It is also possible to travel by road from North Hamgyong to Rason (page 245), from where you can overland to China on foot (page 249) or Russia by rail (page 248).

CHONGJIN (청진 시)

A small fishing village before the arrival of the Japanese, Chongjin transformed itself over the course of the 20th century to become a major industrial city and port. This 'City of Iron', as locals often call it, also proudly promotes itself – in somewhat unique socialist-romantic tones – as being a 'Grand Ferrous Metallurgical Base', with massive complexes such as the Kim Chaek Iron and Steel Complex and the Puryong Alloy Steel Complex making great chunks of this city of 668,000 look like a Lowry artwork.

The economic collapse of the 1990s devastated Chongjin. At first the factories struggled and people became malnourished, but as time went by many plants shut up shop completely. Those who were young, or savvy enough, managed to adapt – just – by engaging in pursuits such as private enterprise and smuggling, or by simply foraging for food in the hills. However, many of Chongjin's residents, who had only ever known a system where the state provided all and only knew to do as they were told, ultimately starved. The city seemed to have been forgotten by the state and by Pyongyang, and left to fend for itself. The worst was over by the turn of the century, but Chongjin looked in parts like a dystopic wasteland – a forest of scrap metal and sea of cracked concrete, with smoke and dust heavy in the air.

Over the last ten years or so, however, Chongjin has slowly begun the long process of picking itself up, dusting itself off and getting back to work as the country's unofficial northern capital. Factories are slowly coming back online, more traffic – including the previously semi-dilapidated trams – can be seen on the streets and, perhaps most tellingly, the people that call this struggling city home seem happier and more optimistic – like a great weight has been lifted from their shoulders. As the province looks to the possibility of doing serious business with Russia and China (Vladivostok and the massive Chinese city of Changchun are both closer than Pyongyang is), prospects in Chongjin can surely only improve as time goes by. But for now, it feels that every tourist dollar spent will likely do more good here than anywhere else in the country.

🏠 **WHERE TO STAY** *Map, page 234*
In this rarely visited corner of the country there is little choice and where you ultimately stay may be up to your local chaperones. All options are, in Western terms, basic, but memorable.

🏠 **Chongjin Foreigners' Lodgings**
(33 rooms) In the grittier Songpyong District of the city, near the Kim Chaek Iron & Steel Complex, this is an old option that has only recently started to welcome conventional tourists – in a former life, foreign engineers working at the steelworks lodged here. While arguably the best option in town, the rooms are still basic, but expect, like anywhere in Chongjin, good food & service. **$$**

🏠 **Chongjin Tourist Hotel** (28 rooms) The most commonly proffered place to stay for tourists in Chongjin, this hotel was built in 1985 & is very tired. A stone's throw from the station, those who don't want to be woken by passing trains should ask for a street-facing room. Hot water is unlikely to be possible but the sauna *may* function, for a fee. The *pièce de résistance* that makes a stay here so worthwhile is the on-site micro-brewery, with

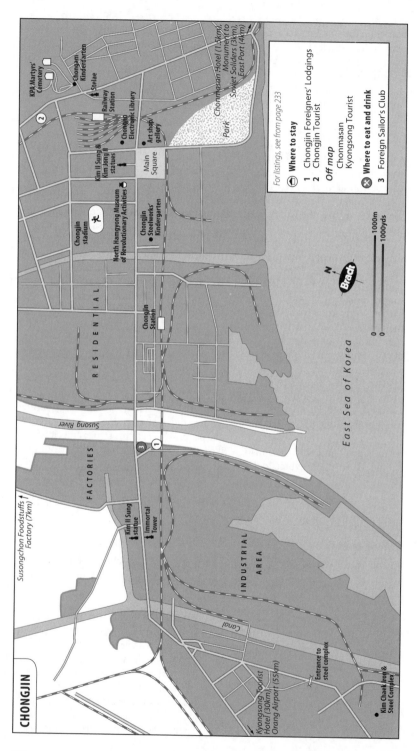

CHONGJIN

Susongchon Foodstuffs Factory (7km)

Kim Il Sung statue
Immortal Tower

FACTORIES

Susong River

Chonsam Kinderdarten

KPA Martyrs' Cemetery

Stelae

Railway Station

Chongjin Electronic Library

Art shop/ gallery

Chonmasan Hotel (1.5km), Monument to Soviet Soliders (3km), East Port (4km)

Park

Kim Il Sung & Kim Jong Il statues

Main Square

Chongjin Steelworks' Kindergarten

North Hamgyong Museum of Revolutional Activities

Chongjin stadium

RESIDENTIAL

Chongjin Station

East Sea of Korea

N

Bradt

0   1000m
0   1000yds

Kyongsong Tourist Hotel (30km), Orang Airport (55km)

Entrance to steel complex

Canal

INDUSTRIAL AREA

Kim Chaek Iron & Steel Complex

For listings, see from page 233

ⓘ **Where to stay**
1 Chongjin Foreigners' Lodgings
2 Chongjin Tourist

Off map
Chonmasan
Kyongsong Tourist

✖ **Where to eat and drink**
3 Foreign Sailor's Club

prices so cheap that hot water, or the lack of, will hopefully be forgotten. **$$**

🏠 **Chonmasan Hotel** (22 rooms) Near the East Harbour, this is another option of old that has only recently started to accept conventional tourists. The quality here is similar to the Chongjin Tourist Hotel but, being away from the railway tracks, you may get a sounder night's sleep. **$$**

🏠 **Kyongsong Tourist Hotel** (14 rooms) In Kyongsong County, roughly halfway between Chongjin & Orang Airport, this basic option is more commonly used as a lunch stop for people passing through, but those who prefer a more rural setting may opt to stay here. The staff will likely lay on meals of epic proportions &, while the electricity may not be constant, hot water should not be a problem – after all, Kyongsong is a spa town. **$–$$**

✖ WHERE TO EAT AND DRINK *Map, opposite*

Besides meals in your hotel, the only option in Chongjin itself is the **Foreign Sailor's Club**, a complex with a restaurant, bar, billiards, sauna and shop that goes by a few similar names, including the Seaman's Club, Fisherman's Club and a few other synonyms for 'sailor'. This is well worth a visit for an hour or 2 of an evening and offers, hopefully, something for everyone. If staying in Kyongsong, the accommodating staff at the Kyongsong Tourist Hotel can lay on, with enough notice, a barbecue or picnic lunch at the Yombun or Jipsam Revolutionary Site – essentially scenic coastal spots.

WHAT TO SEE AND DO Your most likely point of arrival into the region will be **Orang Airport**. Built by the Imperial Japanese Army, this is now essentially a military airport, with no regular scheduled flights. The airport is awash with ageing MiG fighter jets and it is common when arriving in Orang to see, up close, these vintage aircraft practising touch-and-go landings. Given the alleged lack of jet fuel in the country, some have suggested that these drills are timed to take place so that the few tourists passing through get to see the full might of the Air Force; a shame then that photography is not permitted. Depending on your arrangements in the region, and where you are travelling on to next, it is possible that you may pick up altogether new guides here, or an additional local escort to add to your entourage from Pyongyang. The local guides in North Hamgyong can be somewhat 'old-school' compared with their modern Pyongyang counterparts, and are typically a little stricter in their interpretation of dos and don'ts. Hopefully as time goes by they will lighten up a little.

Leaving the airport, you will pass through the small town of Orang and head north on roads that are largely unpaved. There are two options leading to the first main town – Kyongsong: an inland road and a coastal road, which offers up the most interest. The difference in distance is minimal, but a 10km drive from the airport on the coastal road will lead to the **Yombun Revolutionary Site**, also known as Yombunjin. While the historical interest here is negligible (essentially Kim Il Sung and Kim Jong Suk visited in 1947), the main draw is as a short stop to take in the rocky coastal scenery and to stretch your legs. Pressing on, the road passes an attractive sandy beach, home to the concrete shell of a long-abandoned hotel project. From here the road slowly heads inland, passing the small Kyongsong Chuul Airport. After 12km of driving from Yombun you will arrive in quaint and sleepy **Kyongsong**, a famous spa resort and centre of ceramics. A historical town now overshadowed by Chongjin, Kyongsong offers up a few things to entice the lingering visitor (including a small hotel), with the possibility of heading to the forlorn South Gate of Kyongsong, which dates all the way back to 1107, the small and stern Kyongsong Revolutionary Museum, or to either the Kyongsong Hot Spa or Onpho Hot Spa for a genuine local experience – guaranteed hot water at last!

Other than the possibility of a 13km round-trip detour from Kyongsong to visit the **Jipsam Revolutionary Site**, a coastal spot that is only really worthwhile if you have time to kill and want an additional dose of propaganda, the logical step from here is to press on to Chongjin. While the city centre is 30km away, the southern environs of Chongjin will come into view after just 16km, upon passing the brow of the hill just beyond **Sungam**, which is home to the Sungam Ni Airport; keep your eyes peeled here and you may catch a glimpse of some truly ancient military aircraft and crop-dusters overhead.

Slowly descending into Chongjin, now on a paved road, you will pass through the Ranam District of the city, home to a lonely Russian Consulate. Together with the Chinese Consulate these are the only diplomatic representatives in town and unlikely to be of any assistance to travellers, although the Chinese consul here has been known to issue five-day transit visas in emergencies. The city's tram and trolleybus network starts here in Ranam, with both options slowly trundling towards the central city at little more than a jogger's pace. As the landscape becomes increasing urban the sprawling **Kim Chaek Iron and Steel Complex** comes into view to your right, its long conveyer belt and rusting sea of metal a sombre contrast to the gleaming bronze statue of Kim Il Sung that can be spotted on the opposite side of the road. Before crossing the Susong River and entering the central city in earnest, there are two possible stops on this side of the river, with the **Foreign Sailor's Club** (page 235) being a recommended visit at some point while in the city, to enjoy a few drinks in the wonderfully retro bar or to soak in the waters of the piping-hot spa, easing away the aches and pains that will have built up as you have bounced along the pot-holed roads of the region to get here. Approximately 7km north from here, not far from Chongjin Prison (which you will most certainly not willingly visit), the **Susongchon Foodstuffs Factory** is more fun than it sounds. After touring the small plant's museum and production line, the short tour culminates in a rather polished song and dance routine in the factory's very own little theatre. It has been known for the managing director to take to the stage, lower his guard and perform like an early Elvis Presley, much to the amusement of all. The factory normally has a small selection of their produce available, as good a place as any to stock up on snacks, spirits and savouries.

On crossing the Susong and coming into the central part of the city you will likely come first to the **main square** and its twin monuments of, you guessed it, Kim Il Sung and Kim Jong Il. You will normally here be asked to bow at the foot of these foreboding bronze statues, which were renovated in 2014 when the statue of Kim Il Sung was joined by his most esteemed progeny. To the west of the square lies the somewhat Orwellian **North Hamgyong Museum of Revolutionary Activities**; you may be obliged to pop in here for 20 minutes or so, even if you have not requested to, but you will thankfully typically take in just one of the mere 46 exhibition rooms, which are packed to the rafters with sometimes dull and occasionally droll exhibits pertaining to the region's revolutionary history. To the east of the square is the more interesting **Chongjin Electronic Library**, where local schoolchildren can learn basic computer skills and engage in extra-curricular classes, taught by local teachers and through remote learning via the much-lauded domestic intranet. Visitors can enjoy half an hour or so more or less freely exploring the small library where the children, like anywhere in the world, pretend to look busy the moment visitors enter the room. Across the road, to the southeast of the main square is a provincial **art shop/gallery** with a good selection of socialist-realist artworks for sale, together with a display of paintings depicting the leaders which will not be sold for love or money. By prior arrangement, transport enthusiasts or those wanting something a little different may be able to enjoy a brief **trolleybus tour** of the central city, which will likely start from near the main square.

There are two **kindergartens** in the city centre: these days most visitors are taken to the Chongam Kindergarten near the Chongjin Tourist Hotel, but another almost identical kindergarten close to the steelworks is occasionally visited. They are often collectively referred to as the Chongjin Steelworks' Kindergarten and both options are near identical in content. After touring the classrooms and likely seeing the rooms where children learn about the lives of the Kim family in something akin to a Bible studies class, you will almost certainly enjoy a staggeringly well-polished song and dance routine from the tiny whippersnappers in an ever-changing repertoire that should leave you in complete awe. It has become customary here to give the chronically underfunded kindergarten a gift at the end of the tour, by way of a staff member, with stationery, sweets and toys being the norm.

Finally, the last sites you will likely be able to visit will be near the East Port, just over 4km southeast of the main square. In this rather low-rise and tired part of the city the view from the **pavilion** on **Komalsan Hill** down to the harbour is an interesting spot to stop and watch the world pass by and the boats come and go from, but the main draw here is the nearby and rather forgotten **Monument to Soviet Soldiers**. Here your Korean guides, who are typically rich fonts of knowledge on all facets of North Korean 'history', will be *extremely* vague about the Soviet involvement in the post-Japanese years of transition, making the presence of the Red Army sound so negligible that you may question why they even deserve a monument.

HOERYONG (회령시)

Very sleepy in comparison with Chongjin, Hoeryong is the only other city in all of North Hamgyong that it is permissible to visit. The population is reported to be approximately 154,000 but appears much smaller in this compact little town, which could well be the first or last city you visit in the country due to its proximity to a rare permitted border crossing with China at Namyang.

The city itself does not offer a great deal to visitors, as it is essentially a transit point for those en route elsewhere. However, due to distances and the somewhat dilapidated roads in the region, anybody passing through will almost certainly be obliged to stay overnight here before moving on.

Sitting on the southern bank of the Tuman River and facing a small Chinese village on the opposite riverbank, Hoeryong's history is essentially one of a border town. With the frontier far less porous these days than it was in years gone by, a somnolent atmosphere prevails. While visitors aware of any of the many tomes relating to Korean defectors will find the natural 'Berlin Wall' that is the Tuman River of prime interest, the city is chiefly famous among Koreans for two things: Kim Jong Suk and apricots.

The saving grace for the city and people of Hoeryong in contemporary North Korea is that it is the undisputed birthplace of Kim Jong Suk, wife of Kim Il Sung, thus mother of Kim Jong Il and grandmother of Kim Jong Un. Owing to it birthing this 'revolutionary immortal', it would not be deemed appropriate for the city centre to be too shabby; the infrastructure and facilities are thus generally better than elsewhere in the region, with much development and modernisation having taken place in 2010, in the lead up to an official visit from Kim Jong Il.

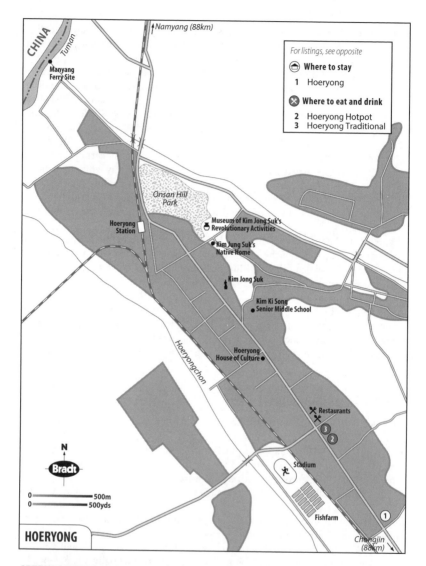

Inside the map:

Namyang (88km)

CHINA

Tuman

Manyang
Ferry Site

For listings, see opposite

Where to stay
1 Hoeryong

Where to eat and drink
2 Hoeryong Hotpot
3 Hoeryong Traditional

Onsan Hill
Park

Hoeryong
Station

Museum of Kim Jong Suk's
Revolutionary Activities

Kim Jung Suk's
Native Home

Kim Jong Suk

Kim Ki Song
Senior Middle School

Hoeryongchon

Hoeryong
House of Culture

Restaurants

3
2

N

Bradt

0 —— 500m
0 —— 500yds

Stadium

Fishfarm

1

HOERYONG

*Chongjin
(88km)*

GETTING THERE AND AWAY

From the south From Chongjin, the 88km 'road' to Hoeryong has to be one of the worst in the country, with the only respite from this backbreaking dirt track being stretches of attractive rural scenery mixed with a few sights relatively unique to North Korea. Expect the jarring drive to take almost 3 hours as you slowly head northbound, passing by a number of tiny hydro-electric stations and irrigation canals and trundling through towns such as Puryong and Komusan, where the Komusan Cement Factory cakes the depressing town in a thick layer of carcinogenic dust. At times the 98km hydraulic pipeline that transports slurried iron ore concentrate from the city of Musan (home to one of the world's largest iron ore deposits) to Chongjin will skirt the road and blot the landscape, but the pipeline branches off to the west near Sosang, while you continue on in a northerly direction, arriving at a logical spot to break the journey after 54km at a small spring water bottling plant and shop. Bumping onwards, the final 34km is increasingly rural and doesn't sound like far – but it will be another hour of perdition before arriving in Hoeryong.

North to China One of the few things that entices people to pass through Hoeryong is that it is possible to travel between North Korea and China from here, by being driven the 85km to Namyang and here parting with your escorts at the border before you walk, unchaperoned but under the watchful eyes of border guards, across the bridge spanning the Tuman River to the Chinese city of Tumen. The journey from Hoeryong to Namyang, which at times hugs the Tuman River, should take a couple of hours, but those visiting this remote northern tip of the country would be remiss to bypass the Wangjaesan Grand Monument, a 40km round-trip east from Namyang, via the town of Onsong. Here stands the second-tallest bronze monument in the country, built to commemorate 1933's Wangjaesan Conference, an important chapter in North Korea's often-fabricated revolutionary history. The monument is impressive enough, a striking last hurrah for visitors at the end of their time in the DPRK, or an arresting first impression for those who have just arrived. Lunch in a simple guesthouse in Onsong or Namyang is normally the order of service before moving on. Those crossing this border, regardless of the direction, should factor in spare time for delays and check *all* logistical issues carefully – the border is only open during set hours and is used rarely. Expect customs to be thorough.

WHERE TO STAY *Map, opposite*

Hoeryong Hotel (33 rooms) The only option in town is the imaginatively named Hoeryong Hotel, one of the first buildings you will come to as you enter the city from the south. This 4-storey hotel is basic yet functional. It has a small stage in the main banquet hall where groups can, for a fee, normally enjoy a traditional Korean song & dance performance. **$$**

WHERE TO EAT AND DRINK *Map, opposite*

While you may be scheduled to dine at the hotel, Hoeryong does offer two modern restaurants, very close to each other on another ingeniously titled spot in the city – Hoeryong Food Avenue. With no clear names, these restaurants can best be described as the Hoeryong Traditional Restaurant and the Hoeryong Hotpot Restaurant.

Hoeryong Hotpot Restaurant In the 'do it yourself' bracket that Koreans adore but leaves some visitors befuddled, this restaurant is the better of the 2 options available. Friendly staff will assist those who find preparing their own food a little too taxing. **$$$**

Hoeryong Traditional Restaurant Serving traditional Korean food, this restaurant is friendly enough, although very similar to what you will encounter elsewhere in the country. One redeeming feature is the beer made on-site, which always seems to go down a little too well after what will have been a long drive to get here. **$$$**

WHAT TO SEE AND DO Half a day is more than enough time to see the key sights of the city itself, and tours will normally always start with a bow before the **bronze statue of Kim Jong Suk** – likely to be your last showing of obeisance in the country (what a relief!) or, if coming from China, your first (what fun!). After paying respects to the statue of the lesser-mentioned member of the founding triumvirate you will be led to her preserved birthplace at **Kim Jong Suk's Native Home** for further deference, before the propaganda is cranked up to eleven at the **Museum of Kim Jong Suk's Revolutionary Activities**. While the aforementioned revolutionary sites *may* be of interest, most find a visit to the **Kim Ki Song Senior Middle School** much more rewarding. Kim Ki Song was the brother of Kim Jong Suk and at this flagship school visitors will normally have the opportunity to interact with the students, possibly over an English-language class or a kickabout in the playground.

The **Manyang Ferry Site** is equally rewarding and lies in the northern outskirts of town. While it does have some revolutionary historical relevance relating to the life of Kim Jong Suk, it is of prime interest due to its proximity to the Chinese border, being on the southern bank of the narrow Tuman River. If lucky, you may well see Korean and Chinese border guards guarding their respective banks of the Tuman; if very lucky, you may be obliged with a wave from a perplexed Chinese border guard. Keep an eye out for the simple border defences of raked sand and rustic nail traps, as they will most certainly not be pointed out to you. While there is a border crossing visible from here it is, for now, for local traffic and freight only. The only reason why visitors are allowed so close to the border here is that this is the very spot from where Kim Jong Suk departed Korea in her youth, fleeing the Japanese occupiers in her homeland for Manchuria, where she eventually fell into the arms of anti-Japanese guerrillas and met her husband to be, Kim Il Sung. The preserved rowing boat in which she crossed the river, which appears suspiciously new, is lovingly preserved beside the riverbank.

MOUNT CHILBO (칠보산)

Mount Chilbo (or Chilbosan), literally the 'mountain of seven treasures', is a remote and undeveloped area of dramatic coastline, jagged peaks and steep valleys, part of the volcanic Paektu chain that stretches all the way from Mount Paektu to Ulleung Island in South Korea. Millennia of weathering on the basalt, trachyte and other igneous rock has wrought the landscape, the provincial propagandists will tell you, 'into fantastic forms and sheer cliffs, which present beautiful and original scenery in good harmony with the East Sea of Korea'. A bit of a mouthful, but a spot-on description. Like Mount Kumgang, this area is also divided into three parts: Inner Chilbo, Outer Chilbo and Sea Chilbo.

The area, which became a UNESCO Biosphere Reserve in 2014, is best visited from early May to mid-October, but there is something to be said for visiting at the bookends of this window, which allows you to see the very best of the spring or autumn colours. Regardless, as long as it's not shrouded in mist, the scenery in this national park will be memorable: 503km² of craggy mountains that rise to 1,103m above sea level, blanketed in dense forest, save for when the gravity-defying rocks jut skywards.

FLORA AND FAUNA Heavily forested with coniferous, mixed and lowland pine forests, the region is home to 827 species of plants, including 16 endemic to Korea and ten threatened species such as Sakhalin cork trees (*Phellodendron sachalinense*) and *Exochorda serratifolia*, commonly referred to as a Snow White tree. Koreans get extremely excited about Mount Chilbo's delicious pine mushrooms (*Tricholoma matsutake*), a highly sought-after fungus that, when sanctions aren't in place, are sold by the boatload to the Japanese for sky-high prices.

The mountains are home to 192 species of bird, 39 species of mammals and 21 species of amphibians and reptiles. Some of the more exciting birds that may be seen include the goldcrest, common kestrel and sparrowhawk, while mammals include plentiful roe deer and wildcats. Threatened animals known to exist in Mount Chilbo include the Japanese black bear and the black woodpecker. The locals will also insist Amur leopards still live in these mountains. In reality, you are more likely to be invited around for afternoon tea with Kim Jong Un than spot one of these beautiful creatures.

GETTING THERE AND AWAY Mount Chilbo is only accessible if coming from the north, ie: Orang or beyond. From Orang, there are two roads – most journeys will take the coastal route but an inland option also exists. The coastal option is arguably the more scenic of the two, but it may be worth asking to travel down one way and back the other for a spot of variety, although the road chosen is usually based on the driver's knowledge of conditions at the time. Regardless of the route taken, expect a bumpy and dusty/muddy journey from Orang on unpaved roads. The distance from Orang to Chilbo ranges from 80km to 110km, depending on the route chosen and your precise destination, and can take up to 4 hours.

The coastal road down Departing Orang you will be driven south. The road initially follows the coast for 10km before arriving at a junction from where you will either continue straight for the inland option, or bear left for the coastal route. It will be the driver's prerogative, so if you have a strong preference of route do try to raise it in advance.

The coastal road passes salterns before arriving at Mugye Lake; from here you slowly leave agricultural land behind as the road ascends into densely forested hills. For the next 3 hours or more, the road curves up, down and around these densely forested hills, through a series of slow switchbacks. The coast will rarely be more than 2km away and, from time to time, dramatic vistas will unfold on the bends and brows of hills. The road occasionally dips down to near sea level as it passes small fishing villages and secluded sandy bays, but is generally at an elevation of a couple of hundred metres, affording good views when the coast does come into view. There is no sudden boundary marking the start of Mount Chilbo; when your guides start to relax a little on photographic restrictions and suddenly take you to an unscheduled little waterfall or the like, you will have effectively arrived.

The inland road back up This road, dependent on where you have been in Mount Chilbo, is generally longer in distance but is unlikely to take any more time than the coastal option as it courses a flatter and straighter, less sinuous route. Heading inland from Mount Chilbo, you leave the hills behind and return to agricultural land before arriving in Myongchon, a small town on the main Pyongra railway line that links Pyongyang with Russia. Slumbersome Myongchon is about as close as you can get to the Punggye-ri Nuclear Test Site, making travel on this route a bonus or deterrent, depending on your outlook. From here, you press northwards for a good couple of hours through farmlands and small towns such as Ryongban and Hwasong, before the road abruptly reaches the coast in the southern fringes of Orang.

🏠 **WHERE TO STAY** Luxury this is not, but if you can put up with the journey to get here you should be able to cope with either of the two choices available. If staying in Mount Chilbo for more than one night it is common to spend one night in each option, but it's up to you.

🏠 **Chilbo Homestay** (20 homes) The only 'homestay' in Korea, this collection of 20 buildings is within walking distance of the beach at Pochon-ri. Local families were gifted these new homes

While international politics won't permit North Korea, like India and Pakistan, to be classed as a 'nuclear-weapon state', the country of course became one in all but name on 9 October 2006, when it detonated its first nuclear device. Five subsequent tests of increasing yield have taken place since then, with the most recent in September 2017 promoting the DPRK into the thermonuclear club, with the detonation of a hydrogen bomb.

While North Koreans will never show any emotion other than absolute pride in their tenacious nuclear achievements in the face of adversity, one thing they bizarrely have no idea of is the actual location of their test site. In a country where one knows from a young age not to ask too many questions, asking the location of the test site will draw a blank from any Korean, much like how the site actually appears on maps – it doesn't.

The Punggye-ri Nuclear Test Site is located in mountainous terrain in Kilju County, North Hamgyong. This rural area, likely chosen for its remoteness, is not all that far from Mount Chilbo, so while visitors may know that they are driving within 30km of a top-secret nuclear test facility, your local escorts will likely be totally oblivious. Likewise, the nearby Tonghae Satellite Launching Ground at Musudan-ri and the Sohae Satellite Launching Station in North Pyongan on the west coast are major military sights that locals know of, but haven't the foggiest idea of where they are situated. In May 2018 the tunnels of the Punggye-ri Nuclear Test Site were reportedly destroyed, a conciliatory gesture to the West that was overseen by a select number of foreign journalists. Crucially, the relevant experts and inspectors were kept away from Punggye-ri, so whether the site has indeed been demolished, or is just temporarily offline, is the million-dollar question.

As rocket technology develops in Korea, the government's next step, it seems, is to be able to deliver any missile from any location they wish. In 2016, while travelling from Pyongyang to Kaesong I was delayed due to an unspecified 'problem on the road'. That evening, with the local TV news roundup, essentially the only news, on in the background of the hotel bar, the reason for our little delay became clear – three Scud-ER missiles, believed to be nuclear-capable, had been launched from transporter-erector-launchers (TELs), from the very road we had been travelling on; quite possibly the most bizarre excuse for running late I will ever be able to give. For the first time in his life my friendly guide could pinpoint exactly where a military test had been conducted, although we mutually thought best not to discuss it – his wry, knowing glance said it all.

on the understanding that they should keep a room available for foreign guests as & when required. Given the dearth of guests, this was a great deal. The 20 homes, some of a Korean style (ie: floor mattresses) & some of a Western style, are spread out in 2 neat rows, with a small courtyard containing a restaurant & shop located in the middle of the cluster of houses. Guides are generally more relaxed here than elsewhere in the region & you should be free to wander at will between your homestay & the beach. If going out after dark, a torch is essential as locating your particular homestay among 19 other similar buildings will be a challenge without one. Once tucked up expect a peaceful night; with your window open you should be able to hear the waves lapping at the nearby shore. By local standards these homes are great, but do remember where you are; don't expect hot water, constant electric or other luxuries. All of your meals will be included

& are typically taken in the restaurant so you will likely have limited time to engage with your host family, but a phrasebook will come in handy, as will some drinks or small token gifts to help break the ice. In warmer months, meals in the restaurant are occasionally replaced by a BBQ on the nearby beach – a most enjoyable way to spend an evening. **$$**

Oechilbo Hotel (25 rooms) Also going by the name of Chilbosan Hotel & a couple of similar variants, this option is approximately 7km inland & well hidden away, positioned in an attractive forest clearing surrounded by rocky peaks. A few rooms are attached to the main restaurant by a short covered walkway, but most are in separate chalets. Hot water is almost guaranteed not to materialise & power cuts can be expected, but the staff – who must go for weeks without any custom – make an effort. Keep your headtorch & insect repellent to hand. **$$**

✖ **WHERE TO EAT AND DRINK** The only options here are to eat at the hotel or homestay, and both should be able to arrange a packed lunch for you if you are off out exploring for the day. Staff at the Chilbo Homestay will also likely be able to arrange a picnic barbecue on Pochon-ri Beach – a lovely way to spend an evening and to sample local favourites, including pine mushrooms and raw sea urchin.

WHAT TO SEE AND DO The order of service will very much depend on the season, weather and time available. Many visitors just spend one night in Mount Chilbo, but given the journey time in just getting here, having two nights and thus one complete full day to explore is strongly recommended. While a couple of villages can be found within Chilbo they remain very much off-limits – almost all of the sightseeing here relates to simply taking in the natural beauty. This typically involves short drives and brief walks to take in small waterfalls, rocky panoramas, sandy beaches and coastal outcrops. Once here the going is pretty soft; those looking for serious hiking would be better off with a visit to Mount Myohyang (page 173) or Mount Kumgang (page 201). No, coming to Mount Chilbo is all about a gentle little foray into nature before returning to the monuments, marching, factories and fun that lie elsewhere.

In **Sea Chilbo** the big draw is the scenic and sandy **Pochon-ri Beach** near the Chilbo Homestay (page 241). From the beach you can swim in the often-chilly waters or just relax at leisure. One or two fishermen may materialise touting short boat trips for a nominal fee, while local lads may scout the group for suitable opponents in a light-hearted wrestling match or game of volleyball. Heading inland, you will be taken to a variety of stops and lookout points to take in the breathtaking scenery of jagged rocky outcrops, dense forest and burbling brooks. Stops in **Outer Chilbo** are likely to include Hadok Falls (vaguely reminiscent of a small waterfall in the Scottish highlands), the natural rock arch known as Kansgon Gate and the hilltop viewing platform at the Joyak Pavilion. If you don't mind pushing a short distance up an overgrown path, you may also have the chance to see the twin pinnacles of Ssangji Rock, which jut skyward so precariously that the next nuclear test may well send them crashing down.

The prime scenery in the region can be found in **Inner Chilbo**, a few kilometres further inland from Outer Chilbo. Arguably the only cultural draw in all of Mount Chilbo, **Kaesim Temple** is a surprisingly well-preserved and charming little Palhae Dynasty temple that dates to AD826. The small temple grounds are home to three halls, two shrines and a pavilion, together with a 180kg bronze bell that dates to 1764. A short drive from Kaesim will bring you to the modern viewing platform known as **Sungson Pavilion**, from where you will have a commanding view over the rocks and region, with seemingly every protuberance steeped in some legend or other. Rocks with names such as Couple Rock and Wedding Rock provide clues to who the protagonists in such legends may be. Should you be inclined to ask, you may regret your query – some of these tales tend to drag and get a little lost in translation.

13

Rason Special
Economic Zone
(라진선봉 경제특구)

The 746km² Rason Special Economic Zone lies in the extreme northeast of the country, bordering China and Russia. This curious corner of an already bizarre nation came into existence in 1991 when Pyongyang, in reaction to the economic reforms that were taking place in China, decided to flirt with trials of a more open financial system. As global communism essentially collapsed and economic chaos was unleashed from the Baltic Sea to the Bering Strait and beyond, Pyongyang's main trading partners fell, one by one, by the wayside. The Cold War was over and old allies were embracing a new economic era: capitalism.

While many of these former communist nations went through an economic 'hard landing' in the 1990s, the DPRK, as with nearly all things, decided to try and usher in these much-needed changes under draconian controls. Rather than roll out nationwide reforms it was decided that a litmus test was required, something that the old guard in Pyongyang would be able to swallow – and where better to trial a more open system than in the remote northeast. With the gift of hindsight, we now know that the attempt at these reforms in the wake of communism's global collapse was too little, too late: North Korea went through the hardest landing of all in the 1990s, decimating the country. The counties of Rajin and Sonbong (the name Rason deriving from the 'Ra' of Rajin and 'Son' of Sonbong) were part of the economic basket case that was North Hamgyong until this special zone came into existence.

On paper, Rason offered everything to seemingly keep all parties happy: a distance from Pyongyang; a rail link with Russia; an ice-free port; and a border with China's Yanbian Korean Autonomous Prefecture. A good analogy for the aim of Rason is to compare it with how things work in China and its Special Administrative Regions of Hong Kong and Macau. Rason, like Hong Kong, has, on paper, some form of semi-autonomy with different laws, rules, regulations, customs and visa requirements from the rest of the country which all, purportedly, make it more open for business with the outside world than the rest of the country.

Separated from the rest of the country, a country within a country almost (with a border fence to prove it), Rason opened for investment. Of course, little came. Foreign speculators would be taking major risks by investing here, and the majority of the 'businessmen' that can be found here today would be called 'traders' by most. Yes, some business has come; the Russians have been trickling money into developing the rail infrastructure and the aforementioned ice-free ports, while

China, Mongolia and others have dipped their toes into certain other waters, but most of the business is still small scale and speculative, with many of those who have decided to try their luck in Rason having political or ethnic ties to the DPRK.

While Rason strives to become a bustling hub of business in this self-proclaimed 'Tuman Triangle', where China, Russia and the DPRK meet along the Tuman River, it is, in reality, a sleepy and picturesque corner of the country, with some of North Korea's best sandy beaches, photogenic lagoons and green hills, all of which can be visited with relative ease. The atmosphere is different here, somewhat more relaxed, and the different setup for tourists (see box, page 248) makes a visit to Rason of particular interest to those who may have already been to North Korea and want to see an alternative version of how things could be. While three or so days is more than enough time for most visitors, the relaxed nature of the zone does allow for the possibility of longer leisurely trips – perhaps to soak up the summer sun or to focus on special interests, such as cycling and fishing.

While Rason may be rooted to its two namesake counties, both of which having a town of the same name, Sonbong is a lethargic underling compared with Rajin, which is the only town of real note. Accordingly, Rajin is the logical base for exploring the region, as any corner of Rason can be visited from here on a day trip. More of a town than the city it strives to be, central Rajin is quite walkable, although you will likely be obliged to drive from point to point. Being an autonomous capital of sorts, Rajin is slowly being upgraded and now has, by North Korean standards, a comparatively affluent air about it. The town develops from one year to the next as money, particularly from China, comes in. The state too now affords Rajin with more importance than it may have had in the past; the bustling Rajin Market and showcase foreign-language school highlight that Pyongyang may not be completely closed to the idea of rolling out wider economic reforms. Life here may still be hard, but on the face of it few North Koreans will have seen such an improvement in their lives over the last 30 years or so as those of Rajin have done, as it has transformed from being a remote backwater to being admired, somewhat begrudgingly, by the top-of-the-pile Pyongyangites.

GETTING THERE AND AWAY

FROM ELSEWHERE IN NORTH KOREA Of course, it would be too much to expect that a 'special economic zone' in Korea would have its own airport. The quickest way to get to Rason from Pyongyang these days is to fly into Orang Airport (page 235) and press on by road – note that it's not permitted to drive all the way from Pyongyang to Rason.

The Orang–Chongjin–Rason road opened to tourists in 2012. The drive from Orang Airport to Rason is approximately 150km and there are no 'open' sites on the journey during the slow and bumpy 88km stretch between Chongjin and Huchang, the customs/border post on the southern boundary of Rason. Assuming all your permits and papers are in place it should take around 30 minutes to pass through this internal border, regardless of the direction. The road between Chongjin and Huchang is poor – expect this stretch alone to take 2½ hours.

Like with Hamhung and Chongjin, tourists may also arrive in both Rajin and Tumangang on one of the rather infrequent and somewhat rustic international trains (page 248) that operate between Pyongyang and Russia. The 802km journey from Pyongyang to Rajin is scheduled to take just under 24 hours, while the additional 60km to Tumangang, the final stop before the Russian border, will somehow add another 1¾ hours to the journey.

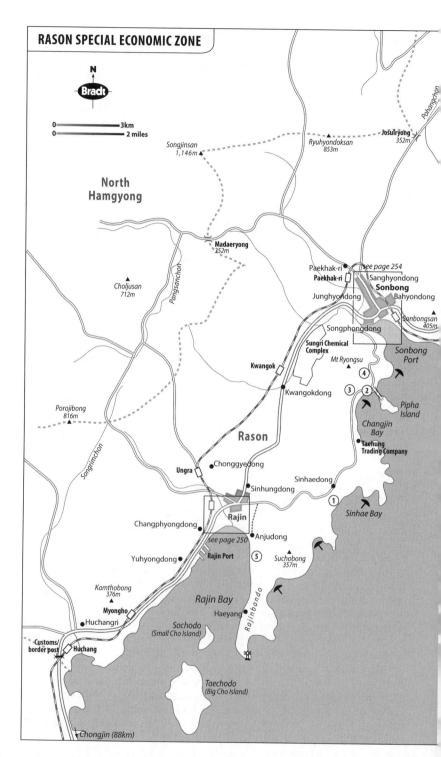

RASON SPECIAL ECONOMIC ZONE

N

Bradt

0 ——— 3km
0 ——— 2 miles

North Hamgyong

Songjinsan
1,146m ▲

Ryuhyondoksan
853m ▲

Josulryong
352m

Pohangchon

Madaeryong
352m

Paekhak-ri ●
Paekhak-ri ⌂

see page 254

Sanghyondong
Sonbong
Bahyondong

Junghyondong

Sonbongsan
405m

Choljusan
712m ▲

Pangsanchon

Songphongdong

Sungri Chemical Complex

Kwangok ⌂

Mt Ryongsu ▲

Sonbong Port

Kwangokdong ●

④

Porojibong
816m ▲

Songrimchon

③ ②

Pipha Island

Changjin Bay

Rason

Taehung Trading Company ●

Ungra ⌂

● Chonggyedong

● Sinhungdong

Sinhaedong ●

①

Sinhae Bay

Changphyongdong ●

⌂ **Rajin**

see page 250

● Anjudong

Suchobong
357m ▲

Yuhyongdong ●

🚢 **Rajin Port**

⑤

Kamthobong
376m ▲

Myongho ⌂

Rajinbando

● Huchangri

Rajin Bay

Haeyang ●

Customs/ border post

⌂ **Huchang**

Sochodo
(Small Cho Island)

Taechodo
(Big Cho Island)

Chongjin (88km)

For listings, see from page 249

Where to stay

1. Chujin Bathing Resort
2. Emperor Hotel & Casino
3. Pipha
4. Pipha Folk
5. Tongmyongsan
6. Songbyok

NOTE
DPRK–RUSSIA RAIL
CROSSING POINT
FOR TOURISTS

China/DPRK border
(for tourists)

Sahoe

CHINA

Chonghak
o Mineral Spring

Hongui

Honguiri ● □ Jokji
Mulkol

Tumangang

Tumangang

Khasan

DPRK–Russia
Friendship House

RUSSIA

Hukji

Puphori

Josan-ri

Tuman

Hwadaesan
891m

Rason

o Sonbon Spring

6

Kuryongphyong

Mt Kuryong
266m

Rason Migratory
Bird Reserve

Sobon Lagoon

Sungjondae
Pavilion

Yondubong
120m

Sungjondae

Ungsang

Lagoon
Man

● Ungsangdong

Kulphori

Tongbon
Lagoon

Kalumdan

Pulgun Island

Mt Uam
(Uamsan)

Khunsom

● Uam Seal
Sanctuary

Cherry
orchards

beach   beach

Uam-ri

Ophodan ●

Sukgun Islands

Al Islet

East   Sea

of   Korea

247

TO AND FROM RUSSIA   Rail is the only means of crossing the 17.5km border between North Korea and Russia. Besides the infrequent long-distance Russia-bound trains that pass through Rajin and Tumangang, such as the epic 10,214km Pyongyang–Moscow service (the world's longest single-ticket rail journey), a more regular and reliable train runs seven times a month between Rason and Russia. While the days of operation do jump around, train 651, which typically comprises just two carriages, shuttles a tiny number of passengers across the frontier. When it does run, the northbound service currently departs Tumangang at 15.00 (Korean time) and arrives into Khasan, an hour ahead and 4km away in Russia, at 18.45 local time, meaning it takes almost 3 hours to cross the border and go through all the formalities before you disembark. There is essentially nothing in Khasan itself, so those arriving in Russia may well consider travelling onto Ussuriysk, near Vladivostok, where this service terminates at 00.54 the following day. In reverse, train 652 is scheduled to depart Ussuriysk at 05.29 and Khasan at 10.29, before arriving into Tumangang at 11.15. Anybody travelling on any train in either direction will of course require visas, permits, a degree of flexibility, an open mind and lots of patience.

EXCEPTIONAL EXCEPTIONS

Rason is different from the rest of the country so, of course, things are a little different for the handful of tourists that come here each year. In the spirit of openness, you do not even need a North Korean visa to visit, just a special permit (that still must be obtained in advance of travel). Once here, things are supposed to be more relaxed, and *theoretically* foreigners can more or less go where they wish in Rason, albeit with a guide. Therefore, *theoretically* once again, foreign visitors can go into 'normal' shops, 'normal' restaurants and even visit the bustling market in Rajin, the only market in the entire country accessible to tourists. Visitors may even use North Korean won, and a trip to the bank is actively encouraged – although once you have won in hand you will discover that all shopkeepers openly admit that they would prefer Chinese currency.

In reality, while the foreigners working in Rason are freer, the tiny number of tourists that come this way are put on a bit of a leash, and the larger the group the tighter the leash. The local and compulsory Rajin-based guides are generally inexperienced and somewhat wary of relaxing their grip. While sitting shoulder to shoulder with locals and tucking into a bowl of cold noodles in the Rajin Market would be a genuine cultural experience, and is – again – *theoretically* permissible, you are more likely to dine in an empty restaurant where you can be kept an eye on. On every visit I have made to Rason I have had to be rather dogged with my obdurate escorts to get the most out of it; this is all a great shame, as by taking away the unique possibilities that exist in Rason, the local tour operators are taking away the chief reason to visit.

However, there is a light at the end of the tunnel; being a zone open to foreign business means that the government no longer have a monopoly on inbound tourism to the region, and a couple of small foreign-owned enterprises in Rason are trying their hand at tourism. Being foreign owned, these companies seem to have a far better understanding of what the intrepid traveller is actually looking for, giving the state travel company a good run for its money. Hopefully this will spur innovation through competition, something that is sadly lacking in most of the country.

TO AND FROM CHINA Thankfully, the region is well connected with China. The 48km journey from Rajin to the border crossing at Wonjong is now on a paved road. From here, travellers can enter China over the Tuman River Bridge, arriving in Quanhe on the opposite bank.

Much like the border crossing between Namyang and Tumen (page 239), entering or departing North Korea by this route requires preplanning and patience; the border *should* be open daily except Sundays, but operating schedules can change, particularly on and around public holidays in both countries. Double and triple check everything – this is not a border that you want to get stuck at.

Once in China, the infrastructure is (unsurprisingly) decades ahead of the DPRK and well-paved roads slowly turn to dual carriageways, meaning that travel to the cities of Hunchun (45km away), Tumen (110km) or Yanji (145km) should take no time at all when compared with travel on North Korean roads. All three aforementioned cities are now also connected with China's impressive and ever-improving rail network, with the fastest trains at the time of writing covering the Hunchun to Beijing route in under 10 hours. From Yanji, the capital of Yanbian, a number of airlines operate out of Yanji Chaoyangchuan Airport (YNJ) to Beijing, Shanghai and other Chinese cities, as well as to South Korea.

 # WHERE TO STAY *Map, pages 246–7, unless otherwise stated*

For a relatively compact area there is a surprising and slowly increasing number of accommodation options available. For a spot of variety and novelty you can also arrange to move hotels part way through your time in Rason. However, while you may of course request your preferred place to stay (and the chance of any hotel ever being full is slight), local tour operators have a nasty habit of switching accommodation on arrival for a range of spurious reasons; you may have to stick to your guns to avoid being billeted elsewhere.

In addition to those listed below, the Singang Company Inn, Piphasom (Pipha Island) Hotel and Uamsan Hotel have essentially fallen into disrepair and are only likely to be used in extenuating circumstances or when they finally undergo long-overdue renovations.

IN RAJIN

Namsan Hotel [map, page 250] (31 rooms) In a former life a Japanese officers' guesthouse, this is the most central option in Rajin & is comfortable enough after a recent refurbishment, with 17 rooms now designated as being 'suitable' for foreign guests. Those visiting during warmer months have the bonus of being able to pop out, unchaperoned, to the main square to enjoy a cold beer or street food from the Chinese & Korean vendors that set up here. The big-screen television adorning the front of the hotel blasts out propaganda from early morning until late at night, so earplugs (or requesting a room at the rear) are recommended. **$$$**

Rajin Hotel [map, page 250] (90 rooms) A large hotel on the southeast edge of town, the Rajin is pretty tired these days; it seems like almost nothing has changed here since the 1980s. Still, it is perfectly acceptable for a night or 2 given where you are in the world, & is arguably a more authentic Korean experience than the alternative backup option, the Tongmyongsan. **$$**

OUTSIDE RAJIN

Emperor Hotel & Casino (90 rooms) Paid for & operated by the Hong Kong-based Emperor Group, this hotel opened in 2000 after an alleged investment of US$64 million. The sole aim of this place was to attract gamblers from China, where gaming laws are more rigidly controlled. The money rolled into Rason (& straight out again) before a change in Chinese regulations and declining relations made coming here a less attractive prospect. While you must purchase

US$500 of chips just to get into the casino itself, the staff are normally happy to let the occasional tourist explore this expensive & often-deserted hotel, where there really is no reason to stay other than for the novelty value. **$$$$$**

🏠 **Chujin Bathing Resort** (30 rooms) On a sandy bay approximately 10km out of Rajin, this small & basic beach hotel is a logical option for those who visit in the summer months & want to enjoy some downtime on the beach. Friendly staff & good seafood. **$$**

🏠 **Pipha Folk Hotel** (7 rooms) This tiny hotel, designed to look like a traditional Korean home, is rarely used but is a viable option for those who really want a bit of peace & quiet. Facilities are limited, but both the Pipha & Emperor hotels, & thus their facilities, are a very short drive away. **$$$**

🏠 **Pipha Hotel** (53 rooms) In a wooded area near Pipha Island, roughly halfway between Rajin & Sonbong, this comfortable hotel is let down by its poor location, away from both the town & the beach. Friendly staff make an effort & the restaurant offers up a dazzling range of seafood dishes. **$$$**

🏠 **Songbyok Hotel** (10 rooms) Near the east shore of Sobon Lagoon, approximately 6km from Tumangang & 2km from the Sungjondae Pavilion, within view of China & Russia (& in range of their mobile networks). This rarely used hotel is meant to resemble a mock-up of the Great Wall of China. Quite why it was decided, in this scenic area of lagoons & wetlands, that the restaurant should be in the basement is beyond the comprehension of even the local guides. Undergoing expansion at the time of writing. **$$$**

🏠 **Tongmyongsan Hotel** (58 rooms) Opened in 2012, the Tongmyongsan is a couple of kilometres outside of Rajin, in a relatively undeveloped area on the east coast of the bay. Unless you are looking for somewhere very quiet there is little reason to stay here, but the choice may not be yours. Still, it is the 2nd-best option in Rajin. **$$$**

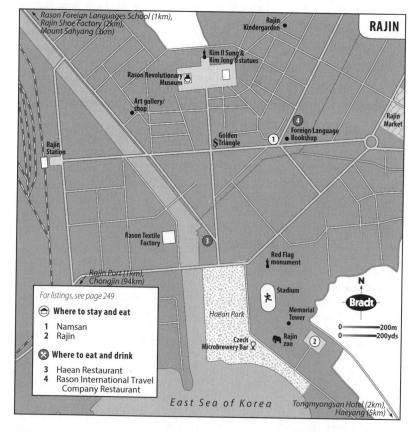

✖ WHERE TO EAT AND DRINK *Map, opposite*

Thanks to its more relaxed economic setup, there is, arguably, more choice for food in Rason than almost anywhere else in the country, with seafood being *de rigueur*. All aforementioned hotels will of course be able to rustle up a meal, but numerous other restaurants such as the perfectly acceptable but rather lacking in character **Rason International Travel Company Restaurant** and **Haean Restaurant** (both $$$) are likely to be chosen for you. Should you have the gift of the gab, you may well be able to convince your local guide to let you go to a genuine locals' restaurant, have a basic meal in the Rajin Market or even to pick up supplies from the sprawling market in order to arrange a picnic or barbecue in the park, mountains or beach – just as the locals would do.

WHAT TO SEE AND DO

IN AND AROUND RAJIN Entering from North Hamgyong, the customs post at Huchang is essentially a border, and you will likely here change vehicles, meet with new and part with old guides (as it is very difficult even for your Pyongyang- or Chongjin-based government guides to be granted permission to visit Rason). With your new hosts handling all the bureaucracy the barrier will eventually be lifted and – hey presto! – you will be in Rason.

Rajin Port It's 11km to Rajin Bay along a road that largely hugs the coastline, where your first port of call (excuse the pun) will be ice-free Rajin Port. This port is arguably the prime reason for the existence of this special economic zone; complications of doing business with North Korea aside, it is logistically and economically beneficial, for example, for coal from northeast China to be shipped from Rajin rather than to be transported hundreds of kilometres overland to China's nearest viable shipping point. As already mentioned, the Russians are investing in the port and upgrading its rail connection to Russia (as its ice-free status is coveted), but for now it is rather sleepy – with most of the ships being tired fishing vessels. Still, 30 or so minutes to explore is worthwhile, and an interesting lesson in the economic ambitions of Rason.

West Rajin Back on the road, which is now paved, a further 1km will bring you into the compact city of Rajin. A visit to the **Rason Textile Factory** in the west of the town is often included on most itineraries, and while it does have the feel of a sweatshop, the staff are probably happier working here than they would be out in the fields. Eagle-eyed visitors may spot the 'Made in China' labels being sewn into the clothing and the finished goods being boxed up ready for shipping and marked, 'Made in China, Destination: USA'. The west of the city is also home to the Japanese-built **Rajin Station**, an attractive red-brick building, and an **art shop/ gallery**, which doesn't seem to have as wide a selection as some other galleries, but is still worth a quick visit.

Central Rajin The city centre is, of course, home to some quasi-obligatory propaganda sites such as the twin statues of the leaders and the **Rason Revolutionary Museum**, but these are near identical to every other such war museum and monument between here and Pyongyang and thus only worth a visit if you have not yet called in on one of these elsewhere – unlikely. Other such sites scattered through Rajin include the Kimilsungia-Kimjongilia Greenhouse and the Mosaic Portraits of President Kim Il Sung and General Kim

Jong Il – worth a visit only for the inquisitive or those who desperately desire to display deference.

Of more interest in central Rajin is the **Golden Triangle Bank**, where visitors can exchange money into Korean won at what is essentially the real exchange rate, enquire about opening a bank account or even purchase a prepaid charge-card for use within Rason. A few hundred metres south from here, **Haean Park** is a good spot for people-watching and popular with locals in the early evenings. The park is now home to a **Czech Micro-brewery Bar** and a small **waterpark**, which is sadly almost never open.

East Rajin Slightly east of central Rajin, the **Namsan Hotel** (page 249) is located on one of the main road junctions in the city. The area around here is busy in the warmer summer evenings with a few stalls, barbecue stands and restaurants plying their trade. It is very easy to while away the hours of an evening from this spot and watch the world go by – you can very easily forget where you are. A **foreign-language bookshop** can also be found nearby, but the selection is far more limited than in Pyongyang, although they occasionally stock some books and pamphlets specific to the region.

This part of the city is home to **Rajin Market**, which for many is one of the highlights of Rason, being the only market open to tourists in the entire country. From a global perspective, the expansive market is not unique in any way – it is similar to any of the bustling markets that can be found across Asia, full of piled-high goods; dispensing almost anything and everything imaginable, from pets to pushrods, apples to zippers. No, what makes this market so unique is that it is in North Korea, a country that we are led to believe has no private enterprise, just state department stores lined with empty shelves. This is the best place in the entire country to stock up on snacks, supplies and unconventional souvenirs, and prices are very reasonable. There is even a rustic canteen serving up basic local food, and some ramshackle counters selling snacks and drinks such as ice cream and home-brewed beer. While the conditions throughout the market seem sanitary enough, the public toilets are so abhorrently malodorous that they could indeed be a gateway to Hades – it goes without saying that they should be avoided. Sadly, photography in this market is off-limits and this is a real shame; the market truly highlights that there is flourishing private enterprise within the DPRK. Your guide will likely try to keep a close eye on you, but push for more time to visit if you can – it is an eye-opener.

North Rajin Heading north from the city centre, the **Rajin Shoe Factory** is a bizarre feature on many itineraries that the local tourist board promotes as a 'must see site' (this is essentially a load of old cobblers), but by pressing on 1km beyond the factory, you will arrive at **Mount Sahyang**. A relatively easy round-trip hike from here through forest to the summit should take a couple of hours, but of course you can never totally escape the propaganda – the hike takes in a small monument, the Sahyangsan Revolutionary Battle Site, that even your guides find hard to get excited about.

South Rajin Heading along the eastern flank of Rajin Bay, you may visit the fishing village of **Haeyang** and the Haeyang Revolutionary Site. Should you ignore the revolutionary nature of the area it is a quaint fishing village, and the 6km road here from Rajin will, on a clear day, afford good views of Rajin Port and the bay, as well as the currently inaccessible Socho and Taecho islands.

Other sights Those wanting to interact with the next generation should consider requesting a visit to one or some of the sites in the city that highlights the many talents of the region's youth, such as **Rason Foreign Languages School** in the northwest suburbs, or the more central **Rajin Kindergarten**. If you haven't yet been to a kindergarten in the country they are all very similar (one is enough!), but the language school *is* impressive. The students here, at least on my visits to date, seem to have a good grasp of conversational English, and your visit will likely be the focus of an English class as you enjoy 20 minutes or so freely chatting with the polite, smart and inquisitive students. Sadly, visitors are not invited to join in with the grenade-throwing exercises that seem to be incorporated into the gym class. Other interactive possibilities include the chance to take in the **Sports Academy** or the **Taekwondo School** for a display of sporting prowess, or for special-interest groups to partake in multi-day training programmes.

BEYOND RAJIN

The road to Sonbong Travelling north from Rajin, a well-paved inland road leads for 16km to Sonbong, whereas the drive along the coastal road is a bumpier 27km, taking you past the turnoff to the relatively isolated bay, beach and hotel at the Chujin Bathing Resort (page 250) and leading onto the **Taehung Trading Company**, a seafood processing factory and one of the largest business enterprises in the region. You can, by appointment, pop in here for a tour. The road beyond Taehung leads to **Changjin Bay** and all the associated sites around here (see below), so it is well worth asking your driver to arrange a circular tour from Rajin, otherwise you will almost certainly travel out and back along the quicker inland route.

As you depart Rajin on the inland road north, the route gently ascends into the hills; it is worth making a photography stop from the top of the pass to look back down over the city, before you push on. Just 7km from central Rajin, a right turn takes you over a poor section of road into the Changjin Bay/Pipha area, home to a number of hotels, including the Emperor Hotel and Casino (page 249). Besides visiting or staying in these hotels, the only thing of note here is the boat trip that travels from the north shore of **Pipha Island** (connected to the mainland by a short causeway) to visit the **Uam Seal Sanctuary**. Boats do not run to any schedule, but if enough people are interested the captain will materialise and take you out for a trip of approximately 45 minutes (and approximately 100 yuan per person) to see the seals.

Back on the main Rajin to Sonbong road, shortly beyond the Changjin/Pipha turnoff you will pass the **Sungri Chemical Complex**. This sprawling, rusting oil refinery closed its doors back in 1995 and talks with various investors to get it back online still continue. You will not be allowed to tour the complex, but ask nicely and your driver may permit a brief detour along some of the public roads that crisscross the plant.

Sonbong In Sonbong itself there is not much permitted for tourists to see in what is a picturesque enough little town. Sonbong Port is essentially off-limits and the Rason Exhibition House, one of the largest buildings in town, is normally only opened to investors for the annual Rason International Trade Exhibition. Still, if you haven't yet been to a kindergarten, you can always opt to visit the **Sonbong Kindergarten**. The only way visitors are normally permitted to see much of Sonbong is by including a visit to the centrally located **Junghyon Ondok Revolutionary Site**, the location where Kim Jong Suk and Kim Jong Il, they say, first landed upon their returning to Korea from exile in 1945.

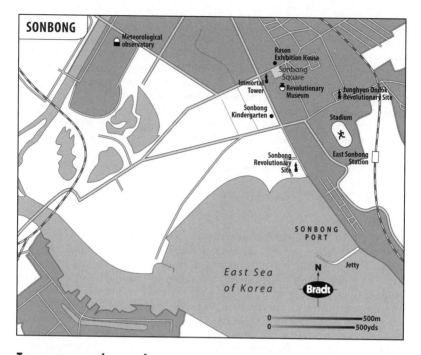

SONBONG

Meteorological observatory

Rason Exhibition House

Sonbong Square

Immortal Tower

Revolutionary Museum

Junghyon-Ondok Revolutionary Site

Sonbong Kindergarten

Stadium

Sonbong Revolutionary Site

East Sonbong Station

SONBONG PORT

East Sea of Korea

N

Jetty

Bradt

0 — 500m
0 — 500yds

Tumangang and around Pushing on, two 'main' roads lead on from Sonbong: one is a paved road that heads in a northerly direction for 35km to the Chinese border at Wonjong, passing the Chonghak Mineral Spring en route; the other is a poor-quality dirt road that heads for 31km northeast to Tumangang, the frontier with Russia. The Russia-bound journey is the more scenic of the two, as you pass through the 32km² **Rason Migratory Bird Reserve**, focused around the three lagoons of Man, Tongbon and Sobon. You will skirt alongside Man and Tongbon lagoons before arriving in the largely deserted border town of Tumangang. The last few kilometres of coastline between Sonbong and Russia are beautiful; one secluded bay and sandy beach after another. Quite understandably, they are essentially off-limits, but it cannot hurt to ask if it is possible to visit **Uam** and the sandy strip of beach near here, the last sliver of land before the border, which many moons ago was used by tourists from the USSR.

   Tumangang itself is practically devoid of life save for when a train passes through; unless you are fortunate enough to embark or disembark here you will likely be whisked through the town very quickly indeed. Slightly beyond the town, just 800m from the border, the **DPRK–Russia Friendship House** is a curious building near the Friendship Bridge, which has hosted meetings between the two nations and is now a museum of sorts, with a preserved meeting room and photographs of various summits and meetings held between the two nations – certainly worth 10 minutes or so to look around. Driving for a further 5km you will pass through the small village of **Josan-ri** and arrive at a panoramic viewing platform beside the **Sungjondae Pavilion**. The pavilion can be found next to the small **Victory Monument to Admiral Li Sun Sin**, who was credited as the designer of the *Turtle Ship*, a Korean warship often recognised as being the first armoured vessel in the world. However, of prime interest for most is the sight of the **Three Country Border**, as from the pavilion you will be afforded a view into both China and

Russia, although asking your guide to pinpoint exactly where the three countries converge is a tad confusing (it's at a point in the middle of the river, approximately 200m upstream from the Friendship Bridge).

Unless you are travelling onto Russia, you will likely be returning on the same road back to Rajin, although while in this extreme corner of the country, where three nations converge, you may as well pop into the **Songbyok Hotel** (page 250) for a nosey around and to look at the shallow and marshy Sobon Lagoon before setting off on the bumpy journey south. Salty Sobon is the largest lagoon in the country at just over 16km^2 and is inhabited by various species of fish including grey mullet, dace, shellfish and shrimp. The management of the Songbyok Hotel is striving to attract visitors for fishing tours in the area, but to date have landed very few.

Appendix 1

LANGUAGE

As you will probably not be able to take this guidebook with you into North Korea (see box, page vii), providing anything more than a few cursory words within these pages would be a pointless exercise. Your affable hosts in Korea will be on hand and translate everything. Accordingly, as you are so well attended to, there will be little need or indeed chance for you to speak Korean. However, for those who want to make the effort (which always helps break the ice, no matter how poorly your words are articulated), phrasebooks and dictionaries from the likes of Tuttle Publishing and Collins can be purchased in advance of travel (albeit always with a South Korean slant). Alternatively, Pyongyang-published language aides can be picked up in bookshops across North Korea for a pittance.

COURTESIES

English	Korean	English	Korean
yes	*ye*	let's go	*kasipsida*
no	*ani/aniyo*	let's have a rest	*swipsida*
good day	*annyonghasimnigga*	excuse me	*mianhamnida*
glad to meet you	*pangapsumnida*	with pleasure	*osoyo*
please	*juseyu*	my name is …	*jega … imnida*
thank you	*kamsahamnida/*	comrade	*tongji/tongmu*
	gomapsumnida	waiter/waitress	*chopdaewondongmu*
goodbye	*annoyghi*	guide	*annaewondongmu*

EATING AND DRINKING

mineral water	*yaksu*	fork	*pok*
tea	*cha*	rice	*pap*
coffee	*copi*	salt	*sogum*
beer	*mekju*	meat	*gogi*
knife	*kal*	fish	*mulgogi*

DAYS

Monday	*wolyoil*	Friday	*geumyoil*
Tuesday	*hwayoil*	Saturday	*toyoil*
Wednesday	*suyoil*	Sunday	*ilyoil*
Thursday	*mogyoil*		

MONTHS

January	*ilwol*	April	*sawol*
February	*iwol*	May	*ohwol*
March	*samwol*	June	*yuwol*

July	chilwol	October	shibwol
August	palwol	November	shibeelwol
September	kuwol	December	shibeewol

NUMBERS

1	hana	6	yosot
2	tul	7	ilgop
3	set	8	yodop
4	net	9	ahop
5	tasot	10	yol

Appendix 2

FURTHER INFORMATION

BOOKS An exponentially growing cornucopia of books on North Korea seem to be published from one year to the next, such is the growing fascination with the nation. The following list is just the tip of the iceberg, but are all titles that either myself or co-author Neil Taylor consider particularly noteworthy.

Korea prior to the Japanese occupation

Barr, Pat *A Curious Life for a Lady* (Biography of Isabella Bird) Secker and Warburg, 1970
Bird, Isabella *Korea and her Neighbours* John Murray, 1898 (many recent reprints)
Griffis, William *Corea, The Hermit Nation* Harper & Bros, 1905
Hamel, Hendrik *Hamel's Journal and a Description of the Kingdom of Korea 1653 – 1666*
    Royal Asiatic Society Korea Branch, 1994

The Japanese occupation

Uchida, Jun *Brokers of Empire: Japanese Settler Colonialism in Korea 1876 – 1945* Harvard East
    Asian Monographs, 2014

The Korean War

Brands, H W *The General vs the President: MacArthur and Truman at the Brink of Nuclear War*
    Anchor, 2017
Cumings, Bruce *The Korean War, A History* Modern Library, 2010
Farrer-Hockley, Sir Anthony *A Distant Obligation: British Participation in the Korean War*
    Stationery Office, 1990
Hastings, Max *The Korean War* Simon & Schuster, 1987
Millett, Allan A *Short History of the Korean War* IB Tauris, 2018
Van Tonder, Gerry *North Korea Invades the South* Pen and Sword, 2018
McLaine, Ian *A Korean Conflict: The Tensions between Britain and America* IB Tauris, 2018

History, daily life and contemporary DPRK

Baek, Jieun *North Korea's Hidden Revolution: How the Information Underground is Transforming
    a Closed Society* Yale University Press, 2017
Beal, Tim *North Korea: The Struggle Against American Power* Pluto Press, 2005
Bonner, Nick *Made In North Korea: Graphics from Everyday Life in the DPRK* Phaidon Press,
    2017
Boynton, Robert S *The Invitation-Only Zone: The Extraordinary Story of North Korea's Abduction
    Project* Atlantic Books, 2016
Buzo, Adrian *The Guerrilla Dynasty* Westview Press, 1999
Cha, Victor *The Impossible State: North Korea, Past and Future* Ecco Press, 2012
Chon, Tuk Chu *Die Beziehungen zwischen der DDR and der KDVR* Minerva, 1982

Chung, Chin O *Pyongyang Between Peking and Moscow: North Korea's Involvement in the Sino-Soviet Dispute* The University of Alabama Press, 1978

Corfield, Justin *Historical Dictionary of Pyongyang* Anthem Press, 2013

Cumings, Bruce *Korea's Place in the Sun: A Modern History* Norton, 2015

Cumings, Bruce *North Korea: Another Country* The New Press, 2004

Fischer, Paul *A Kim Jong Il Production: The Extraordinary True Story of a Kidnapped Filmmaker, His Star Actress, and a Young Dictator's Rise to Power* Flatiron Books, 2015

Frank, Rüdiger *Die DDR und Nordkorea* Shaker, 1996

Hastings, Justin V *A Most Enterprising Country: North Korea in the Global Economy* Cornell University Press, 2016

Hoare, James and Pares, Susan *Conflict in Korea* ABC-CLIO, 1999

Hoare James and Pares, Susan *North Korea in the 21st Century: An Interpretative Guide* Global Oriental, 2005

Iverson, Shepherd *Stop North Korea: A Radical New Approach to the North Korean Standoff* Tuttle, 2017

Kirkpatrick, Melanie *Escape from North Korea* Encounter Books, 2014

Lankov, Andrei *Crisis in North Korea: The Failure of De-Stalinization* University of Hawaii Press, 2007

Lankov, Andrei *From Stalin to Kim Il Sung: The Formation of North Korea 1945 – 1960* Hurst, 2002

Lankov, Andrei *The Real North Korea* Oxford University Press, 2015

Maretzki, Hans *Kim-ismus in Nordkorea* Tykve Verlag, 1991 (an account by the last GDR Ambassador in Pyongyang)

Morris-Suzuki *Exodus to North Korea: Shadows from Japan's Cold War* Rowman & Littlefield Publishers, 2007

Myers, B R *The Cleanest Race* Melville House Publishing, 2012

Natsios, Andrew S *The Great North Korean Famine: Famine, Politics and Foreign Policy* United States Institute of Peace Press, 2011

Seth, Michael J *North Korea: A History* Palgrave, 2018

Smith, Hazel *North Korea: Markets and Military Rule* Cambridge University Press, 2015

Springer, Chris *Caught in Time: Images of War and Reconstruction* Garnet, 2009

Springer, Chris *Pyongyang: The Hidden History of the North Korean Capital* Saranda Books, 2003

Tudor, Daniel and Person, James *North Korea Confidential* Tuttle, 2015

Personal accounts

Abt, Felix *A Capitalist in North Korea: My Seven Years in the Hermit Kingdom* Tuttle, 2014

Albright, Madeleine *Madam Secretary* Harper Perennial, 2013

Bucher, Lloyd M and Rascovitch, Mark *Pueblo & Bucher* Michael Joseph, 1971

Demick, Barbara *Nothing to Envy, Real Lives in North Korea* Granta, 2010

Everard, John *Only Beautiful Please: A British Diplomat in North Korea* Brooking Institution Press, 2012

Harrold, Michael *Comrades and Strangers* John Wiley & Sons, 2004

Ishikawa, Masaji *A River in Darkness* Amazon Crossing, 2017

Jang, Jin Sung *Dear Leader* Atria, 2015

Jenkins, Charles Robert and Frederick, Jim *The Reluctant Communist* University of California Press, 2009

Kang, Chol-Hwan and Rigoulot, Pierre *Aquariums of Pyongyang* Basic Books, 2001

Kim, Suki *Without You, There Is No Us* Rider, 2015

Kim, Yong *Long Road Home* Columbia University Press, 2017

Lee, Hyeonso *The Girl with Seven Names* William Collins, 2015

Park, Yeonmi *In Order to Live* Penguin Random House, 2015

Schumacher, F Carl *Bridge of No Return: The Ordeal of the USS Pueblo* Harcourt Brace Jovanovich, 1971

Tudor, Daniel *Ask A North Korean: Defectors Talk About Their Lives Inside the World's Most Secretive Nation* Tuttle, 2018

WEBSITES Please note that North Korean-run websites are very slow and occasionally down for prolonged periods of time.

W **38north.org** Informed analysis of North Korea.

W **38northdigitalatlas.org** A digital atlas of the country.

W **airkoryo.com.kp** Website for Air Koryo, the national carrier.

W **chosonexchange.org** Supporting entrepreneurs in North Korea (page 51).

W **dailynk.com** A South Korean news service covering the North.

W **engagedprk.org** Interactive map of foreign engagement in the DPRK.

W **en.nknet.org** Network for North Korean democracy and human rights.

W **hrw.org/asia/north-korea** Human Rights Watch page for the country.

W **kcna.co.jp** Korean Central News Agency – official news from the North.

W **Korean-books.com/kp** Publications of the DPRK – many can be downloaded.

W **kp.one.un.org** Website of the United Nations in the DPRK.

W **libertyinnorthkorea.org** Organisation assisting North Korean refugees hiding in China.

W **lovenkchildren.org** UK-based charity providing food to impoverished children across North Korea.

W **naenara.com.kp** Official web portal for the North Korean government.

W **nkeconomywatch.com** Economic news.

W **nkleadershipwatch.org** Research and analysis on the DPRK leadership.

W **nknews.org** A subscription news service providing in-depth coverage.

W **northkoreatech.org** Consumer electronics and technology developments.

W **rodong.rep.kp** Official news page for the Central Committee of the Workers' Party of Korea.

f **@RusEmbDPRK** Facebook page of the Russian Embassy in Pyongyang.

W **uriminzokkiri.com** North Korean news service.

W **vok.rep.kp** Website for Voice of Korea (formerly Radio Pyongyang).

W **who.int/countries/prk/en** World Health Organization in North Korea.

Index

Page numbers in **bold** indicate main entries; those in *italic* indicate maps

INDEX OF ADVERTISERS